Deviance *and* Social Control *in* SPORT

MICHAEL ATKINSON, PhD

Loughborough University

KEVIN YOUNG, PhD

The University of Calgary

Human Kinetics

Library of Congress Cataloging-in-Publication Data

Atkinson, Michael, 1971-
  Deviance and social control in sport / Michael Atkinson, Kevin Young.
      p. cm.
  Includes bibliographical references and index.
  ISBN-13: 978-0-7360-6042-4   (hard cover)
  ISBN-10: 0-7360-6042-1 (hard cover)
  1. Sports--Sociological aspects. 2. Deviant behavior. 3. Social control. I. Young,
Kevin, 1959- II. Title.
  GV706.5.A88 2008
  306.4'83--dc22

                                                         2008015958

ISBN-10: 0-7360-6042-1
ISBN-13: 978-0-7360-6042-4

The Web addresses cited in this text were current as of May 9, 2008, unless otherwise noted.

Acquisitions Editor: Myles Schrag; **Developmental Editor:** Judy Park; **Assistant Editor:** Lee Alexander; **Copyeditor:** Jocelyn Engman; **Proofreader:** Joanna Hatzopoulos Portman; **Indexer:** Joan K. Griffitts; **Permission Manager:** Dalene Reeder; **Graphic Designer:** Bob Reuther; **Graphic Artist:** Patrick Sandberg; **Cover Designer:** Bob Reuther; **Cover Image:** Georg Eisler, Hillsborough, 1989, Oil on canvas, National Museums Liverpool, Walker Art Gallery with permision of Dr. Alice Eisler, Vienna; **Photo Asset Manager:** Laura Fitch; **Photo Office Assistant:** Jason Allen; **Art Manager:** Kelly Hendren; **Associate Art Manager:** Alan L. Wilborn; **Illustrator:** Denise Lowry; **Printer:** Edwards Brothers

Printed in the United States of America   10 9 8 7 6 5 4 3 2 1

Human Kinetics
Web site: www.HumanKinetics.com

United States: Human Kinetics
P.O. Box 5076
Champaign, IL 61825-5076
800-747-4457
e-mail: humank@hkusa.com

Canada: Human Kinetics
475 Devonshire Road Unit 100
Windsor, ON N8Y 2L5
800-465-7301 (in Canada only)
e-mail: info@hkcanada.com

Europe: Human Kinetics
107 Bradford Road
Stanningley
Leeds LS28 6AT, United Kingdom
+44 (0) 113 255 5665
e-mail: hk@hkeurope.com

Australia: Human Kinetics
57A Price Avenue
Lower Mitcham, South Australia 5062
08 8372 0999
e-mail: info@hkaustralia.com

New Zealand: Human Kinetics
Division of Sports Distributors NZ Ltd.
P.O. Box 300 226 Albany
North Shore City
Auckland
0064 9 448 1207
e-mail: info@humankinetics.co.nz

To our students, both past and present, for teaching us how much we enjoy, and have learned from, thinking sociologically about deviance.

Contents

Preface

The idea for a book on deviance in sport emerges from our frustrations over the years with a number of classroom conundrums where teaching certain aspects of the sociology of sport are concerned. Pedagogically, we have experienced difficulty in finding a contemporary, substantively diverse, and theoretically holistic book that offers a decent sweep of the literature in a way that gels with how we want to approach the subject matter. In the subfield of criminology, deviance, and social control, sport is rarely considered seriously, despite the many and varied controversies, corruptions, and illegalities *out there*. Where the sociology of sport is concerned, faculty and students have been reluctant to accept that crime, deviance, and social control should appear on the research agenda at all. Our view is that this reluctance stems from a rather limited and short sighted way that sport-related behaviors have been approached, and by a certain protectionism toward the unsavory aspects of sport, even by those who claim to study it critically.

Our main frustration, then, is with the missed opportunities to develop and expand sociological understandings of sport deviance through cross-fertilization between these two subdisciplines. Little direction on this matter can be gleaned from either literature, because rarely is the idea even proposed. When, for example, sport is mentioned in criminology/deviance texts, or when deviance is addressed in sociology of sport texts, little clear conceptual distinction is made between hard-line actions that fall under the purview of the law as crime and softer manifestations such as violations of norms or mores. In other words, neither area (criminology/deviance, sociology of sport) has taken a systematic look at how the subject matter may be defined, theorized, and investigated. Occasional summaries of or references to (criminal or norm-breaking) rule violation in sport may be found in the respective literatures, but they usually serve as small case examples, empirical oddities, or points of discussion rather than legitimate academic concerns explored in depth. The lack of attention paid to sport deviance is particularly flagrant in the parent discipline of sociology, and perhaps reflects a larger neglect of the subject of sport itself (Dunning 1999). For example, most introductory sociology textbooks published in North America contain stand-alone chapters on many obvious social institutions and social problems—family, youth, media, economy, religion, globalization, health, and ethnicity—but almost never sport. For such a culturally significant social institution, this is a remarkably asociological trend. Quite clearly, if something matters socially, it should matter *sociologically*.

During the last two decades, however, the sociology of sport has grown quickly and developed impressively. There has been an outpouring of books on specific elements of social problems in sport, such as violence (Bridges 1999; Dunning 1999), drugs (Hoberman 1992; Mottram 2005), racism (Lapchick 2002), sexism/genderism (Lenskyj 2003; Messner 2002), Olympic scandals (Roche 2002) and numerous other topics. Many of these books—and far more journal articles and book chapters—have implied and inferred the concept of deviance, usually in a cursory, taken-for-granted manner. None, to our knowledge, has focused specifically on deviance and social control with the notable exception of Blackshaw and Crabbe (2004). And none employs the sort of interdisciplinary orientation we adopt here to understand sport-related *deviances* and their regulation.

Audience and Approach

This book is intended to challenge taken-for-granted understandings about what deviance related to sport is, and to offer a modest conceptual template on which work in the subfield of the sociology of sport might build in the future. Scholars, journalists, sports officials, politicians, and athletes have all been, and are, involved in debates on the issues we examine. For instance, of enduring importance in the deviance and criminology literatures is the analysis of how people become rule breakers. The value of deviancy and criminological research in contemporary sociology has been judged by how well our theories offer viable explanations and predictions of who turns to deviance as a response to prevailing associations, social conditions, and cues.

Yet the theoretical and substantive over-emphasis on how people become rule breakers, labeled as deviants, and then disciplined within social settings often encourages sociologists of crime and deviance to overlook the many ways in which unsavory, reprehensible, surreptitious, or immoral acts may be either ritually tolerated by people or embraced as outright thrilling (Stebbins 1996). A consistent theme running throughout this book is that while players, coaches, referees, fans, sponsors, and others might agree that a particular behavior in a sport violates a rule, canon, code, or law, such deviance might add a social, psychological, or emotional layer of excitement or intrigue to the sport. For example, the November 2007 indictment of Barry Bonds on charges of lying to an American grand jury regarding his (alleged) steroid use, might be stereotypically dissected by sociologists of crime and deviance as a case study in how athletes "go bad" in sport (i.e., a case of player pathology), how the social structure in baseball produces (and therefore must determine a method of disciplining) drug cheats, or how players like Bonds are stigmatized through public labeling processes. A far less common approach to studying case studies like this commences by interpreting drug use in sport as a form of *socially wanted* deviance, which adds a layer of excitement and significance to the game.

Across the chapters in this book, we examine and interlace empirical snapshots of how people learn to commit rule-violating acts as part of sport processes, how these acts are reacted to by certain audiences and empowered stakeholders, and how athletes come to align their rule violations with their identities over time. Perhaps most important, microanalyses of sports such as ice hockey, baseball, soccer, rugby, skateboarding, and Olympic sports illustrate how participants learn to normalize rule violations based on insider conventions as well as audience acceptance of certain contra-normative acts by athletes as *wanted* and *tolerable*. Case examples gleaned from the sociology of sport literature on the development of hubris in sport cultures and its link to rule violation are highlighted in the process of illustrating the *differential associations* (Sutherland 1947) and *career contingencies* (Prus 1987) involved in becoming a rule violator.

Taking the lead from several decades of research on how sport deviance is expressed as a group practice, we examine empirical examples of entire subcultures or, in process sociology terms, *figurations* (Elias 1994), of individuals involved in sport deviance. Our goal is to illustrate how deviance, and in some cases criminal activity, does not occur because of the concerted efforts of a small handful of individuals in sport; rather, it happens and is culturally supported through sophisticated networks of interdependent social actors and structures, many of which enjoy otherwise respectable and revered reputations in the world of sport and the wider community. Information about the prevalence of entire cultures of drug consumption in sports such as track and field suggests how sport figurations develop their own, often subterranean (Matza 1964b), codes of conduct. We suggest that deviance in sport is a co-operative and multilevel phenomenon with deep historical significance and enduring social implications. Rejected are the so-called individualistic *rotten apple* types and levels of explanation for deviance in sport. That is, we favor a far more *sociological* approach: a nuanced and integrated explanation of sport deviance that accounts for behaviors and practices by looking at whole networks of social relationships and how they produce, define, and police rule violation and rule violators.

How This Book Is Organized

In the chapters that follow, we explore a number of expressions of sport deviance, the prospects for curbing it, policing it, and designing inter-institutional efforts to deal with serious offenders. We summarize and critique the major institutional mechanisms in sport worlds for policing unwanted or deviant behavior, offering a close scrutiny of the ethical standards of play (and lifestyle) advocated in minor, amateur, and professional sport figurations. It is important that the question of who has the legitimate mandate to police sport deviance is rarely addressed in sociological (and particularly criminological) theories of deviance. Therefore, we question whether the institutional autonomy over the definition and adjudication of sport deviance held by leagues and organizations work in practice, and if more transparent and public forms of policing might be explored. The idea of a globally instituted athletes' bill of rights is examined within a general discussion of how local, national, and international sport figurations must strive to ensure the safety and well-being of participants.

Special Features

This book draws together empirical research we have conducted, both separately and collectively, over the last decade and a half. The book is unique in that rather than collating papers from separate authors, or using research examples from others as the primary case studies, this book is based on the authors' firsthand empirical research experience on deviance in sport cultures. Each of the chapters presents a case study of a form of wanted or unwanted deviance in sport. The case studies are driven by a single theory, or range of integrated theoretical approaches, to encourage students and colleagues to think conceptually, innovatively, and diversely about deviance in sport cultures. Across the chapters, we encourage contemporary theorists to revisit many of the important *classical* theories of crime and deviance, and challenge *traditionalists* to explore the analytic promise of poststructural, postmodern, and other contemporary theoretical streams. On a substantive note, we include case studies on topics that have received considerable debate in the sociological literature such as ice hockey and pain/injury, alongside others that have received minimal attention, such as terrorism in sport or animal abuse in or as sport. Data for the case studies were generated through a range of interpretivist research methods, including participant observation, interviewing, media and discourse analysis, narrative methods, and historiography.

We ultimately offer this book as a theoretical bridge-builder for those interested in the sociology of sport deviance. Our aim is to encourage sociologists of sport to explore the dimensions and analytic merit of a full spectrum of crime and deviancy theories and, to stimulate a broader discussion of how and why rule-breaking in sport should matter to deviancy and crime researchers. To this end, we have written the book in, what we feel, is an accessible but conceptually engaging manner. Questions and recommended readings included at the end of each chapter are designed to stimulate critical thinking and research on sport deviance. We hope that *rookies* to the subfield and seasoned research *veterans* will explore, debate, and challenge the lines of argument we present in *Deviance and Social Control in Sport*.

Acknowledgments

This book would not have been possible without the support of many people whose interest, encouragement, and enthusiasm helped transform the idea of looking at sport through the lenses of two different sociological subdisciplines into a manuscript. Because so much of *Deviance and Social Control in Sport* grew out of empirical and ethnographic research conducted in the trenches of sport, we need to thank the respondents and subjects of our various research ventures for their time and willingness to share their experiences and for speaking so candidly using their own terms and categories. We are grateful to the Social Sciences and Humanities Research Council of Canada for their support, especially of the fieldwork for chapter 7. We owe a debt of gratitude to Myles Schrag of Human Kinetics for his patience and stewardship in the early phases of this project and to Judy Park for marshaling us through the subsequent stages of manuscript preparation. Finally, if we owe thanks to the respondents in our various research projects for contouring the empirical dimensions of this book, for its theoretical impetus, we need to acknowledge our students in both sociology of sport and sociology of deviance for their interest and engagement in two subfields that, in our view, so obviously and critically overlap. While particular theoretical approaches appeal to us more than others do, we have come to understand from our students the breadth, depth, and potential of all criminological thought and its strangely unexplored applicability to other social arenas, such as sport.

Deviant Sport Conventions

Before we can address the myriad forms and faces of deviance in sport, we must attend to definitional and conceptual issues about what constitutes *deviance*. A review of the historical approach to the subject of deviance—recently dismissed as conceptually vacuous (Best 2000)—in the sociology of sport provides further direction of how we may innovatively interpret social processes of rule violation. In chapter 1 we review the sociological ideas underpinning the concept of deviance and address how and why certain cultural behaviors in sport become stigmatized while others are supported as conventional or tolerable. In this chapter we present a central idea in our work: certain behaviors may be subjectively defined as deviant or unconventional but nevertheless may be socially *wanted* in (sport) cultures. In chapter 2 we collate, synthesize, and critically dissect how sociologists of deviance in sport have theorized deviancy and review the methods researchers have deployed in order to study the subject area. Toward the conclusion of chapter 2, we introduce the eight houses of deviancy theory that we employ across the case studies presented in this book.

The Normal and the Pathological in Sport

Since Smith's (1983) and Hughes and Coakley's (1991) landmark discussions of violence and deviance in sport, few sociologists have systematically studied contranormative behaviors in sport realms with the aim of generating new theoretical understandings of these behaviors. Young (2002a) offers an initial framework for conceptually understanding and compartmentalizing sport deviance by melding sociological and criminological perspectives, but no truly integrated and interdisciplinary exposition of sport deviance exists in the literature to date. On the one hand, sociologists of deviance and crime have viewed sport deviance as empirically inconsequential or have relied heavily on social-psychological theories to explain individual acts of sport deviance; on the other hand, sociologists of sport have viewed deviance and crime theories as overly traditional and of little consequence.

Through our separate experiences in teaching the sociology of sport and the sociology of deviance, we have questioned why researchers in the various branches of the parent discipline rarely dialogue. Sociologists of sport scarcely venture into the world of sociological deviancy theory, while sociologists of deviance clearly discount sport as a legitimate realm of research in rule violation. Substantive research on sport deviance and explanatory theories of deviant or criminal behavior are indeed two solitudes within academic practice. In order to reconcile the puzzling divide between deviancy theory and the sociology of sport, it is useful to examine what sociologists currently know regarding how, when, and why a particular sport behavior is negatively labeled as *contranormative* at various institutional levels such as teams, sports leagues, or schools.

In this chapter, we begin with Durkheim's (1958) early sociological notion of the normal and the pathological and then move to Stebbins' (1996) concept of tolerable deviance in order to outline how and why sociologists may pursue integrated theoretical explanations of sport deviance. Most forms of sport deviance are broadly tolerated both within and outside of sport, a fact that perhaps explains why sport deviance has fallen off the radar screen in mainstream deviance and criminology theory. Subcultural attitudes of tolerance rather than disdain tend to prevail across social institutions when making decisions about what constitutes deviance in sport. The broad tolerance of sport deviance, we argue, should not be conflated with a lack of norms in sport or a theoretical position advocating the abandonment of the very concept of deviance. We conclude our introductory chapter by outlining how several houses of deviancy theory might be explored in the process of understanding how and why rule violations in sport matter sociologically.

The Pathological as Normal

Structural-functionalist explanations of the role of crime and deviance in social life have been critiqued by contemporary sociologists as rigid and conservative, masculinist, and empirically flawed (Atkinson 2003). While we are not structural functionalists, we believe that the academic short shrift the theory has received for more than two decades in North American sociology of sport unfairly rejects the important insight deviancy scholars such as Émile Durkheim, Robert Merton, and Talcott Parsons offer regarding rule violation and its regulation. Thus the inattention to this theory neglects its explanatory potential vis-à-vis sport.

Durkheim (1958) establishes a concept of deviance that is transcontextually and transhistorically important to any sociologist. He flatly rejects any definition of crime or deviance that views the subject matter as universally harmful to a society. Rather, he contends that the only common characteristic of all crimes or forms of social deviance is that they are acts disapproved of by members of a given community. Durkheim understands crime and deviance as behaviors that are historically and culturally determined and as behaviors that depend on situated actors' interpretations. The functionalist framework he uses to describe crime further defines it as that which shocks public or cultural sentiment. Deviance is an affront to the collective conscience and demands stern reprisal. Durkheim does not, however, suggest that an act shocks the common conscience because it is criminal or deviant. Rather, it is criminal or deviant *because it shocks the common conscience.* From any theoretical perspective in the sociology of deviance, this point has enduring analytical merit.

Crime and deviance, argues Durkheim (1958), are not unique or disastrous outcomes of human interaction. Rather, they are universal features of all societies and all cultures, of course to a greater or lesser degree. They represent a patterned *social fact.* From Durkheim's vantage point, the consistency of crime across communities indicates its key role in all human organization and expression. Given the robustness and durability of crime and deviance, both must serve a vital social function. For example, the punishment of offenders clearly marks the moral boundaries of a community and reinforces attachment to these boundaries. Punishment strengthens social solidarity by reaffirming moral commitment among the conforming population that witnesses the punishment of the offender. The morally good or law abiding are thus reassured of their social worth, and the integrity of the normative and penal systems is galvanized as deviants become publicly identified and sanctioned.

For Durkheim, the elimination of crime is virtually impossible. People in all societies will identify differences within and between themselves and others, no matter how small, and will mark and police these differences in some way. In the everyday practice of cultural life, people evaluate differences in behavior and assess them as good or bad, as normal or abnormal, or as natural or unnatural. Lemert's (1967) labeling theory is perhaps borne out of Durkheim's thoughts on the public identification and policing of deviant identities. Elias and Scotson's (1965) established and outsiders theory of group labeling as a power strategy also pays homage to the early ideas of Durkheim.

If, as Durkheim contends, crime and deviance are *functional*, then they must play a role in the maintenance of social communities. The control of crime and deviance demonstrates a society's capacity for flexibility and durability in the face of internal and external change. For Durkheim, contrary to the conventional view that crime is a social (or an individual) pathology, crime is a normal phenomenon and a social fact. Deviant acts should be punished if they offend the collective conscience, but the act itself should not be viewed as an emblem of cultural or structural illness. Deviance and crime are problematic, however, when cultural and legal rules are violated without control, indicating an inherent dysfunction of the collective culture and a lack of social organization bonding people together in normative behavioral patterns (Durkheim 1958).

It is easy to misread Durkheim's (1958) ideas as overly static conceptualizations of the deviance process, as so many subsequent sociologists and deviancy theorists have done. But we find merit in Durkheim's stance on the functional potential of deviance and argue that the mosaic of social institutions and actors in sport does create and enforce normative standards (though varied in form and application) for the participants as a community-based process similar to the one Durkheim outlines. Norms, folkways, conventions, mores, and institutionally codified laws in sport cultures certainly create a semblance of order, but we cannot assume that behavior perceived as deviant is pathological; neither should we assume that deviance in sport is utterly polysemic, fabricated by the media, or subject to boundless definition. As sociologists of deviance, we find it particularly interesting how groups of actors jointly define certain behavior as unwanted or threatening on the one hand while viewing other behavior as wanted or even socially beneficial on the other.

Wanted and Unwanted Deviance

We must not conflate wanted deviance with normative behavior. Wanted deviance is a behavior, thought, or symbol that violates an accepted social or cultural standard. Wanted deviance tends not to be defined as proper or just and is generally understood by perpetrators to be controversial. As Durkheim (1958) notes, wanted forms of social deviance invariably provoke social correction by recognized authorities. When wanted rule violations are relatively controlled, predictable, and rationalized, they are not seen as being emblematic of a pathological cultural or structural condition—yet, neither are they viewed as fully socially acceptable.

Plenty of evidence suggests that rule violation in sport is wanted by players, leagues, audiences, and other stakeholders. Watching forms of deviance, such as a fistfight in ice hockey, can be physiologically pleasurable and thus emotionally meaningful for audiences. The violation may thrill, intrigue, question, and reinforce meaningful social allegiances between participants and audiences. Nevertheless, rule violators are not always excused of their wrongdoing or granted an unchecked license to thrill with their particular form of wanted deviance—witness the increasing intervention of the authorities into the violence in ice hockey (see chapter 7).

An example of wanted and unwanted deviance in sport more clearly establishes their differences. Although certain actions are strictly prohibited by the rules governing a sport, such as Olympic sprinting, there is an unspoken degree of wanted rule violation among participants, coaches, and spectators. The public interest in a sport such as sprinting is partially driven by participants' abilities to set new standards, such as new national or world records. Compounding the desire of athletes and spectators to establish new standards is the technoscientific culture of training and competition that encourages the use of performance-enhancing drugs (Waddington 2000). Therefore, while many athletes are regularly suspected of being drug cheats, audiences appear willing to temporarily excuse illegal performance enhancement in sprinting, especially if national kudos (i.e., winning for the country) is at stake. Drug testing in track and field inevitably uncovers cheating, but rarely do rule violators receive the full weight of punishment from their athletic federations. If this is less true today due to the more sophisticated policing methods available to testers and perhaps to public pressure to blow the whistle on cheats, it has certainly been true throughout the history of the sport, which has hardly been rigorous when policing cheating. Only recently, for example, have elite athletes, such as the American runner Marion Jones, been pursued legally and criminally sentenced for cheating in sport. Considerable evidence suggests that Jones' 2007 admission of taking the drug tetrahydrogestrinone (THG) while competing and the International Olympic Committee's (IOC's) removal of her medals have less to do with internal policing in the sport and more to do with years of public debate and media allegations about her drug use. In this vein, Maughan, Burke, and Coyle (2004) raise the controversial but legitimate question of why drug-using athletes are not arrested, fined, or imprisoned in countries where the possession, distribution, or consumption of illegal performance enhancers is a criminal offence.

By comparison, the symbolic or actual presence of recreational drugs that have no obvious link to performance enhancement is consistently condemned by sports insiders and outsiders. English Premier League football player Robbie Fowler of Liverpool F.C. received a six-game suspension for a 1998 postgoal celebration in which he lowered his body to the ground and pretended to sniff the white touchline after scoring, thus mimicking the nasal inhalation of cocaine—a drug he was associated with in his personal life. Even though the celebration produced a chorus of cheering from amused spectators, Premier League officials were less than impressed by a professional footballer pretending to snort cocaine on the field of play and in full view of the thousands of people at the game and the many more watching on television. Earlier that same year, IOC officials stripped Canadian Olympic athlete Ross Rebagliati of a gold medal in snowboarding won at the Nagano Winter Games after he failed a drug test for tetrahydrocannabinol (THC), which is found in marijuana. Marijuana is not recognized as an official performance enhancer in sports such as snowboarding. Its consumption is deemed unwanted (and is prohibited outright by sports organizations such as the IOC), as it conjures unsavory images of social deviance in Western nations such as the United States, Canada, and the United Kingdom.

The lines demarcating wanted and unwanted deviance in any sport are not universal; nor are they negotiated by athletes, coaches, officials, or league administrators with reckless abandon. In power and performance sports such as rugby, ice hockey, basketball, and football (both European and North American versions), there is considerable tension regarding the tactical use of wanted deviance by coaches and athletes in the throes of competition and its mass mediation by sport promoters (Coakley and Donnelly 2005). Marketers of North American ice hockey might find permissible, on-ice violence hard to sell if both wanted (e.g., body checks or fist fighting) and unwanted (e.g., stick swinging leading to injury) forms of deviant violence in the game did not create excitement and tension for audiences. To make sense of such accommodations and contradictions, figurational sociologists suggest that the emotional tension-balances of safety, risk, and competition underpinning competitive sports are a defining feature of their allure in Western cultures (Dunning 1999; Elias and Dunning 1986, 21).

Marxist and neo-Marxist sociologists of sport, including Gruneau and Whitson (1994), caution figurationalists and others to acknowledge the groups who are hurt by the mass marketing of and audience fascination with wanted and unwanted deviance in sport. Both types of deviance are lucrative for the established capitalist hegemony in sport, a hegemony in which business policy monitors standards of play and influences cultures of violence embedded in sports like ice hockey. Profit-driven entrepreneurs in sport know that deviance sells seats and encourages the public consumption of sport media, which in turn fuels advertising and promotional revenues. North American sports fans pay huge amounts of money to watch or read about crime and deviance involving athletes. Ironically, those paying the heftiest price for deviant behavior may be the athletes themselves. Professional cyclists are banned for taking drugs despite institutional networks that place enormous pressures on racers to push past the barriers of human ability and establish new records (Atkinson 2007b). In American basketball, players such as Allen Iverson and Ben Wallace are fined thousands of dollars for brawling on court despite their corporate branding, and consumption, as thugs (Wilson 2006), and in ice hockey, enforcers are punished for their coach- and peer-approved brutality, which routinely shows up as Hits of the Day segments on television news and sport programs. While owners, sponsors, and officials prosper from on-field deviance, athletes are fined, suspended, dismissed, or banned permanently from competition when their behavior is perceived to cross the ambiguous line from wanted to unwanted. The contradictions and hypocrisy are obvious.

Certain forms of deviance are wanted by media promoters and audiences but are socially embarrassing and even disgraceful for sport insiders. The Skategate controversy at the 2002 Salt Lake Olympic Games, centering on inconsistencies in judging during the pairs figure skating finals, drew millions of viewers but unwanted attention to the Games' organizers and sponsors. Canadian skaters Jamie Salé and David Pelletier performed a technically flawless routine in their final skate and were thought to be the favorites for the gold medal. Yet the gold medal was awarded to Elena Berezhnaya and Anton Sikharulidze of Russia. Following an immediate public outcry, allegations of contest rigging were launched against one of the judges, Marie Reine le Gougne of France. The global media accused le Gougne of trading votes with Russian judges (who had alleged connections with organized crime in Russia) in the pairs ice-dancing competition. Skategate placed much unwanted public attention on pairs figure skating, judging-based sports, and the Olympic Games themselves (Sheppard

2002). As Durkheim would explain, it was morally imperative that the sport's adjudicating body identify and severely sanction deviant targets in order for that body to retain its own legitimacy and image of integrity.

A curiosity in our research efforts on deviance in sport cultures is why athletes, who are keenly aware of the social and material consequences of their wanted and unwanted rule violations, walk the deviancy tightrope and risk their careers. Even the most basic sociological insight leads us to consider the role of athlete socialization and how players learn to use, interpret, and rationalize wanted and unwanted deviance in their respective subcultural settings (Hughes and Coakley 1991), or—in extending our analogy—how the pathological is normalized as functional and appropriate in sport.

The Sport Ethic and Institutional Frames

The dramaturgist Erving Goffman (1974) describes how interpretive frames emerge within group settings and create guidemaps for social interaction. Following Goffman's lead, Hughes and Coakley (1991) explain how athletes in competitive amateur and professional sports learn such interpretive frames and use these frames to gauge commitment to the group and sport. The authors describe how athletes are taught to strive for distinction, accept no limits as players, make sacrifices for their sport, and play through pain and injury as part of an overarching sport ethic. While not all athletes are socialized quite so completely or assess all social interactions and athletic performances in relation to this sport ethic, this maxim is so pervasive that most athletes must encounter it and reconcile themselves to it at some point in their sport careers.

Hughes and Coakley (1991) suggest that the bulk of athlete behavior observed during competition and training or in social settings outside of sport jibes with the requisites of the sport ethic. The authors illustrate athlete behavior on a statistical normal curve (the terminology used here illustrates a clear influence from Durkheim and structural functionalism) and locate everyday athlete behavior at the heart of the curve (Hughes and Coakley 1991). Athlete behavior that deviates from the sport ethic is located at either tail of the normal curve. Hughes and Coakley view sport deviance as statistically rare. On the one tail, they place a category of behaviors they refer to as *positive deviance.* These are athlete behaviors that pursue the principles of the sport ethic to an unhealthy extent. An example of positive deviance is dangerous weight loss (for instance, through dehydration strategies) in order to make a weight category in boxing or wrestling or in order to please judges in an appearance sport such as gymnastics or figure skating. On the other tail, Hughes and Coakley describe *negative deviance.* These are athlete behaviors that overtly reject or dismiss the importance of the sport ethic. Disobeying a coach's instruction to attend every practice session or to work hard in training is an example of negative deviance.

One of the main contributions of Hughes and Coakley's (1991) deviancy classification system is the idea that sports insiders decipher rule violation subculturally. In sport settings, deviance is micrologically defined and controlled by situated actors who understand the customized principles of their own sport ethic. Thus we must direct empirical attention toward how decisions about wanted (positive) deviance versus unwanted (negative) deviance are negotiated. However, Hughes and Coakley do not ask why athletes commit either form of deviance with any theoretical consistency and thus leave sociologists of deviance with a series of unanswered questions regarding the etiology of rule breaking in sport cultures. From their very useful typology, however, we appreciate how athletes are taught to rationalize rule breaking or excessive behavior as a normal and acceptable aspect of sport culture through a set of neutralizing techniques familiar to all in the sport (Sykes and Matza 1957).

Smith's (1983) work on how cultural standards of play in sport as well as civil and legal codes figure into the policing of sport deviance might question Hughes and Coakley's theoretical emphasis on how rule violations are controlled in-house and are always dialogical with a sport ethic. Through the study of violence in ice hockey and other contact sports, Smith asserts that definitions of wanted and unwanted deviance are not singularly constructed within sport cultures and institutions. He classifies sport violence into four types and illustrates how both within-sport and extra-sport constructions of rule violation help determine what constitutes wanted versus unwanted violence in sport as well as in the wider community in which sport is played.

Smith (1983) describes the first category of sport deviance as *brutal body contact* and views this type of deviance as integral to certain sports. Such violence is permissible according to the rules of the sport and the civil and legal codes. Smith's examples of legitimate violence are found in ice hockey, rugby, American football, and boxing. Participants in these sports, by the very act of taking part, implicitly consent to the inevitability of rough contact. The second category of sport deviance, called *borderline violence,* consists of behaviors that violate the official rules of the sport but are culturally understood by players and fans to be wanted deviance. Such behavior—a fistfight in ice hockey is the author's main example—may be punished by referees or league officials but is widely accepted within player and fan culture. In many circumstances, officials allow it to take place if it is enacted by players of approximately similar physical stature and fighting ability. This observation in and of itself speaks clearly to the borderline status of this outside-the-rules behavior.

Smith (1983) sees the behaviors that make up his third category of sport deviance, termed *quasi-criminal violence,* as a more serious form of rule violation (although perhaps still wanted), as these behaviors violate both the formal rules of a sport and the social legal codes. Instances of quasi-criminal violence may symbolize a lack of concern for safety in and around the sport and generally produce serious injury for those victimized. Quasi-criminal violence typically provokes a formal, immediate, and severe response within the respective sport jurisdictions. An example of quasi-criminal violence is Michael Simko's assault on fellow ARCA race car driver Don St. Denis at the 2006 Budweiser Glass City 200. The two collided during lap 112, and both racers' cars were rendered immobile. Simko emerged from his car and attempted to kick his way through St. Denis' windshield. Simko dragged St. Denis from his car, and the two men exchanged punches on the track's infield while the race continued. In response to the incident, ARCA suspended each driver for the remainder of the 2006 season. Video footage of the event not only appeared on global newscasts for a week but also became the most downloaded video clip on the Internet do-it-yourself video site, YouTube, during all of September 2006. This fact confirms the public appetite for wanted but socially controlled sport violence.

Finally, Smith (1983) places certain acts of extreme, unwanted violence in sport in the category of *criminal violence*. This category includes behaviors that so flamboyantly shock the collective conscience of the sport, audience, and legal institutions that immediate serious criminal charges are warranted. For example, Manchester United player and French international captain Eric Cantona received a 9-month suspension, was permanently removed from the French national team, was assessed a £20,000 fine, and was sentenced to 2 weeks in prison for delivering a judo-style kick to Crystal Palace fan Matthew Simmons during a 1995 Premier League game. Cantona's kick was interpreted by fans, players, and league officials as so obviously outside the conventions of wanted aggression in the sport that a strict penalty was needed from the outset.

In sum, the respective subcultures and subcontexts of sport serve an important role in defining what counts as deviance and what is excused and condoned within each respective institutional setting. Though there may be overlaps among sport settings in how the sport ethic articulates itself, each sport tends to develop its own version of acceptable and unacceptable behavior. Over time, these attitudes become established aspects of the patterns, rhythms, and values of the sport and its associated fan culture.

Sport Deviance as Tolerable

The clear reluctance of the public to address sport-related problems, including, in Smith's (1983) terms, *criminal violence*, is not entirely explained by the degree to which normalizing frames within sport subcultures obscure what counts as a norm violation within games, leagues, or institutions. The reluctance to define a range of sport activities as unwanted deviance is an outgrowth of sport being viewed as a separate social world with its own allowable rule violations.

In this respect, we argue that many forms of sport deviance are quintessential examples of what Stebbins (1996) calls *noncriminal tolerable deviance*. A culturally tolerable deviance violates a normative code but is not interpreted by audiences as a legitimate threat to the collective (or moral) good. Tolerable deviance, Stebbins (1996) argues, may be undertaken for personal pleasure or private experimentation. It encompasses moderately proscribed deviant behaviors in Western cultures, such as sexual activities including cross-dressing, watching sex (e.g., striptease, pornography), swinging, group sex, and nudism; binge drinking; gambling; and the use of cannabis and other mildly psychotropic drugs. We contend that a wide range of sport behaviors may also be viewed as tolerable deviance. Stebbins (1996) himself acknowledges sport as a site of tolerable deviance, noting how athletes in risky sports such as snowboarding or mountain climbing pursue extreme challenges. These behaviors may oppose common sensibilities for self-protection, responsibility, and personal care but are tolerable because they pose little risk to broader populations outside of the individual participant or sport.

Stebbins' (1996) emphasis on tolerable rule violation most likely resonates for anyone who has participated in or studied sport cultures. Tolerable deviance is connected conceptually with our descriptions of wanted forms of rule violation in sport because it adds excitement in the sporting context—it adds what Katz (1988) calls *sneaky thrills* or what Hagan (1991) terms *disreputable pleasures*. In this way, sport deviance may provide an emotional double whammy for audiences since the tone and content of the rule violation poses little public threat and the act (i.e., a particularly brutal and rule-violating hit in American football) may be culturally and emotionally fascinating for those drawn to the aggressive dimensions of the game.

As both researchers and participants, we believe, based on our separate and joint ventures in sport, that sport deviance (in most forms) is viewed as tolerable by audiences for seven principle reasons. We refer to these reasons as *arguments* and summarize them as shown in table 1.1.

Hierarchy of Social Problems Argument

The criminological literature on police work shows that any urban police force creates a hierarchy of crimes to investigate (Knapp Commission 1972; Alpert and Dunhamn 1997; Kenney and McNamara 1999). Serious crimes such as murder, sexual assault, drug trafficking, child abuse, and armed robbery regularly appear at the top of these lists. Other behaviors, such as shoplifting or other common forms of theft, exist either in the middle or toward the bottom of these lists. The ranking of each crime on such lists is, of course, influenced by the perspectives of powerful social lobbyists and moral entrepreneurs (Becker 1963), including collective interest groups, economic stakeholders in the community, corporations, private citizens, and even targeted criminals. Control agents in a community simply do not possess the resources to monitor all instances of rule violation, and therefore certain criminal problems receive relatively little attention. From a cultural problems perspective, when communities face more pressing social and physical problems such as health and disease crises, unemployment, environmental degradation, and discrimination, issues that may be perceived as only mildly criminal or culturally problematic receive minimal public attention. Social problems involving statistically few members of a population also tend to be placed at the bottom of the agenda for social control.

Underscoring how a hierarchy of social problems argument might resonate for sport is the fact that social psychologists have uncovered troubling cultures of body distortion and self-starvation among female athletes in sports such as gymnastics, figure skating, and track. By investigating girls' eating pathologies (such as bulimia and anorexia) as conceptual types of body dysmorphic disorder,

TABLE 1.1   *Seven Arguments of Tolerable Sports Deviance*

Argument	Summary
1. Hierarchy of social problems	Social control agents cannot monitor all instances of rule violation. Behaviors on the crime agenda are prioritized. Certain social problems are heavily policed while others receive relatively little attention.
2. Internal policing	Sports teams, leagues, and governing bodies receive and use discretionary power to police themselves using nuanced insider understandings of the act.
3. Mimesis	Figurational sociologists view sport as mimetic because it resembles a safe yet warlike competition. Sport is significant to individuals because it elicits excitement through controlled violence and is structured by an understanding that it is not as perilous to the participants as actual war.
4. Athletes as a special population	Because they are seen as representatives of the community and are culturally revered, athletes who behave badly are protected as a special population.
5. Isolated offender or *rotten apple*	The indiscretions of athletes, however statistically typical, are individualized and viewed as unrepresentative of the wider sport culture.
6. Impossibility of legal intervention	Aggressive and violent behavior in sport is dismissed by the public and the agents of social control due to a belief that convincing judges and juries that sport deviance constitutes criminal behavior is unlikely.
7. Overamplification of sport problems	Athletic deviants are villainized in the media through sensational reporting. Over time, their disreputable images galvanize as they become notorious cultural figures. At the same time, the public becomes desensitized to their behaviors.

Reinking and Alexander (2005) show how certain athlete personalities are more predisposed to eating problems than others are. The extent of eating disorders in young female sport, or in general sport, is not known, but it seems unlikely that anorexia in female sport is any more pressing than obesity in adolescent populations in North America and elsewhere. From this perspective, it might be argued that time and money are better directed toward understanding and countering more common eating, body, and weight problems in the broader population than in the relatively smaller athlete populations.

Internal Policing Argument

In 2003 Dr. Wade Exum, the former director of the drug control administration for the United States Olympic Committee (USOC), spoke to a global television audience about the extent of drug cheating in American track and field. As a longtime insider to American track and field, he controversially released private files indicating that 19 American medalists were allowed to compete at various Olympic Games from 1988 to 2000 despite having failed drug tests leading up to the respective competitions (Knapp 2003). Exum alleged that more than 100 American athletes in several different sports tested positive for banned substances between 1988 and 2000. The athletes were cleared by internal appeals processes within respective sport federations such as the USOC, IOC, International Association of Athletics Federations (IAAF), and the World Anti-Doping Agency (WADA). Acclaimed American sprinter Carl Lewis was 1 of 3 Olympic gold medalists who tested positive for banned stimulants (pseudoephedrine, ephedrine, and phenylpropanolamine) in the months preceding the 1988 Games. In Seoul, Lewis originally finished second but was eventually awarded the gold medal by default when Ben Johnson of Canada was discovered to have failed a drug test.

Exum's files, summarized in an April 12, 2003 *Orange County Register* exposé, sent shock waves through the Olympic community (Knapp 2003). Critics of the U.S. dominance in track and field demanded intervention in order to eliminate drug cheating in the sport. Nearly half a decade later, no such external intervention has been initiated in amateur sports in the United States. The long-standing argument, promulgated by the USOC and IAAF following Exum's claims, is that only sport federations themselves understand how to police their own forms of deviance. At the minimum, Exum's files should have encouraged critics to ask how the extensive network of drug consumption and distribution within sports like track and field has avoided legal scrutiny (Knapp 2003). Given that steroid possession and distribution violates criminal law in the United States and other countries, why do sport federations continue to receive discretionary power to enforce, or ignore, antidrug rules?

The answer to this question in part lies in the way that sport federations such as the IAAF and IOC scapegoat particular athletes (e.g., Canadian sprinter Ben Johnson, whose gold medal in the 100-meter sprint at the 1998 Seoul Games was ironically later awarded to Carl Lewis) and cite their punishment as a measure of institutional efficacy. For example, Irish swimmer Michelle Smith won four medals (three gold and one bronze) at the 1996 Olympic Games in Atlanta. During her two previous Olympic Games, Smith's best result was a modest 17th place in the women's 200-meter backstroke. In the time leading to the Atlanta Games, Smith won three European swimming titles and trimmed more than 17 seconds from two of her personal bests in the pool. Following these unheralded performances, the Fédération Internationale de Natation (FINA), the governing body of amateur swimming, suspected Smith of doping. FINA expressed concern to the IOC that Smith refused out-of-season drug testing in 1995. FINA testers surprised Smith at her home in 1998 and requested a urine sample. The tests found a bizarre alcohol concentration in her urine sample, and FINA testers concluded that Smith doctored the sample by adding whiskey as a masking agent before submitting it. FINA immediately suspended her from international competition for 4 years. The sleuthing of Smith's doping practices was lauded by the IOC and WADA as an example of how internal control in amateur sport functions effectively. The sports world is filled with teams, leagues, and administrative structures that justify their internal policing by pointing to individual cases when many more cases involving precisely the same behaviors escape such close scrutiny. The controversial world of North American ice hockey, in which both inside-the-rules and outside-the-rules violations occur routinely, is a case in point. An assessment of the internal policing argument is offered by Young (2004a, 346-349).

Mimesis Argument

Elias and Dunning (1986) and Dunning and Rojek (1992) argue that a primary role of sport within complex societies is to take the routine out of social life. Sport is a social theater in which spectators are deliberately aroused by the tension-balances created through athletic contests. Figurational sociologists describe sport as *mimetic* because it deliberately resembles warlike competition. It is socially and emotionally significant to individuals because it elicits excitement through controlled violence in a battle that is not as perilous to the participants as an actual war. Spectators are excited by the often rough and rule-violating competitive exchange between the participants yet feel neither guilt nor repugnance in watching the action since the struggles are not real acts of war (Goodger and Goodger 1989; Sheard 1999).

The figurational construction of mimesis is pivotal for grasping why sport deviance is tolerated or promoted as wanted. For example, using the car as a battering ram in American NASCAR racing is a mimetic form of interpersonal violence in the sport. During a race, drivers illegally push, nudge, or crash into each others' vehicles as a maneuvering and jockeying strategy. High-speed crashes, rollovers, and multiple-car pileups occasionally result from the bumping. In a 2003 NASCAR race in Miami, Juan Pablo Montoya clashed cars with Ryan Newman. Newman bumped Montoya at high speed and sent his car head-on into the track's inner wall. Montoya, a former Formula One (F1) race car driver, received only minor injuries from the incident, even though flames engulfed his car shortly after the crash. Newman received no reprimand from NASCAR officials for the accident.

The promise of a crash caused by dangerous driving during a NASCAR race does more than draw audiences. For many decades, the video replay of death-defying crashes has been big business (Atyeo 1979). In 2007, a nonscientific search of Web sites devoted to NASCAR crashes produced more than 1.8 million relevant sites. Despite the tragic on-track death of racing legend Dale Earnhardt Sr. in 2001, an event that underscored the dangers of considering sport deviance as wholly mimetic, NASCAR audiences continue to derive considerable excitement from the occurrence of "controlled" crashes in the sport, even when these crashes are outcomes of rule-violating behaviors.

Athletes as a Special Population Argument

Another sport perspective views athletes as a special population with a license to participate in rule-violating behavior. Athletes, especially young males participating in power and performance sports, are socialized into believing that they are special people whose social transgressions in and around the playing field will be excused by parents, coaches, teachers, and even police (Benedict 1997). Athletes who participate in highly visible and culturally revered sports, even at young ages and amateur levels, may become celebrities in their communities. The public fall and punishment of an athlete–celebrity because of rule-violating behavior not only challenges cultural constructions of the athlete's moral character but also challenges cultural ideals about sport itself as a virtue-producing social institution (Miracle and Rees 1994). Coakley and Donnelly (2005) describe how hubris germinates within athletes who feel as if their actions are beyond reproach.

Bissinger's (2000) ethnography, *Friday Night Lights*, exposes how residents of the small town of Odessa, Texas, excuse local high school football players' disobedience as an act of community solidarity. Since high school football is so closely aligned with the town's collective identity, prosecuting the players' illegal behaviors is tantamount to condemning the town in general. Robinson's (1998) analysis of sexual assault in junior ice hockey reveals how Canadian communities tend to rationalize the criminal behaviors of young players. Teenage athletes accused of sexual misconduct are protected within small towns in order to avoid destroying their careers, and community leaders sidestep critiques stating that ice hockey culture is sexually exploitative of young women. Studies by Bissinger (2000), Robinson (1998), and others underline the degree to which communities remain willing to overlook the deviances and crimes of athletes who are protected as special populations.

Isolated Offender Argument

The indiscretions of athletes, however common and statistically typical, tend to be perceived as unusual and unrepresentative of sport culture by people termed *sport apologists*. Pete Rose's (baseball) or Michael Jordan's (basketball) gambling is defined as atypical, Michael Irvin's (American football) or Theoren Fleury's (ice hockey) use of recreational drugs is interpreted as individually problematic but not widely victimizing, and the spousal abuse perpetrated by star athletes such as O.J. Simpson (football), Sugar Ray Leonard (boxing), and Stan Collymore (English soccer) is interpreted with rotten apple rather than spoiled barrel logic. By pathologizing individuals and not the cultures that help produce their psychologies, characteristics, and patterns of action—in Elias' (1991) terms, their *habituses*—sport advocates deflect attention away from sport as a system of values that allows certain behaviors and personalities to emerge, endure, and remain relatively immune from sanction.

A recent and widely broadcast example of pathologizing the individual athlete rather than the broader sport culture was the 2003 sexual assault trial of Kobe Bryant. A Los Angeles Lakers basketball icon, Bryant faced an arrest and trial after Katelyn Faber, a 19-year-old hotel employee of Eagle, Colorado, accused him of sexual assault. Faber alleged that Bryant had forced sexual intercourse on her at the hotel of her employment. A global scandal resulted, and basketball advocates on both sides of the Atlantic were quick to divorce Bryant's actions from the culture or image of the National Basketball Association (NBA) and the sport of basketball (Reid 2004). Bryant and Faber eventually settled the dispute out of court; the terms of the settlement were not publicly disclosed.

Impossibility of Legal Intervention Argument

Smith's (1983) and Barnes' (1988) respective work on sport violence led them to conclude that criminal deviance in sport is difficult to establish. As we discuss throughout the book, sport is one of the few remaining social institutions that consistently escapes the modern reflex toward settling order and controlling problems litigiously. One of the most cited reasons why the police and criminal prosecutors avoid cases of violence and aggression in sport is the perceived lack of criminal intent in a player's actions, the inherent risks and dangers in competitive sport, and the apparent consent players give to being hurt during play (Barnes 1988). A considerable amount of sport violence is summarily dismissed by agents of social control due to a belief in the impossibility of convincing athletes, spectators, judges, and juries that sport deviance actually constitutes criminal behavior. More than a century's worth of case examples of failed police intervention into North American athletics supports this claim (Barnes 1988; Young and Wamsley 1996; Young 2004b).

Consider the example of the beanball in American baseball. Pitchers deliberately throw fastballs at opposing batters' heads as a tactic of competition, retribution, or revenge in the sport. Legendary pitchers Bob Gibson, Nolan Ryan, Roger Clemens, and Randy Johnson are among the most infamous pitchers throwing beanballs in the sport's history. The beanball is an especially dangerous rule violation, as a batter's reaction time at the plate—and ability to dodge such a pitch—is a matter of microseconds. The problem of beanballs developed pathologically, in Durkheim's (1958) sense of the concept, throughout the 1950s. The Major League Baseball Players Association instituted a mandatory helmet rule for players. Rather than crack down on rule violators and ban the practice altogether, improving equipment that allowed the practice to continue—in this case encasing players' heads in tough plastic—was easier. One of the most notorious examples of the beanball in the modern era occurred during the 1981 World Series. Pitcher Goose Gossage of the New York Yankees intentionally hit Ron Cey of the Los Angeles Dodgers in the head with a fastball, knocking Cey off his feet and concussing him. Given that athletes like Cey disavow their own victimization and consider such rule violations as just part of the game, legally intervening into sport violence cases becomes extremely complicated, and the successful prosecution of offending players becomes extremely unlikely (Young and Wamsley 1996; Young 2004a).

Overamplification of Sport Problems Argument

Cohen's (1972) account of how community folk devils are constructed through amplified media reports emphasizes the role of moral entrepreneurship in the deviancy process. It also highlights the processes by which the public may grow numb toward social deviance due to its ongoing, spectacular representation in the press. Deviants are first villainized in the media through secondhand and thirdhand accounts of their activities, and their disreputable images galvanize over time as they become notorious cultural figures. Cohen identifies a potential discrepancy between the actual frequency and threat of deviant behavior among those labeled as folk devils and the media-amplified significance of the act itself. He understands the media's willingness to report, and overreport, deviant behavior by folk devils as a means of selling copy. Criminologists studying media-influenced crime waves, such as Fishman (1978) and Sacco (2005), support Cohen's claims about the mass media's commercial interest in amplifying deviancy problems. According to Sacco, the media often hyperbolize cases of rule violation and crime, thus distorting public understanding of social problems in the community. Sacco notes that with such media overexposure, grand claims about the sheer presence of deviance, and sensationalization of deviance, people become accustomed to seeing deviance in everyday life and thus are less shocked by its occurrence.

The Nike corporation experienced intense global media scrutiny in 1996 following troubling reports detailing worker victimization in several of the company's manufacturing facilities located in developing countries. Disturbing accounts of corporal punishment, sexual abuse, slave wages, dangerous and unhealthy working conditions, and forced labor to exhaustion surfaced out of countries such as South Korea, Thailand, Pakistan, China, and Vietnam (Frisch 2004). A subsequent global Anti-Nike, Boycott Nike, and Just Don't Do It social movement and a massive media blitz into Nike's corporate practices demanded that the company and certain nations, including the United States, initiate immediate industry reform. Nike acknowledged problematic behavior in a few regions but maintained that several alleged and isolated cases of (especially female) worker abuse were overamplified by the global media. Apparently consumers of Nike products agreed, as the company set profit records during the second half of the 1990s (Firsch 2004).

The remainder of this book discusses the complex interplay of how deviance matters sociologically in sport cultures, how cultures of tolerance develop toward certain acts of sport deviance, and how the current institutional and social control mechanisms regulate sport deviance. One of our main goals in writing this book is to reposition sport deviance on the theoretical map and to argue that we all may learn far more sociologically about deviance by exploring its conceptual parameters rather than rejecting its empirical presence.

Discussion Questions

1. Can you think of any act of sport deviance that might be considered universally wrong? Why or why not?
2. Do you think that we have missed, in our seven arguments, any reason why athlete deviance is not considered problematic in sport?
3. Select a sport and examine what is defined as tolerable or intolerable deviance in that sport. Consider the roles played by all of the people involved (players, administrators, fans, and so on) that help the issue to be seen as tolerable or intolerable.

Recommended Readings

Durkheim, E. 1958. *The rules of sociological method.* Glencoe, NY: Free Press.

This is one of Durkheim's foundational texts on the ordering of social life and the influential nature of group norms and laws. It is also a treatise on how social facts emerge as part of collective life. This text stands as a seminal theoretical pillar in the sociology of deviance.

Hughes, R., and J. Coakley. 1991. Positive deviance among athletes: The implications of overconformity to the sport ethic. *Sociology of Sport Journal* 8:307-325.

This article established the analytical tone and content for sport deviancy researchers for nearly two decades. In it, the authors link athlete socialization to rule violations in respective sport cultures. They argue that deviance exists on a continuum and tends to be rationalized by athletes as hypernormal or hyperdeviant.

Sacco, V. 2005. *When crime waves.* Thousand Oaks, CA: Sage.

Sacco's book is a critical analysis of how, when, and why certain social problems are picked up and amplified by the mass media. As such, it examines how public stakeholders and interest groups selectively police social problems through the media and how cultural constructions of crime reflect the ideological standpoints of moral entrepreneurs.

Smith, M. 1983. *Violence and sport.* Toronto, ON: Butterworths.

The typology of sport violence that Smith presents in this book is still used by sport researchers in many countries. Smith demonstrates how norms, conventions, and laws both inside and outside of sport help frame acts of violence and aggression between players as normatively deviant or intolerably deviant.

Stebbins, R. 1996. *Tolerable differences: Living with deviance.* Whitby, ON: McGraw-Hill.

Stebbins problematizes the simplistic idea that good and bad exist as binary opposites in everyday life. He argues that deviance is far more contextual and open to social construction than we often think it is. He also argues that while we may recognize a behavior as deviant, we may not punish the people committing the act since associated rule violations pose little moral threat to the wider society.

CHAPTER 2

Sport, Deviancy Theory, and Sociological Research

© Greg Trott/Getty Images Sport

In 1976, Landers edited a volume titled *Social Problems in Athletics: Essays in the Sociology of Sport.* His preliminary examination of controversial sport behaviors was updated in the United Kingdom by Kew in his 1997 book, *Sport, Social Problems and Issues.* Neither book systematically discusses the relationship between the sociology of deviance and the sociology of sport. Both were very much investigations into social problems and were theoretically uninspiring. While there are several texts that include chapters on aspects of sport deviance and social problems in sport focusing on various sport-related controversies (these discussions are usually found in introductory sociology of sport texts), no one apart from Landers (1976) and Kew (1997) has rigorously explored how a full scope of crime and deviance theories may be applied in the sociology of sport.

Substantively driven textbooks in the sociology of sport literature on behaviors such as rape and assault, white-collar crime, and cheating in university sports certainly exist, but no book covers a wide range of *criminal* and *deviant* topics in a theoretically holistic and comparative manner. With this in mind, we feel that the legitimate place of deviancy theory within the sociology of sport is yet to be determined. While the respective fields of criminology and deviance continue to flourish in the sociological discipline, generations of sociologists of sport have exscribed deviance from their research. Authors such as Blackshaw and Crabbe (2004) and Coakley and Donnelly (2005) reject the conceptual underpinnings of the term *deviance* as overtly hegemonic, preferring not to explore whether classic deviancy or crime theories offer sport researchers anything innovative or helpful. What these and other authors are rejecting is the supposed value-laden character of the concept of deviance rather than the theories of deviance per se. Our intent throughout this work is to illustrate how sociologists of rule-breaking and contranormative sport behaviors might step back and examine whether deviancy theory has a legitimate place in sport research.

Further, we see merit in mining deviancy theory from the parent discipline because the empirical analysis of contranormative sport and sport behaviors is extremely common. The term *deviance* is rarely inscribed into such research as a meta-analytic tool; nevertheless, the emphasis on norm and rule violation—the cornerstone property of deviance—in and through sport is apparent. Consider some of the following ways in which deviance exists in and around sport.

EXAMPLES OF DEVIANCY

On April 21, 1980, Rosie Ruiz, a 23-year-old New Yorker, crossed the finish line as the women's winner of the prestigious Boston Marathon. She not only won her gender category but also set the third fastest time ever recorded for a female runner (2:31:56). Those involved in the event remarked how fit Ruiz appeared, especially when she approached the winner's podium relatively relaxed and free of sweat. Ruiz was a virtual unknown in the world of distance running, was not noticed as a front-runner during the race, and stunned the running world with her unexpected victory. However, spectators later approached race officials to testify that they had witnessed the runner entering the race illegally during the final mile and sprinting to the finish line.

Race officials of the Boston Marathon disqualified Ruiz from the race and soon after discovered that she had also cheated during the earlier New York City Marathon. Ruiz used the same tactic in New York, riding the subway from the starting line to a stop near the finish line. In a shocking repeat of Ruiz's rule violation, the winner of the 1991 Brussels Marathon, Abbes Tehami, cheated to win the race by having his coach run nearly two-thirds of the race for him. Tehami leaped into the marathon toward its end and claimed victory. He was also later disqualified.

Justin Fashanu was the first player of African descent to receive a £1 million salary in British soccer. He shot to prominence as a promising young player in 1980 and signed an unprecedented deal with the Nottingham Forest F.C. Shortly after signing for Nottingham, however, rumors of his homosexuality affected coaches' and teammates' treatment of him. Amid alleged homophobic and racist taunting by Nottingham staff and supporters, several on-field injuries, and media hounding, Fashanu failed to perform as a player. He spent the bulk of the 1980s being transferred from club to club in the United Kingdom (Southampton, Notts County, Brighton and Hove Albion, Manchester City, West Ham United, Ipswich Town, Leyton Orient, Southall, Leatherhead, Newcastle United, Toquay United, Heart of Midlothian, and Plainmoor), North America (Los Angeles Heat, Edmonton Brickmen, Atlanta Ruckus, and Maryland Mania), Sweden (Trelleborg), Australia (Adelaide City), and New Zealand (Miramar Rangers).

Fashanu "came out" in 1990, becoming the first prominent player in English soccer to disclose a gay identity while still playing. Colleagues lashed out in anger, and his brother John publicly labeled him a *poof* (Marshall 1991). Fashanu spent the 1990s attempting to find a welcoming home in the professional game, but constantly met with open discrimination and hostility. Following allegations of sexual assault made in 1998 by a 17-year-old American male, Fashanu hanged himself in a garage in London. His life and death serve as a reminder that gay and lesbian lifestyles remain taboo and "othered" in mainstream sport.

Debates about the representation of aboriginal and indigenous peoples in sport surfaced in the late 1970s. For more than 100 years, and especially in the United States, Little League, school, amateur, and professional sports teams have used images of native peoples as team logos or mascots, including traditional native peoples stereotypically adorned with headdresses, feathers, war paint, and loincloths. Such teams have native-sounding names, such as *Warriors, Braves, Chiefs, Tribe, Redmen, Savages, Redskins,* and *Squaws.* Since the 1950s, every version of the Cleveland Indians' baseball uniform has included their red-faced, smiling mascot Chief Wahoo. At different points in the history of the Atlanta Braves professional baseball team, the organization's publicity and promotion staff used the slogan "Take me out to the wigwam" to boost ticket sales. At one point the Braves employed Chief Noc-A-Homa as a human mascot. The owners erected a makeshift tepee in the bleachers near the field, and each time a Braves player hit a home run, Chief Noc-A-Homa emerged and danced for the crowd.

Although largely unchallenged throughout the history of North American sport, the use of Native American icons and mascots came under intense scrutiny in the last three decades of the 20th century as aboriginal activists across the United States and Canada increasingly protested, "We are people, not mascots" (King 2004). While professional sports teams have to this point successfully defended their legal or cultural use of Native American mascots, U.S. colleges and universities have proven to be a battleground of controversy. The University of Oklahoma discontinued its use of the Little Red mascot, Marquette University stopped using its Willie Wampum mascot, Syracuse University terminated its use of the Saltine Warrior mascot, and the University of Tennessee discontinued the Chief Moccanooga mascot. Recently, the University of Illinois discontinued its highly controversial support of the Chief Illiniwek logo and mascot. This decision came after nearly two decades of intense lobbying by organizations including the National Association for the Advancement of Colored People, the National Education Association, Amnesty International, the Modern Language Association, the Society for the Study of the Indigenous Languages of the Americas, and the North American Society for the Sociology of Sport. Similar stereotyping and use of exploitative native imagery at the Olympic Games have been studied by Forsyth and Wamsley (2005).

Tim Gmeinweser, a volunteer ice hockey coach of the Knights of Columbus Sabres (Edmonton, Canada), removed his 13- and 14-year-old players from the ice during a game against a team from New Sarepta, Alberta. Gmeinweser's team was losing by a score of 7 to 1 during the second period of the game. Several of his players, including his own son, had been injured during the match, and he feared for the safety of the rest of his team. From his perspective, the violence in the game had escalated without effective control and intervention from the officials.

Anticipating the injury of more players, Gmeinweser called his players off the ice and forfeited the contest. In response, Gmeinweser received a 1-year suspension from the Edmonton Minor Hockey Association (CBC News 2003). Charlene Davis, the president of the association, remarked that "coaches, who are volunteers, can't be made responsible for players' safety" (CBC News 2003). Several weeks later, Kent Willert, head coach of the Knights of Columbus Thunder peewee ice hockey team (players aged 11-12), received a 1-year suspension from the Edmonton Minor Hockey Association for similarly removing players from the ice for safety reasons.

Consider that in a single month (July 2007), numerous athletes from a host of sports were identified as rule violators. Professional cyclist Michael Rasmussen of team Rabobank was fired from the team, removed from the Dutch national team, and dismissed from the Tour de France (while holding the leading yellow jersey late in the event) for repeatedly missing competition drug tests. National Football League (NFL) player Michael Vick of the Atlanta Falcons was arrested for operating an illegal dogfighting ring. NBA referee Tim Donaghy was accused by the FBI of gambling on games in which he refereed. The FBI filed reports that New York Giants' professional football player Jeremy Shockey deliberately dropped passes during games in 2006 in order to win a fantasy league football pool in which he was entered.

These concrete examples only scratch the proverbial surface of everyday rule violating in and around sport. From a review of these cases and similar episodes, we have compiled a preliminary set of substantive areas, or categories, pertinent to the ongoing analysis of sport deviance (see page 26). The list is far from exhaustive, but we are struck by how little empirical research exists on most of the behaviors included on this list. We are equally curious about the lack of theoretical understanding advanced on each and the degree to which mainstream sociologists of crime and deviance have also ignored these behaviors. We provide this list only as a means of encouraging students and researchers to explore, with greater empirical force and theoretical rigor, the many manifestations of sport behavior across and within the 10 listed categories. The case studies we offer in the following chapters of this book are examples of how to explore only small portions of the deviance on this list.

Each of these 10 empirical categories of sport deviance could spawn hundreds of small research ventures across the globe to better understand the behaviors of those involved. A few of the empirical categories (e.g., insider misconduct, gender, sexualities, ethnicities, fan and crowd disorder) have received disproportionately more research than the others have received. A problem related to the lack of firsthand descriptive research on a majority of the 10 types of deviance is the lack of theoretical diversity or innovation within research on sport deviance.

Researchers interested in each of the 10 substantive areas have accomplished little to generate innovative or transcontextual theoretical understandings of sport deviance that could be utilized to study a wide range of sport deviance. In the bulk of the existing literature, a few theoretical usual suspects are dragged out and uncritically applied to cases of sport deviance. A majority of these theories are individualistic, oversimplify issues related to deviance in sport settings, or were not developed as theories of deviance or crime per se. For the sake of conceptual convenience, we bracket existing approaches in deviancy research into four main conceptual categories: *violence and aggression theories, subculture theories, identity politics theories,* and *victimology theories* (see figure 2.1). In the following discussion, we consider each category in turn and explain what we have learned about deviance in sport through each.

Traditional Strands of Sport Deviancy Theory

In the remainder of this chapter, we address and critique the four traditional strands of sport deviancy theory. Our intent is to highlight the degree to which sociologists of sport currently but unsystematically explain sport deviance under a variety of conceptual labels. In building this discussion, we review how sociologists have developed a set of methodological preferences for studying sport deviance. Toward the end of the chapter we introduce a blend of eight traditional and contemporary types of deviancy and criminology theory that could be explored in future research on sport deviance. The case studies we present throughout this book systematically apply these eight theoretical houses.

Violence and Aggression Theories

Deviance in sport is often perceived to be synonymous with violence and aggression in sport. Whether showcased as eye-catching behavior during a Highlight of the Night feature on sport television or critiqued in popular media as reprehensible, on-field and off-field violence involving athletes, fans, and

(Continued on page 28)

EMPIRICAL CATEGORIES OF SPORT DEVIANCE AND SAMPLE BEHAVIORS OF EACH

1) Alternative Sport Cultures
- Snowboarding
- Surfing, windsurfing, and water sports
- Skateboarding and other forms of street boarding
- X Games
- Ecoendurance sports
- Extreme fighting cultures and mixed martial arts
- Antijock movements
- Sport video games
- Yoga and new age athletic cultures
- Sport for All and Fair Play Leagues for children
- Le Parkour
- Animal blood sports

2) Health, Drugs, and Doping
- Steroid abuse
- Gene manipulation
- Corruption in drug-testing policies and organizations
- Use of painkillers and other masking drugs
- Olympic controversies
- Recovery from illness and disease
- Whistle-blowing
- Clearing of injured athletes by sport doctors
- Obesity and sport cultures
- Body pathologies
- Use of marijuana, alcohol, and non-performance-enhancing drugs
- Use of legal supplements and fitness products

3) Insider Misconduct
- Cheating during play
- Egregious or violent fouls
- Abusing officials
- Taunting and celebration rituals
- Hazing and initiation cultures
- Athletes and rape cultures
- Sexual abuse of and by athletes
- Education, athletes, and academic misconduct
- Athletes and partner abuse
- Overtraining, injury, and self-abuse
- Sport and criminal prosecutions for violence
- Player gambling and point-shaving

4) Olympic and Global Sport Controversies
- Host city bidding and bribery scandals
- Terrorism, militarism, and global games
- Judging and referee controversies
- Professional athlete participation in amateur games
- Local resource depletion
- Host cities and postevent debt
- Anti-Olympic movements

5) Fan and Crowd Disorder
- Stadium tragedies involving spectators
- Postevent rioting
- Field invasions by fans
- Missile throwing
- Fighting between players and fans
- Ethnographies of sports fans
- Vandalism traditions
- Sports, parents, and fighting
- Antisport social protests

6) Gender
- Sport opportunities in the educational system
- Funding equality and legislation
- Differential rule and pay structures
- Women, men, and hypersexuality
- Women in men's sports leagues
- Coaching and ownership inequalities
- Media coverage of women's sport
- Female sportscasters and male sports

7) Sexuality
- Homophobia
- Openly gay athletes
- Lesbian, gay, bisexual, and transgender (LGBT) sports leagues
- Gay Games
- Transsexual athletes
- Coach–player sexual relationships

8) Ethnicity
- Integration through sport
- Racial profiling and stacking
- Team mascots
- Cool pose and popular culture style
- Commercializing and exploiting ethnic athletes
- Minority coaches, managers, and owners
- Race and the biology of performance
- Sport and at-risk ethnic youth
- College, graduation rates, and ethnic minorities
- Globalization and migrant ethnic athletes

9) Corporate Sport
- Government sponsorship and subsidization of players and teams
- Commercial branding of athletes
- Drafting young and amateur athletes
- Media broadcasting rights
- Sport and transnationalism
- Disappearance of indigenous folk games
- Corporate stadia
- Monopolization and antitrust violations
- Equipment manufacturing in developing nations
- Ticket distribution and scalping

10) Sport, Civility, and Social Ethics
- Sport in educational systems
- Government-sponsored gambling
- Sport and political defection
- Animal rights and blood sports
- Environmental effects of sport
- Access to sport for all citizens
- Sport and religious expression
- Bill of rights for athletes
- Player unions
- Urban planning, sport, and gentrification

(Continued from page 25)

officials is the subject of widespread and prolonged public debate. Numerous sociologists of sport have theorized the causes of violence and aggression and related sociocultural experiences in a variety of games. But many scholars inside and outside of the sociology of sport continue to conflate the study of deviance in sport with the study of violence in sport.

There is no definitive work on either aggression or violence in the sociology of sport literature. However, a review of that literature reveals that the term *aggression* is typically conceived of as behavior that intentionally threatens or inflicts physical injury on another person or thing. The definition of aggression may include assertive behaviors (such as a verbal attack), discriminatory behaviors, or economic exploitations that need not produce physically injurious outcomes.

Olweus (1993) suggests that the term *violence* is confined to the use of physical force. He defines violent behavior as aggressive behavior in which perpetrators use their own body as an object to inflict discomfort or injury upon an individual. With such a definition there is an obvious overlap between violence and, say, bullying in sport, where bullying is carried out via physical aggression. Guilbert (2004) expands on traditional definitions by naming certain forms of sport intimidation as violence. He classifies *hard* violence as actions designed to impose pain and injury on opposing players and *soft* violence as verbal, symbolic, and psychological actions.

Many attempts to understand violence and aggression in sport focus on how situations of emotionally intense competition trigger aggressive cues within individuals. For classification purposes, we call these *biopsychological theories* of violence and aggression. Dollard and colleagues (1939) offer some of the earliest theories of aggression that social psychologists of sport have used to explain acts of on-field violence. They explain all forms of aggression and violence as a product of situationally experienced frustration, particularly frustration arising from blocked goals. From this perspective, a wide range of violent acts on the playing field, from *beanballs* in baseball to fistfights in hockey to two-foot and cleats-up tackles in soccer, can be explained as emotional responses to conditions of frustration occurring between players. Violent outbursts between athletes are explained as natural phenomena that occur in social spaces defined by intense competition for an object or a prize. Frustration may also manifest itself in response to officiating that is perceived to be inept or biased or as a result of taunting by other players.

Central among theoretical accounts that emphasize the biopsychological dimensions of sport violence is the Freudian-inspired instinct theory. Popularized by the ethological ideas of Konrad Lorenz (1963), instinct theory explains violence and aggression as Darwinian struggles for social superiority. Lorenz posits that violence and aggression occur naturally in any competitive context, and he attributes the manifestation of aggression in competition to its role in clarifying the ranking of the members of a group (such as a sports team). Lorenz and other instinct theorists also suggest that frustration is a motivator to participate in close, hand-to-hand struggles as a form of instinctual release. Given social rules curtailing the use of aggression and violence in everyday cultural life and the degree to which the instinct to aggress continues to underpin the human psyche, contexts like sport allow individuals to cathartically vent natural drives toward aggression.

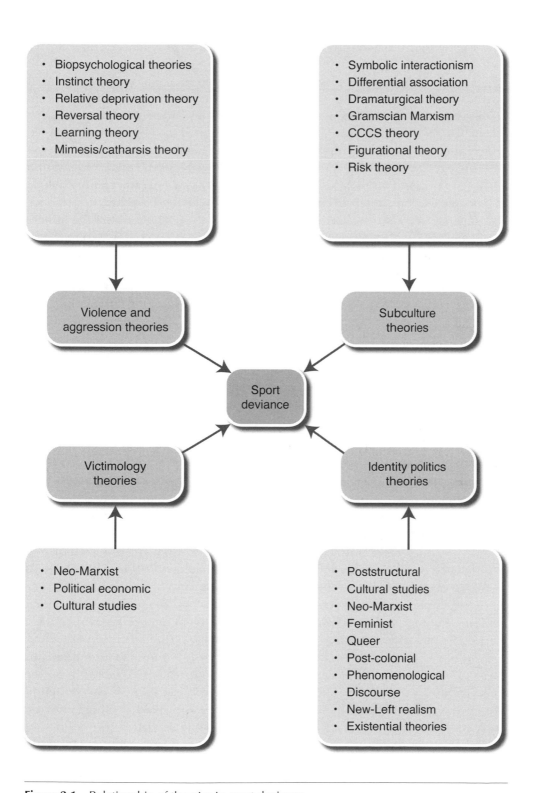

Figure 2.1 Relationship of theories in sport deviance.

A second category of violence and aggression theories commonly employed in the sociology of sport literature is social psychological in orientation. This category includes Gurr's (1970) relative deprivation theory, originally published in his book *Why Men Rebel.* Relative deprivation has been used to explain grievance, social hostility, and aggression. Gurr defines relative deprivation as "actors' perception of discrepancy between their value expectations and their value capabilities" (Gurr 1970, 24). In other words, relative deprivation is the gap between that "to which people believe they are rightfully entitled" and that which "they think they are capable of getting and keeping" (24). Deprivation leads to frustration and aggression and is not based on wants or needs alone but on wants and needs that people feel they deserve. Therefore, an athlete who feels that his performance warrants victory also feels a sense of entitlement to accolade. What the athlete thinks he is able to accomplish as a logical outcome of success is also relevant. When an entire group such as a sports team holds a similar skill–outcome mindset, a collective sense of entitlement toward winning, recognition, and success develops. If success is not forthcoming (if, for instance, it is unjustly blocked by a referee during a competition) and the individual or team feels deprived by the outcome, violence may result toward the source of the perceived deprivation as one, or several, of the participants responds.

Kerr's (2004) reversal theory attempts to explain why athletes or spectators may conform to rules in one context but revert to violence and aggression in others. He outlines a number of what he calls *bipolar meta-motivational states.* These states determine passive or aggressive behavior in any sport setting and are quickly altered due to factors such as frustration and satiation. He identifies four meta-motivational states: telic-paratelic, conformity-negativism, mastery-sympathy, and autic-alloic.

Kerr explains violence in sport by arguing that aggressors spend more time in a particular combination of meta-motivational states than in any other combination; namely, they spend more time in paratelic (risk-taking), negativism (norm-violating), mastery (dominance), and autic (self-concerned) states. The crucial point for Kerr is how such states are cognitively and physiologically experienced when combined with arousal and what he calls the *hedonic tone.* To be relaxed is to be in the telic state with low arousal and high hedonic tone. For Kerr, the combination of meta-motivational states and the feelings they create explains the motivation behind aggressive or violent acts of sport deviance. Kerr explains forms of soccer hooliganism in this way.

Bandura's (1973) more sociological account of aggression is summarized in the book *Aggression: A Social Learning Analysis.* Bandura uses his learning theory to describe how punishment and reward play an important role in the modeling of all behaviors. He argues that violence and aggression, like any other behavior, are learned through observation and imitation. While accepting the Skinnerian view that people learn through direct reinforcement of their responses to stimuli, Bandura adds that people also learn to aggress by observing the consequences of others' actions. His theory, not entirely dissimilar to Sutherland's (1947) theory of differential association, suggests that people imitate aggressors who are similar, who are rewarded for their actions, and who hold a revered social status. He concludes by observing that aggressors continue with violent behavior if it leads to a positive self-evaluative reaction. Simply put, if aggression is defined as pleasing or rewarding to the self, it will continue. Students of on-ice violence in Canadian hockey have contended that fistfights and vicious checking are learned in precisely the sociopsychological manner that Bandura outlines (Robidoux 2001).

Finally, process sociologists (Elias 1994, 1996; Elias and Dunning 1986; Dunning 1999) have examined the role of violence and aggression in arousing emotion and creating an exciting significance for spectators. A central principle in figurational research on long-term civilizing processes is that Western societies have become relatively unexciting social environments. With the general pacification of cultures that occurs over time, a collective need to devise and institutionalize cultural activities that strike a balance between personal pleasure and restraint arises. As outward displays of emotion are pushed behind the scene of social life (Elias 1994), individuals pursue a full range of activities that elicit exciting significance in highly controlled contexts of interaction (Maguire 1992).

Elias and Dunning (1986) argue that sports involving a moderate degree of physical violence (including rule-violating violence) are predominantly tolerable, thereby allowing individuals to participate either as competitors or as spectators in behaviors that are taboo in other social spheres. In the words of figurational sociologists, sports contests are situations in which there is a *controlled decontrolling* of emotions (Elias and Dunning 1986). Implementing such an approach, Atkinson (2002) analyzes how spectators' enjoyment of contact sports in North America seems to be increasingly influenced by the level of safe violence displayed through competition.

Subculture Theories

Influenced by social anthropology scholars of the early 20th century such as Park (Park, Burgess, and McKenzie 1925), Shaw (1930), and Whyte (1943) of the famed Chicago School, sociologists have studied groups of sports and athletes as distinct subcultures replete with their own subterranean values. For some authors, such as Fine (1987), a sport subculture might be a Little League team that shares esoteric perspectives on its characteristics and values. Chicago School symbolic interactionism (Blumer 1969) focuses on how people in everyday life define their social realities as meaningful and act according to shared and learned ways of viewing the self and the surrounding social world. Children in Little League sports such as baseball or ice hockey, for instance, are analytically approached as special populations, distinct in their shared statuses, identities, and collective rituals. Symbolic interactionism highlights the uniqueness of sport subcultures in the process of describing what it means to be a member of such an esoteric group.

Others have explored theoretical offshoots of symbolic interactionism, such as dramaturgy (Goffman 1959, 1963), in order to learn how definitions of normativity and deviance are negotiated within sport subcultures. Pike (2005) offers a grounded investigation of the ways in which traditional and alternative medical ideologies clash and are negotiated between injured rowers and their chosen physicians. She shows how female rowers occasionally define their available health care as restrictive (or as medically deviant) and pursue unorthodox health care strategies as a subcultural solution. Atkinson (2000) blends symbolic interactionism with ethnomethodology to study the deviant street subculture of ticket scalpers in Canada. His Toronto-based study focuses on how scalpers define the activity as tolerable deviance (Stebbins 1996) and devise subculturally appropriate means of conducting illegal trade.

One of the rare clear links between the sociology of deviance and the sociology of sport emerged in the 1980s and later as sport researchers tapped subcultural research initiated at the University of Birmingham's Centre for Contemporary Cultural Studies (CCCS). Members of the CCCS used a blend of Gramscian Marxism, semiotics, and labeling theory to conceptualize subcultures as reaction-formation groups that form in response to collectively experienced social or material problems (see chapter 3). Subcultural participants symbolically illustrate collective alienation through physical styles and social practices not found in the mainstream (Hall and Jefferson 1976; Hebdige 1979). The early work at the CCCS provided key theoretical insight into understanding why youth subcultures adopt flamboyant styles to represent their ideological positions. There is perhaps no more seminal a text on how subcultures utilize style as resistance than Dick Hebdige's (1979) *Subculture: The Meaning of Style.*

By the 1980s, sociologists of sport began adopting the CCCS interest in the politics of subcultural style and group disaffection to explain how specific youths utilize sport as a site of resistance. The CCCS-inspired perspective views do-it-yourself (DIY) youth sports with avant-garde styles as symbolic gestures of opposition toward sport orthodoxy. Beal (1995) understands skateboarding as a strategy of resistance against mainstream competitive sports that stress middle-class, White, and male norms. Wilson (1997) deconstructs the use of particular athletic footwear and uniforms by urban Black basketball participants as a symbol of racial resistance to White hegemony in the sport, and Thornton (2004) views the development of ultimate Frisbee subcultures as part of the early eco- or envirosport movement.

Although rarely viewed as such, the University of Leicester's Department of Sociology produced yet another stream of subcultural research on sport deviance in the 1980s. The department became internationally recognized for its study of football hooligan subcultures (Dunning, Murphy, and Williams 1988; Murphy, Williams, and Dunning 1990; Williams, Dunning, and Murphy 1984). Led by Eric Dunning, the Leicester School produced a range of subcultural and historical studies of deviance using the work of Norbert Elias. Their figurational approach emphasized the sociopsychological meaning of football hooliganism over time and its relationship to ongoing social and structural processes of industrialization, class gentrification, and community deterritorialization brought on by globalization. Figurationalists explained the violence expressed through hooligan subcultures in numerous ways: as unintended products of urban expansion, as working-class masculine frustration and anxiety experienced in an economically fragmented postwar Europe, as ethnic diversification in the United Kingdom, and as part of the broader sportization of English folk games.

A turn to risk theory (Beck 1991) in sociology has encouraged a recent generation of sport researchers to view thrill seeking via dangerous forms of athleticism as an example of deviance. Risk theorists in sport research seek to explain the cultural allure of extreme sports. During the 1990s, the term *risk* became associated with a sizeable corpus of research in the sociology of sport, and risk ascended to become one of the most popular research areas within the subdiscipline. Of particular interest are accounts of risk mentalities in sport, lifestyles of athletic risk taking, and the rise of extreme sports. Authors such as Rinehart and Sydnor (2003) and le Breton (2000) deconstruct sports insiders' ideologies of risking the body through surfing, hang gliding, skydiving, and backcountry snowboarding as a type of symbolic death and power game. The term *deviance* rarely appears in analyses of the risk, extreme, or death sports, but the empirical works in this theoretical vein nevertheless typically classify willful risk taking as contranormative, alternative, or marginal activity.

Identity Politics Theories

Dunn (1998, 20) defines identity politics as the process of aligning oneself with others who share feelings of marginality and oppression. Eschewing conventionally ascribed characteristics revered by dominant social hierarchies such as White or heterosexual, individuals engaged in identity politics struggle to redefine personal (and collective) identity in the process of winning space (Cohen 1972). In this process, violating dominant norms, values, and beliefs that provide the ideological support for cultural practices is critical. The sexual revolution, civil rights movement, and women's liberation movement (all gaining cultural momentum in the 1960s) were all forms of collective social activism aimed at bringing about social change and yet at their roots were campaigns of identity politics. That is, they reclaimed and redefined collective identities (race, sex, and gender identities in particular) through the subversion of hegemonic constructions of these categories.

Such cultural battles between normative and oppressed identities have been played out through sports for decades. Tommie Smith's and John Carlos' raised fists gesturing Black Power at the 1968 Olympics in Mexico City, Billie Jean King's 1973 Battle of the Sexes tennis match against Bobby Riggs, and Greg Louganis' 1994 public declaration of his sexual orientation were all heralded as symbolic challenges to dominant ways of thinking about race, gender, and sexuality in sport. They were also, from a certain perspective, deviations, or rule violations, of commonly expected sport performances and identities.

We are reluctant, however, to conceptualize race, gender, or sexuality politics in sport as forms of social deviance since there is an inherent tendency to pathologize and discriminate against what is labeled as deviant. Nevertheless, we approach the deliberate resistance against oppressive ways of seeing and doing race, gender, and sexuality through sport as a type of difference if not deviance in sport. In other words, we view this resistance as a technique for challenging how power inside and outside of sport is structured and mediated by ascribed social statuses. When we include identity politics in deviancy research zones, the true extent of the core concept's relevance to sport research becomes clear. Research on identity politics in the sociology of sport is so important that it has been tackled via a wide array of approaches, including postmodern and poststructural theories, cultural studies, neo-Marxism, political economic theories, feminist theories, queer theories, post-colonial theories, phenomenological theories, discourse theories, New Left realist theories, and existential theories (Atkinson 2007a).

Researchers interested in the expression of identity politics through athleticism have most consistently focused on the reproduction and contestation of dominant gender codes. Gender-power objectivists examine how opportunities for participation and leadership in sport (i.e., access to sport for men and women, coaching and administration opportunities, economic power positions in sport, and so on) are structured rigidly by traditional ideologies that place masculinity (i.e., strong, powerful, aggressive, authoritarian, intelligent) as the gender norm and femininity (i.e., weak, passive, dominated, domestic) as the deviant gender. Messner's (2002) book on gender in sport paints a sobering portrait of the structural barriers that remain for female athletes and the ways in which women are systematically marginalized in sports organizations. Simon's (2004) historical review of American legislation designed to remedy gender inequality in sport, including Title IX, suggests that even formal attempts to correct gender discrimination in sport receive limited public support. With this in mind, there is little surprise that the 2007 decision to award equal prize money to the men's and women's winners of the Wimbledon tennis tournament became international headline news and a hotly debated topic.

Gender-power subjectivists, by contrast, examine how dominant gender logics are negotiated or resisted in sport contexts. Theberge's (2002) research on femininity in Canadian ice hockey and Williams' (2003) analysis of women's football in Britain show how aggressive or contact sports provide contexts for consciously subverting cultural constructions of the passive woman. Theberge and Williams underscore how women come to associate athleticism, as well as the ability to exert power over others in athletic competition, with the performance of gender identity in sport. Rail's (1990) research on the experience of masculine-like physicality in women's basketball also explores how participants receive physical, psychological, and emotional satisfaction by culturally standing out as powerful figures. Young and White's (2007) volume on the identity politics of gender reproduction and resistance in sport examines how deviant gender performance is deliberately choreographed by athletes. Kestenbaum's (2003) research on a traditionally docile and feminine sport—figure skating—also reveals how young female athletes assert agency and individuality in their sport to an unprecedented, and heretofore deviant, degree.

Racial and ethnic discrimination is also an important dimension of gender politics in sport. Wiggins and Miller (2005) provide a detailed overview of how pseudoscientific discourses on the genetic basis of sport performance influenced more than 100 years of structured inequality in North American athletics. Individuals who were not Caucasian were systematically excluded from sport participation on the grounds that genetic inhibitors prevented them from appreciating complex rule structures demanding self-restraint and that their biologically primitive bodies provided an unfair edge in competition (Rhoden 2006). For more than 50 years, racialized athletes have been portrayed as deviant and as biologically gifted (Entine 1999; Hoberman 1997) or as part of a criminal or bestial athlete underclass characterized by hubris and aggression (Miller 2003). Similar research has been conducted on the systematic exclusion of Latinos (Mangan and DaCosta 2001) and Native Canadians (Paraschak 2007) from mainstream White, middle-class sport cultures in North America and elsewhere. Studies of racial stacking in sport (see Woodward 2004), which illustrate how athletes and coaches are assigned positions in team sports on the basis of perceived race and related physical and cognitive ability and status, arrive at similar conclusions about race, ethnicity, and ability. Rushton's (2000) inflammatory report, *Race, Evolution and Behavior,* concludes that the genetic characteristics that give Black athletes a physiological advantage in sport are linked with criminal predispositions that eventually manifest themselves in problems for the authorities.

Contemporary research on definitions of ethnicity and the politics of doing race through sport excavates ways in which minority identities are asserted publicly as nondeviant through sports practices. Embedded cultural antagonisms toward Asian, Indo-Asian, African, and other minority ethnicities in the West have been exposed and challenged through sport research (Coakley and Donnelly 2005). Pluss' (2005) study of cricket in China or Gillespie's (2000) analysis of cricket in Canada draw attention to how sporting excellence is produced on playing fields without mainstream cultural recognition. Cashmore (2002) argues that the systematic public underappreciation of non-White sports is a measure of a broader cultural exclusion of minorities and that their continuance indicates minority resolve. At the same time, minority groups have publicly confronted racist and ethnically insensitive representations in mainstream White sport, such as those found in the previously discussed team mascot images. The efforts of groups promoting Native Americans, such as the Society for the Study of the Indigenous Languages of the Americas, to eliminate the racist use of Native American names, images, and iconography in sport show how some people envision sport as a key location for negotiating minority rights (King 2004).

Identity politics continue to be the dominant focus of research on the exercise of heteronormativity of sport (Eng 2007). Heteronormativity is an ideology and a set of disciplinary practices that enforce heterosexual relations and related gender roles in social groups. Griffin (1998) describes sport as a heteronormative *deep closet* for the ways in which gay and lesbian athletes have been culturally and structurally ostracized. By interrogating how gay, lesbian, and transgender identities and symbols have been historically denigrated in sports worlds, authors such as Anderson (2005), Cauldwell (2006), and Pronger (1990) reveal how Western sport cultures remain some of the last bastions of overt and socially tolerated homophobia. Queer identities and sexual preferences were, until relatively recently, blatantly denied, excluded, and even aggressively marginalized in the masculine and heteronormative world of sport (Eng 2007). Even today, gay and lesbian identities are among the least publicly acknowledged and celebrated within, for instance, the sports media.

Collective expressions of queer politics in public spaces, including those of visionary and activist Tom Waddell (creator of the Gay Games), signal resistance to heteronormative politics in sport (Lenskyj 2003). Public and media awareness campaigns and gay, lesbian, and transgender sports leagues in Canada, such as the Toronto-based Front Runners and the Cabbagetown Group Softball League (Jarvis 2007), demonstrate not only that gay men and women exist and are active in sport but also that the absence of homoerotic desire and expression in sport is more myth than reality. Queer activists in the sports world endeavor to disrupt the essentializing constructions of sexuality in sport, the exclusionary White and heterosexual norms underpinning most sport practices, and the cultural tendency to deny sport as a site of multiple sexual experiences. McDonald (2007) presses for a further examination of how gay and lesbian experiences in sport may encourage a larger critique of the (White) hetero–homo, normative–deviant binary lines of identity construction. Theorists such as McDonald encourage innovative conceptualizations of how identity is constructed along sexual lines, suggesting a complete destabilization of the ways in which we assign and hierarchize athlete identities.

Finally, Howe (2004) and other scholars analyze sport as an institution that promotes normative constructions of bodies with differing ability. Joukowsky and Rothstein (2002) reflect on how traditional Western conceptions of sporting excellence offer little room for bodies with disability. Culturally revered athletic ideals revolve around images of the body as the pinnacle of human development and performance. Sport has been a terrain of cultural exclusion for people with disabilities and a tool for defining bodies of different abilities as deviant. In the first half of the 20th century, athletes who were blind, hearing-impaired, or paraplegic had relatively few opportunities to participate in sport. Certainly, the creation of the Special Olympics in 1962 and the Paralympics in 1960 and amateur athletic federations such as Disabled Sports USA and World T.E.A.M. Sports gave an entire generation of athletes with disabilities hope for future participation opportunities. Yet critics of the separate-but-equal system of competition formed through disability teams or leagues suggest that polarizing athletes into binary categories once again reproduces ideologies of normative and deviant bodies in sport.

Hoyle and White (1999), like Howe (2004), show how athletes with disabilities use sporting practices to prove their mental and physical strength. These athletes now use, both proactively and resistantly, the same cultural ideologies of athletic excellence that served to marginalize bodies of different abilities throughout the past. Further, athletes with disabilities now proclaim more frequently that, in Butler's (1993) terms, their bodies matter in sport and elsewhere.

Indeed, in North America some of the most inspiring athletic performances in recent memory have been produced by athletes with disabilities. In 1980, Terry Fox started his Marathon of Hope for cancer research, aiming to run one marathon (42.4

kilometers) a day across Canada. Fox, who had experienced cancer and a leg amputation, shattered images of athletes with disabilities as being passive even though he eventually had to abandon his run in late 1980 due to incapacitating lung cancer. Fox died tragically in the summer of 1981, but he is celebrated annually as one of the most inspirational athletes in Canadian history. Between 1985 and 1987, Canadian Rick Hansen logged more than 40,000 kilometers in a wheelchair journey across 34 countries to raise money for spinal cord research. American cyclist Lance Armstrong shocked the world of body normativity in sport by winning seven consecutive Tour de France races between 1999 and 2005. Three years before the 1999 Tour, Armstrong had cheated death by recovering from testicular, lung, and brain cancer (see chapters 5 and 6). Allegations about and inquiries into how Armstrong's illness had been cheated (and racing victories won) underline the fact that deviancy processes often form complex webs of social action. They also suggest that laudable and widely respected athletic performances may not exist independently of rule-breaking behaviors, such as the use of banned substances. The multiple dimensions of Armstrong's story also illustrate the links connecting the various parts of this book.

Victimology Theories

A radical departure from existing thinking about deviance in sport, victimological perspectives encourage us to focus on people who are affected firsthand by rule violation (Young 1991; Young and Reasons 1989). Victimology is rooted in the idea that people who participate in sport hold inherent rights to freedom, safety, and personal welfare. Moreover, athletes who are paid to participate in sport and are members of complex economic organizations should be viewed as workers who deserve institutional and legal protection. Early victimological research in the sociology of sport displayed Marxist and cultural studies leanings, addressing the myriad ways in which athletes or other sports insiders are systematically victimized, whether physically, socially, economically, or psychologically, by exploitative and corporate sport hegemonies (Young 1991).

Victimologists shift attention from the expression of deviance to the pressures placed on individuals in certain settings to behave in certain ways. For example, victimological studies of sport violence like those of Young (1991) and Young and Reasons (1989) challenge labor officials and courts to view the exploitation of athletes as a type of white-collar crime. Practices such as requiring that athletes gain or lose an unnatural amount of weight in the off-season, asking or even forcing athletes to play while injured, or implicitly threatening their job security if they do not play while in pain may be considered exploitative and a violation of their rights (Young 1993). Unfortunately, few sociologists of sport have pursued a victimological perspective; far more emphasize the subcultural kudos athletes receive for competing while under physical, emotional, or psychological duress (Howe 2004; Young et al. 1994).

Psychologists and sociologists of sport do, however, study sexually abused athletes from quasi-victimological perspectives (Brackenridge 2001). Pastiche analyses of the sexual exploitation of young players by coaches have been organized through psychoanalytic and feminist readings. David (2005, 12) identifies the sexual and physical abuse of children in sport as a theoretical *black hole*. He argues that the abuse of children in local or global sport cultures is relatively ignored and that sports insiders in highly competitive athletic circles rarely question whether intensive training, ideological indoctrination into winning at all costs, isolation from nonathletes, emotional manipulation, dietary control, sexualization, and corporal punishment for performance failure are appropriate for youths.

Contemporary research on nationalism and globalization attends to how the mass commercialization and market expansion of Western sport creates victim communities in economically developing nations (Sage 1999). The labor practices of corporations such as Nike, the spread of professional sports cultures into new regions, and even Olympic movements are linked to the economic exploitation of indigenous labor (through product development, facility construction, and gentrification) in countries like Mexico, Argentina, Brazil, South Africa, Indonesia, China, and Pakistan (Liao 2006; Maguire 1999). Other scholars address the non-human victims of global sport through their investigations of the environmental effects of organized sports like golf. Hyun's (1995) account of the golf industry's contribution to deforestation, water pollution, energy consumption, and the destruction of wildlife exemplifies how sport victimizes a range of sentient life forms and in return faces minimal social, legal, or cultural accountability.

Victimological research is cutting edge in the parent discipline of sociology and certainly in the field of criminology, but it has been underutilized in the sociology of sport. We revisit victim-oriented approaches to the study of sport deviance toward the conclusion of this book.

In what follows, we build on our review of how deviance is theoretically bracketed in the sociology of sport by addressing how researchers measure or evidence the practice of deviance in sport. We ask you to consider the links between the aforementioned theories and the methods used to study sport deviance.

How to Research Sport Deviance

Researching sensitive matters such as rule-violating and socially disreputable behaviors poses a series of practical and ethical problems for sociologists. While sociologists of sport may be interested in a substantive topic in the field of deviancy, their empirical work may be untenable for a host of reasons or, if practically plausible, complicated by social, cultural, and academic factors. For example, a researcher may be personally and professionally inclined to study partner abuse committed by athletes. While there is a range of theories explaining why athletes abuse partners and how partner abuse is patterned in sport, it is naive to think that persons involved in such disreputable or illegal behaviors will simply open up to researchers who may later publish work that gives them away or turns the spotlight on them. Similarly, why would a track athlete, swimmer, or bicycle racer who relies on performance-enhancing drugs speak freely to a stranger whose work may jeopardize his career and reputation? Thus, how does the researcher access the perpetrators and victims of sport-related deviance to either test or develop a theory? Excellent research ideas and the theories supporting them—including all of the theories covered in this book—are useless if they cannot be translated into feasible research projects. Given social sensitivity on issues such as abuse and cheating, which perpetrators are often fully aware of; ethical concerns about researcher safety and the protection of subjects; and the potential fallout of findings, deviancy is inherently difficult to interrogate and to report. In brief, while some subjects are amenable to examination for sociological research, deviance research often proves tricky.

However, for those researchers committed to the empirical analysis of rule violation in and around sport, methodological strategies *are* available. These include certain design strategies, methods of data collection, and modes of analysis that allow us to assess how deviance in sport is socially structured, culturally patterned, reproduced over time, personally experienced, institutionally managed, and reported in the mass media. In the discussion that follows we offer a brief overview of the salient approaches within deviancy research, compartmentalizing a variety of research design, data collection, and analysis strategies into three main methodological groups: structuralist methods, interpretivist methods, and critical methods.

Structuralist Methods

Decisions about an empirical procedure for studying deviance in sport largely reflect the researcher's ontological and epistemological assumptions. Ontological concerns relate to the nature of social reality and how this reality affects human group life. Structuralists, for instance, believe that there is an objective and patterned social reality that operates in a lawlike fashion, thereby determining all human behavior. Sports deviance, like any other social behavior, is systematic and is processually patterned by psychological, emotional, social, and cultural variables that theory can outline and explain.

Epistemological concerns deal with what researchers view as legitimate sources of knowledge about the way social behavior (like deviance in sport) unfolds. Methodological structuralism—not to be confused with the far more critical structuralism derived from linguistic theory (see Derrida 1978)—posits that we may know the lawlike nature of sport deviance by studying aggregate numerical trends in behaviors (e.g., the rates of fouls committed by soccer players, the emotional states of soccer players that lead to violence on the field, or the rates of cheating, such as diving in the professional game).

Structuralist research questions generally take the form of definitive causal hypotheses that can be supported or disconfirmed by empirical, often demographic, data. For example, a structuralist might hypothesize that basketball players from the southern United States commit more on-court fouls than athletes from the western United States. The data collected are fragments of evidence indicating whether patterns among variables exist in the social world as predicted by the theory. Structuralists, for example, assume that knowing the causal factors that lead to a rule violation in sport (taken as an objectively measurable social fact) allows us to predict who becomes a rule violator, what contexts generate rule violations, and, perhaps most importantly, how to control systematic rule violating.

Structuralists test theories and the hypotheses related to them by utilizing standardized and quantitative modes of data collection and analysis. Preferred modes of data collection include official statistics and secondary data analysis, surveys, and experiments or evaluation methods. The data gleaned are transformed into easily comparable numbers and are analyzed systematically through statistical programs such as SPSS, SAS, R, or STATA. As a means of illustrating how structuralism works in research practice, let's consider sport and the environment.

At present, research on the interface between climate change, environmental pollution, and sport and leisure is predominantly underpinned by a particular line of thinking. A review of the sparse literature on sport and environmental damage reveals that, with few exceptions, sociologists of sport focus on how climate change and pollution negatively affect the sport experience for participants (Wheaton 2004). Subsequently, they focus their concern about environmental damage on repairing the earth so that participants may perform even more sport. Almost completely ignored are the effects that sport and leisure have on our natural habitats and, more consequentially, the separation of the needs of humans and the needs of the earth that is found in most sport cultures (Petrovic 2004). Despite an abundance of evidence suggesting that sports such as golfing, skiing, football, ice hockey, cycling, and fishing as well as tournaments such as the Olympic Games have massive and potentially irreversible effects on habitats and ecosystems, no one has studied environmental destruction via sport as a patterned and enduring form of social deviance or has studied this subject using deviancy theory.

Structuralists might commence research into sport and environmental destruction by testing whether a particular deviancy theory helps identify environmentally problematic sports and explain whether sports dominated by particular social groups are among the most hazardous to the environment. Turk's (1969) version of culture conflict theory might be utilized to predict that middle- and upper-class sports that are marketed to tourists are the chief offenders. As a preliminary step, secondary data (i.e., existing statistics) on highly commercial upper-class tourist sports in countries like the United States and Canada might be used to examine any systematic patterns regarding environmental impact. From these data, the environmental effects can be communicated as standardized numeric figures (i.e., gallons of water polluted, amount of carbon dioxide emissions created, kilograms of pesticide used, or acres of forest cleared) that provide a descriptive summary of sport's contribution to habitat degradation.

Other structuralists might mail questionnaires to members of major sports organizations such as the PGA, NHL, FIFA, and IOC to test a given theory, such as Turk's. Since surveys are often used to measure how people's attitudes shape their social practices, a questionnaire would be useful for gathering information on how and why sports organizations pollute. Hypotheses from

Turk's conflict theory could be encoded into the survey through questions focusing on the organization members' awareness of the environmental effects of sport, the ways that the power elites in the sports manage concerns from environmental lobbyists, the role of environmentalism in sport marketing, and the institutional policies designed to protect the environment from sport. Additionally, researchers might mail a different questionnaire to a range of amateur or professional participants in the given sports. Such a questionnaire might focus on the awareness or concern the players and spectators have for environmental damage, their contributions to environmental pollution and repair, and their assessment of how to improve the environmental footprint of sport.

Finally, structuralists might use methodology from the natural sciences to conduct a social experiment regarding the effect of a sport's organizational policy on environmental awareness and practice within a specific group. This type of experimental design is referred to as *evaluation research*. Here, social scientists are asked to assess whether or not an institution's policy—in experiment language, an institution's treatment or intervention—influences behavior in the manner intended. The introduction of a new policy is, in effect, a social experiment designed by an organization to alter human behavior in some way.

Let's imagine that a private golf resort in British Columbia, Canada, or Colorado Springs, United States, develops a multipronged environmental program to reduce its environmental pollution and disruption by eliminating pesticide use on the course, by watering the greens fewer times per week, and by introducing only local flora and fauna. The program also aims to promote environmental responsibility among club members through awareness fact sheets and signs posted in the clubhouse, increased availability of refuse containers on the course, and package-free snacks and meals on the course. A sociologist of sport might be asked to gather related data and analyze (most likely through surveys) whether the resort's new policies actually work with respect to the stated initiatives. That is, the sociologist of sport must determine whether the signage increases members' awareness and whether the additional refuse bins and package-free foods reduce litter in the area. These are some concrete ways in which a structuralist methodological approach might help in the study of sport deviance.

Interpretivist Methods

Like structuralist methods, interpretivist methods are also underpinned by a series of philosophical assumptions about reality and social knowledge. Interpretivists stress that we can only understand the lived, created reality of deviance by collecting information on the mind-sets of the rule violators (e.g., how they define rule violating, why they commit a particular act of deviance, or what it is like to be labeled as a social transgressor in sport). Interpretivists phrase research questions as guiding propositions or sociological problems for *exploration*. For example, an interpretivist might ask, "What is it like for a woman to play in a sport culture dominated by men?" Thus, interpretivist forms of data collection must tap into how people understand, communicate, and respond to deviance in sport. Interpretivist data—evidence fragments collected by asking people to describe their sport experiences—provide tentative portraits of how deviance is experienced and understood by people within certain groups or institutional settings.

Interpretivism is predicated on the idea that social scientists seeking to understand people's lived actions must first understand social behaviors, thoughts, and systems of representation actions *from the participants' perspectives.* Social researchers should methodologically get as close to those perspectives as possible without arriving at a conclusion before completing investigation. Interpretivism denies that an objective reality exists independently of people's thoughts and actions. Interpretivism does not, therefore, concern itself with searching for broadly applicable laws about the form, content, and expression of deviance in sport. Rather, it seeks to produce descriptive analyses that emphasize deep, interpretive understandings of what people inside and outside of sport understand as *social deviance.* Interpretivist methods of data collection and analysis tend to be inductive, exploratory (or descriptive), and generally qualitative.

With respect to research design, interpretivists generally employ one of three data collection and analysis strategies. Each is based on the principle of *analytic induction* (Glaser and Strauss 1967). Simply put, each uses data collected from the empirical ground up to build concepts and theories about group life. A popular method of induction-oriented interpretivist research is interviewing. In an open-ended interview, researchers ask specially identified informants about their experiences with, attitudes toward, and activities pertaining to a given topic. Interviews are designed to resemble informal conversations between the participants and the interviewers and are often organized by only a few general research questions. Participants are encouraged to speak freely about a subject and to describe what they know about it using their own vocabularies. The interviewees' words, stories, and thematic tones become the researcher's sources of data. There are many varieties of interviews apart from the standard one-on-one format employed by social scientists. These include focus-group interviews, memory-work interviews, and computer-assisted or computer-mediated interviews.

Interpretive sociologists of deviance have also relied on ethnographic methods. In ethnography (also referred to as *field research, participant observation,* or *observation),* the researcher becomes a part of what is being studied. Here, the researcher may actually participate in the activity to experience it firsthand (i.e., become a football player to study football culture) or hang out with a group of people as a loose participant (i.e., go to the beach every day to speak with and watch surfers). Behind ethnography is the idea that only by directly engaging in a given setting can researchers truly understand insider perspectives and activities. Data take the form of conversations between people (which may, and often do, include interviews), observations, field notes, pictures, video, and physical artifacts gathered in the field. Ethnographic studies strive to provide richly detailed representations of life in a particular social milieu.

Of growing popularity among ethnographers are two particular methods of field research: autoethnography and visual or documentary analysis. Autoethnography seems to be used more widely in the sociology of sport than in the sociology of deviance. It is a research design in which the researcher is the subject of the study and provides a narrative account of involvement in a particular social activity. The goal is to represent sociological knowledge about the world in an alternative social scientific format—one in which narratives about life are not distorted by sociological theory. In the sociology of sport, for example, we have Hockey's (2005) account of running while injured. Hockey offers an emotional narrative about what it is like to feel a moving but damaged athletic body. Visual ethnography or documentary analysis presents alternative ways of seeing and knowing social life. Researchers use pictures and video (principally) to represent lived experiences beyond the written text. Classic sport documentaries such as *Hoop Dreams* (1994) are powerful ethnographies that allow audiences to gain entrée into the lives of the actors and to literally *see* their social worlds unfold.

Maguire (1999) studies the global migration of professional athletes among sports leagues. Often lost in the mass media stories about player salaries, transfer fees between teams, and a player's effects on a particular team are discourses on what migration through sport is like for athletes. Maguire argues that ethnic minority players who migrate to nations like Canada, the United States, and England to play are often alienated, ostracized, and ridiculed as deviant within the cultures of their new teams and broader host nations. Maguire does not offer this but an exploratory, interview-based study of how particular athletes experience migration and ethnic othering in a sport like American baseball could shed light on a private aspect of professional sport that audiences know very little about. Further, by asking participants how they experience and understand sport as a migrant, foreign national, or ethnic other, we could learn a good deal about how foreign identities are assessed and are responded to in particular settings.

An ethnographic analysis of ethnic othering in professional or global sports migration might prove difficult unless the researcher is already a professional athlete. However, if interested in minority sport experiences, ethnographers could join an ethnically homogeneous team at the recreational level, such as a local softball team, tennis club, or swimming league, and choose a team where they would be a visible minority. The goal of such a research venture might be to understand how it feels to be an outsider in a small setting, to understand how sport institutions help mediate ethnic differences between people, or to understand how sport cultures reproduce, negotiate, adapt, or resist ethnic differences between athletes and fans. Such a project could also be amenable to autoethnographic approaches.

Critical Methods

One outgrowth of the ethnographic work of the famed Chicago School began in the 1970s around the time of the publication of the landmark criminological text *The New Criminology: For a Social Theory of Deviance* (Taylor, Walton, and Young 1973). In this outgrowth, sociologists of crime and deviance increasingly explored what may be broadly called *critical theory* in the study of rule-violating behaviors. Theoretically influenced by the Frankfurt School (especially the works of Adorno, Horkheimer, and Marcuse), Gramscian (1971) hegemony theory, and the discourse theory of Foucault (1979) critical theory emerged as an attempt to deconstruct the antecedents and outcomes of cultural power and knowledge. The term *critical theory* has proven difficult to define, but certain strands of cultural studies, literary and feminist theory, ecocriticism, postfeminist theory, music theory, queer theory, and postmodernist theory are examples of the critical approaches that have influenced sociological research. As Andrews (2006) notes, the general field of critical theory is now prominent in the sociology of sport.

Critical criminologists and sociologists of deviance typically interrogate how systems of social control (such as the state, the educational system, or the media) work separately and in tandem to reproduce forms of social stratification, exclusion, and dominance and, in the process, to identify normal and deviant (Best 2000). In academia, the project of critical theory is to challenge taken-for-granted assumptions about what and who is deviant and to give voice to alternative ways of knowing the world around us. In doing so, critical theorists concerned with the sociology of deviance deploy a series of methodological approaches to expose how power-ridden social codes are meted out in the practice of everyday life.

Critical methodologies show how mediated discourses and other collective cultural representations naturalize and reinforce power and inequality among people. Common are media analyses (television programs, print advertisements, movies, songs, and so on) of how images of normativity and difference are circulated as objective or factual. The emphasis is given to exposing the preferred meanings of power and authority encoded into a text and evidencing how both subtle and overt forms of power (hegemony) operate within it (Hall 1980).

A related hermeneutic methodology popular among critical theorists is *standpoint methodology*. An offshoot of critical feminist theory, standpoint methodology takes the epistemological position that the bulk of social scientific research produced on deviance or any other sociological subject is androcentric. Standpoint methods allow for data collection (using interviews, ethnography, performance ethnography, documentary, literature, and other representational methods) on the ways in which gender influences our conceptions of knowledge, the knowing subject, and the practices of inquiry (Reinharz 1992). Practitioners of standpoint methodologies argue that dominant research practices disadvantage women by excluding them from inquiry, denigrating their feminine cognitive styles and modes of knowledge, producing theories of women that represent them as inferior or deviant, and developing theories of social phenomena that render women's activities and interests invisible or marginal.

One of the most complicated but popular of the critical methodologies is *deconstruction*. Based on the philosophical work of theorists such as Heidegger (1993) or Derrida (1978), deconstruction locates and dissects the concepts in a social text that serve as the axioms for thought both within and outside of that text. In the study of the sociology of deviance, deconstruction projects might aim to expose the inherent rules of normality and deviance encoded in a particular text. For example, in 1996 an entire issue of the *Sociology of Sport Journal* was devoted to deconstructing Michael Jordan as both a legitimate and a deviant American sporting, ethnic, and gender symbol. Related to deconstruction are the Foucauldian (1979) genealogical and archaeological methods currently popular in the sociology of sport. Genealogical and archaeological methods examine how particular historical discourses of truth, knowledge, reason, and social ethics—discourses that frame how we are able to understand deviance and social control—continue and discontinue over time.

Here is a research example illustrating how critical methodologies might be incorporated into the study of sport deviance. Imagine that you are interested in studying homophobia in sport cultures, and you select women's golf as a case example. You gained an initial interest in the subject by reading Guiliano and Knight's (2003) article on the way that the media coverage of women's sport encourages heteronormativity and heterosexism in athletic practices and thereby reinforces dominant relationships of power and authority between sexed men and women. From the article, you speculate that there may be present but unstated tones of homophobia in media coverage of women's sport, and so you seek to explore the idea through media-based research on women's golf in the United States. For this study, you decide to use Internet news stories about women's golf and golfers, national television coverage of LPGA tour events, and sport periodicals focusing on professional golf in the year 2007. You are interested in collating hundreds or even thousands of textual descriptions, visual representations, and other symbols of gender, sexuality, and homophobia in media coverage of women's golf to examine whether any relevant patterns emerge from the data.

When conducting the research as a critical theorist, you might be methodologically influenced by discourse analysis. You assume that the newspaper discourses about particular female golfers, the language employed in the television coverage of women's golf, and the narratives provided by the players in media texts contain both manifest (denotative) and latent (connotative) social codes about gender and sexuality. You examine whether dominant cultural expectations regarding heteronormativity (Cauldwell 2006) are structured into the discourses and representations of women's golf and, if homophobic sentiment is found, determine whether it is overtly or subtly present. As a critical theorist you might then question what effects heteronormative discourses have on the world of golf. For example, a critical theorist might inspect whether writing and representing heteronormativity and homophobia in the sport maintains power balances between straight and gay communities in the United States and male and female players in sport.

A deconstructionist approach to the media treatment of homophobia and heteronormativity in women's golf might seek to destabilize the taken-for-granted homophobic assumptions embedded in golf discourses. Here, deconstruction of U.S. media texts pertaining to women's golf could help dissect why players such as Natalie Gulbis, Annika Sorenstam, or Michelle Wie are used so frequently to promote the sport. A critical theorist might be led to deconstruct texts regarding Gulbis, Sorenstam, and Wie and expose if their representation or popularity is tied to a showcasing of their stereo-typical femininity. A systematic deconstruction of the fundamental cultural assumptions upon which the texts are written could yield significant insight into how heterosexism and homophobia are produced through images and discourses that privilege the players who abide by the norm. As in the case of discourse analysis, deconstruction is not only a practice of data collection but also a mode of cultural analysis.

Finally, if you adopted the standpoint methodology you might be inclined to interview a sample of female professional or amateur golfers and use their knowledge of gender and sex as an interpretive frame for understanding how power operates within the sport. From a standpoint methodological perspective, you may feel that media coverage of women's golf obfuscates the ways in which homophobia and heteronormativity exist in the sport. You could conduct interviews in order to tap women's unmediated stories and knowledge regarding sexuality and its enforcement in golf. This method would be geared toward providing women with voices in the production of theory and fashioning a grounded sociological understanding of gender and sex norming in sport using women's standpoints first. A standpoint methodologist might then compare and contrast women's stories about gender and sexuality in golf against mass mediations of gender and sexuality in golf to look for inconsistencies between insider and outsider interpretations.

In sum, as you read through the chapters in this book, you should do so with an eye for the connections among research questions, method, evidence, and knowledge. No method or source of evidence on the presence and meaning of deviance in sport is exhaustive, but some tend to be more efficient than others given the obvious practical problems addressed by the researchers. The case studies offered in this book are based on firsthand empirical research efforts but are not methodologically perfect by any means; nor do they represent the full spectrum of potential research methods undertaken by sociologists of sport. They illustrate, we hope, how theoretically informed research problems are pursued through active empirical research and how claims about the practice and meaning of deviance in sport should be grounded by solid research techniques and practice.

Moving Backward and Forward With Theory

In an attempt to break ground in the theoretical and methodological study of sport deviance, we have decided to revisit traditional theories of crime and deviance as well as review more contemporary thinking about deviance processes. We have learned a great deal from the concepts and theories that abound in the study of sport deviance, but we feel that there is a dearth of theoretical consistency, dialogue, and development within the literature on sport deviance.

In the remaining chapters of this book, we present a series of case studies selected from our own research on sport deviance in order to unpack how criminological and deviancy theories can be explored with concerted intent and purpose. Through our past research ventures, we have come to develop particular sociological curiosities of how deviant sport communities exist, how individual and collective bodies are made deviant in sport settings, and how mass mediations of deviance play active, not passive, roles in establishing what counts as deviance. To this end, we include Le Parkour and greyhound racing as case studies of deviant sport communities; drug use, emaciation, and illness transgression as case studies of body pathologies in sport; and ice hockey violence and terrorism at the Olympics as case studies of the intricacy of media deviance through sport.

In each chapter, we review where the subjects emerge in the sociology of sport and the sociology deviance literatures and then review the empirical details and theoretical interpretations we have made of the cases. At the end of each chapter, in a section titled Theoretical Intersections, we suggest potential interpretations of the cases and future directions for research in the area by examining eight theoretical ways of seeing the cases. The eight houses of theory we apply represent a range of traditional and more cutting-edge criminological and deviancy ways of understanding sport deviance. To date, these houses are predominantly untapped in the literature on the sociology of sport deviance. Respectively, these houses are as follows:

1. Functionalism and Strain theory
2. Conflict theory
3. Interaction theory
4. Social control theory
5. Classical theory
6. Critical theory
7. Gender and Feminist theory
8. Integrated theory

For every case study, we select existing work from within each of the houses to demonstrate how we might approach the study of deviance in sport using a particular criminological or deviancy model. The principal goal of this format is to encourage students and colleagues to think reflexively about how a broader range of theories might be used in research on sport deviancy.

Discussion Questions

1. From your perspective, which of the theoretical approaches we have summarized in this chapter best captures the essence of sport deviance?
2. Review the list of sport deviance acts we have provided in this text. Ask yourself if we have missed any or if you would delete any from our list.
3. If you were to conduct research on deviance, which methodology would you choose? Why?

Recommended Readings

Blackshaw, T., and T. Crabbe. 2004. *New perspectives on sport and deviance.* London: Routledge.

> This book offers a contemporary and theoretically innovative examination of deviance as a social and political construction. The authors deconstruct deviance as an ideologically loaded cultural term and suggest that collective understandings about what constitutes bad behavior in sport is more of a media fabrication than an objective social reality.

Dunn, R. 1998. *Identity crises: A social critique of postmodernity.* Minneapolis: University of Minnesota Press.

> Dunn's text represents thinking among identity and postidentity researchers in sociology. It explicates the centrality of identity as a chief determinant of social behavior and as a social symbol of human interaction. Along these lines, the author addresses how debates about and negotiations of identity are part of the everyday social fabric of life.

Hebdige, D. 1979. *Subculture: The meaning of style.* New York: Methuen and Company.

> Hebdige's seminal text underlines the importance of how subterranean youth cultures construct and deploy style as a means of articulating resistance to mainstream cultures and politics. The author theorizes how youth groups transform from resistance-oriented protestors to mainstream cultural icons and commodities.

Lenskyj, H. 2003. *Out on the field: Gender, sport and sexualities.* Toronto, ON: Women's Press of Canada.

> Lenskyj's book problematizes taken-for-granted assumptions about gender, sexuality, and heteronormativity in sport. It illustrates how sport is a significant cultural battleground with regard to how social power is exercised through gendered and sexualized bodies.

Young, K. 1991. Violence in the workplace of professional sport from victimological and cultural studies perspectives. *International Review for the Sociology of Sport* 26:3-14.

> In this article, Young provides one of the first victimological approaches to the study of sport violence in the sociology of sport. Building on a Marxist and cultural studies framework, he questions what would become of sport if we considered athletes as workers possessing the same rights to health, safety and other civil liberties that employees in other workplaces possess.

PART II

Deviant Sport Communities

The heart of the sociological enterprise is understanding the dynamics of group life. We use a range of terms to define the groups that sociologists study, including *dyads, families, peer affiliations, subcultures, communities, institutions, nation-states,* and even *global networks.* Both chapters in part II examine how two distinct sport communities may be studied as deviant along a series of theoretical lines. In chapter 3, we tackle a popular subject in the sociology of sport—deviant youth subcultures. We present the case study of Le Parkour as a means of inspecting how youth resistance to mainstream sport cultures and contemporary social neoliberalism in major urban areas has been problematized in the late-modern era. In chapter 4, we examine a relatively underexplored deviant sport community—the greyhound racing community. Chapter 4 includes a critical analysis of animal blood sport cultures and discusses how the scholarly neglect of this dimension of sport deviance reflects a broader speciesist tendency found throughout sociological theory.

Youth Tribes in Sport

Throughout the 1980s and 1990s, a spectrum of radical youth sport and leisure practices emerged. While there is little empirical evidence to suggest that mainstream youth sports in North America, including baseball, football, ice hockey, and basketball, waned in popularity during this time, the institutional model of youth sport (that is, the traditional way of thinking about and structuring sport for young people) clearly lost its status as the *only* model of sport mentoring for youths. Exploring do-it-yourself athletic endeavors such as skateboarding, rock climbing, and wakeboarding led sociologists of sport to reconsider the varied roles that sport may play in youth socialization as well as the extent to which cultural ideologies are impressed upon young people through their involvement in sport.

A theme emerging in the study of these radical youth sports was that of social resistance. Rinehart and Sydnor (2003) summarize how sociologists of sport started to understand the creation of sport and leisure forms, both by youths and for youths, as an innovative means of rejecting dominant social codes and power structures in sport as well as beyond sport. For example, sociologists of sport began to understand skateboarders as protestors against the confining ways in which urban space is traditionally used and policed, windsurfers and surfers as opponents to corporate waste and environmental damage, and ultimate Frisbee players as critics of sports that disrespect safety and fun. At the same time, embedded within each of these activities are fundamental social positions on questions of class, race, and gender (Rinehart and Sydnor 2003).

By the turn of the 21st century, however, youth resistance studies in sociology of sport seemingly lost favor (Atkinson and Wilson 2001). Many sociologists using a wide range of theories decried an overreliance on *resistance* as a meaningful conceptual tool and stressed how the social politics of demonstrating identity through acts countering hegemony are best studied as floating, hypersubjective, and polysemic acts of personal representation. From this point of view, there is no objective or even intersubjective deviance through resistance in alternative youth sport, as one person's act of resistance may be interpreted as another's act of conformity.

In this chapter, we argue that youth resistance intentionally crafted through sport and leisure is alive and well but requires theoretical reassessment. The case study of Le Parkour is employed to examine the complex ways in which youth subcultures use sport and athleticism to negotiate and struggle for cultural space and social legitimacy in urban settings.

From Resistance Subcultures to Lifestyle Sports

The concept of subculture continues to be used widely within studies of youth deviance, despite suggestions that it no longer bears empirical validity (Muggleton and Weinzrel 2004; Atkinson and Young 2008). Atkinson and Wilson (2001) point out that, rather than abandoning the concept outright, sociologists of (sport) deviance have reformulated it and its implementation. One such example is the emphasis on social resistance as a marker of what constitutes a subcultural formation. Here, subcultures are social groups whose members consciously, and often flamboyantly, violate class, gender, race, ethnic, sexuality, or religious norms and often intend, in their process of disrupting culturally taken-for-granted ways of seeing the world, to challenge the power base of a society that creates social stratification.

Throughout the early and mid-1990s, considerable sociological research was conducted on youth subcultures in sport as being resistance-oriented (see figure 3.1). Surfers, BASE jumpers, kite surfers, hang gliders, beach volleyball players, ultimate Frisbee enthusiasts, skateboarders, BMX riders, rock climbers, windsurfers, and even street lugers have been studied as youth sport formations with unambiguously oppositional tendencies (Maguire 1999). Each developed particular athletic preferences and practices, esoteric styles of language and dress, music preferences, and other group-signifying practices. Rinehart and Sydnor (2003) show how such groups, who sociologists of sport almost unanimously believed, at first, to reject mainstream sport values and ethics, ushered in a new set of sporting sensibilities and possibilities to North American youths. Referred to as *alternative, resistant, whiz, extreme, edge,* or *postmodern* youth sports, each was categorized as fundamentally oppositional to the dominant sport and social orders (Wheaton 2004).

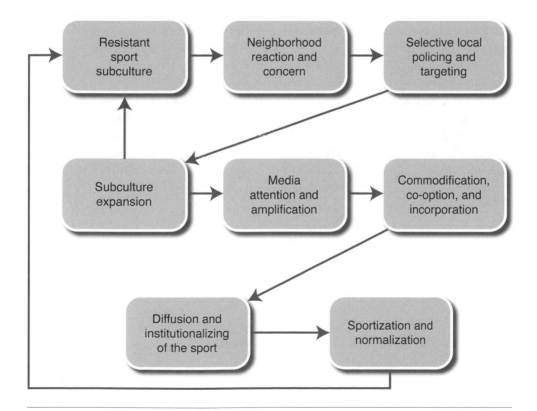

Figure 3.1 Emergence of resistance-oriented youth subcultures.

Perhaps most importantly, the new cadre of resistance sport enthusiasts seemingly disavowed parent-controlled, heavily competitive, rule-bound, commercial, authoritarian, and exclusionary forms of organized sport like football, baseball, and basketball. Skateboarders, in particular, were heralded as the working-class youth sports heroes of the 1970s and 1980s, as they used free forms of athleticism to carve out socially marginal athletic identities. Becky Beal (1995), whose research on skateboarding is foundational in the subcultures literature, was one of the first to document the group as countering hegemony and therefore being socially resistant. Her research showed how skaters reject White, hypermasculine, and middle-class jock cultures, preferring instead to explore the liminal (Shields 1992) possibilities of sport through highly individualized, creative, autonomous, rebellious, and personally authentic skateboarding tricks and techniques performed in a variety of public spaces. Groups such as skateboarders were identified as the urban rebels of the 1990s and were often targeted by police and other control agents for disrupting social spaces such as parking lots, public parks, and shopping malls. The persistent targeting of participants by authorities encouraged a generation of young skateboarding enthusiasts to emblazon the slogan "Skateboarding is not a crime" across their T-shirts.

Until the turn of the 21st century, sociologists of sport in many countries clamored to analyze youth resistance in a wide variety of sport settings. The notion of cultural resistance strongly impacted the sociology of sport discipline in the 1990s, contouring many of the ways researchers examined sports during that time. Youth sports were no exception. Wilson (2002) argues that within only a brief time frame, however, the analytical tide turned and sociologists of sport began to question the viability of youth sport groups as *resisting* anything at all. Like Rinehart and Sydnor (2003), Wilson suggests that most alternative sport groups not only contain residual elements of mainstream sport cultures but also, as time passes, come to resemble mainstream sport groups themselves. In an earlier subcultural study using Canadian university rugby as a case example, Young (1983) had similarly underscored the simultaneously resistant and co-optive or incorporative potential of sport.

From where did the original theoretical inspiration to understand sport subcultures as resistance emerge, and what is the current status of youth resistance research in sport studies? Arguably, Albert Cohen's (1955) early analysis of subcultures encouraged sociologists of youth culture to interpret a variety of social practices as resistance. Perhaps the most influential of the early American subculture theorists, Cohen suggests that subcultural activities are generally oriented toward resolving problems with youth status or identity frustration. Because status criteria, or the means of achieving social status, are defined and protected by middle-class standards, working-class youths are often excluded from legitimate opportunity structures for achieving social status. The deviant subculture serves as a collective solution for working-class youths, as the goals, standards, and identities that are established in the subculture can be achieved through the local means available. Since subcultural formations are derivations of parent cultures (and their social class trappings), they express a symbolic opposition to the dominant culture.

Although Cohen's subculturally sensitive version of strain theory is theoretically foundational in many ways, subsequent sociologists of sport who studied resistance in sport subcultures throughout the 1990s drew most heavily on Marxist cultural studies. As mentioned in chapter 2, during the 1960s and 1970s a core group of scholars in the United Kingdom built on Cohen's assessment of youth subcultures and pioneered innovative studies of how youth styles articulate social difference and forms of opposition. Established in 1964, the Centre for Contemporary Cultural Studies (CCCS) at the University of Birmingham went on to become the intellectual hub of research on culture and subculture. Much of the early subculture research conducted at the CCCS (Hall and Jefferson 1976; Hebdige 1979; Williams 1977) held that any given social structure does not contain one monolithic culture; rather, it contains several main (class) cultures, with one holding authority as the ruling culture. Key CCCS subculture texts, including Hall and Jefferson's seminal *Resistance Through Rituals: Youth Subcultures in Post-War Britain* (1976), outlined how subcultures arise in response to socially structured class relations: "[R]elative to these cultural-class configurations, *sub*-cultures are sub-sets—smaller, more localized and differentiated structures, within one or other larger cultural networks" (13).

According to the CCCS work, in order to understand the *structure of feeling* (Williams 1977) in any given subculture, we must first analyze its multilayered or doubly articulated nature, locating the subculture in relation to its original parent culture (such as working-class culture) and referencing the parent culture within larger social relations. In CCCS-inspired research, this typically meant that studies were anchored by the analysis of how working-class subcultures engage in social resistance against more autonomous middle-class customs and traditions.

Focusing on how British youth subcultures such as the teddy boys, mods and rockers, and skinheads were social constructions, Dick Hebdige (1979) demonstrates how resistant behaviors tend to be accompanied by a specific, and usually flamboyant, style. According to Hebdige, style is created to signify both in-group cohesiveness and disassociation from the dominant culture. Further, it is constructed from a range of available cultural commodities that have preexisting (i.e., dominant or preferred) meanings. The Italian theorist Eco (1972) calls this process *semiotic guerrilla warfare.*

Hebdige (1979) believes that it is necessary to decode the constitutive elements of style because the objects hang together as part of an overall *homology.* Intergroup experience is represented through the homology, and "each part [of style] is organically related to the other parts and it is through the fit between them that the subcultural member makes sense of the world" (113). However, Hebdige also forecasts that socially alternative subcultural styles are ultimately appropriated within a dominant culture. The clothing, language, or music of subcultures becomes fashionable in the larger culture, and the widespread distribution of style as a commodity minimizes its resistant or subculturally authentic nature through seemingly inevitable mass incorporation.

The two most prominently studied youth sport subcultures during the 1990s (and later) influenced by CCCS theory are undoubtedly skateboarders (see Beal and Wilson 2004) and snowboarders (see Heino 2000). With respective roots in the 1960s (skateboarding) and the 1970s (snowboarding), these sports emerged in North America as direct rivals to mainstream middle-class sport ethics and practices. Participants devalued authority in sport, reveled in a do-it-yourself style of baggy and pastiche (antiuniform) dress, and generally articulated ennui with dominant sporting forms. The subcultural *noise* (Hebdige 1979) they created through movement and style attracted new generations of youth sport participants and encouraged these new participants to *keep it real* by experimenting with sports on the edge. But, as the CCCS researchers predicted, there were subcultural costs to mainstream popularity.

Humphreys (1997) argues that with the rise of extreme sports cultures in the 1990s, the development of the American television station ESPN2 as a platform for rebel sports, the commercialization of the X Games, and the boom in magazine and video game representations of sport cultures, resistance sports like snowboarding were entirely co-opted into the mainstream American culture. In a later assessment of skateboarding as a form of social resistance, Beal and Wilson (2004) contend that if skateboarding culture resisted the mainstream, it did so only momentarily. With the popularization of the sport and the *Tony Hawkification* of its culture into a globally marketed and prepackaged commodity, the quintessential antisport showed all of the trappings of mainstream commercial sport by the late 1990s. Through such studies of youth sports, argue Rinehart and Sydnor (2003), sociologists of sport initiated a sobering second look at youth sport as resistance (Atkinson and Wilson 2001). Indeed, Wheaton (2004) and others have suggested that the CCCS stream of subcultural research in sport overly romanticized the degree to which youth sport subcultures operate as meaningful forms of social resistance. The notion of hyperbolizing sport's potential for social empowerment is not new. For instance, several critics (see Dunning, Murphy, and Williams 1988; Young 2000) of Ian Taylor's subcultural work on British football hooliganism (see Taylor 1971) have argued that Taylor's insistence on an early 20th-century *participatory democracy* in which ordinary fans allegedly shared power over the game with players and owners was at odds with actual structures of control at that time. Nevertheless, most sociologists continue to agree that *romantic* social research tends to be inaccurate and misleading, and it is certainly true that much of the sport subcultural work has been critiqued in this way.

Maffesoli (1996) and Muggleton (2000) contend that with the current development of more eclectic and fragmented ways of life, resistance has become difficult since the distinction between alternative and mainstream cultures is increasingly blurred. As class, race, and gender boundaries collide and fuse, so do the boundaries of traditional subcultures. It may be impossible to ascertain what a specific style communicates, as no truly dominant interpretation of the style exists either inside or outside of a subculture. If, as Polhemus (1994) claims, there is a current gathering of the subcultural tribes and a stylistic exchange between youth groups, authenticity is engulfed by a sea of mass-marketed commodities and images. In the youth tribe supermarket of style (Polhemus 1994), individuals are free to select from a plethora of products to paste together hybrid styles. From this point of view, youth never need to become genuine members of a subculture, since they can simply purchase membership through commodities and thus look and act like a member.

The case study of snowboarding may also reveal that sociologists have over-interpreted youthful resistance through sport. As Popovic (2006) shows, considerable evidence suggests that first- and second-generation snowboarders were never a fully *resistant* subculture; rather, they were a product of more mainstream values sympathetic to a market economy. Snowboarding has always been a commodity culture in this respect, organized by snowboarding manufacturers to be a style tribe for all; and an expensive one. Further, Popovic contends that snowboarders never intended the practice to be subculturally *tight*. Instead, it was intended as a competitor sport to skiing and a form of leisure geared toward creating a particular youth style. For Popovic, the emergence of popular snowboarding icons like Olympic hero and corporate spokesperson Shaun "The Flying Tomato" White illustrates the degree to which snowboarders seek to create a global market niche for the sport in a commercial and hardly oppositional way.

Also important is the question of whether the measures that sport subcultures take to internally police the styles they create allow them to retain their authenticity in a commodity-based culture. Thornton's (1995) and Sardiello's (1998) statements on the complex processes by which members of subcultures assess the authenticity behind mass-marketed style aside, many postmodernists (including those conducting sport research) reject any sense of subcultural integrity given the increasing interest in extreme sports. Subcultural boundaries are now fuzzy, permeated by anyone able to draw upon physical props, language, and body movements to emulate the original subculture's style. Since identity in the postmodern era is defined by purchasing power and the consumption of signs and imitation without understanding, being an authentic member of a youth sport subculture is not as important as looking like one. As long as youths wear the right snowboard boots, use the right surf wax, are versed in the latest skateboard lingo, or mountain bike on the best off-road trails, they are subculturally *down*—at least to the point where subcultural identity testing commences (Donnelly and Young 1988).

In building on the work of Maffesoli (1996), Bennett (1999) maintains that youth subcultures are ephemeral social groupings, since members enter, withdraw, and ultimately disband. Bennett uses Maffesoli's term *neo-tribe* to refer to youth subcultural formations in order to stress the transitory nature of subcultures such as skateboarding or snowboarding, in which there are few core ideologies, lifelong participants, and committed, noncommercial rebels. Bennett claims that neo-tribes are lifestyle groups, in that members immerse themselves temporarily and then move on to another leisure pursuit. In the context of sport subcultures, many young people immerse themselves in an extreme sport or two, adopt the group's commodified physical and ideological markers of resistance, and then migrate to the next neo-tribe when doing so is culturally en vogue.

A cluster of researchers, including Wheaton, Booth, Kay, and Kusz (see Wheaton 2004), build on Bennett's emphasis on sport subcultures as lifestyle groups while minimizing the theoretical focus on subcultures as inherently oppositional. In referring to windsurfers, rock climbers, ultramarathoners, and others as *lifestyle sport participants,* analytic attention is given to how sports are not necessarily valued by participants for resistance but for the way in which the sports fit homologically within participants' alternative lifestyles and identities. Lifestyle sport enthusiasts define their identities by extensive participation in respective sport settings, valuing the roles and statuses of their lifestyle sports over all others. Sociologists of lifestyle sport also direct attention to how "just being there and doing it" as everyday life (Wheaton 2004, 8) is gratifying for participants and how long-term commitments to marginal or less intensely commercialized sports crystallize as a central component of self-identity.

We might add that the turn to lifestyle sport is occurring at a time when an ethos of neoliberalism appears to be growing within North American sport, health, and leisure cultures. Leading theorists of neoliberalism in sport, including Silk and Andrews (2006), argue that late-modern or postmodern capitalist cultures are saturated by do-it-yourself ideologies of personal enhancement, consumption, and self-responsibility. Andrews and Silk provide a detailed analysis of how and why a broad range of sport enthusiasts view physical activity in terms of individual but not necessarily social benefit. Sport, as well as the associated health it fosters, becomes a matter of personal choice and construction—buttressed, normally, through specific commodity consumption—with less of an overt emphasis on creating potentially subversive identity through nonmainstream sport. Directly in league with analyses of lifestyle sports, neoliberalist deconstructions of contemporary sport and health preferences focus on how individuals are encouraged to rely less on state or institutionally regulated forms of social interaction and more on personally designed ways of achieving health and wellness goals.

The case study we discuss in the remainder of this chapter describes how classical resistance theories of youth subculture may be coupled with analyses of lifestyle sports to produce novel ways of viewing resistance in youth sports and leisure. Specifically, we analyze Le Parkour as a deviant youth subculture and alternative sport culture.

Le Parkour

During the past two decades, cities such as Paris, London, New York, Copenhagen, and Toronto have become hotbeds for a form of urban running, gymnastics, and martial arts known as *Le Parkour* (or simply, *Parkour).* Contemporary Parkour, introduced by French practitioners David Belle and Sébastien Foucan in the mid-1980s, is a practice and an ideology of athleticism focusing on uninterrupted gymnastics performed over, under, around, and through targeted obstacles (both man-made and natural) in the urban environment. Parkour movement comes in the form of running, jumping, or climbing or a combination of these techniques.

The ultimate (physical) goal of the Parkour lifestyle is to adapt one's body to quickly pass any urban obstacle and hone one's evasion, avoidance, and flight capabilities within a city.

Practitioners of Parkour refer to themselves as *traceurs, free runners,* or *urban free-flowers.* They poach cityscapes (often to the dismay of local authorities) as training grounds of innovative body discipline. Traceurs are urban explorers and *bricoleurs* in this regard, approaching the highly capitalized and commercially sanitized inner city as a site of physical jouissance (Fiske 1989). Typically, traceurs reject other sporting forms as contrived, unnatural, overregulated, and heavily constricted by the exclusionary codes and practices of late-modern sport (Giddens 1991).

Becoming Parkour

In the summer of 2005, we started collecting data on traceurs in Toronto, Canada. Atkinson launched the project by hanging around with a core group of four traceurs in an eastern borough of the city. He first encountered a traceur in an undergraduate course he taught in Hamilton, Ontario, who invited him to watch a traceur training session involving 13 traceurs in Toronto. By July of 2005, Atkinson found himself fully immersed in the local crew, investigating the meaning of Parkour for the young men on a firsthand, participatory basis.

Although difficult to quantify, the number of traceurs in Toronto appears to be growing. During his 12-month participant observation of traceurs, Atkinson met nearly 300 local practitioners in the metropolitan area and formally interviewed 17. Through participant observation and interviewing, he found several important sociodemographic commonalities among the traceurs. Nearly 90% of the traceurs Atkinson encountered were male, 86% lived in the urban core of the greater Toronto area, 72% were middle class, and 64% were White. The mean age of the group was 21, and nearly all of the traceurs had played in a traditional sport during their adolescence. The mean Parkour experience of the group was 3 years, and the skill level within the group varied considerably.

The general ethos among the traceurs reflected stereotypical resistance subculture attitudes toward mainstream sport. Traceurs expressed disdain for highly organized, scripted, contained, authoritarian, competitive, and consumer-based sport experiences. They preferred free, creative, and liminal forms of athletic movement. Those studied saw Parkour as a method of personal exploration through movement, a do-it-yourself form of urban gymnastics, and a rejection of traditional ways of seeing and training the body. When discussing their playing field, the traceurs described a need to "take back" local city space for their own purposes and to use their "natural environment" to meet their own physical, emotional, and psychological needs. Most described Parkour as a way of life and as an ideology permeating all of their thoughts and actions.

In Western cultures such as those found in North America, which are increasingly criticized for hyperindividualistic and greedy consumption ideologies, we often ignore how small clusters of like-minded actors such as traceurs use athleticism to actively resist capitalist pressures. Sociologists have studied, for instance, how certain religious groups reject mainstream consumption and body indulgence via the practice of asceticism, or, simply put, through a morally grounded lifestyle predicated on notions of body purification, restriction, and control (Atkinson 2006). Ascetics approach the body as a natural entity needing protection from noxious physical pollutants (e.g., drugs, alcohol, disease, and, in some cases, medicines) and from risks posed to its moral integrity by cultural norms (e.g., sexual or eating norms). Often, an ascetic philosophy is buttressed by a belief that it is the human duty to align pure body practice with pure spirit.

Shepherd's (2002) analysis of the Australian anarcho-environmentalist movement suggests how resistance to environmental degradation may be waged through intense physical discipline. The group Shepherd describes rejects mass consumption in favor of a less-is-more approach to resource use. In the hope of minimizing their collective environmental footprint, group members neoliberally practice Spartan discipline on their own consumption and attempt "a moral [environmental] regeneration of the social world" (142). According to Shepherd, the way that members self-police and advocate for social change is a contemporary, secular example of collective asceticism.

Toronto traceurs believe that mainstream (middle-class) lifestyles in North America promote both personal and environmental pathologies. They frequently juxtapose their own training practices and body discipline against trends of obesity, inactivity, and social degeneration in the broader population. Viewed from such a resistance perspective, Parkour is a novel case example of youth subcultural innovation.

Thus we may explore how a lifestyle and resistance sport movement such as Parkour promulgates a regeneration of moral cultural practice; that is, we may explore how the resistance is performed publicly through the body as a collective process of habitus reformation. Despite Melucci's (1996) and Gitlin's (1991) belief that new social movements rarely include a collective desire to alter social practices or norms, Parkour is designed, at least for some practitioners, to better the self via physical awareness and self-discipline. Common in much of the literature on new social movements is, unfortunately, a dismissal of the interest of youth groups to reform collective habituses (i.e., toward promoting self-discipline and control) in these ways (see Castells 1996; Diani 2004). Lifestyle sport movements such as Parkour are generally discounted as Maffesolian neo-tribes, and their members are described as ideological poachers and poseurs.

The resistance philosophy within Toronto Parkour lifestyles is likely a product of the networked process through which most traceurs find the practice in the city. With only a few rare exceptions, traceurs are recruited into a crew or are sponsored in by a long-term advocate. As Sutherland (1947) explained more than half a century ago in his account of how differential association works in practice, birds of (ideological) feathers do seem to flock together in Parkour figurations. The apparent similarity in the perspectives of Toronto traceurs might be an anomaly, though, as the group is relatively small in comparison with other Parkour scenes worldwide and is rather sociodemographically homogeneous. All anecdotal evidence on the global spread of Parkour suggests that factions develop and split as a greater diversity of traceurs enters into a crew.

What follows is an introduction to Parkour. In particular, we focus on the origins and alternative basis of Parkour as a youth lifestyle sport.

Parkour Lifestyles and Resistance Philosophies

The philosophical roots of Parkour as an athletic practice date back more than 100 years. Parkour grew out of a style of physical training and moral development called *Hébertism*. Hébertism emerged in the late 19th century through the physical training philosophies of Georges Hébert, a French naval officer. Hébert exerted a major influence on the development of physical education in France during the later years of the 19th century. As a naval officer, he traveled throughout the world and was struck by the physical development and skill of indigenous peoples across the African continent.

Hébert was stationed in St. Pierre, Martinique, during 1902, when the town was hit by a catastrophic volcanic eruption. Hébert himself coordinated the evacuation of nearly 700 people from a local village. The experience had a profound effect on him and reinforced his belief that athletic strength and skill must be combined with courage and altruism in order to be socially useful. Hébert came to believe that physical fitness should be a common cultural goal, not only for merely aesthetic or competitive purposes but also for the collective good (Delaplace 2005).

Upon his return to France, Hébert tutored at the College of Rheims, where he struck a new path in physical education. He created a series of apparatuses and exercises to teach what he dubbed the *natural method* of physical training. Hébert believed that individuals should train in nature as an animal species traversing landscapes and physical obstacles. He rejected remedial gymnastics and the popular Scandinavian methods of athletic training, which seemed unable to develop the human body harmoniously with nature to prepare his students for the moral requirements of life. Hébert believed that by concentrating on competition and performance, mainstream sports diverted physical education from both its physiological ends and its ability to foster moral values.

The natural method cultivates muscularity and speed so that a person is able to walk, run, jump, climb, balance, throw, lift, defend, and swim in practically any geographic landscape. In a liminal and energetic sense, the natural method demands that the person possesses sufficient energy, willpower, courage, coolness, and *fermeté* (hardness/firmness/strength) to conquer any physical or mental obstacle. In a moral sense, by experiencing a variety of mental and emotional states, such as fear, doubt, anxiety, aggression, resolve, courage, and exhaustion, during natural training, the person cultivates confidence and self-assurance.

Hébert became the earliest proponent of what the French call *parcours* (obstacle course) training. Indeed, woodland challenge courses and adventure races comprising balance beams, ladders, rope swings, and obstacles are often described as *Hébertism* or *Hébertisme* courses both in Europe and North America. It may even be possible to trace a full array of modern adventure playground equipment to Hébert's original parcours designs of the early 1900s. The French government named Hébert the Commander of the Legion of Honor in 1995 for his lifelong commitment to the physical and social skills of its people.

The contemporary moniker *Parkour* thus derives from the French term *parcours du combattant*. During the Vietnam War, French soldiers were especially inspired by Hébert's work and used the natural method to hone skills for jungle warfare. Among the French soldiers exposed to the natural method was Raymond Belle. Belle taught his son, David, the principles of the natural method following his tour of duty in Vietnam. The younger Belle participated in activities such as martial arts and gymnastics as a young teenager. After moving to the Paris suburb Lisses, David Belle explored the rigors and benefits of the natural method and continued his journey with others—most notably, his friend Sébastien Foucan. By age 15, Belle and Foucan had developed their own suburban style of Parkour. In the 2003 BBC documentary *Jump London,* Foucan described Parkour as a physical and spiritual style of movement in which "the whole town [Lisses] was there for us; there for free running. You just have to look and you just have to think like children. This is the vision of Parkour."

By the late 1990s, the media in France, the United Kingdom, and the Netherlands documented the emerging Parkour movement and highlighted the countercultural coolness of the practice. Hinting at the potential for the commodification of all alternative subcultures, Belle later described Parkour's insertion into the media as part of a "prostitution of the art" (BBC 2003). Foucan and Belle disagreed vehemently over the vision and purpose of the practice. Belle continued, at least for a time, to adhere to the original principles of Parkour, pioneering a more risky and aesthetically oriented lifestyle of Parkour now referred to as *urban freeflow* or *free running.*

As noted, the ideological split between Belle and Foucan and the severing of the Lisses crew into separate Parkour factions are rather predictable for a youth lifestyle or subculture movement, especially in the wake of the lifestyle's mass mediation and popular cultural ascendance in commodity form (i.e., Parkour clothing, language, moves, and jargon). What is interesting is that Belle and his followers attempted to subculturally police the Hébertism essence of Parkour and publicly rejected its popularity as a style or commodity culture. Picking up on themes of subcultural testing raised earlier by Donnelly and Young (1988), Thornton (1995) points out that subcultures are indeed able to internally distinguish and externally label participants as either authentic or inauthentic. Foucan and his converts, by contrast, have aggressively sold Parkour to global audiences through television commercials and documentaries, movies, clothing lines, training schools, video games, and even international competitions. While Belle's loyalists remain somewhat resistance-oriented and purist (calling Parkour an *antisport* and a *subaltern lifestyle),* Foucan's brand of Parkour continues to undergo sportization (i.e., formalization, rationalization; Dunning 1999) as so many other resistance sports have done throughout the past several decades.

Parkour in Toronto

Despite ideological and technical differences between traceurs in Europe and traceurs elsewhere, practitioners in Toronto certainly agree that Parkour is both a moral and an athletic cultural form qua Hébert's and Belle's original visions of the natural method. The bedrock philosophical elements of Parkour in Toronto, although perhaps difficult for the average resident in cities like Toronto to understand while watching practitioners leap across cityscapes, are what classify the practice as a lifestyle sport in Wheaton's (2004) terms.

David Belle suggested that the *yin and yang* relationship of mind–body balance is a defining feature of Parkour philosophy, and traceurs in Toronto clearly agree. During training sessions, traceurs perform soft gymnastic movements involving fluidity and ease and then contrast the movements with acrobatics involving heavy impacts on the ground, on buildings, or on other stationary structures. Traceurs utilize such techniques to understand how to move, think, feel, and reflect in a range of physical and psychological situations. A common belief among traceurs in Toronto is that by preparing their body and spirit to adapt through movement, they train the mind to adapt to any condition of living. To be fluid through Parkour is to be fluid in life.

The founding fathers of Parkour, Belle and Foucan, described the ultimate goal of Parkour as finding a new way of urban living. Their *way* is one resistant to lethargy, physical atrophy, hyperindividualism, and consumption. The Parkour way also extolls the virtues of connecting the mind, body, and spirit with the intimate physical and social environment. These interconnections are fostered through intense training jams in urban settings. Toorock (2005) argues that Belle and Foucan, in their construction of the way, found influence in Chinese Taoist doctrines. Taoist concepts of flow, harmony, and the way are evident in and represented by traceurs in Toronto and other major cities such as London, Brussels, Glasgow, New York, Amsterdam, Paris, and Sydney.

While ultimately the connection with the environment is individual, traceurs can often be found in what they call *clans* or *crews*. Practicing with a number of other traceurs in training sessions (known as *jams)* is encouraged so members can help one another progress. Toronto traceurs are careful to point out that the philosophy of Parkour should not involve competition or bravado; rather, everyone should improve and evolve at their own pace, step by step and leap by leap. The emphasis is to conquer the surrounding obstacles, not one another in a traditional competitive sense. In this way and others, Parkour is clearly a lifestyle sport that rejects the conventional philosophy of dominating opponents that characterizes traditional sports.

Building upon these philosophies, traceurs in Toronto stress athletic fluidity and flow in everyday life rather than sport-related conquest and competitive opposition. A review of the literature on resistance sports (see Rinehart and Sydnor 2003; Wheaton 2004) demonstrates how their advocates often eschew traditional Western sporting doctrines of ultracompetition. For traceurs in Toronto, a person is skilled in the art of Parkour when movement becomes effortless and natural. They compare the physical prowess of a skilled traceur to water flowing over rocks, not only because water implies grace and artistry when moving over rocks in a stream but also because the flowing water seems to effortlessly pass across, under, over, or around any environmental obstacle it encounters.

The flow that traceurs in Toronto revere is accomplished when they are immersed in a Parkour jam to such an extent that absolutely nothing else matters and they move and react on *autopilot*. The concept of flow was popularized by the Hungarian American psychologist Csikszentmihalyi in his book *Beyond Boredom and Anxiety* (1975). Central to the attainment of flow for traceurs is the physical and psychological match between the perceived demands of Parkour and the skills the traceur possesses to perform as water and to understand the way. This match promotes harmony of mind and body through movement and relaxed effort and produces a Zen-like state.

During the flow experience of Parkour, traceurs relinquish self-consciousness and doubt and become one with their activity. This engenders a biopsychological state in which the traceur is rewarded solely by movement and flight and not by extrinsic (i.e., competitive) rewards. Parkour is somewhat deviant, then, as a sport practice, as it rejects performance-oriented rewards based on judging or evaluation. In other words, in Parkour there are no trophies, awards, or cash prizes. Although athletes in mainstream sports may also refer to *flow* and to *being in the zone*, the flow experience seems to be highly coveted but rarely attained by elite athletes—perhaps due to a psychologically embedded focus on extrinsic rewards that somehow mitigates the experience (Wheaton 2004).

For traceurs in Toronto, flow experiences are enhanced by the controlled risks inherent in urban Parkour movements and tricks. In an analysis of symbolic death sports, le Breton (2000) argues that the burgeoning interest in flow experiences in natural and untamed environments (versus contained gymnasia and sport facilities) is a sign of postmodern anxiety and isolation. As such, the booming interest in urban, athletic risk-taking like Parkour may reflect cultural fragmentation, normative uncertainty, heightened alienation, and disenfranchisement among youth practitioners (i.e., in their search for a new physical and emotional way). The search for personal flow experiences as a lifestyle pursuit acts as a surrogate for dismantled cultural connections or fractured social absolutes. Akin to the triathlon lifestyle discussed in chapter 5, the Parkour way is a personal and collective search for a new lifestyle predicated on using athleticism as a vehicle for subcultural experimentation and connection.

Toronto traceurs also described Parkour as a context for achieving personal efficacy. Flow performances are characterized by a supreme sense of control or connection, to the degree that the person need not mentally or physically focus on moving at all. Once they have mastered the basic Parkour techniques, traceurs often articulate feeling as if they possess a total connection with their mind, movement, and physical environment. For Toronto traceurs, being in control of the self, honing flow through Parkour, and developing connection with the urban landscape are certainly forms of social resistance. These traceurs believe that most people are motivated and moved by forces beyond their control (i.e., market capitalism and consumption), and that their inability to move as thinking, autonomous actors manifests itself as personal feelings of inadequacy, fear, and alienation. By contrast, highly skilled traceurs talk about feeling invincible during a particular jam or even in everyday life. Such a sense of control frees them from fears of personal failure and social impotence and creates an enduring feeling of empowerment.

Of course, we are reporting here simply what a relatively small group of Canadian traceurs have claimed. From their studies of the social implications of sport involvement for young female athletes, Young and White (1995) and Young (1997) caution that the equation of participation with self-worth and personal success does not necessarily take place in and through sport: To claim such would be to possibly overestimate the power of human agency in sport and the wider social implications of something as broadly praised by athletes as flow.

Nevertheless, as a traceur learns to perceive competence and flow during training, concern for the self often disappears. As a traceur becomes one with the urban environment, concerns about athletic performance are abandoned. Csikszentmihalyi (1975) suggests that after a flow experience in which the rational, other-oriented, and calculating self is relinquished, self-perception is strengthened. By temporarily removing doubts, anxieties, fears, and frustrations, a training jam psychologically refreshes the traceur. Such a flow experience is precisely what Hébert taught through his natural method. Parkour is a designed autotelic activity, then, in which flow liberates the individual. Traceurs learn to switch off peripheral distractions and focus solely on enjoying the task at hand.

The idea of flowing through the city as a traceur is ultimately demonstrated through the basic moves of Parkour. Moves such as the cat leap, monkey vault, and cat balance mimic animal movements that enable traceurs to efficiently travel over and between urban obstacles. When executed effectively, these somewhat seemingly unnatural athletic movements, which include jumping from wall to wall, cascading off of a three-story building onto the ground, and balancing on a ledge 80 feet in the air, appear aesthetically beautiful. The traceurs' physical and aesthetic appreciation of Parkour parallels the appreciation found in modern dance and movement cultures such as the Brazilian dance and martial art capoeira, but it also involves obvious elements of risk.

Traceurs in Toronto believe that flow cannot occur unless they achieve a deep appreciation for their place in nature as an embodied and interdependent being. Parkour forums on the Internet representing crews from around the globe stress the need to look after the body and protect the environment. Articles on healthy eating, proper stretching, warming up, and safety are common. Dan Edwardes of the Urban Freeflow Network (see: www.urbanfreeflow.com) suggests the need for a sustainable mind–body–environment practice:

> The qualification is that your training must be sustainable. And, quite simply, in order for Parkour practice to be truly sustainable it must not detract from your overall physical health or environment in any way. Is this possible? The good news is YES, it is—in fact, good Parkour training should actually enhance your vitality and strengthen your life all round. How is this possible? Through having a complete, holistic approach to your practice that both prepares and maintains your body for the duration of your training career. A telling measure of the true effectiveness of any discipline—and of its practitioners—is its sustainability. If a training method enables you to perform some amazing feats for a short period and then results in premature degeneration, it is probably not being done right or done well, or both!

Interaction between the self and the natural urban environment is so crucial that a city's architecture determines the fundamental techniques that traceurs practice. Reflecting Hébert's philosophy, traceurs develop physical skill sets not in opposition but in relation to the surrounding physical environment; that is, they become physically adept in moving through, in, and around their immediate structural environment. With respect to Elias' (1978) or Bourdieu's (1984) understanding of how the body is conditioned by environmental influences, a traceur develops skill as part of a broader habitus cultivated by a Parkour lifestyle.

A superficial examination of the recent popularity of Parkour might provide empirical support of Maffesoli's (1996) arguments about the evolution of youth subcultures into temporary style cultures. Even though the traceurs interviewed in Toronto adopt Parkour as an athletic lifestyle, others are drawn to the practice because of its cultural difference and coolness, and they wear Parkour clothing styles or hang around in Parkour crews in order to attain subcultural capital (Thornton 1995). But there is little evidence, at least from our research in Toronto, to demonstrate that traceurs are unable to internally distinguish between those committed to Parkour as a lifestyle and those merely sampling it through commodity fetishization. Those committed on a lifestyle basis tend to simply move, be, and enact Parkour in a Zen-like fashion without any need to prove commitment on a material or a public basis. Simply put, participating in movement or hanging in a crew is not the defining feature of Parkour group membership, and traceurs reflexively understand who *gets* flow and who does not.

THEORETICAL INTERSECTIONS

Stebbins' (1996) conceptualization of tolerable deviance may seem obsolete among those who believe that deviance is dead. If cultural absolutes and metanarratives have disappeared in the postmodern era (Muggleton 2000), there is neither tolerable nor intolerable action, only polysemically relative behavior. The preceding analysis of Parkour in Toronto, however, suggests that groups of like-minded actors do collectively perceive and interpret social behaviors and ways of life along lines of normativity and contranormativity. While our discussion of Parkour focused on how traceurs engage the lifestyle as a prosocial form of resistance and personal liberation, outsiders to the group often express opinions regarding the intolerability of the behaviors and their associated lifestyles. In the remainder of this chapter, we analyze Parkour from a range of theoretical perspectives to suggest how alternative youth lifestyle sports remain a cultural battleground and are not merely meaningless examples of pop cultural consumption. Each theory underscores how we may understand the ways in which traceurs use urban space creatively, and each, in turn, shows how the traceurs' apparent transgressions on public or commercial property are deviantized by agents of social control.

FUNCTIONALISM AND STRAIN THEORY

In 1992, Agnew updated classical strain theory in his article "Foundation for a General Strain Theory of Crime and Delinquency." His revisions of Merton's work in particular address several important points. Agnew notes that strain in an individual's life does not merely result from the failure to achieve culturally defined economic goals. According to his general strain theory, there are four types of strain: the failure to achieve positively valued goals or personal accomplishments (e.g., economic success, status, and personal autonomy), a perceived sense of social injustice, the loss of positive stimuli in life (e.g., severed bonds, status loss, or economic hardship), and the introduction of negative stimuli (e.g., abuse, illness, neglect, adverse relations with significant others, negative social experiences, neighborhood decay and crime, or homelessness).

Agnew's strain theory focuses on negative relationships with others—relationships in which a person is not treated in a way that he expects or wants. He argues that people are pressured into criminal or deviant acts by negative states, such as anger, which further erode their existing relationships. He also notes that an individual's anger amplifies when she blames negative life circumstances and relationships on others. However, as Agnew points out, deviance and crime are not the only responses to strain. Individuals may cope with strain in a variety of ways. There are three different types of coping strategies: cognitive (i.e., rationalizing and understanding strain as acceptable), emotional (i.e., managing strain through anger-purging activities like exercise, relaxation, or meditation), and behavioral (i.e., avoiding negative stimuli and seeking positive stimuli). Each coping strategy can be used on its own or can be combined with others to reduce the amount of strain in an individual's life.

Dennis, a 17-year-old Toronto traceur, suggests that Parkour is a significant stress-reducing practice for him. Over the course of 2 years, Dennis lost his father to cancer, moved from Vancouver to Toronto, and dropped out of high school to join the workforce. He found Parkour through friendship networks in the city, and he uses his weekly *jams* to help manage his feelings of abandonment and isolation. For Dennis and other traceurs, the Parkour lifestyle is an emotional and a behavioral coping mechanism. Rather than channeling anger and frustration into personally and socially destructive forms, traceurs like Dennis cope using socially reintegrative forms of athletics. He interprets the flow that he experiences through Parkour as a tolerable social activity. Research on other lifestyle sports like Parkour could, using Agnew's version of strain theory, strive to understand how apparently alternative sport and leisure activities are prosocial and functionally tolerable adaptations to strain.

CONFLICT THEORY

Spitzer's (1975) article, "Toward a Marxian Theory of Crime ," suggests that a capitalist economy creates a surplus population of workers. The current stage of the modern industrial economy, which Marxist criminologists like Spitzer term *monopoly capitalism* (meaning the world economy is dominated by a relatively small number of multinational corporations), subjugates the majority of workers, including youth workers. Spitzer argues that in monopoly capitalism, the less educated and less skilled are an increasingly superfluous population. As these individuals recognize and internalize their status as irrelevant, they become socially dangerous. Stakeholders in the capitalist system (including agents of social control) must minimize the threat (i.e., crime and deviance) from this surplus population in order to maintain the status quo.

In Spitzer's rendition of Marxist criminology, he describes members of dangerous social classes as either *social junk* or *social dynamite*. Social junk populations are nonproductive members of society (i.e., youths from the working class or lower-middle class who drop out of educational and work streams). They are often homeless, unemployed, sick, and therefore costly to larger society. Members of social dynamite populations first emerge as social junk but become radically (and often criminally) oriented when they recognize the extent of their social alienation.

Traceurs in Toronto have been classified by agents of social control as *both* social junk and social dynamite. Between the summers of 2004 and 2006, traceurs were the cause of several moral panics in the local media. Reports about the disruptive and aggressive tendencies of these urban gymnasts were broadcast on evening news programs and printed in popular newspapers such as the *Globe and Mail* (Law 2004, D9) and the *Toronto Star* (Wortz 2006, C1). City councillors and police officers decried the traceurs' use of city space for sport and leisure as intolerable and likened their activities to youth panhandling and the street squeegee business (Law 2004). Traceurs are viewed as social junk because their running, jumping, and climbing through the city produces little economically, detracts from the normal business culture in the downtown core, and falls outside of the purview of authoritarian sport institutions that restrict youth expression in predictable ways. They are simultaneously deemed social dynamite because their lifestyles are believed to be pervaded by illegal drug use and other forms of deviant activity (Wortz 2006). From Spitzer's (1975) theoretical position, an analysis of discursive battles over the value of traceurs within a city might shed light on how targeted youth groups become ostracized as political and economic waste in modern capitalist societies.

INTERACTION THEORY

Garfinkel's classic *Studies in Ethnomethodology* (1967) provides an analytical template for understanding how people make social sense out of everyday life. The term *ethnomethodology* simply means the study of the ways in which people assign meaning to action in the social world. Garfinkel believes that social order (i.e., patterns of relatively predictable social interaction) is produced when people define the social world as real, assigning what is referred to as *typifications* or *recipes of knowledge* to everyday interaction. He suggests that individuals bring order to or make sense of their social world using a psychological process he calls the *documentary method*. This method consists of selecting certain facts from a social situation that seem to conform to a pattern (typifications) and then making sense of these facts in terms of an interpreted pattern (resulting in recipes of knowledge). Once the pattern has been established, it is used as a framework for interpreting new facts that arise within the setting.

An important dimension of the documentary method is indexicality. The term *indexicality* simply refers to how people make sense of a remark, sign, or particular action by referring to the context in which it occurs; that is, they ascribe it to particular circumstances of the situation. Garfinkel suggests that we constantly use the documentary method in our daily lives to create a meaningful and predictable world. To test such a theoretical proposition, ethnomethodologists like to perform breaching experiments, in which they temporarily disrupt the taken-for-granted world we live in and then inspect how people react to confusion and anxiety. The point of a breaching experiment is to expose background assumptions that underpin social reality.

The philosophical foundation of Parkour, as an urban resistance activity, might be understood as a breaching experiment par excellence. The lifestyle sport not only seeks to disrupt what many consider to be tolerable sport but also asks people in urban centers to question what constitutes the natural and constructed environment in which they live, as well as its appropriate use. Akin to one of its subcultural predecessors, skateboarding, Parkour might be studied as a sporting form that intentionally breaches common typifications of city space and cultural recipes of knowledge for its ongoing development. Audience ethnography on Parkour might, for example, explore how nontraceurs react toward and negotiate with traceurs in an attempt to determine acceptable use of urban space.

SOCIAL CONTROL THEORY

In revisiting longitudinal data on youth crime collected between 1925 and 1960, Sampson and Laub (1993) pioneered what is now referred to as *life course theory*. Their work is a response to Gottfredson and Hirschi's (1990) theoretical assertions regarding the stability of criminal personalities after childhood. Sampson and Laub demonstrate that while there is a measure of continuity in criminal or deviant behavior among those who start early as offenders, criminality over the life course is also mediated and potentially halted by forms of social bonding during adulthood.

Sampson and Laub hypothesize that while antisocial behavior during childhood (measured by official delinquency statistics and self-report data, parent, and teacher reports) leads to generally higher deviant and criminal involvement in adulthood, this tendency can be counteracted by the informal social controls of job stability, commitment to occupational goals, and attachment to a partner. In accordance with variants of social control theory, Sampson and Laub argue that strong social bonds in adulthood reduce offending, while weak social bonds in adulthood accelerate deviance. While an individual might begin life as a youth on a criminal trajectory, transitions between life courses, such as work, marriage, and peer bonding, may stimulate normative social behavior in later life. Sampson and Laub thus believe that deviants can be resocialized throughout the life course and become law-abiding citizens.

An extended longitudinal research project on Parkour in Toronto or elsewhere might focus on the life-course transitions and trajectories that members experience and investigate if these in any way alter their social careers as traceurs. Accepting, for the moment, that Parkour is a form of social deviance might allow researchers to analyze the members' extra-group relationships and bond attachments throughout adulthood in order to grasp whether outsider social forces encourage desistance among members. Evidence from our Toronto study suggests that a certain degree of risk taking and a relaxed self-restraint characterize practitioners' personality types. Of interest might be whether, through intensive bonding during later stage life-course transitions, risk-taking mentalities are altered by work, family, and other civic responsibilities. A trend that has not been fully explained to date in the sociology of sport literature is the demographic drop in membership within most lifestyle sports among people past their late teens and in their early 20s. While member attrition might be simply attributed to the physical demands of many lifestyle sports, Sampson and Laub (1993) would offer a much more long-term argument regarding member resocialization.

CLASSICAL THEORY

Shaw and McKay's *Juvenile Delinquency and Urban Areas* (1942) claims that delinquency is not caused at the individual level but is a response by individuals reacting to structural conditions in urban areas. Building on Park and Burgess' (1924) ecological model of social development, Shaw and McKay argue that individual deviance can be explained by studying the social environments in which the individual resides.

Shaw and McKay use official police and court data from the city of Chicago to make pin maps, spot maps, rate maps, and zone maps of urban growth and crime. Their theory of social disorganization states that "traditions of delinquency are transmitted through successive generations of the same [city] zone in the same way language, roles and attitudes are transmitted" (1942, 28). They loosely define the term *social disorganization* as the inability of local communities to realize the common values of their residents or solve commonly experienced problems. The three traditional sources of social disorganization are residential instability or mobility (high population turnover), racial or ethnic heterogeneity (cultures living in close proximity but in interactive isolation), and poverty. Social disorganization theorists sometimes call this causal chain the *gradient tendency* because of the sequential way in which successive declines in neighborhood effectiveness lead to amplified rates of delinquency.

A social disorganization theorist could conceive of Parkour as a manifestation of urban breakdown and cultural fragmentation. Even though Parkour crews are found in the suburban periphery of cities, a significant amount of urban jams take place within the central business district in the downtown core. From a classic social disorganization point of view, it is precisely the unruly use of public parks, buildings, and pedestrian walkways by groups with alternative values that make the urban core undesirable. Traceurs in Toronto, who openly express a desire to create cultural noise (Hebdige 1979) in urban settings, might cause cultural disorganization for local residents by expressing differential value systems. Perhaps Parkour members and other groups of urban youths might encourage residential mobility in central business districts by influencing people to leave city areas experiencing value conflict. Additionally, Parkour crews might find suitable contexts for the activity in already socially disorganized settings. Traceurs in Toronto, for instance, might travel from the suburbs to practice in disorganized areas because these areas are fair game for whatever use the traceurs may put them to.

CRITICAL THEORY

Critics of urban surveillance, governmentality, and modern state policing have undoubtedly encouraged criminologists to reinvestigate mainstream methods of urban policing. Hebert (2001) notes that criminologists in the 21st century are particularly skeptical of the neoliberal approach to urban policing, which encourages (or demands) that inncer city communities devise their own strategies to solve their local street crime problems such as drugs, gangs, gun violence, and so on. Hebert and other sociologists are especially critical of the neoliberal staple ideology in the do-it-yourself policing debate: Kelling and Wilson's (1982) popular broken windows theory.

Crime theorists Kelling and Wilson published an article in the *Atlantic Monthly* that advocated a crime theory known as *broken windows.* According to the theory, "If the first broken window in a building is not repaired, then people who like breaking windows will assume that no one cares about the building and more windows will be broken. Soon the building will have no windows" (1982, 29).

The theory also suggests that crime results from ineffective and haphazard policing in urban settings. From the broken windows vantage point, strict and consistent law enforcement is the primary ingredient for establishing safe communities. Kelling and Wilson also hypothesize that if loitering youths are left unchallenged, their behavior will likely evolve into more socially consequential offenses such as theft, assault, and drug use. Other targeted broken windows populations in Kelling and Wilson's theoretical model include panhandlers, beggars, muggers, pickpockets, and alcoholics:

> Serious street crime flourishes in areas in which disorderly behavior goes unchecked. The unchecked panhandler is, in effect, the first broken window. Muggers and robbers, whether opportunistic or professional, believe they reduce their chances of being caught or even identified if they operate on streets where potential victims are already intimidated by prevailing conditions.
>
> (*Kelling and Wilson* 1982, 32)

If left in disrepair, a single broken window, such as youth loitering, causes local neighborhood inhabitants to lose community pride and respect. Because of the residents' collective retreat into their homes and decreased civic participation, other windows break. Beginning with youth disorder and disobedience, crime levels rise. The effort and cost to fix the condition become insurmountable in the eyes of the police, and the community is compromised as a culture of deviance takes root.

If youth disorder and disobedience are broken windows, then Parkour can be understood as at least a cracked pane. Seemingly innocuous youth misbehaviors such as jumping over park statues or running down stair railings cannot be tolerated for fear of escalating behaviors. Tolerating Parkour stands as an affront to the conventional stewardship of public buildings and revered spaces. Local police and city officials in Toronto have condemned local residents who allow Parkour to exist in their neighborhoods. City councillors have implied that city members who complain about drugs, guns, and youth violence need only to examine their own tolerance of broken windows (such as traceurs and other youth groups) to understand why urban crime problems are flourishing (Law 2004; Wortz 2006). Critics of neoliberal philosophies of crime control like the broken windows theory quickly suggest how shifting the cause of crime and the responsibility for crime reduction from the state to everyday citizens obfuscates broader crime-related problems like unemployment, unequal access to education, race and ethnic discrimination, and cultural intolerance, and does little, in the end, to reduce crime.

GENDER AND FEMINIST THEORY

As an ecofeminist understanding of how environmental movements form, Shepherd's (2002) work illustrates how the politics of class, gender, and environmentalism are embedded in social constructions of deviance. Through her analysis of the Australian anarcho-environmentalist movement, Shepherd suggests how resistance to environmental degradation may be waged through personal and collective asceticism. Anarcho-environmentalist groups (often influenced by ecofeminist constructions of how the environment is victimized by patriarchal social orders and capitalist agendas) are at the radical end of the spectrum of those involved in the environmental movement. These groups oppose the hierarchical organization of social order, believing it to be inherently exploitative, destructive, and consumption oriented. They express disdain for the pursuit of profit and the related destruction of the environment. Their preferred mode of action is to participate in nonviolent, direct behaviors that challenge and resist capitalist ideologies and practices.

The group of anarcho-environmentalists Shepherd (2002) describes rejects capitalist philosophies of mass consumption in favor of a less-is-more approach to personal resource use. To minimize their collective environmental footprint, anarcho-environmentalists restrict their own forms of consumption and attempt to initiate "a moral [environmental] regeneration of the social world" (Shepherd 2002, 42). According to Shepherd, the way in which members police themselves and advocate for social change is a contemporary secular example of feminist-inspired asceticism.

In many ways, traceurs in Toronto might be conceptually understood as an anarcho-environmentalist collective that envisions urban styles of life as intolerable. Traceurs in the city are highly critical of the disembodied modality of urban living and of the extent to which urban residents are seemingly disengaged with the realities of life beyond everyday work routines. For traceurs, today's transportation, technological interface at work, virtual existence and interaction through cyberspace, and even exercise involving machines at the gym punctuate how modern cultural life is antithetical to the natural body. Traceurs' guerrilla urban gymnastics could be studied as a collective reminder of the separation between urbanites and their natural physical needs, capabilities, and interdependence with the living physical environment that sustains life. If we use Shepherd's model as a guide, we might interpret Parkour as a lifestyle sport designed to stimulate a moral regeneration of urban life and to radically reorient urban residents' mind-sets toward mind–body–environment holism.

INTEGRATED THEORY

Wilson's study of the Canadian rave culture in his book *Fight, Flight, or Chill: Subcultures, Youth, and Rave Into the 21st Century* (2006) proposes a working set of integrated theoretical propositions for re-envisioning subcultural resistance. Rather than adopting a dogmatic or rigidly traditionalist (e.g., CCCS-oriented) perspective that views youth subculture involvement as class-based resistance, Wilson draws on a blend of Birmingham-inspired subculture theory, symbolic interactionist theory, and poststructuralism to argue that youth resistance tactics are far more diverse, conservative, and potentially small scale than previously theorized. He presents five integrated theses on youth subcultural formation that outline how members' lifestyle activities may at once articulate purposeful and tactical social resistance, adaptive and reactive resistance, socially trivial resistance, self-aware nonresistance, and reaffirmation of dominant cultural norms, values, and beliefs. Wilson's position is anchored by the theoretical belief that resistance orientations still matter within lifestyle or subcultural groups but that resistance is neither homogeneous within such groups nor static over time. From his integrated position on resistance, we learn how subcultural members may resist social codes in one social context but accept them uncritically in another.

Wilson's position on youth resistance poses a certain paradox for lifestyle sport theorists. Traceurs, on the one hand, often resist mainstream definitions of sport and city space. But on the other hand, most of the Toronto traceurs do not attempt to replace traditional sport models. Rather than characterizing resistance as an all-or-nothing practice, Wilson might encourage students of Parkour to see the multilayered nature of conformity, negotiation, and resistance in the lifestyle and to realize the extent to which resistance is enacted on a situational basis. If we utilize Wilson's model of resistance as a theoretical guide, we appreciate how subcultural resistance may be far more (consciously) situational and temporary than often theorized in the deviancy literature.

Discussion Questions

1. Locate a sport subculture of your choice in your own community. Conduct some preliminary research on where, when, and how the subculture formed.

2. The debates about subcultures as sites of social resistance continue. Do you think subculture, in any definition of the term, is inherently oppositional?

3. Do you think traceurs should be allowed to use public and private city space to pursue flow in sport? Why or why not?

Recommended Readings

Le Breton, D. 2000. Playing symbolically with death in extreme sports. *Body and Society* 6:1-11.

> This article addresses the rise in popularity of sports that may pose significant physical harm to participants. It analyzes the late-modern cultural ideologies and practices that prepare people to seek out near-death experiences through sport as acts of self-realization.

Maffesoli, M. 1996. *The contemplation of the world: Figures of community style.* Minneapolis: University of Minnesota Press.

> Maffesoli's book helped usher in a new era of theorizing in subculture research. The text questions the nature of subculture as a tight-knit and policed community of actors and argues that subcultures are best conceptualized as more fluid, transitory, and style-oriented flashes of social interaction.

Rinehart, R., and S. Sydnor. 2003 *To the extreme: Alternative sports, inside and out.* Albany, NY: SUNY Press.

> This book summarizes contemporary thinking on the emergence, co-option, and diffusion of sport subcultures. It covers key moments in the development of resistant sport subcultures, and the authors analyze systematic patterns in the common paths that extreme sport cultures follow toward commodification and commercialization.

Wheaton, B. 2004. *Understanding lifestyle sport: Consumption, identity and difference.* London: Routledge.

> Wheaton illustrates how traditional concepts such as resistance and subculture may not reflect contemporary sensibilities about alternative small-group sport clusters. The contributors to this volume explore small sport communities as lifestyle groups whose social identities and practices in sport distance them from mainstream cultures both in their ideologies and affiliations but not necessarily in resistant ways.

Wilson, B. 2006. *Fight, flight, or chill: Subcultures, youth, and rave into the 21st century.* Montreal, PQ: McGill-Queen's University Press.

> Wilson's ethnographic analysis of the Canadian rave scene summarizes and breaks new ground in subcultural resistance theory. Wilson's interpretation of rave as a youth community culminates in the presentation of five theses on the nature of social resistance and the novel ways in which the concept may be employed in contemporary subculture research.

Animal Violence in Sport

Sociologists have been very slow to turn their attention to blood sports involving animals or to activities in which animals suffer neglect and abuse. Although in many countries there seems to be heightened public contempt toward the outwardly cruel treatment of animals in the food industry (such as in eating habits, restaurants, and televised cooking shows) or the entertainment industry (such as in zoos or circuses), we rarely consider how animals may be enmeshed in wider formations of sport-related abuse and violence. In this chapter, we explore the social chains of interdependence that perpetuate tolerable deviance involving animals in sport.

Blood sports are competitions or games that involve animals (and sometimes humans) and carry a risk or probability that one of the participants will be harmed, wounded, or killed during competition. In such sports, animals are chased and killed (e.g., foxhunting) or placed in direct physical combat with one another (e.g., dogfighting). They are called *blood sports* because during competition blood from at least one of the participants may be drawn.

Animal blood sports have deep social roots. Roman gladiators (circa 260 BC) fought wild animals such as lions and tigers at the Colosseum and Circus Maximus in contests called *venationes* (Jennison 2004). The bloody sport of baiting animals emerged around the same time. Baiting is the practice of tormenting chained or confined animals by encouraging another animal (such as a dog) to attack them. A baiting contest ends when the chained or subdued animal is killed. Until the middle of the 19th century, a full range of animals, such as donkeys, tigers, bulls, horses, bears, monkeys, lions, and boars, were used in baiting contests in countries like Britain (Noyes 2006). Before the turn of the 20th century, even insect baiting could be found in China, and camel baiting occurred in several northern African countries. In the Americas, badgers have been used in baiting contests, as have hogs and rats. Following the protests of animal rights advocates principally in the United Kingdom and the United States, most Western nations banned baiting by the middle of the 19th century.

A modern day residue of baiting cultures is dogfighting. Dogfighting, traceable back to ancient Rome and Japan (Jennison 2004), is the act of combat between two dogs for the entertainment and financial profit of spectators. The sport, historically popular in countries such as the United States, the United Kingdom, Afghanistan, Australia, Japan, Argentina, South Africa, Honduras, Colombia, and Brazil, involves placing two dogs into a fighting pit or ring. Handlers release the dogs so that they scratch, claw, and bite one another until one dog either quits or dies. In addition to the dogs, human handlers and a referee typically stay in the pit during the contests. The battles are watched by spectators who bet on the outcomes. Indeed, the cultural purpose of contemporary pit fighting centers as much on the illegal gambling supporting the activity as it does on the animals themselves. American historians of dogfighting, such as Hanna Gibson (www.animallaw.info), tell us that the modern version of the sport was initiated in England in 1835 (ironically, the same year British officials passed the Humane Act prohibiting baiting). It began with the widespread introduction and popularization of two formidably vicious dogs: the Staffordshire bull terrier and the American pit bull terrier. Throughout the 19th century, these breeds were trained to be among the most aggressive of dogs, and they excited fans of dogfighting with their extraordinary aggression and fighting abilities. The breeds joined the ranks of other vicious dogs historically associated with fighting contests, including the Great Dane, Tibetan mastiff, molossus, old English bulldog, and dogo Argentino.

While dogfighting is now illegal in the United States, the activity continues to occupy an underground status in selected states such as Louisiana. Because of the sport's ties to other nefarious cultures in the state, it has been linked to behaviors such as drug trafficking, homicide, illegal gambling, assault, rape, and even weapons trafficking (Forsyth and Evans 1998). The Humane Society of the United States estimates that in 2006 there were 45,000 illegal dogfights performed in the United States alone, and these contests generated more than $5 million U.S. in illegal revenue (*Humane Society of the United States 2007*). In addition to facing brutal violence in the ring, these dogs are often subjected to intense and painful training by their handlers, are often physically abused and neglected when not performing well in competition, and may be force-fed performance-enhancing drugs (Forsyth and Evans 1998). American dogfighting has recently been in the news as a result of the widely documented Michael Vick case. Vick, one of the most high-profile and athletically admired players in the NFL, was charged on a number of counts related to dogfighting, including organizing events and being present at the time dogs died. He is currently serving a 23-month sentence in a federal prison in Leavenworth, Kansas.

An older and a more globally popular form of animal pit fighting is cockfighting. Cockfighting, which is similar to dogfighting except that roosters assume the combat roles, is one of the oldest spectator sports on earth, dating back 6,000 years to ancient Persia (Snow 2004). In human history, it is difficult to find a more widely practiced and watched blood sport than cockfighting. The sport flourished in India (where it is known as *aseel)* and China as well as along the Mediterranean coast during the 4th century BC. It then spread throughout the world during the course of exploration and colonization. Famous military leaders throughout the past, including Alexander the Great and George Washington, were reputed cockfighting enthusiasts, as were many generations of British royalty from the 12th to the 19th centuries (Snow 2004). By the mid-1700s, British nobility had started referring to cockfighting as the *sport of kings.*

Cockfighting remains especially popular in countries such as Belgium, France, Spain, Mexico, the Philippines, Puerto Rico, Guam, the United States, and Haiti. In several of these nations, public stadiums have been constructed to house fights. Just like the dogs involved in pit fighting, gamecocks can suffer horribly during competition. They are bred to be especially combative and aggressive. Parts of their bodies may be removed (including the wattle at their necks) to prevent injury during matches, and they may be fitted around the legs with metal spurs (called *cockspurs)* for gouging their opponents during fights. They are often given drugs that boost their aggression, and they may even have parts of their skin burned with chemicals to harden their flesh and protect them from injury in the ring (Snow 2004).

While animal baiting and animal pit fighting, such as dogfighting and cockfighting, were pushed underground over time, the traditionally English blood sports of foxhunting and hare coursing remained publicly legitimate until quite recently. Foxhunting, the practice of using either sight hounds like salukis or greyhounds or scent hounds like beagles to track and kill a fox, dates back to ancient Egypt (Branigan 1997). Throughout the 14th and 15th centuries, foxhunting ascended in popularity in Britain especially, eventually being viewed by the British elite as a noble and civilized sport (Dunning 1999). Through colonization, the English exported foxhunting to countries such as Canada, the United States, India, and Ireland.

Hare coursing—the chasing of a rabbit in an open field by two dogs with the intention of catching it or making it turn in a particular direction—is believed to have originated in ancient Greece. It, too, has a long history in countries such as England, Ireland, and the United States (Matheson 2005). The oldest form of hare coursing simply involved two dogs pursuing a live hare, with the winner being the dog that caught and killed the hare. There are two forms of what participants call *open hare coursing:* driven coursing and walk-up coursing. In driven coursing, beaters (men who chase the hares out of wooded areas) encourage hares to run toward a designated coursing field. As the hares enter the field, a person known as a *slipper* releases two dogs to initiate a chase. In walk-up coursing, a line of people progresses through the countryside and a pair of dogs is released once a hare is spotted. Coursing fell into considerable disrepute in the United Kingdom and the United States in the 1970s due to the obvious cruelty of the sport (Scully 2004). By 2002, British and Scottish governments banned open coursing through national legislation. In Northern Ireland and the United States, similar attempts by lobbyists such as the Irish Council Against Blood Sports (Ireland), People for the Ethical Treatment of Animals (PETA; United States), and Animal Place (United States) have been unsuccessful in convincing federal legislators to criminalize the practice.

Immortalized by Hemmingway in his 1932 novel *Death in the Afternoon,* bullfighting is one of the most culturally revered and socially ritualistic of all animal blood sports. With roots traceable to the Minoan sport of bull jumping, in which youths hop over charging bulls (this can be found in the United States and Mexico), modern bullfighting is popular in Spain, France, Portugal, Peru, Columbia, Venezuela, India, Ecuador, and Mexico. Spain alone has more than 400 bullfighting venues, and this country is regarded as the modern cultural epicenter of the sport (Levine 2005). As in Portugal and France, in Spain a bullfight *(corrida de toros)* is an enormously popular spectator event deeply encoded with pageantry, ritual, and custom (Scully 2004). Bullfights in Spain are directly linked to times of cultural festival such as *ferias taurinas,* and they are celebrated in the streets of Pamplona through the famous running of the bulls (Levine 2005).

In a traditional Spanish bullfight, a matador confronts the bull in a circular arena surrounded by high walls. He (or, more recently, she) may be supported by a crew of up to six assistants who ride on horseback during the battle. These assistants help deliver initial wounds to the bull using spears, lances, or swords in highly scripted and ritualistic ways. The matador is responsible for delivering the death blow—the *escotada*—after which, the confrontation ends (Levine 2005). Following its death, the bull is normally tied to and dragged from the ring by horses or mules, and it may be immediately butchered for human and animal consumption. There are variations in the precise way a bullfight concludes. In Spain, the bull is killed in the ring, but if the matador does not deliver a mortal blow, in what is arguably one of the most brutal aspects of any sport, an assistant with a shorter blade enters the ring to stab the bull's brain until it dies. In Portugal, the bull is not killed in the ring; rather, it is taken away from audience view and slaughtered by a professional butcher. In countries such as France, the bulls that successfully survive a match are allowed to live and may become legends in the sport. One of the most celebrated bulls of all time in France is Islero, the reputed killer of many bullfighters including the immensely popular Manolete (McCormick 1999).

PETA's informal estimates suggest that 5,000 bulls are killed yearly in contests around the world. Because of the sport's inhumane treatment of the bulls and the painfully slow manner in which the bulls die, antifighting groups have lobbied for the sport's prohibition. Claiming that the law in European countries is speciesist and unfair to animals, groups like No Mas Violencia in Spain have campaigned for economic boycotts of any organization or government supporting the practice (McCormick 1999). In Brazil and Argentina, animal welfare reformists successfully encouraged their governments to ban the sport. The International Movement Against Bullfights and Greenpeace have lobbied globally for the termination of all bullfighting and similar animal blood sports. American bullfighters have responded by pioneering a bloodless bullfight, in which a large piece of Velcro fabric is attached to the back of the bull. The matador then strikes a Velcro-tipped spear against the bull to symbolically represent a death strike (Scully 2004).

In the past several decades, global animal rights activists have challenged the cultural legitimacy of sports like bullfighting, cockfighting, and dogfighting. The 2006 outright ban on foxhunting in the United Kingdom, the end of a centuries-old tradition, underlines how social sensitivities toward the care or suffering of animals in sport are changing. Groups such as PETA in the United States have argued that we need a new perspective on the role of animals in sport and entertainment. Among other things, PETA argues that animals are not placed on earth for human entertainment, torture, or amusement. Animals, like all other creatures, are subjects of their own lives and have physical and emotional needs. PETA argues that because humans are creatures with an advanced capacity for caring, it is the social responsibility of humans to protect rather than injure animals and to respect them rather than hurt them or treat them cruelly. These are elements of blood sports that enthusiasts have always found a way to rationalize.

Animal Sports and Social Justice

Sociological investigations into blood sport cultures in North America and elsewhere are rare. Especially absent are in-depth investigations of blood sports using criminological theory. We find this phenomenon rather curious on several grounds, especially since illegal gambling cultures related to such sports in the United States and elsewhere have received considerable criminological attention. Nevertheless, minor streams of research in the existing literature provide a degree of conceptual direction for thinking sociologically about animal blood sports.

Figurational sociologists such as Sheard (1999) and Dunning (1999) illustrate how animal sports in the United Kingdom have become less violent over the course of civilization and time (Cunningham 1980; Holt 1990). Sports involving animals, such as foxhunting and bird twitching, are understood as killing (or hurting) by proxy, in which social desires to witness and actively participate in violent sport or hunting may be explored symbolically. In considering the social history of animal blood sports around the globe, figurational sociology is helpful in demonstrating how animals are inserted into the civilizing of events and practices and how they become tools for helping humans practice self-restraint and emotional control.

Empirical accounts of animal abuse in sport in North America and continental Europe (i.e., outside of the United Kingdom) typically take a radically different tack than figurational studies take. Largely informed by symbolic interactionist or social constructionist perspectives, research efforts have been aimed at conceptualizing how economies of underground animal blood sports survive despite negative public labeling and social control efforts. In examinations of dogfighting (Forsyth and Evans 1998), cockfighting (Darden and Worden 1996; Hawley 1993), rodeo (Rollin 2001), trophy hunting (Kheel 1999), and bullfighting (Mitchell 1991), authors tend to focus on the social constructions of animal abuse in deviant sport subcultures. Rationalizations and subcultural perspectives of animal abuse have been interrogated, and detailed descriptions of violence have been offered. Among other things, authors have explained the ways in which organizers use particular techniques of neutralization (Sykes and Matza 1957) to justify the cruelty and criminality of the sports. In a study of dogfighting in Louisiana, for example, Forsyth and Evans (1998) show how dog owners, dog trainers, and fight spectators rationalize the cultural traditions associated with the sport and defend the practice using a differential association perspective on social deviance (Sutherland 1947).

In addition to this research and the trends described, empirical investigations of animal blood sports have been tied loosely to emerging academic and political discourses on the ethical and moral treatment of animals. As Regan (2000) notes, animal exploitations in a full range of social spheres, including sport and entertainment, should be comparatively analyzed in order to grasp how animal mistreatment figures into everyday human group life. Wise (2000) and

Beirne (1999) also argue for a nonspeciesist cultural approach to animal rights in sport and elsewhere, particularly emphasizing increased animal protection by law. Ecofeminist scholars such as Kheel (1999) contend that the legal welfare of animals in sport and other social spaces will not change, however, unless communities develop more holistically balanced perspectives on the place of animals in the broader global environment. Most of these perspectives believe that animals will remain relatively unprotected by law as long as prevailing cultural norms promote the exploitation of the marginal in business and entertainment practices.

According to Bermond (1997) and DeGrazia (2002), the historically pervasive view that animals do not experience pain as humans do (that is, reflexively or emotionally) and are not sentient living things with moral rights allows for animal commodification in sport and elsewhere. Preece and Chamberlain (1993) employ a political economic perspective to show that cultures of human mastery over animals (culminating in the mass production and use of animals as a food source) are based on the philosophical and pseudoscientific standpoint that animals do not and cannot suffer emotionally or psychologically in the same way as humans. From this perspective, cultures of mastery over animals transform into economies based on animal suffering. Animals become viewed as commodities to be inserted into a full range of human market exploits, including scientific testing (Regan 2000), decoration in zoos (Lindburg 1999), and personal companionship (Shepard 1996). Rollin (2001) argues that animals are objectified as inanimate objects and are used to confirm the intellectual, moral, and spiritual superiority of humans.

Predictably, perhaps, individuals inside and outside of animal sport cultures tend to adopt a *don't ask, don't tell* standpoint when it comes to animal suffering. Dominant views appear to adhere to the following logic: "We do not believe animals feel pain or should be morally protected from victimization, but neither do we wish to observe the actual violence occurring on farms, in laboratories or in zoos" (Lindburg 1999, 18). Apparently, sport audiences across the globe concur that if we do not see animals being openly victimized in sport—even though we may anticipate its occurrence in the inevitable back regions of such activities (Goffman 1959)—animal sports, including the bloodiest versions, can be rationalized and tolerated. In Stebbins' (1996) terms, by secluding violence against animals to the social periphery or the back regions of everyday life, we position blood sports as unsavory but tolerable forms of culture.

In the following section of this chapter, we examine greyhound racing as an extended case example of an animal blood sport. We show how speciesist ideologies regarding violence, victimization, and crime are embedded in greyhound racing. We argue that deviance in any animal blood sport does not occur through the concerted efforts of a few *bad apples* but rather through extended and complex chains of social interaction involving large numbers of people operating at several levels of activity. Such interaction tends to be knitted together by ideologies that reject the notion that animal athletes have social rights of health and safety.

Greyhound Racing

Although much has been written about abusive and victimizing violence in mainstream sports, violence against animals is, at best, haphazardly inserted into analyses of violence occurring in and around the sports field. Identified by Young (2001, 2007) as a blood sport in his matrix of sport-related violence (SRV), contests involving potentially harmful animal pursuits for the entertainment of participants or spectators may be linked, in both ideology and practice, to more mainstream sports and SRV activities (see Malcolmson 1973). Since greyhound athletic contests, first through coursing and then through formalized racing, symbolically resemble killing-based competitions, they are a clear example of what Elias and Dunning (1986) refer to as *mimesis*. Greyhound racing involves the cultural pursuit of contests representing controlled bloodletting, and it does so in a way that effectively exploits and endangers the participants.

For more than 8,000 years, greyhounds have featured in human communities. The ancient Egyptians, Romans, and Greeks revered the greyhound, which is the world's oldest purebred dog, as a companion, hunter, and religious icon (Barnes 1994; Branigan 1997). Indeed, such was early Christian respect for the breed that the greyhound, according to Branigan (1997), is the only dog mentioned by name in the Christian Bible. British monarchs from the 6th to 18th centuries (e.g., Canute, Harold, and Edward III) elevated the greyhound's revered status through legal code (i.e., the early forest laws) and convention as *the* companion and trusted hunting animal (see Baker 1996).

By the turn of the 18th century, Western civilizing processes and colonial expansion transformed the cultural status of the greyhound. Greyhounds were used less for hunting game and more for taming colonized peoples of the New World (Sullivan 2000). By the 1720s, greyhounds were imported in large numbers to the colonies. Noblemen from England brought the emerging tradition of greyhound coursing to North America (circa 1840s) and exposed popular audiences to the breed through early dog shows (Finch and Nash 2001; Jones 1997). After a series of failed attempts to create a bloodier coursing culture, Owen Patrick Smith helped establish the first modern greyhound racetrack in 1910 in Oakland, California. Several years earlier, Smith had introduced a primitive form of coursing and racing in which greyhounds were released in sealed pens with live hares. In response to the crowd's horror at the carnage that normally ensued, Smith, an engineer, developed the first electronic lure—a device he called the *inanimate hare conveyor*—to pacify the event (Samuels 1999).

In the 1930s, working-class crowds flocked to makeshift racetracks across the southern United States. Races were billed as humane versions of traditional coursing and as events that were more culturally and economically accessible than upper-class horse racing (Branigan 1997). Until the 1990s, greyhound racing served as a staple of American sport betting and was ranked among the most popular spectator sports (GreyhoundracingSUCKS.com 2007). Throughout the bulk of the 20th century, greyhound racing held a central position in the American gambling community and as a tourist attraction, especially in the southern United States.

Fundamental dimensions of the current greyhound figuration in the United States (the world's largest racing community) and the number of dogs involved are revealing. According to the National Greyhound Association (NGA), approximately 34,000 racing greyhounds are born in the United States each year, and 28,000 are registered to race every year. Estimates suggest that 50,000 to 60,000 greyhounds are used as racers each year in the United States. At the time of this writing, 46 tracks are operating in 16 American states, generating more than $100 million U.S. in revenue per year. However, other and more sobering racing statistics may be offered. For instance, estimates published by the Greyhound Protection League suggest that nearly 30,000 greyhounds are killed in America every year at a very young age (from 3-5 years) when they are no longer able to win or place. From 5,000 to 7,000 farm puppies are culled annually, and still more simply vanish without being registered to an owner (GreyhoundracingSUCKS.com 2007).

The sheer number of greyhounds killed in racing (either through early identification as unsuitable racers while still puppies or through lackluster results on the track) is only part of the overall abuse and violence found in the sport, just as the butchering of animals ending up as food products in the supermarket is merely the end result of tolerated and sanctioned violence against livestock (DeGrazia 2002). Clearly, closer inspection of the varied violence against greyhounds is required. We argue that racing greyhounds in North America face four types of violence: breeding violence, training violence, housing violence, and disposal violence. In order to understand the social processes involved in greyhound racing as SRV, we examine (1) the management of greyhound racing as a form of mimesis; (2) the development of greyhound racing as an activity that harms dogs; (3) the contexts, conditions, and ideologies of violence against greyhounds in creating exciting significance in the sport; and (4) the current trends in greyhound racing, suggesting the demise of the sport in North America.

Greyhound Racing as Mimesis

As discussed in the first two chapters, an undercurrent in Elias' writings (cf. 1994, 1996) on long-term civilizing processes is that modern Western figurations have produced relatively unexciting social environments. With the general pacification of figurations that occurs over time, a collective need to devise and institutionalize cultural activities that balance personal pleasure and restraint has occurred. Locating sport in the category of activities that elicit a high level of socially accepted excitement, Elias and Dunning (1986) note that sport provides a context in which a moderate degree of violence is both permissible and encouraged. Thus sport allows individuals to participate in activity that is less condoned or strictly taboo in other social settings (Dunning 1999). In the language of figurationalists, sports contests provide an interactive opportunity for "controlled decontrolling of emotional controls" among participants and spectators (Elias and Dunning 1986, 44).

Elias and Dunning (1986) and Dunning and Rojek (1992) further suggest that a primary role of sport within complex figurations is to take the routine out of social life. In the social theater of sport, spectators are aroused by the tension-balances created through athletic contest (Dunning 1999; Elias and Dunning 1986; Maguire 1999). Sports such as greyhound racing may be considered mimetic because they deliberately resemble warlike competition. Individuals find these sports to be socially and emotionally significant because they elicit excitement but are also structured by an understanding that their outcomes are not as perilous to the participants as are the results of genuine war.

The social history of the greyhound exemplifies how animals have been inserted into the mimetic sporting pastimes of Westerners. From early coursing to later racing, greyhounds have been prized for their ability to hunt. The long-term custom among European and North American upper classes of using the hounds to track game recreationally made them ideal animals for violent-looking dog racing among the American working classes and lower middle classes. Aligned with broader civilizing processes, athletic contests involving greyhounds came to symbolize a habitus categorized by affective restraint and the pursuit of exciting (or mock violent) social activities. Through the formation of the International Greyhound Racing Association in 1926, greyhound racing developed a sporting and civilized facade, and the association's rationalized rule structures and specified outcomes minimized and even obscured the often harsh experience of the races. In this way, violence mocked in greyhound racing not only provided *bread and circuses* for spectators but also became carefully structured by emerging codified rules.

The focus on the financial outcomes and statistical chances of the races adds another important, and in some contexts unsavory, dimension to modern greyhound racing. Rather than emphasizing the ability of the competitors, the concern for financial gain among gambling spectators often deflects attention away from the health and well-being of the dogs, as occurs in other blood sports such as dogfighting or cockfighting (Wise 2000). Audience satisfaction at the track is tempered by financial wins and losses and not by interaction with or empathy for the contestants. Thus greyhound racing is unlike other mimetic sporting competitions in which spectators socially, culturally, and emotionally align with players. Further, while gambling occurs in many sports, greyhound racing is set apart from other sports in that the vast majority of spectators attend races with the sole purpose of betting. The races are only a means to an end of possible financial gain. Mimesis in greyhound racing partly occurs through the multileveled process the audience uses to distance itself from the competing athletes. In this case, distancing is easily facilitated by the use of animals rather than humans in the competition.

In brief, a sport-as-mimesis process has flourished historically in greyhound racing, as it has in other animal-oriented sport cultures (Darden and Worden 1996; Forsyth and Evans 1998; Shepard 1996), perhaps as a result of the relative lack of victim vocalization and representation within the racing community.

As nonhuman competitors, greyhounds obviously do not possess the ability to recount or oppose their experiences with pain. For this reason and others, as long as the demands and effects of competition (anxiety, pain, and injury) are hidden from spectators, greyhound racing is not problematized as victim producing and thus retains its acceptability in the public realm (Beirne 1999; Gold 1995).

Networks of Pain and Violence

Contemporary greyhound racing is formed through the interwoven actions of seemingly disparate players operating at different levels of the figuration. Bullfighting is another animal blood sport that exemplifies this phenomenon. Even though a bull dies at the hands of a single matador, the bull ends up in the ring through the cumulative efforts of numerous social actors operating at multiple levels of the bullfighting figuration (Rollin 2001). Many more actors beyond the bull and the matador are involved in the social organization of an event that may be perceived as exciting, sporting, and tolerable, and it is clear that many people are similarly required to support the figuration and stage the contests of greyhound racing (see table 4.1).

TABLE 4.1 *Actors in the Greyhound Racing Figuration*

Contexts players	Conditions players	Regulation players
Track owners, both local and international	Breeders	State legislators
Track promoters, scouts, and marketers	Trainers	NGA and other greyhound associations
Spectators	Dog owners	Antiracing groups
Gamblers	Kennel owners	Animal rights activists
Betting establishments	Track workers	Adoption and rescue agencies
Betting industries and tourism services	Veterinarians	Private adopters and foster families
	Disposers	
	Medical organizations	
	Universities and research centers	
	Hunters	

In table 4.1, individuals are categorized according to the roles they play in the racing figuration. *Contexts players* are those responsible for establishing the supply of and demand for the races. These individuals seek to normalize the sport in varied social spheres and act as the primary definers of greyhound racing. For the most part, they are responsible for circulating the following techniques of neutralization (Sykes and Matza 1957). The dogs are treated humanely, the racing is healthy and exciting for the dogs, the sport is exhilarating for the audience, and the sport is a suitably monitored and civilized cultural pursuit. Through covert facilitation and rationalization, contexts players form the basis of the greyhound racing economy, supplying the structural resources (i.e., tracks and promotion) and financial resources (i.e., breeding and wagering monies) needed to fuel the industry.

By contrast, *conditions players* are more directly involved in physically harming the dogs. From breeders to trainers to medical professionals who experiment on retired racers, conditions players are the unseen members of the figuration. They operate in Goffman's (1963) *back regions*, overseeing the daily care and handling of the racers. An obvious parallel may be found in circus and carnival cultures, in which there is also a contrast between what is seen on the front stage of an animal showcase and what the handlers and trainers do to care for the animals backstage after the audience is gone (Wise 2000).

Regulation players comprise the figuration members responsible for policing any alleged abuse against racers. Consisting of individuals such as state regulators (who establish gaming laws and animal abuse codes), police officers, members of national greyhound associations (such as the American Greyhound Council), and animal rights advocates, regulation players pursue a mandate to control unwanted abuse in the sport. Historically speaking, this mandate has been exercised somewhat passively, at least in the U.S. racing figuration.

A mere glance at the existing research is all that is necessary to see how some racing greyhounds endure lives of pain and abuse through the cooperative efforts of the main players in the sport. In the following discussions, we outline four ways in which a greyhound might suffer in the business of racing.

Breeding

Greyhounds encountering abuse during their racing careers typically do so at an early age. Along with neglecting the greyhounds, breeders may kill or simply abandon puppies they deem to be unsuitable for racing or dogs that wash out after failing to succeed at local racing school. Estimates received from informants place this number at approximately 1 in 10 dogs bred every year. The industry refers to this process as *farm culling:*

> Culling happens, it really does. As a breeder, one of the skills you acquire is the ability to look at a pup and watch its gait for potential. Dogs who don't have the instinct [to chase] or the tools to be a consistent winner—well, a good handler can spot it a mile away. . . . Most of the time, I'd drown the pups.
>
> (Breeder, age 39)

Such justificatory accounts are clearly motivated by the greyhound marketplace. According to a breeder in our own empirical research, if the dogs are successful, they are typically isolated from human contact during training and crammed into pens with other greyhounds. Reports of improper, suspect, or flagrantly inhumane housing facilities abound in the southern United States (the location of some of the most cash-strapped tracks in the entire U.S. racing industry), with descriptions of dogs kept chained outdoors or left to roam without proper feeding or care. In some rare cases during the breeding process, the dogs are trained using live animals such as hares as bait (an illegal practice in all states sanctioning greyhound racing). Transportation of the dogs between their breeders and their eventual owners (kennel owners at tracks or other private owners) may also prove perilous. Greyhound advocacy groups have reported more than a dozen cases of transportation-related deaths since .1993, and our research leads us to strongly suspect that far more dogs face a similar fate. Deaths may occur when greyhounds are left unattended in small caravans or wagons in extreme heat. In such cases, the dogs die of either heat exhaustion or dehydration. Allegations of greyhound abuse along these lines are maintained in the *back regions* of the racing figuration or are disregarded in more public venues as merely atypical or exaggerated.

Training and Racing

The on-track training and racing of greyhounds may also lead to significant physical abuse and harm. While it is commonly suggested by trainers and has been set as a historical precedent that each dog be raced 2 or 3 times per week, track averages vary enormously and can peak well beyond this limit (up to 7 times per week). Information provided by former track workers and other insiders and verified by racing cards indicates that some dogs may be raced up to three times the recommended level. Due to overuse and the intensity of the races, pain and injury inevitably occur. Like some human athletes, some greyhounds live through pain on a daily basis. Broken bones, torn ligaments or muscles, back and neck injuries, lacerations, and facial abrasions caused by muzzling are common.

Why do owners and operators allow their investments to be injured or jepoardized? In practice, a simple economic equation answers this question. Treatment of the animals often proceeds if the benefits outweigh the costs. If a successful racer experiences an economically minor injury (as assessed against what a successful racer may yield each year), medical attention will likely result. But since many dogs crash out after 2 to 3 years of racing and there is a surplus of younger dogs to promote to regular racing tracks, owners may find it more economical to run an injured racer until it can no longer perform and then relegate it to a lower grade track where it will finish its career.

Unsurprisingly, as part of their daily training maintenance, greyhounds require a substantial amount of food. Rather than feeding the dogs a high-caliber diet, some low-budget tracks utilize what has been termed *4-D meat* (dead, dying, downed, and diseased meat) to minimally sustain the greyhounds' nutritional requirements. Such meat is often rife with *E. coli* toxins and may not be sold commercially according to USDA standards. It is illegally purchased for pennies per pound, and its consumption may lead to a skin condition that handlers refer to as *Alabama rot* (a condition featuring open lesions and ulcers) or an intestinal problem referred to as *blow-out* (which includes chronic vomiting and diarrhea that lead to death from dehydration). Insider estimates suggest that 15% to 20% of racing greyhounds have consumed 4-D meat at some point in their careers. In the words of one of our respondents,

> You know that saying, "Not even fit for a dog"? Well, the food we used to give them takes that saying to a whole new level. The so-called *4-D meat* is disgusting, for sure, but [Alabama] rot is the worst thing I've ever seen in an animal.

Other greyhounds may be injected with anabolic steroids such as methyl testosterone to improve their on-track performance. Some greyhounds, as indicated by recent allegations against greyhound tracks in Florida such as the Naples Fort Myers Greyhound Track in Bonita Springs, are even injected with cocaine as a performance enhancer or painkiller (Seitlin 2004).

Again, these sorts of practices, pushed behind the scenes of everyday life in the greyhound figuration, demonstrate how greyhounds in contexts of economic and social neglect may be treated. As part of the mimetic process, this backstage behavior is undertaken to lower the overhead costs of the races and is hidden from public view to avoid scandal.

Housing

The housing of greyhounds at racetracks often reflects a cost-cutting, low-overhead mentality and, with the use of sometimes brutally inhumane care, further objectifies the dogs. At any given time, a greyhound track may house hundreds of dogs in a complex of kennels. A kennel operator is in charge of all the dogs in a specific kennel, which can amount to anywhere from 10 to 100 or more dogs. The dogs are often kept in rows of stacked cages for nothing more than space considerations—sometimes, a cage may be only 24 inches (61 centimeters) in width—and may be housed or muzzled for up to 22 hours per day (see GREY2K USA 2007). Squeezing dogs into cramped kennel spaces allows more races to be run every day, thus increasing track efficiency and revenue. The dogs are turned out several (1-4) times per day to urinate or defecate and are usually freed once to eat and receive water. Due to the stacked cages and the wire mesh structure and lack of proper flooring in the kennels, greyhounds in the bottom rows are showered with the waste of others. At some of the more disreputable tracks, music is blasted into the kennels to drown out the incessant barking or whining. None of this happens accidentally. As a 40-year-old former track worker told us,

> . . . we'd never listen to them howling on end for hours. All you can do is close the doors, turn the radio up, and walk away. At first we turned it to lite music stations cause we thought it might calm them down a bit. But that only seemed to make them madder. We tried heavy metal, classic rock, and even Latin, and nothing worked. . . . Rap is about the only kind of music louder and more obnoxious than barking!

Under such conditions, some greyhound kennels become infested with fleas and ticks. As a result, greyhounds from particular tracks carry skin, blood, heart, and respiratory diseases such as canine ehrlichiosis, *Ehrlichia equi,* canine babesiosis, and Rocky Mountain spotted fever. Due to dismal sanitary conditions at the low-budget tracks, greyhounds may suffer from hookworm, tapeworm, whipworm, and giardia. Since the turn of the century, outbreaks of kennel cough in American racetracks have killed several dozen greyhounds (see GREY2K USA 2007). On-track conditions, however, may be no kinder to the dogs. Many die each year from racing collisions and falls (often, smaller females are trampled in races with larger males) or from electrocution by electrical lure systems.

Release

Recently circulated stories about the release or the retirement of racers have prompted close scrutiny of the racing industry in the United States and abroad (especially in Ireland, the United Kingdom, and Spain). When racers no longer win, they are downwardly discarded through the racing system, competing at tracks of lower status and grade. When they have finally reached the end of this career spiral and are no longer financially worthy of housing at any racing level, they are replaced and disposed of rather unceremoniously. In the words of another track worker, "I think racers know their time is up. They won't 'bring it' to the races anymore and act uninterested. Shortly after, they'll start to lose at every track, and then they're done for good." While increasing numbers of greyhounds are now fostered out through developing greyhound adoption agencies such as Wings For Greyhounds, thousands of racing hounds are also euthanized annually.

Disposal of the dogs varies considerably, but two noticeable trends (other than adoption) are evident in dumping processes. The first is the individual killing of greyhounds following their retirement as racers. Colloquially referred to as *going back to the farm,* death may be very cruel. Racing greyhounds in the United States may be bludgeoned, hanged, starved to death, abandoned in a field or woods, decapitated, electrocuted (with a device called a *Tijuana hot plate),* sold to fishermen to be used, for example, as shark chum, sold to hunters, or sold to medical laboratories for research purposes.

Second is the even more disturbing microtrend of the mass killing of racing hounds. Since the mid-1990s, antiracing organizations have reported the discovery of so-called *killing fields* of dog carcasses in the United States and Europe (especially Spain). Greyhounds have been found dead in rural grasslands, tied to railway tracks, or stacked in local dumpsters (People for the Ethical Treatment of Animals 2007). Medical laboratories and a handful of American universities have been targeted as mass killers of greyhounds, and the entire racing industry has been labeled by groups such as PETA as abusive and inhumane.

Changing Climates for Animal Sports

In light of such evidence, it is clear that abuse in the greyhound figuration occurs through a multilayered constellation of efforts made by many actors. While one individual may directly starve a racer, fail to treat its wounds, feed it spoiled food, or euthanize it inhumanely, numerous others are complicit in these acts through cooperative behavior or through turning a blind eye. Each of the contexts, conditions, and regulation players contributes, although clearly through different means, to the process of greyhound abuse, with physical acts of neglect and violence as the end result of their actions. Animal abuse is not unique to the world of greyhound racing; rather, it is one of numerous contexts in which animals suffer from selective mistreatment in the name of sport. Figure 4.1 illustrates this network of relationships that culminate in abuse.

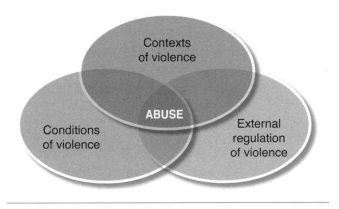

Figure 4.1 Abuse and interdependence in greyhound racing.

In North America, however, the greyhound racing industry appears to be in a state of decline. There are several reasons for this possible demise. First, the boom in casino gambling in the United States has partly muscled out the racing industry in stronghold states such as Florida and Alabama (Samuels 1999). Second, animal advocacy and vegan lifestyle groups such as PETA have attained increasing media attention and public legitimacy throughout the past several years (Dillard 2002). As a result, public discourses on greyhound racing are replete with chilling accounts of dog abuse and the public is more informed than ever before.

Third, and reflective of ongoing civilizing processes in Western cultures, of which the rise of animal rights groups is a component (Dunning 1999), many North Americans are increasingly concerned with animal cruelty, especially through seemingly trivial sport contests (barring hunting, rodeo, and horse racing, which continue to thrive on the continent). In particular, the youngest generations of North Americans are raised in social spaces with new habituses that are more compassionate and politically correct regarding animal cruelty (see Armstrong and Botsler 2003). Fourth and finally, the demise of greyhound racing may be occurring simultaneously with the ongoing legitimization of SRV in other sport spheres. As Young (2000, 2001) suggests, today there are other forms of mimetic sport violence available that are apparently more palatable to Western audiences than are animal competitions. These kinds of sport violence may be found in mainstream contact, collision, or otherwise high-risk sports or in sports involving, for example, vehicles driven at high speeds.

Despite noticeable decline in the U.S. greyhound industry and progressive attempts to remedy its abuse and violence issues (American Greyhound Council 2004), we can draw lines of comparison between the neglect in greyhound racing and the systematic mistreatment of animals in other settings such as laboratories (for experimentation), zoos (for gaze), factory farms (for mass consumption), pet stores (for companionship), and hunting fields (for sport killing). The conceptual figuration of actors described in this chapter may be compared with a plethora of other contexts in which animals are subject to neglect, abuse, or violence (see Shepard 1996). Each context contains its own indigenous contexts, conditions, and regulation players who perform various roles in the abuse and violence process. In some cases, such as hunting, figurations are composed of a modest number of actors participating individually or in small groups, while in others, such as bullfighting or rodeo, figurations include larger and more complex chains of participants who directly and indirectly contribute to harm against animals that becomes rationalized and normalized over time.

THEORETICAL INTERSECTIONS

We believe that greyhound racing is a social activity that straddles the balance beam of wanted and unwanted deviance. On the one hand, greyhound racing can be exhilarating and even aesthetic to watch. The mock hunt in racing symbolizes an instance of killing by proxy and, as such, is certainly wanted deviance by many. Greyhound racing could, when operated safely and with due care for the dogs, be a quintessentially civilized and doubly mimetic sport (Atkinson 2002)—doubly mimetic since the historically bloody form of greyhound coursing is a cultural stand-in for battles between groups of people and since the pacified greyhound race is a more civilized instance of field coursing. In other words, greyhound racing is a representation of a representation of battle. However, given the cultural dynamics at work in the greyhound community in the United States and abroad—Ireland, England, Spain, and Portugal are known worldwide for their disreputable and cruel greyhound racing cultures—there are many empirical grounds to suggest, as we have in this chapter, that even the most mimetic of sports may have violent and tragic consequences. Even doubly mimetic sports, then, produce unwanted deviance.

With regard to mimetic social activities in sport, Dunning (1999, 248) asks whether future historians will examine the social and cultural practices of the 20th and 21st centuries and refer to people as *late barbarians*. While groups of sociologists suggest that Western nations, including the United States, Canada, the United Kingdom, and others, are either postmodern or poststructural, Dunning questions if such labels are too hasty, arguing that social institutions in the West are beset with modernist tendencies of production and consumption and that Western cultural practices continue to heave with rather barbaric tendencies. Sport is but one example of social behavior designed and perpetuated within groups to showcase blood, violence, aggression, fear, anxiety, and a host of other emotions that have primitive undertones. Human cultures cannot be postmodern if they have not eclipsed, in social practice or thought, even premodern behavioral codes. In what follows, we ask you to consider eight different theoretical perspectives and to ponder whether they support or refute the concept of late barbarianism.

FUNCTIONALISM AND STRAIN THEORY

In 1937, the American sociologist Kingsley Davis published an innovative and controversial analysis of prostitution. For Davis, prostitution, while an overt criminal act, serves a social purpose if it provides a sexual outlet for individuals who are otherwise blocked from more socially acceptable sexual opportunities. Davis postulates that such people might become psychologically and emotionally frustrated without the illicit gratifications offered through prostitution, and that they subsequently seek to find emotional or physical release in more socially destructive ways.

Greyhound racing, and animal blood sports more broadly, might also be understood as a cathartic social safety valve. As social psychologists of sport violence like Kerr (2004) argue, watching violent or aggressive sport (especially forms framed around real or otherwise mimetic killing) tends to elicit mass spectator arousal. Thus blood sports allow audiences to witness forms of (largely taboo) violence. Davis or other functionalists might make a case for animal blood sports by arguing that because they direct aggressive human impulses toward other species, they may functionally serve to channel natural human emotions in socially safe ways. Attributing such a meaning to animal blood sports could potentially explain (and help rationalize) why they have remained popular across cultures for more than 2,000 years.

CONFLICT THEORY

Stanley Cohen's (2003) study of how Westerners frequently deny the existence of human suffering and atrocity rather than seek to eliminate them via collective action offers an innovative conflict theory of victimization and suffering. In *States of Denial: Knowing About Atrocities and Suffering*, Cohen questions why so many people who witness injustice or suffering acquiesce to them rather than oppose them or engage in social activism. He suggests that most citizens in affluent nations are bystanders to dominant systems of social oppression. Because most of us are required by power elites to conform and are intimidated or embarrassed by the possibility of becoming entangled in controversy, we rarely tell the truth about pain and suffering when we witness it and we rarely become a whistle-blower or call attention to a prevailing condition of exploitation or violence. Using a theoretical framework based on a sociology of denial, Cohen contends that the real power of social control lies in the ability of the power holders to persuade people to relinquish their roles as moral or political watchdogs and to embrace a culture of civic irresponsibility over political intervention.

According to the rhetoric of animal rights advocates, Cohen's ideas about cultures of learned passivity jibe with mainstream thinking about animal abuse and neglect in sport. Even though the plight of entertainment animals has been well documented over the past several decades and has been debated in the public sphere, there are very few organized social movements dedicated to the elimination of animal sports. It seems that the knowledge of suffering is not enough to combat bystander cultures in the West. Further, given that increasingly ubiquitous media and the Internet present audiences with a range of social atrocities to ponder, it is possible to understand how mass murder, war, gun violence, drug use, sexual assault, terrorism, or human torture might become prioritized over cases of animal abuse in sport. Cohen theorizes that with the media's consistent emphasis on crime, deviance, and social problems (as the well-known axiom states, "If it bleeds, it leads!"), we frequently feel culturally and emotionally overwhelmed with victimization narratives and scarcely believe that individual action could ease collective suffering, even in obvious cases where large numbers of animals suffer.

INTERACTION THEORY

Sutherland's (1973) *Principles of Criminology* outlines the theory of differential association. According to Sutherland's theory, people learn criminal (or non-normative) behavior through interactions with deviant others. We learn our attitudes about what is acceptable group behavior from family, friends, coworkers, and other intimates we socialize with regularly. Sutherland believes that people learn normative values that either support or oppose crime and deviance. His principle of differential association states that individuals who are exposed to an excess of ideologies supporting rule violation will themselves become rule breakers compared with those who are exposed to values favoring conformity. From this view, people are cultural sponges who predictably uphold or violate the law or dominant social norms because they have been socialized to act in these ways.

Sutherland's differential association sheds light on how blood sport advocates and organizers might justify violence against animal *athletes*. Just as British foxhunting enthusiasts are typically from rural locations or affluent social classes (that is, from settings where people are taught early in life that such activities are meaningful and acceptable), trainers and handlers in greyhound racing typically are raised in close proximity to the sport or possess family affiliations with the sport. Generations of trainers and racing enthusiasts linked by sanguine ties are not uncommon in the southern United States.

On a more sweeping cultural scale, entire cities or regions, such as Seville or Andalusia in Spain, develop their own blood sport traditions—and techniques of neutralization—that become tied to celebration or nostalgia or to codes of gender and honor. Within both rural and urban contexts, communities pass on the social rituals of the blood sport to successive generations, link the sport to collective identities, and help frame the practice for neophytes as a tolerable cultural pastime.

SOCIAL CONTROL THEORY

Extending the boundaries of traditional social control theories is Fromm's (1973) social psychological understanding of human aggression. In *The Anatomy of Human Destructiveness,* Fromm describes a particular problematic social act of violence—malignant aggression. This type of aggression exists in two main forms: sadism (the desire to control other beings) and necrophilia (the desire to destroy life).

Malignant aggression is linked to what Fromm calls *character-rooted passions.* Fromm believes that humans have existential needs, such as the need to be socially bonded to others, to enhance agency through bonding, to develop meaningful ways of life, and to achieve a sense of collective purpose or unity. If people are socialized into bonding communities, they adopt biophilous passions of belonging, compassion, equality, justice, and the desire to nurture life. When personal needs are frustrated, bonding is low, and existential needs are frustrated, people adopt character passions of hate, greed, jealousy, envy, cruelty, narcissism, and destructiveness. The desire to control others (sadism) or to inflict pain as a form of social control or self-control (necrophilia) stems from—in the conventional language of social control theory—ineffectual social bonding and inhibited self-control.

Fromm's approach could explain why humans would create animal blood sports as a malignantly destructive form of social entertainment. By using Fromm's ideas, we could explain human dominance over animals in sport as a form of necrophilia undertaken by groups with similar character passions derived from low levels of normative social bonding. In particular, Fromm believes that humans create their own social drama when their lives are filled with frustration and outlets for wielding malignant aggression are desired. Animal blood sports provide people with a patterned context for not only seeing but also participating in the aggressive dominance over other species. Blood sports, while varying in the degree to which animals experience harm during competition, are flavored by the participants' collective desire to produce and consume suffering and destruction.

CLASSICAL THEORY

Inspired by the utilitarian theoretical tradition in criminology, Lo (1994) describes the human decision to engage in deviant behavior as a carefully weighed process involving a balance of personal choices and constraints. Her economic theory of crime contends that potential criminals assess the relative costs, risks, opportunities, and benefits of deviance and then follow the most attractive line of behavior. Deviance is explained in the same way that normative behavior is described: as a consciously calculated, pleasure-generating experience for individuals. From this rather straightforward and perhaps austere theoretical perspective, the choice of deviant or conforming behavior boils down to an economically rationalized decision.

Evidence presented in the case study of greyhound racing illustrates that certain dogs experience abuse as part of the cost–benefit decision making that occurs at racetracks. When dogs perform well and make a profit, they are protected as investments. Further, owners and handlers may invest only the minimum amount needed to keep racers in competitive form, and they may cut costs (of feeding, handling, injury treatment, and transportation) to maximize profits. When the costs of maintaining a loser outweigh the benefits of continued racing, the dog is discarded. Decisions to treat the dogs humanely are therefore linked less to the rights of animals than they are the outcome of an economically determined calculation.

CRITICAL THEORY

Postmodernist sociologists of law and order might encourage researchers of animal blood sports to examine the truth claims that underpin insiders' perspectives on animal suffering. Postmodern criminologists like Milovanovic (1997) view any form of knowledge—such as how we come to know that a blood sport is acceptable as a cultural tradition, know it does not produce animal suffering, or know it involves only instinctually violent animals—as fragmented, partial, and contingent. Milovanovic and others suggest that rather than there being one truth about the cultural place of something like a blood sport, there are many floating, or possible, truths. In this vein of thinking, postmodern criminologists search for the dismissed or subverted knowledge that might change our perspective on how to decide on what is moral, just, criminal, fair, or deviant.

For postmodernist theorists of deviance and crime, knowledge about what is socially acceptable is both relational and positional. Therefore, any way of knowing and talking about a social practice, such as blood sport, reflects the relationship of the speaker to the audience and is predicated on social hierarchies of power. For example, the justifications that support the use of animals in sports are discursively formed truths with their own potential points of rupture only when we consider who is speaking. Someone involved in bullfighting might, from a position of power and authority, draw on the cultural legacy of the sport and its meaning to audiences as a deep symbol of a total way of life. But when deconstructed, such discourses that justify the killing of bulls as a form of cultural affiliation and representation are revealed as nothing more than systems of knowledge that silence other ways of knowing the sport as brutal or inhumane. The primary goal of the critical theorist interested in blood sports is to challenge the legitimacy of taken-for-granted truths about the sports by uncovering alternative perspectives that may destabilize justifications of violence.

GENDER AND FEMINIST THEORY

In their book, *Animals and Women: Feminist Theoretical Explorations* (1995), Adams and Donovan draw on an ecofeminist understanding of social oppression and exploitation in order to deconstruct how, among other things, animals are violently inserted into the entertainment industries. Although not traditional deviance or crime theorists, Adams and Donovan paint a chilling portrait of how mainstream social norms in entertainment may be predicated on the abuse of animals. The spectrum of animal abuse in entertainment circles has widened over time, since not until recently have animals been viewed as things with social rights. Adams and Donovan believe that animals are like other socially marginalized groups and are part of a patriarchal hegemony that ignores the well-being of those not in mainstream White, male, middle-class groups.

Ecofeminists call our attention to the cultural politics of denaturalizing animals and the environment through blood sport. Bulls, bears, greyhounds, dogs, and roosters are taken out of their normal environments and encouraged to act upon what we believe to be their *natural* instincts. We can justify greyhounds running, roosters fighting, bulls charging, or bears attacking because it is what they normally do in nature. The paradox that Adams and Donovan and other ecofeminists find in such a position is that the fights are socially choreographed, the battles are arranged, and the natural fighting for space, food, or survival is exploitatively structured for the profit or pleasure of humans. In short, there is little reason to believe that a greyhound race or a bullfight represents anything *natural*.

INTEGRATED THEORY

In general, the work of Elias (cf. 1991, 1994, 1996) has been untapped in mainstream crime and deviancy research. Elias outlines a metatheory of the civilizing process and offers an integrated theory (that is, a weaving together of biological, psychological, sociological, and historical theories of human behavior) of deviance. In *The Civilizing Process* (1994), Elias emphasizes that the best inhibitor of deviance is self-control and that self-control varies not only individually and culturally within a population but also historically as nation-states develop and interact. He shows how the internalization of self-restraint and the development of stricter normative codes *(psychogenesis)* connect to broader social processes, including transformations in the division of labor, population shifts, the development of peace-oriented cultural ideologies, and industrialism and the growth of cities *(sociogenesis)*. Throughout the history of nations such as England, France, Germany, and the United States, external restraint became less important for social control and became internalized as self-restraint gained prominence. For Elias, this is the heart of the civilizing process. In relatively civilized nations, mimetic social activities are fashioned in order to stimulate dangerous social emotions and aggression prohibited in other social spheres. As noted throughout our case study of greyhound racing, animal blood sports have been considered a prototypical mimetic activities by figurationalists like Dunning (1999).

Discussion Questions

1. What are the main reasons why people are fascinated by animal blood sports? Can sociology help in explaining this fascination?
2. Greyhound racing is certainly not the only sport that involves dogs. Think of at least five sports that involve dogs in any way, shape, or form. Are these sports more or less tolerable than greyhound racing? Why or why not?
3. Propose how you would design and carry out a study of an animal sport culture.

Recommended Readings

Beirne, P. 1999. For a nonspeciesist criminology: Animal abuse as an object of study. *Criminology* 37:117-148.

In this article, Beirne exposes what he calls the essential *speciesist* construction of the law in North America. He questions why criminologists have largely ignored how animals are repeatedly victimized in a range of social settings while the perpetrators go relatively unpoliced.

Branigan, C. 1997. *The reign of the greyhound.* New York: Howell Book House.

Branigan's book is one of the most detailed historical and contemporary accounts of greyhound racing and its cultural significance. It documents the role of the species in human cultures across centuries and provides insight into how the contemporary sport is organized and rationalized.

Dunning, E., and C. Rojek. 1992. *Sport and leisure in the civilizing process.* London: Macmillan.

This book is part of an extended figurational sequence of texts that detail the rise and prominence of sport as a form of social excitement and pacification and a set of institutionalized practices. The authors draw and expand on the work of Norbert Elias to examine the sociological, historical, psychological, and biological significance of sport in everyday life.

Regan, T. 2000. *The case for animal rights.* Berkeley, CA: University of California Press.

Regan's widely cited and controversial book provides one of most compelling accounts of the role of animal suffering and exploitation. It summarizes evidence for and against more humane approaches to animal welfare in the United States and elsewhere.

Snow, R. 2004. *The history and sport of cockfighting.* London: Twiddling Pencil Publishers.

Snow's book is one of the most comprehensive historical and cultural analyses of cockfighting communities. The book presents cross-cultural and historical understandings of the role of this animal blood sport in the confirmation and maintenance of social identities.

III

Deviant Athletic Bodies

The past 10 years have produced a wealth of sociological information on how we define, experience, and police norms regarding body performance and representation in sport cultures. Despite the diversity of body deviance in sport cultures, few sociologists of sport have made use of deviancy theory. In chapter 5, we use a three-pronged approach to address how performance-enhancing drug use, self-aggressed bodies in triathlon, and the emergence of virtual sport cultures illustrate the differences between wanted and unwanted deviance in sport. Through these case studies, we describe how boundaries between normative and deviant bodies in sport cultures are blurred by technological and scientific ideologies in late-modern societies. In chapter 6, we present the case study of diseased bodies in sport as an example of how people may utilize sport to challenge stigmas related to illness in Western cultures. We review narratives of athletes who use their sporting endeavors to disavow the status of the deviant and morally inferior ill body and to critique power and competition ideologies found in mainstream sport cultures.

Body Pathologies in Sport

As social and academic interest in the body expands, the corporeal practices of athletes—whose bodies experience constant public gaze—come under increasing scrutiny (Andrews 2003; Rail 1998). The deviancy literature suggests that body practices within specific cultural contexts may be labeled as *different, contranormative,* or *rule breaking.* Sport contexts are hardly different. Because athletes and audiences are preoccupied with excellence in physical performance, deviations from the ideal athletic form (however defined within a given sport culture) can meet with a range of responses, from complete indifference to scorn and even punishment. When athletic bodies do not measure up to established standards in sport cultures, athletes may be encouraged to violate rules as a compensatory response.

Through sport participation, some athletes are labeled as body deviants. For example, the bulk and musculature perceived as necessary for elite competition in certain sports may elicit stigmatization for female athletes when their bodies violate traditional notions of femininity and sexuality (Markula 2003). Further, research on female rugby players (Chase 2006) shows how body logic in the sport contradicts a body idiom that is established among women (and men) in other social settings. Sociologists of sport have also shown how bodies that are racialized, disabled, or sexualized are often defined as deviant in one sport context or another (Atkinson and Wilson 2001).

Despite recent suggestions that the concept of deviance in sport is no longer useful (Coakley and Donnelly 2005) or that sport deviance is cleverly choreographed by media agents as a carnival-type spectacle (Blackshaw and Crabbe 2004), we believe that critics have overstated their case against the usefulness of the concept of deviance, especially when examining what sports insiders and outsiders classify as *body deviance.* Anyone who studies athleticism and its cultural representations knows that the idea of a normless, forgiving, or totally polysemic sport culture in which anything goes regarding the body is unrealistic. Sport cultures create, monitor, and police normative comfort zones that frame acceptable body appearance and performance, and rule violators are stigmatized with varying degrees of intensity and consequence. Media coverage of sport and athletic bodies certainly inserts ways of knowing corporeal rule violation into the public consciousness, but it is also possible that researchers have exaggerated media influence by assuming that television, Internet, magazine, or newspaper narratives systematically blur, obfuscate, or deconstruct understandings of physical normativity in sport settings (Brookes 2002).

In this chapter, we approach bodies much as Douglas (1970) described them some time ago: as living tableaus, or texts, of culture. Douglas argued that the body is a material symbol of established social rules, values, and hierarchies and that people develop relationships with their body on the basis of cultural norms. An embodied rule violation in sport risks reprimand and a loss of achieved status for an athlete. Further still, the social credibility of a sport may be challenged by flagrant body rule violations among athletes. The rigging of boxing matches (i.e., not physically competing according to ability), the interpersonal violence among professional basketball players (i.e., not showing physical restraint), and the use of marijuana in snowboard cultures (i.e., abusing an athletic body) may all be perceived as body violations that undermine the sport ethic (Hughes and Coakley 1991) and may result in stigmatized sport identities (Goffman 1963). Even a cursory glance at a morning newspaper in sport-hungry countries reveals a fascination with body violations committed by athletes or persons connected to sport.

As Ritchie (2007) has argued, the use of performance-enhancing drugs is now among the most publicly condemned body problems in sport. Sociologists of sport including Waddington (2000), Houlihan (1999), and Beamish and Ritchie (2005) have documented the growing moral panic regarding doped bodies on the playing field and the multi-institutional struggle to clean up sport, especially at the elite level. Discourses about drug use typically include definitions of acceptable and unacceptable embodied practice and frame embodied violations of sport principles as intolerable. Waddington (2000) and others understand the complexity of drug use as a social process and document the social trends in and around sport that counterbalance prohibitionist discourses. Waddington believes that the prevalence of legal and illegal performance enhancers among athletes despite punitive control in most elite sports is produced by three normalizing social trends that help to create new boundaries of drug use: the medicalization of sport, the subcultural traditions of drug use, and the technologization of sport training and performance.

In this chapter, we build on Waddington's approach. We expose the paradox of contemporary body rules in sport through illustrations of how norms of medicalization, subcultural affiliation, and technologization create structural and cultural spaces for athletes to consider non-normative forms of bodywork as meaningful. We believe that contemporary athletes are socially prepared to engage in corporeal sport deviance, given dominant trends in how their bodies are objectified through technomedical sport cultures. Our analysis of body deviance in sport is further buttressed by our own separate and collective research on athletes and training cultures, including qualitative field studies of varsity athletes in a host of sport cultures (from rugby to football to swimming), studies of endurance athletes, and studies of recreational athletes.

This chapter covers three case studies. In the first, we link a discussion of medicalization in sport with a small study of the performance-enhancing drug erythropoietin (EPO) in professional cycling. This is followed by a case study of subcultural preferences for risky and even self-violent management of body weight in endurance sport. In the final case study, we build on Waddington's work to examine the movement toward virtual bodies in sport cultures as a deviant offshoot of technological sport cultures.

EPO in Professional Cycling

Throughout the second half of the 20th century, much of what sociologists traditionally called *social problems* increasingly became identified as *medical problems*. Social injustice, prejudice, intolerance, self-hatred, depression, sexual desire, and interpersonal aggression were increasingly diagnosed and treated using medical paradigms and medical terms. Sociologist of health and illness, Conrad (2005) argues that the tendency to frame social problems under the jurisdiction of objective science is part of an ongoing medicalization of Western cultures.

For athletes, who are both the subjects and objects of medical, kinesiological, nutritional, and psychological sciences, corporeal training, control, performance, recovery, and success are understood as essentially medical matters. Athletic bodies present a panorama of medical puzzles related to physical growth, performance, repair, and longevity. Sociologists of sport such as Butryn (2003) or Miah (2004) contend that modern athletes essentially represent data sources for sport and exercise scientists, as they are mapped, prodded, and medically colonized. Successful training and athletic discipline are often gauged by how well an athlete follows the advice of doctors, trainers, or other sport scientists. Athletes seek medical counsel in order to improve all facets of athletic performance, and the athlete's habitus shifts toward medicine and drugs.

Beamish and Ritchie (2005) maintain that an established medical mind-set in athletic cultures opens the door for increased drug use as a remedy for performance problems. Trainers and coaches may not specifically instruct athletes to cheat and use a drug as a solution to a performance problem, but the idea of using medicine to resolve problems that are also perceived as medical is something athletes clearly learn in the process of constructing an athletic self.

Sociologists interested in drug use suggest it is likely that performance-enhancing drugs have been used since the beginning of organized sport (Waddington 2000). Evidence suggests that such substances were used as early as the 4th century BC in Rome and Greece, at which time there existed substances and methods to create euphoria, decrease fatigue, and increase strength among athletes (Mottram 2005). In recent decades, highly publicized expansion in the use of substances including morphine, codeine, amphetamines, anabolic steroids, and corticosteroids to increase sport performance has underlined the prevalence of medicalization in sport training and performance.

Although drug scandals have pervaded modern sport since the middle of the 20th century, a disturbing number of athletes have been caught with banned substances in their bodies in the past two decades. Our own informal review of amateur and professional athletes that have been caught cheating through illegal drug supplementation reveals a list of more than 650 international athletes (either amateur or professional) from 71 countries caught since 1986. But this is the tip of the iceberg; many more athletes have been caught, and it is likely that far more have evaded apprehension. Patterns in the data suggest that subcultures of drug use exist among athletes in track and field, elite powerlifting, swimming, professional cycling, and numerous other sports. As global sports are medicalized through training and performance analysis, athletes' bodies become sites of pharmaceutical experimentation and self-medication (Monaghan 2002).

One of the burgeoning drug scandals in global sport is the use of EPO by endurance athletes, especially professional cyclists. EPO, a synthetic peptide, is one of the first substances for which medical practitioners found a quantifiable effect on athletic performance (Joyner 2003). The introduction of EPO into sports like cycling (dating back to the 1970s) is unquestionably part of the ongoing medicalization of athletic performance and the quest to push the body to extremes. Since the introduction of EPO into endurance sports, international athletes have achieved shocking performance increases, as evidenced by the rate at which new world records are being set in sports such as swimming, cycling, and speed skating.

EPO FUNCTION

EPO is a hormone produced by the kidneys that promotes the formation of red blood cells in the bone marrow. The synthetically produced EPO is injected under the skin to stimulate red blood cell production in athletes. This is desirable since an increase in red blood cells makes the body more efficient in carrying oxygen to the muscles. The abundance of oxygen-carrying red blood cells delays fatigue so that an athlete can, for instance, run, cycle, or ski harder and for longer durations. Astonishingly, tests have shown that performance improvements observed with 4 weeks of EPO use match those expected after several years of natural training (Joyner 2003). Long-distance runners, swimmers, speed skaters, cross-country skiers, and long-distance cyclists are reputedly the primary consumers of artificial EPO.

A major health risk associated with EPO use is cardiac arrest or even death. Injecting the drug into the body thickens the blood by introducing an abundance of red blood cells. If EPO is overused, the blood becomes so thick that there is a danger of the heart stopping when the body slows down, such as when falling asleep or resting. The likelihood that a long-term user will experience blood clots, heart attacks, and strokes is high (Tokish, Kocher, and Hawkins 2004). Despite the increasing international opposition to EPO use in sport (principally waged by WADA), the condemnation of cheaters by clean athletes, and the highly publicized cases of athlete fatalities following EPO use, there is little doubt that athletes around the globe are continuing to participate in what might be termed the *sport-pharmaceutical body project.*

Cycling has been especially plagued by EPO use among its elite competitors. Racers who have participated in the world's most famous cycling events, the Tour de France and the Giro d'Italia, have routinely reported wide-reaching EPO use at the events. EPO is an especially attractive drug for long-distance cyclists, as it helps red blood cells repair damage caused by grueling endurance events. WADA has described the use of EPO in professional cycling as a *moral epidemic.* The agency claims that unless drug consumption and self-medication among cyclists change, EPO abuse could lead to the demise of the sport (Savulescu and Clayton 2004). Even more tragically, it may lead to the deaths of professional cyclists who use the drug over the long term.

Theberge (2006) also challenges the scientization of high-performance sport. She examines the pervasive risk culture in sport that coexists with a growing medical culture. Athletes seem to be more willing than ever to take risks in the pursuit of sporting excellence. Theberge partly ascribes the heightened emphasis on risk taking to the medicalization of sport, as a full battery of doctors and other physiological experts can be solicited to counsel and repair damaged bodies. We agree with her that it is difficult to separate risk philosophies and the conscious testing of body boundaries through medical and unnatural means.

Deaths related to EPO use are not uncommon in professional cycling. As noted, when the drug is used excessively, it can progressively thicken the blood and clot the arteries. This leaves users susceptible to arterial shutdown, as the thickened blood cannot flow through the body properly. In 2004, the world of professional cycling was shocked when two highly successful riders, Johan Sermon of Belgium and Marco Pantani of Italy, died due to heart failure. Sermon (age 21) and Pantani (age 34) were reportedly both in good health when they died (Tokish et al. 2004), and their deaths signaled something that everyone in cycling knows: EPO use comes with tragic consequences.

Since 2003, seven other professional cyclists have died suspiciously due to heart failure. They include Denis Zanette (Italy, age 32), Marco Ceriani (Italy, age 16), Fabrice Salanson (France, age 23), Marco Rusconi (Italy, age 24), José Maria Jiménez (Spain, age 32), and Michel Zanoli (Netherlands, age 35). Phil Liggett, an international cycling broadcaster, contends that more than 100 cyclists' deaths in the past 15 years might be attributable to EPO use (Fotheringham 2006).

Organizers of cycling megaevents have battled the use of drugs like EPO in the recent past, but allegations of doping have been linked to the Tour de France since it began in 1903. For years, a major scandal related to cyclist drug use was both feared and expected by Tour de France organizers and fans. One of the most infamous cases of illegal drug use in all of sport rocked the Tour as well as all of cycling in 1998.

The 1998 Festina scandal may have tarnished the reputation of professional cycling forever (Hood 2006). On July 8, 1998, French customs officers arrested the Festina cycling team's premiere athlete and potential tour winner, Willy Voet. Voet was found in possession of several illegal drugs, including performance-enhancing drugs, growth hormones, and amphetamines—most notably, EPO. French police subsequently raided the hotel rooms of several other teams, including the remainder of team Festina. Members of both team Festina and team TMV had substantial amounts of EPO in their possession (Hood 2006). Some race participants decried the French police's military-like tactics in raiding hotel rooms and went so far as to boycott the race by refusing to finish. These actions might also be understood as evidence of the willingness of the cycling community to disguise and deny known drug use. Only 100 racers actually crossed the fabled Tour de France finish line in Paris. Partly in protest, on the last day of the Tour, the remainder of the participating riders cycled though the streets of Paris without any deliberate effort, much to the disappointment of the fans.

The Festina scandal resulted in major changes in drug policy and testing that continue today (including the formation of the World Anti-Doping Association itself). Riders now undergo regular, random, and unannounced testing for illegal substances like EPO. Facilitated by the cooperation of regulatory bodies in world cycling, WADA now polices drug use in the sport with considerable force and scope. However, according to anecdotes offered by professional riders (many reported in popular cycle magazines and other media), these measures have not been sufficient in controlling EPO use among elite cyclists, perhaps since athletes in the sport have been so heavily encouraged to cheat in a culture surrounded by medical and scientific discourses of athlete discipline and control (Miah 2004). Two examples illustrate the ineffectiveness of the new rules and procedures.

Just a few years after the 1998 *Tour of Shame* (Hood 2006), the third-place finisher of the 2002 Tour de France was arrested on charges of doping with EPO. In 2004, members of the Cofidis pro cycling team openly admitted to using performance-enhancing drugs, including EPO, during competition (Fotheringham 2006). Particularly disturbing was that Cofidis members suggested that EPO use is far more prevalent than people who control doping in sport even believe, and they predicted more deaths in the sport unless the testing procedures change dramatically.

Only a few days before the start of the 2006 Tour de France, 13 riders were banned from the race due to a Spanish investigation (known as *Operación Puerto*) into doping in sport. The report named nearly 100 world cyclists as suspected users of EPO and other performance-enhancing drugs (Fotheringham 2006). Two race favorites in 2006, Jan Ullrich of team T-Mobile and Ivan Basso of team CSC, were named in the Spanish report and immediately excluded from the 2006 Tour de France. Other notables who were named in the report and dismissed from competition included Francisco Mancebo (team AG2R), Oscar Sevilla (team T-Mobile), Santiago Botero (team Phonak), and José Gutiérrez (team Phonak). Alexander Vinokourov, another race favorite, was not linked to the doping scandal but was forced to withdraw when nearly half of the eligible riders on his Astana-Wurth team were suspended. Following the Spain scandal and the failure of American cyclist Floyd Landis, the leader of team Phonak, to pass a drug test at the end of the 2006 Tour, the Phonak parent company withdrew all of its financial sponsorship of professional cycling and disbanded the team. Interestingly, Landis had been crowned as the outright winner of the 2006 Tour de France just before his test failure surfaced in the press. In 2007, Landis became the only Tour winner to be stripped of his title following failure of a drug test. Critics of sport around the globe decried Landis' test as simply the latest example of body deviance in a sport systematically plagued by cheating.

Arguably, no other cyclist, or indeed athlete, has been accused of using drugs and tested for EPO more than seven-time winner of the Tour de France Lance Armstrong. The American cyclist, who returned to the sport after surviving testicular, lung, and brain cancer in 1998, has never tested positive for EPO or any other performance-enhancing substance. The most serious of the recent allegations came in 2006, when the French cycling newspaper *L Équipe* reported that a laboratory had discovered trace elements of EPO in a frozen blood sample Armstrong gave during the 1999 Tour de France, his first Tour victory (Fotheringham 2006). Armstrong responded to the allegation on his Foundation Web site, claiming that the report was "nothing short of tabloid journalism" (Lance Armstrong Foundation 2007). He continued, "I will simply restate what I have said many times. I have never taken performance-enhancing drugs."

Though both short-distance and long-distance runners, like cyclists, have been targeted for EPO testing in the past decade, only a few have tested positive for the banned substance. The most famous runner caught to date is the American runner Marion Jones. Jones was found guilty of having illegal amounts of EPO in her system in 2006 (Brcic 2006). Jones, a five-time world champion in track and field and a five-time medalist at the 2000 Sydney Olympics, had been suspected of drug use for nearly a decade. In October of 2007, Jones finally admitted to taking banned substances during her illustrious career. On January 11, 2008, she was sentenced to 6 months in prison by a United States court for perjury (to IRS special agent Jeff Novitzky, during the BALCO drug investigation in 2004) concerning her use of performance enhancing drugs such as EPO.

Other athletes caught for drug cheating include Olympic bronze medalist (in the 1,500-meter run) Bernard Lagat of Kenya, Russian runner (5,000-meter run) Olga Yegorova, American cyclist Adham Sbeih, Russian cross-country skier Natalia Baranova-Masolkin, Chinese track athletes Zheng Yongji and Li Huiquan, Moroccan runner and former holder of the world record for the 10K Asmae Leghzaoui, and French cyclist and Olympic bronze medalist Philippe Gaumont. In 2006, members of the Anshan Athletics School, a Chinese athletics institute, were caught with illegal levels of EPO in their blood (Brcic 2006). Apparently, coaches at the institute had been injecting them with the drug and a series of other banned performance enhancers. The story surfaced on the heels of a 2000 drug scandal in China, in which 40 members of the Chinese Summer Olympics team were banned from competition due to EPO use (Brcic 2006). Clearly, EPO use in sport is widespread and envelops a range of sports in a large number of countries.

Equally clearly, the problem of EPO use in sport is linked with what sociologists call the *medicalization of everyday life*. People in many countries are consuming more pharmaceutical products today than ever before. For many of us, taking pills or pursuing medicinal remedies is almost a normal part of our daily routines, and consuming performance-enhancing drugs has certainly become a ritual form of *nutrition* in the world of athletics. Athletes are under intense pressure to perform, are taught to trust the advice of their doctors and trainers, and are encouraged to use medical science to improve their bodies at any cost.

Hoberman's (2005) controversial analysis of gene therapy and drug cultures in global sport illustrates the extent to which scientific ways of knowing the body are embedded in sport. Many involved in sports professionally or at an elite amateur level know that athletes increasingly view their bodies as sites of medical work. Whether athletes seek to improve the speed, strength, and efficiency of their bodies with legal products (those not on the list of forbidden substances for their sport) or with forbidden drugs like EPO, the goal of physical performance enhancement is the same—to push performance frontiers of the human body to new extremes.

Slimming as Self-Violence

Sociological research has contended that pathological dietary practices of female athletes (Davis 2007), the overtraining tendencies of male athletes (Sabo 1986), and the play-through-the-pain mentalities of both male and female athletes (Young et al. 1994; White and Young 1999; Young 1997) are risky and potentially self-destructive. Rarely, however, are pain and discomfort sought willfully through sport conceptualized as socially and psychologically *positive* forms of self-violence.

Sociologists of sport tend to view pain and injury as processes to be avoided, managed, or rationalized as character-building ventures (Young 2004b). Although athletes may adhere to the pain principle (Sabo 1986) and relish in the ability to endure pain as a marker of athletic accomplishment, research has overlooked how the intentional experience of physical, mental, or emotional pain (undertaken by the self, against the self) may be a core motivation for participating in sport. For certain individuals, the phenomenological experience of pain may in fact be *the* purpose for athletic participation. Even though the literature on extreme or high-risk sports such as skateboarding, snowboarding, or skydiving positions athletes as physical risk takers who find sneaky thrills (Katz 1988) in adrenaline-producing contexts, rarely do these athletes express receiving actual pleasure from being hurt (Rinehart and Sydnor 2003; Wheaton 2004).

A large body of psychiatric literature on self-injury, which is also referred to as *self-inflicted violence (SIV), self-injurious behavior (SIB),* or *self-mutilation (SM),* highlights common forms of self-violence such as flesh cutting or burning, hair pulling, skin picking, scarring, anorexia or bulimia, and amputation. The psychology literature invariably suggests that such embodied manifestations of self-violence indicate personal pathology, anxiety, alienation, depression, guilt, or self-hatred. In other words, violence against the self is typically viewed as a psychological deficiency. Medical, social, and cognitive therapy is almost always recommended as a corrective measure (Alderman 1997; Herman 1994).

Favazza's (1996, 1998) seminal research on nonsuicidal forms of self-violence suggests that they are symptoms of deeply rooted personality disorders and that they illustrate the individual's desire to disassociate the body from psychological suffering. Collins'(1996) data on self-cutting shows how self-aggressors feel so distanced from corporeality that they attack the body as if their minds exist independently of the flesh (particularly in the case of self-cutters who have been sexually abused). Sociobiologists like Wilson and Herrnstein (1985) suggest that the release of beta-endorphins and the spike in serotonin produced by self-violence rituals become so exhilarating that a chemical dependency on the behaviors occurs. Favaro and Santonastaso (2000) argue that self-aggressors are generally plagued by obsessive-compulsive disorder, somatization, and low self-esteem.

Despite the long-standing interest in deviant behavior within social science literatures, only a handful of researchers have challenged the medical ways of seeing self-violence as inherently pathological and disconnected from broader social and cultural conditions. In a study of self-cutters and self-burners, Adler and Adler (2005) expand on Best and Luckenbill's (1982) typology of solitary deviants and uncover processes by which individuals learn self-harm. While providing a more sociological basis for psychological models of self-aggression, Adler and Alder portray self-cutters as relative loners. In another study of self-cutting, Hodgson (2004) similarly defines self-aggressors as isolates who learn to manage or negate the social stigmata associated with self-injury.

In his categorization of SRV, Young (2007) includes violence against the self as a type of participant violence. Through this categorization, Young places the self-injurious behaviors of athletes on the analytical table and opens the door for researchers to consider a full range of sport behaviors as self-violent and self-victimizing. Self-aggression, as a form of SRV, may be defined as encompassing self-initiated, intentional, and athletically based practices that directly jeopardize the health and physical, psychological, or emotional well-being of athletes. Although we cannot predict or control the outcome of such activities with precision, athletes undertaking self-aggression through sport subject the body, mind, or spirit to intense strain in order to explore corporeal or psychological limits. Self-violent acts in sport are more than symbolic risk taking (le Breton 2000), as they involve an acknowledged degree of physical, cognitive, or emotional disruption to the individual. Stated differently, the thrills accompanying the activities emerge from the pain, discomfort, and exhaustion involved rather than from the possibility of injury.

Over the past decade, triathlon has ascended in popularity in many countries. With the booming popularity and increased public attention on triathletes as endurance warriors, the sport has come under intense scrutiny for encouraging anorexia, bulimia, and dangerous forms of weight management among elite members (Atkinson 2007). Self-violent maintenance of body weight is deemed pathological and is decried as fatalistic and ill-conceived by trainers, coaches, and athletes. Such concerns are well founded but ignore possibilities that, for example, slimming down in sport is part of carefully undertaken performance practices that not only improve endurance abilities but also act as a component of pleasurable pain and endurance rituals. In what follows, we address slimming as self-violence that is willfully undertaken by some athletes as part of a subcultural logic that pain and suffering experienced through intense body ordeals may be cognitively, emotionally, and socially rewarding.

Triathlon Bodies

> To be a serious competitor in any demanding sport requires that health must occasionally be overlooked. There are times when the line between sickness and health becomes fine. The threat of sickness and injury is often overruled by the desire to excel. When I'm at my fittest, I am at my most vulnerable. (Brendan Brazier, triathlete)

Comments similar to this quote by internationally known vegan triathlete Brendan Brazier summarize what many elite competitors already know: Emaciating the body to the point of sickness can benefit performance. What sociologists of sport currently know about athletes' cultural constructions of the thin triathlon body as normative or deviant is extremely limited.

There exists, however, a burgeoning literature on the occurrence of the female athlete triad—eating disorder, amenorrhea, and osteoporosis—in sport. In particular, sociologists and psychologists of sport have documented high rates of anorexia and bulimia in female sports that require participants to have low body fat, lean muscle, and generally slender physiques (Markula 2003). Researchers have identified how eating pathologies develop among (especially young and female) athletes and how to intervene through sociological, psychological, or clinical measures (Davis 2007).

The general consensus among researchers in sport nutrition is that women account for 90% of athletes with eating pathologies, such as emaciation practices (Hausenblas and Carron 1999). Emaciation can be defined as a deliberate practice to reduce body weight that includes a 10% or greater loss of body weight within 4 to 6 weeks, caloric deficit spending (burning more calories through exercise and work than consumed through diet), and use of dehydration strategies to remain thin. Athletes who practice emaciation in sports like triathlon regularly replace natural or raw foods with exercise supplements (to strictly control caloric intake), avoid eating in social situations when possible (to avoid derision and questioning from others), and overtrain to maintain thinness. Although these practices are undertaken by individuals with various body shapes, weights, and sizes, individuals who practice emaciation over the long term tend to possess a body mass index of 16.5 or lower (Atkinson 2007).

Emaciation is not particularly well understood by sociologists of sport, and it is usually classified as anorexia. Athletes who practice emaciation may experience bouts of anorexia or bulimia, but neither condition is a prerequisite for emaciation. However, the predominant focus of existing research on thinning in sport remains squarely placed on athletes who experience anorexia (a condition called *anorexia athletica*) or bulimia or who engage in emaciation regimes in order to keep their weight low. Researchers have focused on athletes who self-starve or seriously restrict caloric intake, purge or vomit after eating, use heat sources like saunas to drop weight, overexercise, or use diuretics to drop water weight (Atkinson 2007). Dominant explanations for the cause of emaciation point to the social and psychological backgrounds of athletes and the cultural factors encouraging slimming practices (McClelland and Crisp 2001). These include preselection (losing weight to enter into sport), increased exercise (believed to reduce the desire for eating), body dissatisfaction (intense dislike of body shape or ability), belief in the link between performance and thinness (a lower body weight improves athletic performance), and societal ideas of thinness.

Clearly, emaciating the body to a point where it is functionally unable to compete in triathlon is athletic folly. However, thinness experts tend to place athletes into one of two nutritional and psychological camps: the healthy, who are of average weight according to BMI scores and have a balanced view of the body and self, and the unhealthy, who are underweight according to a BMI score of 18.5 or lower and have a sense of body dysmorphia. According to these parameters, a significant number of elite (and even serious recreational) triathletes in North America are deviant and out of personal control. Few researchers have carefully considered whether emaciation is part of a larger subcultural understanding of the social and psychological benefits associated with testing the boundaries of the body as a conscious practice of self-violence. Even fewer have approached willfully orchestrated pain in sports like triathlon as a form of self-work.

Endurance Work as Deep Flow

In order to compete in endurance sports, a body must be trained to suffer. Whether the athlete is young or old, endurance training involves shocking the body beyond comfortable thresholds. Through repetitive training that includes hundreds of hours on the road and lengths in the pool and body minimization through nutrition regimens and ergogenic supplementation, endurance athletes are encouraged to dramatically slim their bodies.

Somatic frames constructing the body as a site of *pain work* permeate talk and thinking among peers, coaches, friends, and fellow competitors. The athlete quickly learns that involvement in endurance sport involves regular pain and suffering (Young et al. 1994). The process involves experiencing the body as a moving, hurting, enduring, and thinning tool of competition.

Along with learning to feel a triathlon body as a device for competition or endurance, the athlete internalizes a set of aesthetic preferences about the appearance of a triathlon body. Lean, toned, and minimized bodies are championed the most, as they signify expertise in training, strict dietary control, and moral willpower to submit the body to constant conditioning and efficiency:

> A huge advantage anyone has in competition is looking fit. Some at the [start-ing] line can be psyched out and thrown off their game just by seeing people who look more like athletes than they do. When my muscles are ready [to compete], my body is efficient, and I can't help but ooze strength. It's noth-ing I ever think about, honestly, your body kind of just feels right. Personally, it's really satisfying having a body toned and tuned to work hard . . . it shows [competence] to everybody.
>
> (Cindy, age 31)

The words of this 31-year-old triathlete illustrate how aesthetics of the flesh crystallize in endurance sport cultures and how codes of body idiom (Goffman 1959) form in the triathlon community. Triathletes experience their bodies as ready to compete and come to associate outward body appearance with being a quality athlete. These perspectives are confirmed and legitimized when the athletes' newfound body capabilities and aesthetics allow them to experience *deep flow* (or, a certain pleasure through pain) in the sport.

As discussed in chapter 3, flow is a state in which the individual's mind, body, and spirit are in sync through active movement (Csikszentmihalyi 1975). During flow, the athlete releases the rational, thinking, calculating, and self-doubting mind and experiences energetic body rhythm and harmony. Maslow (1970) perhaps first outlined the concept of deep flow in describing what he called a *peak experience.* He claimed that from time to time people are able to feel intense joy, excitement, and comfort with the self in a moment of sudden enlightenment. Maslow argued that peak experiences, while often derived from observing beautiful works of art or hearing especially pleasing music, can also come during times of great suffering and fear when people realize that their power is far greater than they previously imagined. He described how the peak experience is emotionally uplifting and transcends the ego; it releases creative energies, affirms the meaning and value of existence, instills the individual with a sense of purpose, and gives a feeling of integration with the universe. Peak experiences can be therapeutic in that they tend to increase an individual's sense of agency, efficacy, creativity, and empathy. Triathletes generally experience deep flow when they are psychologically, emotionally, and physically suffering during training or competition; the ultimate body pleasure is derived from the ability to endure sport-induced physical pain and agony.

Arguably, the booming interest in sports like triathlon may reflect cultural fragmentation and normative uncertainty in many societies that regularly avoid pain, suffering, and ritual ordeals of discomfort. As Bale (2004) showed in his study of distance running, the ability to endure painful body ordeals in sport can serve as a stark measure of existence and of really being present on the earth; for some, it is a definitive flow experience. Endurance sport becomes an affirmation of body efficiency and agency at a time when social experience is framed less by physically interactive experiences and more by fleeting signs, discourses, and textual representations (Baudrillard 1983). Triathletes and other sport participants seek out and learn deep flow or peak experiences less haphazardly than what is usually described in theory. These states are cultivated through years of sport experience, mastery of the physical and emotional skills required for participation, and experimentation of personal limits.

Across generations of triathletes, triathlon is a personal and collective example of what Lyng (1990) calls *edgework,* allowing individuals to experiment with suffering and endurance. The physical honesty and personal truth learned through the deep flow or peak experience to which many endurance athletes refer are also grounded in what Callois (1967) refers to as *voluptuous panic.* While triathlon is not normally as physically perilous as other extreme sports, participants articulate a sense of deliberate stress seeking (Klausner 1968) as motivation for their participation—clearly, reducing body weight to dangerously low levels is part of this process. A peak experience is often cultivated by deliberately placing the body in a context of sporting risk, panic, and stress. In playing with endurance sport as the sort of symbolic death that le Breton (2000) describes (i.e., enduring to the point of complete physical exhaustion and collapse) and as subsequent rebirth (i.e., through surviving), triathletes find flow in feeling the muscles drained, glycogen stores decimated, breath labored, and the mind cracked. For many of the participants, sport-related exhaustion, which is actually delayed for some by their low body weight, is both pleasurable and meaningful as a pathway to deep flow and peak experience.

In *Hello, I'm Special* (2004), Niedzviecki underscores how hyperconsumeristic norms around feeling special (qua individualistic) in countries like Canada propel many people to seek nonmainstream tests of identity, or flow experiences. With the pressure to be unique, individuals are encouraged to constantly redefine the self through progressively more radical forms of embodied action, to innovate ways of expressing self-identity, or to do whatever it takes to be publicly lauded as *special*. For Niedzviecki, though, hyperindividualistic modalities of life heighten cultural fragmentation, alienation, and role and status confusion across social groups. It is precisely this sense of individual and community disconnection that may encourage people to seek out peak experiences in triathlon. In the search for neotraditional communities, individuals locate triathlon clubs or are recruited into such clubs by friends who have found a new family among triathletes. Membership in a sport training and competition culture provides a disciplining set of sociopsychological frames. Training schedules are set and corresponding workouts are provided by coaches. Puritanical eating programs are designed and followed. Races are identified and specially trained for. Regular meetings with other triathletes are maintained. In these contexts, codes of ethics in the sport, commonly accepted rules for training and competition, and relationships are forged between people as disciplined athletes.

The sociopsychological frames that crystallize in triathlon figurations buttress a predominantly middle-class habitus shared among the athletes. Participants typically share a preference for goal setting; attribute moral worth to health, thinness, and vibrancy; preach self-responsibility and self-reliance; and approach embodied performance with rationality in the spare-time spectrum (Elias and Dunning 1986). Working the body through leisure makes intuitive sense within the figuration and reflects white-collar tastes for sport as work.

Replete with middle-class constructions of the will to succeed with humility and perseverance in the face of adversity (White, Young, and Gillett 1995), the social psychology of training, weight maintenance, and competition in triathlon appears to revolve around a construction of maintaining inner restraint as a test of endurance. A slender and toned (read *dangerously lean)* triathlon body is a metaphor of working the self in a distinguished manner.

When an individual triathlete pursues the sport habitually as meaningful endurance work over the long term, changes in self-perception are often noticed. Although a broad spectrum of people participate in the sport—not all of whom experience endurance work as deep flow—triathletes with the longest involvement in the subculture tend to exhibit a final set of learned interpretive frames. These self-reflexive psychological frames develop in the passage from being an athlete who relishes the rigor of triathlon as an endurance competition to being an athlete who values the extension of self-restraint beyond comfort boundaries. A relatively small group of triathletes develop self-reflexive performance frames in which their abilities to endure extreme pain in training and competition become *the* defining feature of their identities.

Among career, non-elite triathletes who pursue the sport as serious leisure (Stebbins 2006), there is no longer a battle to be merely competent or to simply finish well. For athletes approaching the training and competition from intensively self-reflexive standpoints, the triathlon appeals specifically because it is an ultimate test of the self.

As triathletes extend their physical investments in the sport, their bodies become accustomed to general pain and fatigue. Barring injury, extended training invariably builds a more enduring biological body. Given the shift in physical capabilities, a corresponding alteration to the habitus is expected. Yet akin to Becker's (1967) description of how tolerance for psychotropic drugs is learned within groups, triathletes are effectively taught by others in the figuration how to positively perceive and embrace the improvement of endurance thresholds. As a critical part of adopting self-reflexive frames, triathletes learn to interpret physical cues of pain as self-improvement and are thereby taught techniques of extended endurance and body transcendence. As one 34-year-old female triathlete told us,

> Just when I think I've hurt more than I can take, that's when I know I need to train harder. Like I never thought it would be possible to complete a short course tri, then a long course, then an Iron distance. But, I did all of them. I know I'm going somewhere I need to be during training when I start to feel a sort of agony or soreness I've never felt or am smaller than I've ever been and can keep going forever. It's like you feel absolutely wiped, but your body is raging with power. When I train and train, at longer and longer distances, and feel nothing, that's when I worry I'm not doing enough to make it to the next level I can.
>
> (Stephanie, age 39)

Here, Stephanie's words illustrate how particular triathletes configure smallness, pain, and suffering as self-liberating. From her perspective, there is always another level of pain to negotiate and an enduring self to actualize. Once athletes like Stephanie are set on this path, it seems that the quest for new levels of endurance becomes waged privately.

Self-reflexive frames also take form as individuals become more insulated within a triathlon lifestyle and emotionally invested in the sport. Increased involvement in training, competition, and socializing with other triathletes is positively correlated with adopting a triathlete master status. Correspondingly, work and family responsibilities are often neglected by self-proclaimed triathlon junkies, as thoughts of training or competition consume the individual and as time and monetary investments in the sport increase. Consistently self-reflexive triathletes probe for innovative ways to improve or for more challenging races, and they feel (one might argue pathologically) lazy when not training.

As a totalizing triathlon lifestyle becomes embedded in the habitus, athletes increasingly juxtapose their minimized bodies against the (perceived) unhealthy, undisciplined, and nonreflexive bodies of generalized others. As subcultural theorists like Muggleton (2000) and Maffesoli (1996) might argue, members of neotribes that uphold strong ideological standpoints and regimented social practices tend to construct outsiders as unenlightened or ideologically naive. When athletes learn to become extremely self-reflexive, they more frequently contrast their health and wellness pursuits against the perceived self-destructive behaviors of others. This comparison further accentuates their sense of endurance achievements. In Caroline's words,

> I'm sorry, but I have a hard time getting emotional for people who choose not to be fit. All I need is a pair of shoes to run or a cheap swimsuit to hop into a pool. The way a person sculpts her body and maintains it shows inner resolve, and I think people need to take responsibility for themselves, for their own health problems, and do basic nutrition and exercise.

> (Caroline, age 28)

The hyperfocus on health and body that certain triathletes develop penetrates their everyday assessments of others' eating, exercise, work, or relationship habits. When endurance athletes become extremely self-reflexive, they often steer their eating behaviors toward vegetarianism or veganism (which are viewed as more ethical forms of eating). They purchase organic or locally produced training products more regularly, and some refrain from consuming alcohol or other mood-altering substances.

While any triathlete assesses performance and understands the sociality of the sport in self-reflexive ways, a relatively small percentage transform into hyper-reflexive agents whose habituses are strongly shaped by their activities within the sport. These participants downplay the role of interpersonal battles of endurance, become lifestyle triathletes and practice emaciation as a lifestyle. Theirs is a unique interpretive framework in sport, as they understand painful, or deviant, body rituals such as emaciation as austere but rewarding measures of the self.

Technology and Disappearing Bodies

The preceding analyses of becoming drugged or lean in the pursuit of sport are part of a larger discussion on how contemporary athletic cultures are saturated with ideologies and discourses of denaturalized bodies. With the intensified application of kinesiological, biomedical, and other scientific knowledge to athletic performance and possibility, what counts as a normal or natural sports body has been disrupted and called into question. As the sport sciences penetrate the boundaries of the sporting field and colonize sporting bodies as extensions of bioscience, the lines between the sovereign biological body and technology become fuzzy at best (Balsamo 1996). Coakley described the encroachment of technology into sport (and into sports bodies) as a lurking *technosport* culture.

For others, the general tendency to technologize training processes, equip-ment innovation, injury recovery, nutrition practices, and even competition spaces subverts the sporting body as a subject of performance and representation in favor of objectifying the body as a target of scientific discovery. Here, the social practice of sport is stripped, as Pronger (2002) illustrates, of human aesthetic or emotive qualities, which become replaced with an ethos of human-calculated engineering, rationalization, and movement perfection. Such a progression has led theorists like Hoberman (1992) and Miah (2004) to speculate about the transhuman modality of elite sport. The drugged and perfected technosport body is a logical but unintended outcome of long-term scientization in sport. From Hoberman's and Miah's perspectives, the technologically invaded and refashioned body is not a deviant entity, insofar as it is neither human nor machine. Rather, it is a postmodern, Frankenstein-like amalgamation of nature and science. Butryn (2003) calls for the conceptualization of modern athletes as cyborgs—as biological and mechanical hybrids replete with technological support, control, and discipline.

The metanarrative cutting across cyborg research in the sociology of sport is a central questioning of whether technology dehumanizes athletes or liberates them (Rail 1998). In mostly philosophical statements on the role of technology in elite or professional sport, theorists like Bale (1997) address the ways in which athletes become cyborgs, the personal benefits of becoming a cyborg, and the broader cultural logic of approaching athleticism from improvement and perfec-tion standpoints. In the language of deviance research, sociologists of sport are struggling with the issue of whether technology undermines the *human* in the *human performance of sport*.

Butryn (2003), whose research on enhanced athletes is groundbreaking, con-ceives of five technologies that when applied in sport allow athletes to become cyborgs (see table 5.1). In his empirical examination of track and field athletes, Butryn argues that most athlete narratives are replete with cyborg stories. It is therefore difficult, regardless of one's ideological position on the appropriateness of corporeal and technological intersection in sport, to conceive of the cyborg athlete as a deviant body. While Butryn and others map out the philosophical and empirical agenda for cyborg research, Miah's writing on the ethics of modifying the genes of athletes challenges sport and body theory even further.

TABLE 5.1 *Applied Technologies Leading to Athlete Cyborgs*

Technology	Example
Self	Advancements that reshape or redesign the human body
Landscape	Technologies that create competition spaces; artificial earth forms like fake grass
Implement	Equipment used in and for competition
Rehabilitation	Technologies designed to repair the wounded or debilitated athletic body
Evaluation	Biomechanical analyses that identify and reduce inefficient body movements

In 1969, Hirschi challenged criminologists to reconsider the essential socio-logical questions pertaining to rule-violating behaviors. He argued that the fundamental problem facing social theorists is not *why* people break social rules but *why they do not.* He believed that experts in the study of crime and deviance had not addressed the central problem in their research efforts: How are we to stop people from engaging in behaviors that are contranormative but are sought out nevertheless as natural curiosities and personal fascinations?

Miah's (2004) *Genetically Modified Athletes: Biomedical Ethics, Gene Doping and Sport* might affect thinking in the sociology of sport ethic and body modification in the same way that Hirschi's *Causes of Delinquency* altered theory in criminology. Miah's text calls attention to the central themes, issues, and policy problems related to controlling (or even understanding the role of) the scientific manipulation of elite athletic bodies. His work is a postmodern study of the moral philosophies and rational logistics underpinning the institutional regulation of athletes' abilities to compete with modified bodies. Miah's work challenges the taken-for-granted need for curtailing drug use and genetic manipulation in amateur athletics as well as challenges the genetic fair play promoted by antidoping organizations such as WADA. He presents a global portrait of the harmonization process as a dominant justification for the control of genetic manipulation, and through a pastiche of ethics theory, he attacks the position that there should be a moratorium on the insertion of performance-enhancing biotechnologies into sport. Works like Miah's challenge us to reconsider the genetic protectionist mentality encapsulating sports worlds and to question why sport officials have not accepted genetic modification as a normal part of sport, as other social spheres have done throughout the recent past.

Miah and other researchers on the ethics of genetic technology also raise a litany of penetrating questions about the notion of fair play and justice in sport. One of the most pressing issues they address hinges on an interrogation of the essentialist position on athletes' bodies. If athletes are not born with equal physical abilities and thus are not placed on a genetically level playing field, is it fair to hold back the less genetically gifted by banning institutional intervention? What is the purpose of restricting genetic manipulation in sport? Why not develop sports organizations or competitions tiered according to the athletes' degree of genetic manipulation? Why not push the envelope of human performance, just as biomedical research outside of sport has challenged our natural physical abilities to stay young, give birth, or heal following traumatic injury? Since there is already much technological intervention into sport—think of the technology involved in most mainstream sports that enhances an athlete's ability to move or play more effectively—why create roadblocks at the most basic genetic levels?

The development of cyborg or genetically modified athletes in sport has stimulated a recent groundswell of research into sport as a site of technological advancement. However, sociologists of sport have been slow to address how a gamut of virtual sports further dislodge traditional cultural norms about bodies and athleticism by literally removing the natural sporting from of athletic competition altogether.

Virtual sports are symbolic representations of embodied, expressive, and real-world athletic experiences. These sports can involve complete out-of-body practices in which participants play a sport without traditional athletic exertion (i.e., through a sport video game) or more embodied physical activities in which participants perform in a simulated sport environment (i.e., a modified sport setting like a cyclists' wind tunnel). Virtual sports involve human beings as either real or represented athletes in a technologically enhanced setting. Although certain ludic activities such as touch football, pick-up ice hockey, or go-kart racing might be considered as representations of *sport*, virtual sports are those that place embodied or computer-generated athletes in simulated sport spaces. In this way, virtual sports might be considered as deviations from the traditional experience of sport as a flowing, embodied human practice.

By and large, virtual sports have escaped sociological scrutiny. Nevertheless, three types of virtual sports are ripe for investigation. First, and perhaps most commonly, are the virtual sports that abound in home and arcade *video games.* Through the advent of home entertainment systems such as Atari, Intellivision, ColecoVision, and Vectrex in the 1970s and 1980s, sport video games became a staple of both popular and youth cultures in North America. From the 1980s onward, players have competed in virtual sports ranging from hockey to basketball to hunting to skateboarding. Indeed, one of the very first video games commercially marketed in the United States, Pong, resembled a crude form of table tennis. Since then, digitally refined and interactively dynamic computer systems such as Sega, Nintendo, Odyssey, PlayStation, and Xbox have enabled consumers to play practically every mainstream Western sport. Sport games account for approximately 20% of video game sales in North America, the world's largest gaming market, grossing $8 billion U.S. yearly (Liberman 2003).

Second are the physically interactive video games that virtual sport enthusiasts now have access to. For example, players may literally step onto virtual golf courses in the comfort of their own home. The player stands on an artificially turfed tee box, holds a golf club fitted with electronic sensors, and swings at a virtual ball. A simulated ball instantaneously appears on a large video screen situated several feet in front of the tee box and flies down the virtual fairway with force and spin. Individuals may play an entire round of golf on the machine, selecting from any number of well-known courses. People may also use similar machines, to drive virtual race cars, bat against virtual MLB pitchers, shoot virtual basketballs, ride virtual racehorses, or even paddle virtual kayaks.

Third are the simulated sport environments that may be utilized as training tools for elite athletes. Virtual training machines, described by Butryn (2003) as either *landscape* or *evaluative technologies,* carefully monitor athletes' performances in order to study and help improve their physical abilities. For example, swimmers are often placed in current tanks to scientifically evaluate the efficiency of their strokes and pinpoint their $\dot{V}O_2$max. The skating strides of elite ice hockey players are studied technically in laboratories by using treadmills with simulated ice surfaces. Professional cyclists straddle stationary racing bikes in wind rooms and pedal virtual courses they watch on video screens, twisting and turning when they go through turns and exerting effort when tackling hills.

The ascent of virtual sport over the past quarter of a century points to how a host of sociogenic (Elias 1994) shifts within Western cultures have altered our understanding of embodied athleticism. Virtual sports are of increasing importance at a time when both amateur and professional sports are intensely commercialized. Sociologist of sport suggest that, particularly in Western nations with state-sponsored, rigidly institutionalized, and professional sport cultures, the entire sporting experience is fragmented into market commodities, including sport simulations that allow users to become more actively involved fans. As sport is consumed as a popular culture commodity, sports organizations profit by aggressively tapping home entertainment and gaming markets. Global and national sports organizations such as the IOC, NFL, FIFA, MLB, PGA, NHL, and NBA package virtual game experiences for consumers, allowing them to create fantasy leagues and to manipulate player performance at the push of a button or thrust of a joystick.

Athletic contests are promoted globally as mimetic events. Sport marketers sell audiences virtual sports as symbols of emotionally charged and risky yet rule-bound scenarios of physically intense competition. Because of their obvious levels of aggression, struggle, and toughness, sports provide a safe version of exciting significance for audiences. Virtual sport games highlight and exaggerate the taken-for-granted and often extravagantly deviant physicality and mimesis inherent in both mainstream and alternative sports. Extreme hitting, bloodletting, brutal tackling, and flamboyant injuries are common in virtual sport games. Rules are broken without penalty, virtual players do not experience the catastrophic effects of rough play, and users receive reward incentives within games for mastering on-field hits or styles of violence.

The booming popularity of virtual sport games should be understood in terms of what Baudrillard (1983) calls the *simulation* of social reality. Virtual sport games, for instance, create hyperrepresentations of embodied athleticism and transform social constructions of real sport for users. The games not only mimic what actually occurs in sport but also partially define what audiences expect from real sports. Virtual games may be more accessible forms of sport for many users, as users can play dozens of sports regardless of their physical fitness. Further, the user is granted an unprecedented agency to mold the parameters of an athletic contest, including the players involved, physical settings, length of competitions, speed of games, and rule structures. For athletes who are plugged into virtual sport machines, simulated sports fields allow for exertion without the physical dangers of real contact and competition. Sport machines designed for performance evaluation or rehabilitation simulate performance contexts so that athletes may become swifter, higher, and stronger during competition.

Virtual sports also underscore how machines and bodies cybernetically inter-sect in modern cultures. Haraway (1991) notes that the postmodern era is one in which technology increasingly challenges corporeality. For Haraway and others, it is difficult to conceive of any social activity, including sport performance, that has evaded technological improvement, innovation, control, and monitoring.

When individuals are able to kick a soccer ball, catch a baseball, throw a javelin, or perform a ski jump by tapping a computer button or moving the body in front of video sensors, it is impossible to overlook how the contemporary sports world is deeply intertwined with technology and electronics.

The prominence of virtual sports reflects emergent cultural preferences for stationary, home-based digital entertainment rather than embodied action. Virtual sport participation through video games jibes with athletically inactive North American lifestyles. Virtual sports gel with the sedentary lifestyles widely attributed to long workdays, poor dietary practices, and exposure to computers as everyday work tools. At a time when physical passivity in the leisure sphere and overall obesity rates are rising in North America and when physical education programs are disappearing from curricula at all institutional levels, virtual games are becoming a primary form of *sport participation* for growing populations of North Americans (Clocksin, Watson, and Ransdell 2002).

Sociological studies of virtual sports are narrow in both scope and content. The bulk of the limited empirical research on virtual sports suggests that exposure to violent sport games may be causally associated with violent interpersonal behaviors (Bensley and Van Eenwyk 2001). Virtual sports are especially targeted in the contemporary moral panic about youth crime and the consumption of violent video games. Using a blend of sociopsychological, behavioral, and sociobiological theories, researchers argue that virtual sport games desensitize users to extreme violence and confound users' understandings of real-world aggression (Anderson and Bushman 2001). Yet despite nearly three decades of empirical research concentrated on youth violence and video game play, there is no empirical consensus among social scientists that virtual sports actually cause criminal or otherwise unlawful behavior (Sternheimer 2003).

Political economists study virtual sports as vacuous cultural commodities. Authors including Postigo (2003) weave a pastiche of Marxist, cultural studies, and postindustrial theories to show how virtual sports have little use value but great exchange value among youths. Virtual sports alienate users from embodied athletic experiences and diminish the socially interactive aspects of competitive sport. As critics of virtual sport, political economists contend that athletes, teams, and leagues utilize video games to crassly solicit fan investment into athletics. Further, virtual sports like video games discourage the firsthand experience of athleticism in sport and motivate individuals to participate passively via video interface.

Sociologists of sport employ postmodernist theories to examine the effects of computer technology on athlete training, performance, and rehabilitation. Scholars such as Shogan (1999) study athletes' bodies as being fragmented, technologically invaded, and subject to penetration or improvement at the hands of therapists, doctors, and trainers. Athletes, as the subjects of medical knowledge bases, are built as carefully engineered scientific machines instead of existing as free, self-determined, and embodied agents. Virtual sport machines used in athletic training or in recreational leisure pursuits also blur the boundaries between natural sport performances and artificially engineered athletics. The postmodern athlete is a person whose performance is carefully mapped, dissected, analyzed, predicted, and monitored by a full spectrum of computer systems and scientific principles rather than a person whose performance is based on a free human desire to run, jump, and compete.

THEORETICAL INTERSECTIONS

The underlying theme of this chapter is that wherever there are norms about the body and its representation, there is also deviance. Yet, due to the socially constructed nature of deviance, what is deviant in one context may be understood as normative in another. Our sociological research experience on sport deviance has encouraged us to approach body deviance as something that is essentially, as Hebdige (1979) would put it, *poylsemic*—that is, subject to many cultural interpretations. For example, a doped body in sport is not so easy to determine as deviant. It is a polysemic text, representing a violation of a sport's code of practice to some but a normative commitment to winning for others. Still, while athletic bodies may be polysemic texts, particular groups in sport, such as players, coaches, fans, officials, league administrators, promoters, and sponsors, tend to assign meaning to what they feel is normative or deviant with regard to sporting bodies. In the following sections, we review our theoretical intersections and consider Hebdige's emphasis on the polysemic nature of social deviance and how specific sport groups see the body differently with respect to its normative or deviant status.

FUNCTIONALISM AND STRAIN THEORY

One of the classic American statements on strain theories of deviance was offered by the structural-functionalist Robert Merton (1938) nearly a century ago. Merton argued that dominant social and cultural goals such as achieving occupational status or acquiring financial success create lifestyle norms for people and that when the institutional means for achieving them are not readily accessible, a state of normlessness, or anomie, occurs. Here, the terms *goals* and *norms* refer to cultural beliefs and practices, while the term *institutionalized means* refers to the existing opportunities in the social structure. Strain occurs because of the imbalance between the person's internalized cultural goals and the available institutional means for achieving those goals.

The dysjunction between goals and means combined with the accompanying strain weakens social commitment to normative behavior. Merton proposes that in such contexts, individuals will adapt to alleviate strain. He presents five such modes of adaptation. The first, conformity, is the most common mode of adaptation. Conformists accept the goals as well as the prescribed means for achieving those goals. Others who adapt through innovation, the second mode, accept societal goals but have few legitimate means to achieve those goals, and so they fabricate their own, often criminal, means for achieving success. The third mode, ritualism, is a type of adaptation in which individuals de-escalate goals in order to make them more realistic and achievable. The fourth, retreatism, is a form of adaptation for those who give up not only the goals but also the means. Retreaters, such as alcoholics or drug addicts, sever ties from mainstream social groups. Rebellion, the fifth and final mode, occurs when the cultural goals and the legitimate means are rejected outright in favor of an alternative set of goals and means (achieved, for example, through political protest or collective action).

Merton's description of drug use as a form of retreatism has been used in sociological research for more than half a century. High-performance athletes who use performance-enhancing drugs like EPO, however, may not be typical retreaters; rather, they may be innovators. For example, elite cyclists accept institutional sporting mechanisms for success but reject prohibitive cultural frames that criminalize the drug. Whether an athlete uses EPO to level the playing field or to gain an unfair advantage is theoretically irrelevant, since both are a response to strain as Merton defines it. It is interesting how Merton's term *innovation* conceptually overlaps with Hughes and Coakley's (1991) understanding of positive deviance: The latter is applied extensively in the sport deviance literature; the former is not.

CONFLICT THEORY

In their general theory of social problems and claims making, outlined in *Constructing Social Problems,* Spector and Kitsuse (1977) describe how actors, social conditions, or cultural trends become publicly defined as intolerable. Spector and Kitsuse's value conflict theory of deviance identifies claims makers as those who draw attention to the social conditions of deviance or moral problems and demand corrective measure. The authors characterize social problems as subjective and processual social phenomena with potentially no enduring character. Claims makers are thus interest groups of sorts who lobby for social change around their ideological positions and moral frames. Spector and Kitsuse argue that there is no deviance outside of social problem construction and claims making, and they suggest that any interest group (not only privileged class groups or power elites) can undertake this form of moral entrepreneurship.

The study of virtual sports and their supporting cultures reveals an array of claims makers regarding the value of sport technology and artificial training environments. Sociologists of sport ethics might describe the increased intervention of simulated environments into sport training as a deviant athleticism that separates the pure joy of natural movement from the training process. Athletes might decry the technologization of sport as yet another instance of athlete disempowerment and commodification. And imagine what coaches, trainers, and athletes from developing nations participating in the Olympic Games might claim about the deviant advantage members of more developed nations have because of their technologically superior training. Though all of these groups share an interest in assessing the place of technology in sport, each set of claims makers might construct the problem of virtual sport from a different interpretive view.

INTERACTION THEORY

Goffman's dramaturgical model of social interaction, showcased most famously in *The Presentation of Self in Everyday Life* (1959), is an example of how people deliberately manage their bodies in front of others in order to avoid being labeled as a social outsider. Critical for Goffman are the common codes of body idiom underpinning all social interactions (e.g., dress, appearance, comportment, manners, and so on) and the messages about the self conveyed through conformity to—or deviation from—such codes. Goffman's dramaturgy defines embodied interaction as a context-specific social performance constructed to provide others with favorable impressions of the self. Violating body idiom within a group risks social stigmatization, the loss of social status, and, ultimately, ostracism from the group.

The relevance of Goffman's dramaturgical model to the pursuit of thin bodies in endurance sport cultures is clear. Images of athletic proficiency in endurance sport regularly include thin bodies (Hargreaves and Vertinsky 2006). Thin bodies are associated with a wide range of preferred qualities in the sport, ranging from mental and psychological discipline to corporeal perfection. Similarly, athletes who are thin in other sports like gymnastics, running, and swimming exhibit acceptance of codes of established body idiom and illustrate what Goffman might call an *achieved identity*. Researchers interested in the image of a thin body as a marker of athlete identity might also explore social constructions of what being thin means, as well as emaciation practices, in a fuller range of sport settings. They might question whether athletes in power and performance sports requiring more mesomorphic body shapes undertake emaciation as a part of both physical training and dramaturgical performance in their respective sports.

SOCIAL CONTROL THEORY

Hirschi's (1969) *Causes of Delinquency* transformed the theoretical landscape of deviancy research in the 20th century. Rather than focusing on individual personalities, pathological social structures, or subcultural formations as the breeding ground of criminality, Hirschi highlights the primacy of intimate social relationships (social bonds) as a causal factor in deviancy. He builds his theory on the notion that social bonds, especially familial bonds, inoculate people from deviant behavior. His control theory of delinquency assumes that rule violations result when an individual's bonds to family, school, religion, work, or other conformity-producing sites of institutional life are malformed, weakened, or broken. Crucially, Hirschi argues that no special motivational factors are needed to encourage deviant behavior. Only a lack of bonds is required to let loose the socially disintegrative drives that all humans possess (e.g., anger, fear, lust, hunger, and so on) and that lead under certain conditions to crime and deviance, such as assault, vandalism, rape, or theft.

Hirschi explains that bonds comprise four principal components: attachment, commitment, involvement, and belief. The more bonds people have in life, the more they are emotionally, cognitively, socially, and ideologically linked to conforming behavior, and thus the more likely they are to view rule violation as unfavorable. Social control is therefore a function of how external constraints operate through the bonding process and how inner restraints sediment in the psyche through self-alignment with conforming others.

More in league with dominant psychological constructions of emaciation as personal pathology, researchers sympathetic to Hirschi's construction of deviance might interpret an athlete's emaciation as an indication of personal alienation from normative bonds. Freed from constraining social bonds, athletes who emaciate might derive disreputable satisfaction from the practice. Or, an athlete's personal emaciation journey might reflect a lack of learned restraint. If this is the case, research on emaciation in athletics would have to address the personal biography of the athlete practicing emaciation and measure factors such as self-restraint preferences. Key to the research process would be an examination of the relationship between the person practicing emaciation and the parental group and the socializing lessons learned about the body, eating, and control in early life.

CLASSICAL THEORY

Wilson and Herrnstein's (1985) controversial book *Crime and Human Nature* is a modernist theory inspired by classical thinking on the relationship between genetically determined types of decision making and environmental factors. In this book, the authors outline how a small group of repeat criminal offenders (perpetrating street crimes) are both genetically similar (i.e., low birth weight and IQ, young age, and male) and socioculturally alike (i.e., low socioeconomic status, low education, and adopted). The authors set forth the taken-for-granted criminological proposition that an individual is likely to commit a crime if the perceived rewards are greater than the sum of the risks and potential disadvantages. They maintain that the benefits of crime—the release of affect, acquisition of power, or experience of exhilaration—are immediate sources of pleasure and thus are enticing. The search for gratification, then, is a major factor on the pathway into crime. People who are genetically unprepared to control gratification needs or are constrained by poor social conditions to postpone gratification quests are likely to be criminally predisposed. Akin to Hirschi (1969), Wilson and Herrnstein argue that without attachment to an adult primary caretaker and social mentor, a child will develop without a sense of guilt or shame, reveal little concern for social approval, and show little investment in normative social contexts. By contrast, a child learns deferred gratification from adult socializing agents through a process of linking good behavior to social inclusion and punishment avoidance.

Researchers interested in the paradigmatic thrust of Wilson and Herrnstein might approach the analysis of performance-enhancing drug use by first determining which athletes are patterned or repeat offenders. Even though drug cheats are a relatively special population of deviants, there are clearly patterns of team or networked drug consumption in sports like cycling. Proponents of modern classical theories such as that of Wilson and Herrnstein would then have to establish whether recidivists in the sport share common biological traits, have similar family backgrounds with regard to parenting styles, and are exposed to similar environmental conditions. Using the general propositions of the theory, the researcher might also be encouraged to examine the culture of a sport like professional cycling to see whether socialization mechanisms are in place to curb the use of drugs.

CRITICAL THEORY

French philosopher Louis Althusser (1977) introduced the notion of ideological state apparatuses (ISA) as a way of understanding how compliance to dominant power relations is produced within a society. An ISA refers to an institutional social group (such as a religious, educational, family, or legal group) that transmits ideologies encouraging individuals to accept their roles, statuses, and positions within a stratified social hierarchy. People learn to accept dominant modes of thinking and behaving through interpellation within ISAs. Thus, an ISA works to support dominant superstructural modes of power and to persuade populations to view themselves as socially benefiting from—and thus to be in ideological support of—dominant social conditions.

Sociologists of deviance might employ Althusser's concept of an ISA to examine how sport disseminates hegemonic ideologies regarding body medicalization. In this vein, an Althusserian reading of performance-enhancing drug use in sport could reveal the systematic contradictions regarding the regulation of drugs in sports like cycling. The sport-industrial complex encourages the use of science in cycling to produce better athletes and generate more profit within the sport. Possessing both commodified and medicalized bodies, athletes learn to see themselves as workers within an economic system geared toward profiting through winning and as medical subjects with bodies ready for drug intervention as a relatively normative process. Yet the punishment of drug deviants in professional cycling also illustrates the power of a central authority in an institutional sense and thus becomes a metaphor for larger authorities of control, such as the state. Discourses on punishment for drug abusers in professional cycling are composed of themes such as justice, restitution, meritocracy, and the morality of pure competition. Each of the narratives is a neoliberal and capitalist construction of work, power, and social order. The ability of the medical-capitalist complex to influence deviance in cycling is hidden from public view, and cheaters are offered to the public as criminals whose punishment is warranted. Althusser might interpret chemically enhanced cyclists as athletes who are persuaded toward cheating because of the power of sport hegemony, but who also experience guilt and shame when caught.

GENDER AND FEMINIST THEORY

Foucault's concept of technologies of the self is used widely among feminist scholars of bodies inside and outside of sport (Markula 2003). Foucault describes technologies of the self as ascetic and ethical practices of self-formation and personal definition. The word *ascetic* in this context means an "exercise of self upon the self by which one attempts to develop and transform oneself, and to attain a certain mode of being" (Foucault 1979, 282). Foucault insists that technologies of the self can be liberating processes of self-realization, in which ethical self-care of the body constitutes power for the individual and transforms the individual's life. The process of liberation, in Foucault's (1981) model, emancipates the true self from its bondage or repression within conditions of dominant biopower (i.e., emancipates the subjugated, self-surveilling, and docile body that is ordered and disciplined by dominant social discourses).

Markula (2003) outlines how a critical feminist might employ Foucault's technologies of the body in research on emaciation practices in sport. On the one hand, emaciation might be interpreted as a form of biopower or a technique of domination exerted on (typically female) athletes by (typically male) authority figures in high-performance athletics. Gymnastics is a prime example of a sport in which emaciated female bodies are produced through relations of domination. Yet Foucault's work provides, as Markula contends, an understanding of how emaciation might also be configured by female distance runners as an aesthetic and ethic of self-care and as a technique of positively constituting the self through liminal and socially challenging bodywork. Because emaciation transgresses certain body codes in sport—as does the pursuit of sport-related suffering by women as a vehicle of personal growth and reflexivity—emaciation may be constructed as liberating along gender lines. If emaciation is a technology of the self as Foucault (1981) describes them, then female athletes who initiate their own body slimming are conscious social resisters against male domination of their bodies, and these women practice an embodied and a creative form of self-care.

INTEGRATED THEORY

Although Stanley Cohen's *Folk Devils and Moral Panics* (1973) is rarely seen as a major integrated theory of crime, it is perhaps one of the foundational attempts to integrate more than one theory into the analysis of social deviance. Cohen provides an understanding of how the media act in conjunction with local interests groups and agents of social control to label select others as social outsiders (folk devils) worthy of stern reprimand and control. The theory is a complex blend of structural conflict theory, Gramscian hegemony theory, labeling theory, semiotics and media theory, as well as theory on subculture formation. A successful public and media crusade against a targeted group of defined miscreants results in a moral panic, in which the entire spectrum of moral codes, values, and norms are reinvestigated in the process of understanding the emergent group of folk devils. Cohen's work leads sociologists to consider whether the folk devils are legitimate societal threats or whether the public identification and criticism of them by a dominant class is merely a technique for deflecting social attention away from wider processes of power and social control.

Groups of people that labeling theorists call *moral entrepreneurs* have lobbied for heightened public inquiry into the relationship between violent video games (including sport games) and youth violence for nearly half of a century. There are perhaps few forms of popular sport culture that are studied in laboratory settings as widely as the relationship between game play and violence. The general aggression model (Anderson and Bushman 2001) is a favorite scientific theory espoused among (typically) neoconservative, White, Christian social reformists who seek to regulate sport games and label their producers as folk devils. Anderson and Bushman have demonstrated that violent video games influence players' behavior by promoting aggressive beliefs and attitudes, thus creating aggressive worldviews among the players. In the contemporary moral panic over violence in sport video games and other video games, game participation is assumed to be linked to other deviant behaviors such as drug use, truancy, theft, slothfulness, and even sexual abuse. A sociologist employing Cohen's theoretical framework might ask if the emphasis on video games as a cause of social deviance perhaps deflects public attention away from broader social contexts of inequality, youth disenfranchisement, family breakdown, poverty, and racism that might be deeper causes of violence and aggression among young people.

Discussion Questions

1. Can you think of a sport in which a peak experience may be the outcome of deviation from a specific norm, value, or social practice?

2. In this book we have discussed the complex relationship between wanted and unwanted deviance in sport. Considering our review, do you think EPO use in cycling is wanted or unwanted deviance or both?

3. Do you think that the extreme violence often showcased in video sports affects violent behavior among youths? Why do you think the violence in sport video games is so flamboyant?

Recommended Readings

Butryn, T. 2003. Posthuman podiums: Cyborg narratives of elite track and field athletes. *Sociology of Sport Journal* 20:17-39.

> Butryn's article blends the trend toward the use of narration as data with a contemporary critique of the intersection between humans and technology in sport. His analysis of embodiment in sport is a critique of simplistic binary oppositions between athletic bodies and technology.

Le Breton, D. 2000. Playing symbolically with death in extreme sports. *Body and Society* 6:1-11.

> This article addresses the rise in popularity of sports that may pose significant physical harm to participants. Le Breton analyzes the late-modern cultural ideologies and practices that prepare people to seek near-death experiences through sport as acts of self-realization.

Markula, P. 2003. The technologies of the self: Feminism, Foucault and sport. *Sociology of Sport Journal* 20:87-107.

> Markula is widely regarded as a leading expert on poststructural understandings of the body as a site of biopower, agency, and self-exploration. In this article she outlines how Foucauldian analyses of embodiment in sport shed light on how athletic discourses create and exercise power balances between people.

Miah, A. 2004. *Genetically modified athletes.* London: Routledge.

> Miah's theoretical arguments concerning the role of genetic and other biological manipulation among athletes are cutting edge in the sociology of sport. Miah untangles some of the main institutional ideologies prohibiting the advanced biological manipulation of athletes and underlines their inherent contradictions.

Waddington, I. 2000. *Sport, health and drugs: A critical sociological perspective.* London: Taylor and Francis.

> Waddington's book brings together streams of critical thinking on the rising prominence of drugs in sport and drug use as a process related to the ongoing scientization of sport and health cultures.

Illness Narratives
and Sport

Beginning with the early criminologists' fascination with phrenology (the extrapolation of the skull contours to character), physiognomy (the extrapolation of the face to character), and somatology (the extrapolation of the body to character), the body has been connected to how people define deviance and crime. The most infamous example of this connection is perhaps Cesare Lombroso's stereotypical leap from human appearance to criminal propensity that led him to identify signs of atavism and criminality in the thief Vilella, whose face allegedly betrayed numerous stigmata (Deutschmann 2007, 157-165). This early focus on genetic inheritance led to the notion of the *born criminal* and to critics referring to this school of thinking as the *bumps and grunts school of criminology.*

Centuries of research on deviant body forms and associated identities show how differences in appearance, shape, size, race, or functional ability may be interpreted as signs of dubious or disreputable character (Gould 1996). As discussed in the previous chapter, what constitutes a normative or a deviant body is culturally bound and historically specific, and every culture contains examples of socially lauded and socially marginalized body types. A scarred body might be seen as aesthetically unpleasing in one context but be praised in another (Young 2004b). Nevertheless, when a person is labeled with body deviance, the identity attribute may significantly alter the bearer's life experiences. Ellis' (1998) autoethnographic account of lisping as a stigma and Richardson's (2003) account of how 'looking Jewish' may be situationally problematic underscore the influence that even minor body differences may have on social interaction. Various genocides across time are chilling examples of how physical appearance may be linked with far broader social and political actions.

Sociologists of the body, including Markula (2003, 2006), argue that from the 19th century onward, Western cultures have increasingly defined body stigma from scientific and medical perspectives. Particularly influenced by Foucauldian theories of biopower, control, and surveillance, sociologists of scientized bodies point to how sick and deviant and healthy and normal identities are largely formed in and disseminated from institutional sites of medicine. Medical experts wield enormous power to define what constitutes a deviant body and how such a body should be treated. A person need only to think of contemporary discourses related to obesity or anorexia to appreciate how such complex social, psychological, and emotional problems have been defined and addressed predominantly along medical lines. Once bodies are medically dominated, they become, as both Frank (1991) and Couser (1997) argue, docile in that people lose the ability and power to determine what a (deviant) body means to them.

Frank (2004) refers to the process of entering medical biopower networks and the accompanying loss of self to science as *the ride.* He illustrates the ride with the image of a patient passively sitting in a medical apparatus through illness, experiencing the highs and lows of the embodied ride as dictated by medical script. This image is reminiscent of Parsons' sick role (1951). Parsons describes the individual who is diagnosed as sick as having specific rights and obligations in a society. People with illness are immediately exempted from normal social roles and responsibilities and are generally regarded as not being responsible for their condition. Thus, the patient loses normative status as a contributing member of society. Further, the individual is pressured to get well and to seek out and cooperate fully with medical experts to help remedy the illness. Frank (2004) characterizes illness as a journey (i.e., the ride) in which the individual is diagnosed as sick by another, stripped of normal status and agency, and then encouraged to accept further medical constructions of illness by granting medical experts authority to fix the deviant status. The medically dominated body is prompted into action by scientific discourses directing how a body is to move, feel, mature, and mend. Lupton (2003), as well as other sociologists of the body, argues that such medical models alienate people from their own sense of self.

As Little and Sayers (2004) point out, once bodies with illness or disease are diagnosed, they are considered medically unique. They are not viewed as special or to be coveted but rather as deviations from a healthy norm. The broken or otherwise malfunctioning body is by medical standards a deviation from the ideal body and thus a problem to be cured for both practical reasons (i.e., to promote individual health) and moral reasons (i.e., it is the duty of medicine to fix broken bodies in order to, among other things, prevent the brokenness from spreading). But, Williams and Bendelow (1998) contend, broken bodies are socially useful to test the reliability and validity of the medical industry. Therefore, broken bodies heal through medicine, and medicine only advances through the study and mapping of broken bodies.

Once the body is designated as a medical problem, it is also marked socially. Sociologists of death and dying such as Seale (1998) note that signs of morbidity during illness draw the finality of life into sharp relief. An ill body is a problem for the individual, of course, but it is also a sobering symbol of life's harshest reality: death. As figurational sociologists like Elias (1994) remind us, signs and symbols of disease have been increasingly pushed behind the scenes of everyday cultural life for this reason.

If the diseased body is individually stigmatizing and socially disruptive in mainstream cultures, it is perhaps doubly deviant in sport cultures, where images of virile, dominating, and hyperreal bodies reign supreme. The growing sociological literature on pain and injury in sport (see Young 2004b) testifies to how athletes from a variety of sports, social backgrounds, and global cultures are embarrassed to be ill in front of peers, coaches, and fans. Illness or injury may be viewed as a marker of an inability to perform athletically, a failed athletic self, an end of a career, a lack of masculinity or femininity, or even a sexual or an ethnic deficiency. Illness in sport is essentially an unwanted form of body deviance—it symbolizes weakness, frailty, and failure. Smith and Sparkes' (2005) work on male rugby players, Collinson's (2005) autoethnographic account of running, and Pike's (2005) research on rowers show how even speaking about illness or injury is difficult for some athletes. Young, White, and McTeer (1994) describe how athletes go to great lengths to disassociate their identities from illness and injury in order to avoid being stigmatized as deviant athletes.

Although predominantly untapped by sociologists of sport, extensive literature on the psychological effects of being ill in sport cultures is available for study. Hardy's (1992) seminal research reveals how becoming socially stigmatized as injured emotionally stresses athletes. Green and Weinberg (2001) find that athletes with knee injuries are routinely at risk of developing acute depression and enduring mood disturbances. Johnston and Carroll (2000) show how long-term psychological support is often recommended for athletes diagnosed with a serious injury or illness. The double bind for athletes is created when a medical authority defines their body as deviant in a physiological sense and then athletic cultures further stigmatize their body as unwanted for its failure to perform. For many athletes, becoming ill violates the rule of body law established by medicine and by conventional norms of embodiment in perfection- and performance-oriented sport cultures.

Our interest in the sociology of illness in sport comes from our understanding that the conventional medical approach to illness is both reproduced and challenged within sport cultures of the 21st century. In some cases the social construction of illness within sport cultures jibes almost perfectly with Parsons' (1951) understanding of the *sick role* and Frank's (2004) discussion of *the ride*. Some athletes who experience injury or disease are viewed as deviants to a degree and are encouraged to come back as a display of personal fortitude and grit. Other athletes seek to challenge medical and traditional sports world distinctions between ill bodies and athleticism and to challenge the very construction of illness as social deviance. These athletes reject the accepted binary opposition between health and illness and deliberately insert the discussion and representation of illness into sport discourses.

In this chapter, we showcase narratives of illness in sport (figure 6.1). In doing so, we explore how athletes negotiate sick roles on their varied rides through sport.

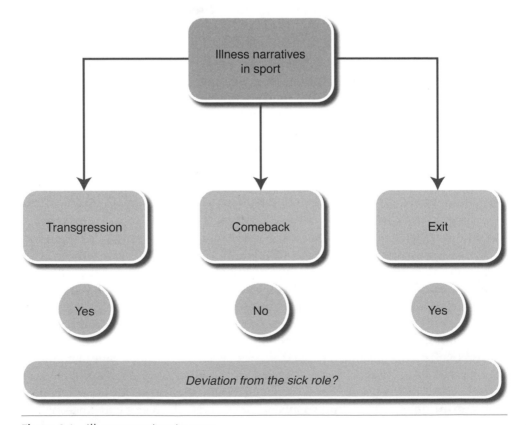

Figure 6.1 Illness narratives in sport.

Narratives of Wounded Athletes

Sociologists are interested in how people talk about everyday life and ascribe meaning to it through storytelling. As such, we are fascinated with how individuals in sport make sense of healthy and ill bodies, how bodies become deviant and problematic for the individual, and how that individual adopts certain strategies to deal with or overcome deviancy. To this end, in this chapter we explore what Frank (1995) might call *wounded storytellers* in sport.

Narratives of combating disease are filled with stories of hope and moral self-repair through wounded storytelling. According to Nelson (2001) and Lupton (2003), narratives of hope offered by patients are cultural countermeasures waged against the medical labeling of sick bodies and identities. Walter (1999) describes the cultural process of recording, disseminating, and celebrating non-medical stories about illness and death as the public *democratization of grief.*

Discourses and narratives offered by people diagnosed with disease are not merely ways of speaking about illness—they are also patient-initiated therapeutic techniques (Brittain 2004). According to Swain and French (2000), people living with and through illness often seek to produce nontragic (i.e., nonmedically deterministic) discourses about illness that highlight how they may emerge from disease as embodied agents of self-determination. Engel (2005) documents how these shared stories reaffirm the power of patients to be truth tellers about illness and how they counter images of the deviant body.

The turn to narrative research on illness is well documented in the sociology of health and increasingly in the sociology of sport (Gillett, Cain, and Pawluch 2002; Sparkes 2004). Following the path-breaking leads of Susan Sontag (1991) and Arthur Frank (1995), studies on illness narratives address how patient identities are reclaimed, resisted, and adapted through situated storytelling. Frank's (1995) work, in particular, describes the ways in which stories about the fragile body reflect the teller's journey through illness and the degree to which the teller configures the body as a problem to be managed. Frank (1995, 23) argues that illness creates a narrative rupture of identity; it is a point that shifts the life course into a new narrative trajectory. From there, bodies are clinically diagnosed as ill and colonized by the technoscientific industry. Illness claims the body at a physical and an emotional level, and medical experts claim control over the body. From Frank's perspective, patients ritually experience a loss of authority for telling personal and emotional stories about their illnesses and identities as they are taught to tell illness through narrative pathography using medical language that emphasizes how the body has failed.

From the narrative wreckage created by exposure to medical discourses, particular illness stories emerge (Frank 1995, 28). The first type of narrative, which is the culturally preferred type, is the restitution variety, in which individuals tell stories about wishes to return to preillness identities. Restitution narratives reaffirm the authority of medical ways of knowing illness and the individual's willingness to accept them. Medicine, the stories tell us, is the only legitimate vehicle through which a normal, preillness condition can be restored. The second type of narrative is a chaos narrative, in which individuals express a lack of certainty about their future. The chaos narrative has a defeatist tone, as the individual is overcome by anxiety, anguish, and despair. Finally, there are quest narratives, in which patients tell stories about illness as a spiritual journey of self-discovery. A quest narrative contains stories about how individuals seize illness as a way of discovering a transcendent and liberated self.

The sports world is filled with restitution narratives offered by players, coaches, and other insiders. As Young et al. (1994) and Sparkes and Smith (2003) show, restitution narratives are common in sport cultures, in which physical adversity is used routinely as an instance of personal growth and character building. One of the most common forms of restitution narratives in sport is *the comeback.*

POPULAR COMEBACK NARRATIVES IN SPORT

- *Nwankwo Kanu.* Kanu, a Nigerian international athlete, was advised to give up soccer in 1997 when doctors discovered that he had a serious heart defect. Determined to continue his career, Kanu underwent major surgery in the United States to correct his cardiac condition. After lengthy recuperation and rehabilitation, he made a full recovery. Kanu signed with the London-based Arsenal F.C. in 1999 and was named African Player of the Year in the English Premier League in 2002.

- *Ludmila Engquist.* Engquist, a former Olympic and world champion in the 110-meter hurdles, underwent surgery for breast cancer in the months leading up to the 1999 IAAF World Athletics Championships in Seville, Spain. Doctors presented the Swedish athlete with a bleak prognosis for a return to sport and suggested that recovering before the Seville competition was not possible. But Engquist managed to regain her fitness before the Seville Championships and eventually won a bronze medal.

- *Mario Lemieux.* In 1993 the Canadian ice hockey all-star Lemieux was diagnosed with Hodgkin's disease. He missed 23 games during the season while receiving aggressive radiation treatment. Incredibly, Lemieux returned to play during the same season and won the National Hockey League's (NHL's) scoring title. He rested for the entire 1994-95 season, recovering from back injuries and other ailments, but returned to the sport to win two Art Ross trophies (as the NHL points champion) and a Hart Trophy (as the NHL most valuable player) before announcing his retirement in 1997. In 2000, Lemieux shocked the sports world once more by retuning to the ice.

- *Bethany Hamilton.* On October 31, 2003, 13-year-old amateur surfboarder Bethany Hamilton was attacked by a 15-foot (5-meter) shark in waters off the coast of Kauai's north shore in Hawaii. The shark bit off her left arm just below her shoulder, leaving Hamilton with an open wound 16 inches (40 centimeters) long and 8 inches (20 centimeters) wide. Hamilton paddled to shore with her remaining arm, losing nearly 70% of her blood along the way. She miraculously survived, and only 4 months after the attack, was back on a surfboard

and performing competitively. She placed fifth in the 2004 U.S. National Surfing Championships and earned a place on the U.S. National Surfing Team that
year. She won an ESPY Award for Best Comeback Athlete in 2004.

- *Niki Lauda.* Track officials administered last rites to Lauda, an Austrian F1 race
  car driver, only minutes after dragging him from his Ferrari following a crash
  during practice at Nürburgring in 1976. Lauda survived the wreck even though
  his body received considerable burn damage and a lung injury. Scarred and
  battered, Lauda returned to competitive racing only 6 weeks later, placing
  fourth in the Italian Grand Prix in 1976. He retired from racing in 1979 but
  returned in 1982 and won the F1 World Drivers' Championship in 1984.

Such stories about professional and semiprofessional athletes are only one type of
comeback narrative. A full range of sporting events have become sites for recording
hope in the face of illness. In particular, a global culture of cause-driven distance running has developed. Races are held around the world to raise public consciousness
and funds for people living with chronic illness. These events typically emphasize
the message that people who are medically diagnosed with an illness can *come back*
and lead rich lives. Nettleton and Hardley (2006) show how cause-driven urban
running has dramatically changed how people think about illness. The events are
staged, run, and represented as contexts of hope and self-reclamation rather than
as competitive sports demarcating clear winners and losers. Races become, as King
(2001) illustrates, public spaces where participants (especially those diagnosed with
disease) are able to suggest, through movement and discourse, alternative ways of
knowing the medically deviant body.

However, not all people who participate in sport do so in order to come back
from illness and to correct the narrative wreckage (Frank 1995) illness creates in
their lives. Others pursue sport in order to embrace its liminal potential (Turner
1969; Shields 1992). Illness disrupts the normal pathway of life, changing the
person's self, roles, and social statuses as well as physical being. The doubt and
uncertainty created through illness are approached by people as an opportunity to construct a new self through sport. In other cases, people are faced with
terminal illnesses and seek out sport as a means of writing an exit script. Both
options are *deviant* to varying degrees, in that sport is not usually a site through
which people explore the parameters of being ill or a place to create public
images of a dying self. Sociologists know very little about how sport, illness,
and death are stitched together narratively by participants.

For the remainder of this chapter, we draw on Frank's (1995) phenomenological understanding of the body as a site of embodied narration in order to
examine athletes' constructions of illness and recovery in and through sport.
Although the standard comeback as restitution narrative is a common script
in sport, we also examine alternative illness narratives in sport cultures that
include negotiating with extreme and even fatal medical conditions.

Meeting Wounded Athletes

We started meeting wounded athletes in 2004 through research ventures in body-building, distance running, and multisport events such as duathlon and enduro racing in Canada and the United Kingdom. In Ontario, Canada, in 2005, Atkinson met an endurance athlete named Ryan who had come to distance running after being diagnosed with, being treated for, and surviving cancer. Atkinson was particularly struck by Ryan's performance ability and enthusiasm for sport, considering that he had not been an athlete before his experience with cancer. Ryan, a 53-year-old sales and marketing executive, is now a competitive runner and triathlete and a recreational rugby player in Canada. He admittedly worries about a cancer relapse but nevertheless embraces athleticism in his everyday life.

Ryan introduced us to three other *reborn* athletes living in the area who had survived traumatic illnesses. One was a 52-year-old woman recovering from a partial stroke, the second was a 46-year-old survivor of a heart attack, and the third was a 23-year-old female who had had breast cancer. As part of their ongoing recovery and life adjustment, each became involved in sport as a postoperative physical rehabilitation tool. Later, each became fascinated with sport-specific training and competition, and they all sought to become grassroots fund-raisers for respective illness initiatives in their communities. Using snow-ball techniques, we asked each of the participants for names of other people who shared illness and survival experiences through sport. We spent the next year developing the snowball sample, and we identified and contacted 19 athletes. By early 2007, we met 4 additional athletes with similar illness experiences through social running networks in the United Kingdom.

The people we have interviewed to date have experienced cancer (8), stroke (2), heart failure (4), Crohn's disease (1), partial paralysis (2), or HIV infection (1). Of the 17 athletes interviewed, 11 were White, 5 were Asian, and 1 was African Caribbean. Their mean age was 44. Twelve were male, and most occupied middle-class or upper working-class social backgrounds. A majority were married (11), and 12 of them had children. Each of the respondents was in recovery or remission at the time of the interview and had no signs of imminent relapse. Over time, we also met a terminally ill athlete named Mary. Mary was a 53-year-old cancer patient who, at the time we met her, had been told that she had only 10 months to live. She had been an avid ice hockey fan her entire life but had never played. When diagnosed, she started a local pickup league in her community so that men, women, and children of all ages could learn to play and enjoy the sport together. In a conversation with Mary, she said that all she ever wanted to do was play one time with her husband and two sons. She participated in hockey for 8 months until she became physically unable to skate. Mary died in the fall of 2006.

We interviewed each of the individuals using an open-ended narrative format. Rather than trying to force a narrative reconstruction of the illness and recovery process via a set of rigidly structured questions, we simply talked to people about their experiences with health, sport, and recovery. The only central theme we initiated during the conversations was the use of sport as a later-life technique of identity reclamation and redefinition. Proponents of narrative and biographic research methodologies (Denzin 1989) stress the need to allow participants to set the tone, content, and flow of narrative memory work. We agree, and we felt that we should allow our participants to reassemble their experienced narrative wreckages (Frank 1995) and express their own logic of storytelling. Our interviews therefore scarcely resembled a traditional interview but instead were respondent-directed storytelling sessions about body experiences before and after illness.

While each story is detailed by the narrator's own biography and storytelling style, there is a common theme of transgression across the narratives, and in Mary's case, we find an exiting narrative. Each of the athletes expressed a desire to no longer be considered as a weak or socially deviant patient diagnosed with illness. They came to sport and used sport as a ritual shedding of their sick roles. Their sport narratives are a denial of the expectation that they will remain a docile patient subject to medical authority. They use moving bodies in sport to testify to their socially transgressive minds, bodies, and spirits.

The stories we present in this chapter thus differ conceptually from the typical restitution or comeback narratives. The stories are offered by athletes who are currently involved in sport as a transgressive form of deviance and illness disavowal. While conceptually similar to Frank's (1995) quest narratives, we refer to such stories as *transgression narratives*. The athletes deliberately come to sport as a means of shedding the social stigma of a body or self at risk of loss, but they do not seek to return to their preillness self through a grueling comeback. Instead, they choose to resist images of the docile patient and to articulate how illness has placed them on a liminal life-course trajectory. Their moving bodies in sport are thereby scripted narrations of self-repair and identity exploration (Nelson 2001).

Before we analyze transgression narratives, we review typical examples of the comeback or restitution narrative in sport. We draw on the well-known case of Lance Armstrong's battle with cancer and return to professional cycling as perhaps the quintessential comeback story. Following this review, we examine transgression narratives and then discuss perhaps the most emotionally compelling narration of illness in sport—the exit narrative.

Comeback Narratives

The comeback narrative is the most common story told about illness in and around sport. The comeback is the positive outcome for a patient who accepts and fulfils the duties assigned to him in the proverbial sick role. The patient accepts medical definitions, works with doctors to treat or cure the problem, and fights to return to a normative, preillness identity. Seale's (2001) review of media coverage of athletes' comebacks from cancer shows how the physical struggles of athletes are symbolically linked to a metaphor of sports battlefield and moral victory. The standard version of the comeback narrative recounts the athlete's tragic encounter with dramatic illness or injury. Through perseverance and dedication, the athlete defies medical odds to return to sport. Narratives focusing on the return of such an athlete reaffirm culturally revered personality characteristics like the sport ethic (Hughes and Coakley 1991) and emphasize how sport brings out the best in the human spirit. In an innovative way, Gillett, Cain, and Pawluch (2002) identify how people with HIV or AIDS use a wide range of sports as complementary therapy in their social comebacks. Patients with AIDS use sport to manage illness and to reclaim the self socially through activity.

LANCE ARMSTRONG'S COMEBACK

Lance Armstrong's comeback is perhaps the most globally told story of its kind in modern sport (Sparkes 2004; Butryn and Masucci 2003). Armstrong's Tour de France victory in 1999 occurred just 3 years after doctors predicted that he would die from cancer. At the age of 25, just as his professional cycling career had blossomed, Armstrong was told on October 2, 1996, that he had stage III testicular cancer. The cancer had spread to his abdomen, lungs, and brain. Armstrong received aggressive chemotherapy in 1997 and returned to professional cycling later that same year. The upstart U.S. Postal cycling team signed Armstrong in 1998, and from 1999 to 2004, he captained the team in six straight Tour de France races. Incredibly, Armstrong won the overall Tour title in each race. In 2005 Armstrong led a new team, the Discovery Channel team, to a seventh straight Tour championship. His unprecedented and record-smashing seven consecutive tour victories—each plagued by unsubstantiated allegations of illegal doping—in one of the world's most grueling sports competitions became symbols of hope to millions of cancer patients.

Armstrong's comeback narrative does not end, however, with his tour victories or the numerous biographies and autobiographies chronicling his life. Armstrong argues (Livestrong 2007) that narrations of his comeback take their most important form through the Lance Armstrong Foundation (LAF). Established in 1997, the foundation is a fundraising, research, interactive outreach, sport organizing, and personal counseling service designed to support people surviving cancer. The LAF raised millions of dollars in cancer research funding and founded counseling programs in American hospitals from 1997 to 2003. Concomitant with Armstrong's ascending global popularity, the LAF launched the Livestrong Web site to promote cancer awareness and mediate survivor stories. In 2004, the LAF worked with Nike in order to create and disseminate the Livestrong wristband. The LAF and its yellow wristband campaign are now among the most recognized support resources for people living with or affected by cancer. Throughout the early 2000s the LAF also worked globally to establish international fund-raising, propose and script national policy plans for increased government funding of cancer research, establish survivor days sports events, create children's survivorship days, promote cancer education programs, and endow young innovator awards to help fight the physical, social, and emotional outcomes of cancer.

Among the pioneering initiatives of the LAF is the use of Livestrong Web space as a narrative resource center for people and families who have survived cancer. The Livestrong site includes space for people to read and share survivor narratives and to join the symbolic LAF survivor peloton (a peloton is group of cyclists riding together in a tight and cooperative cluster). The stories of survival, loss, doubt, hope, and the future are shared through diary entries and personal testimonies. Armstrong's vision for the Livestrong space is clear: It is designed to inspire frontline dialogue about cancer and its effects on people. As the LAF motto states, "We believe in focus: getting smart and living strong. Unity is strength, knowledge is power. Attitude is everything" (Livestrong 2007).

The LAF's showcase of survival narratives certainly fits into—but also breaks new paths within—public discourses of illness and recovery in countries like the United States. Sontag (1991) notes that Western discourses of illness and recovery tend to be underpinned by militaristic languages of battle, warfare, fighting, and survival. The Livestrong Survivorship Center of Excellence Network and Survivor*Care* program, for example, promote discourses of *winning* against cancer by narrating a survivalist ethos among patients. Illness narratives showcased through the LAF advocate personal empowerment and recovery through grassroots *battles* against disease. Patients are discouraged from becoming conditioned as passive victims through medicalization processes, and from telling the docile illness tales common among the chronically ill (Ezzy 2000).

The comeback as a restitution narrative in sport is meaningful because it documents the athlete's successful return to a normative medical state and because it reaffirms body codes associated with the athletic social identity. From both perspectives, the comeback is a transition from distinction through illness to distinction through excellence. A sociological study of the sport comeback should attend to how the restitution narrative frames a set of normative expectations for athletes who encounter body problems and to why a return to sport is the ultimate achievement for the wounded individual.

The comeback as a restitution narrative in sport is also embedded in popular cultural ideas about sport as a site of potential recovery. As mentioned, the growing number of cause-related athletic events held each year in North America and Europe attests to the use of sport as a site of collective recovery work. In many cases, the events are held annually or even more frequently. The Canadian Imperial of Bank of Commerce (CIBC) and Canadian Breast Cancer Foundation have been co-organizers of an annual Run for the Cure since 1992. The annual run and walk, branded by a pink ribbon, raises awareness about breast cancer, honors the memories of family members and friends lost to cancer, and collects funds for breast cancer research. The first event saw 1,500 runners take part in Toronto. By 2007, more than 50 communities in Canada hosted Run for the Cure events involving more than 170,000 participants (CIBC Run for the Cure 2007). Run for the Cure races have even migrated to the United Kingdom, the United States, Australia, and Japan. In the United Kingdom, the BUPA-sponsored Great North Run is the largest half marathon in the world. More than 50,000 runners participate, and the event helps to raise awareness about and funds for children living with leukemia. Acknowledging the importance of talking about illness, the Great North Run Web site (http://gnr.realbuzz.com) also includes narrative space for participants to write their own reflections on the race and on experiences with illness.

In brief, a wide range of comeback stories are told in sport. More than ever before, sports elites, recreational athletes, and everyday citizens use sport settings to work through sickness and to negotiate medicalization. The narratives we outline in the remainder of this chapter break from such a tradition and challenge people involved in sport to reject the deviantization, and stigmas, of illness.

BODY NARRATIVES

Frank's (1991) typology of body narratives is especially applicable to athletes struggling with compromised selves. In Frank's view, there are four conceptual 'types' of bodies: disciplined, dominating, mirroring, and communicating. The *disciplined body* expresses a need for control (as the individual has experienced a loss in control) and performance predictability. A disciplined body lacks self-initiated desire (other than to be in greater control) and is socially closed off and self-alienated. It is a being in itself but not for itself. The disciplined body is a passive body subject to mechanical control by an authority such as a doctor or another specialist whose knowledge base takes over. Young and colleagues (1994) illustrate how athletes develop pain and injury discourses that reveal how deeply their bodies are disciplined by coaches, trainers, and medical staff.

By comparison, *dominating bodies* are in control, are filled by desires to conquer others, are other-related (i.e., in the desire to be in control of others), and are self-alienated (Frank 1991). Many of the endurance athletes discussed in chapter 5 possess dominating bodies. Seale (2001) argues that the classic comeback narrative in sport is overflowing with constructions of the dominating body and is often taught as the preferred body orientation in sport. The ability to endure and to prove oneself as a dominating athlete is such a component of the sport mind-set, argues Shogan (1999), that it might very well be the defining element of the athlete's habitus.

Mirroring bodies are characterized by consumption and public identity work (Frank 1991). All of the self-work the individual undertakes, through a variety of body projects, must be "given" (Hebdige, 1979) to others publicly to reaffirm its investment in preferred gender, race, class, and sexual codes of body idiom. Such bodies are, in Baudrillard's (1983) terms, *hyperreal* and culturally valued for the image they project rather than their corporeal functionality. For example, Smith-Maguire (2007) suggests that slimming through weight training and aerobic conditioning is a culturally meaningful practice because it conveys an investment in the self through capital expenditures (i.e., the consumption of fitness products and services) and because it cultivates revered images of a purchased healthiness. Actual physiological improvements of the heart, lung, or muscles are less important than being perceived to be fit.

Communicating bodies are controlled, other-related, and deeply connected with selves (Frank 1991). In Frank's perspective, these bodies are perhaps the least common, as very few people are able to develop the empathic body orientation and self-awareness required for engaging in communicating body performances. It is possible to view Livestrong testimonials about Lance Armstrong's 2004 and 2005 Tour de France races as communicating body narratives. Armstrong's final two victories expressed a keen sense of his own body awareness, connection, and control but also a desire to give his sporting body to cancer survivors as a symbol of hope. By this stage in his career, Armstrong had little left to prove on a sports field, and therefore he exhibited (especially in the 2005 Tour) a desire to ride and perform for his own communicative purposes.

Transgression Narratives

Louise is a 46-year-old schoolteacher who survived cardiac arrest in 2000. Her heart failure and resulting double bypass created a significant change in her life. Before her narrative break, Louise participated in athletics only sporadically, occasionally riding her bike or swimming with her two children. She considered herself to be a generally healthy person, and she scarcely believed that she would find herself prostrate on a hospital gurney by the age of 40. In our interview with Louise, she noted how the heart attack, surgery, and recovery were physically and emotionally draining, but she spoke about being most unprepared for managing her new identity as the survivor of a heart attack. Louise's heart attack transformed her into a docile person, someone requiring constant monitoring and care. She described being treated like a "porcelain doll" in the first 3 years after the event and of experiencing a ritual dismantling her self and identity.

Louise's description of identity loss through illness is a typical narrative. Elements of Frank's (1995) disciplined body narrative and chaos narrative are evident in her story: The body is dominated by its newly ascribed medical status and is lost in a patient narrative. The illness is a major break in the life narrative, placing the individual in an often "deviant" social identity (i.e., the weak, frail, unhealthy, incapable person). In their study of deviance, Sampson and Laub (1993) describe similar events as life-course transitions that direct people in new social trajectories with their accompanying role sets and statuses. Illness is a transitioning about-face in life, as it sends people down a new and often stigmatized social pathway.

At the age of 27, Hugh became a paraplegic after a spinal injury in an automobile accident. His experience of illness led him to loathe himself and to distance himself from others. He described the hatred for his new identity and the ways in which he became an "obstacle" for his family, friends, and coworkers. Then, in Hugh's words,

> One day, it came to me while I was sitting in my room looking out the window. The snow was falling and a peace came over me, and I knew it right then. I only feel awful about myself because that's how I see myself from other people's eyes. I let other people tell the story of my life; it's like a tragedy that hasn't come to the last page yet, but everyone can foreshadow into the story so they all tiptoe around the ending thinking you don't know it. When other people talk about your life as tragic, you believe it is too and your mind is warped into self-pity. What I had to grab back hold of is the power to define my life in my own terms. When you do that, you're no longer an obstacle to anyone, including yourself.

Hugh's comments clearly illustrate the importance of writing the self by telling stories in everyday life. He sees the power to define the self, as deviant or otherwise, in narration. To venture from a socially marginalized status to one that is empowered is achieved in the process of telling one's *own* story.

But what Hugh suggests about the narrative reconfiguration of identity is not easily achieved for people confronted with illness. Others interviewed in our research suggest that people cannot simply verbally convince themselves of being normal; they cannot lose the stigma of being ill simply by speaking about their normalcy. As Goffman (1963) notes, once a body stigma like illness is applied to an individual, it may be a status carried for life, despite recovery. Ellen, a 28-year-old woman living with Crohn's disease, says that the surest way to break the narrative categorization of life and self as deviant is to initiate yet another about-face through embodied performance. A person cannot convince others of normality simply through talk; a person must demonstrate it through performance.

Rick's story of personal redefinition postdiagnosis is especially indicative of the importance of movement as narration. Rick received his HIV-positive diagnosis at the age of 23. Devastated by what he called a *medical death sentence*, Rick withdrew from social life in fear of ridicule and ostracism. He viewed his body as "rotten on the inside" and, at 25, had given up on life. Following initial shock, anger, and depression, he made peace with his biological illness and started to live again. Rick describes how he felt the need to convince others that he could live a long life despite having HIV.

A close friend of his, who he met in an HIV support group, introduced him to a basketball league for people living with HIV. Paul told Rick about the physical benefits of sport. Gillett, Cain, and Pawluch's (2002) research on men with HIV and AIDS attests to how people like Paul and Rick struggle to find leisure spaces for their ongoing disease management. Rick played in the league after some coaxing from Paul and almost immediately fell in love with sport. Rick had never played in a sports league before this experience, and he soon became hooked. He hired a personal trainer, started to run and swim weekly, and, by the age of 27, completed his first marathon. Rick is now a lifestyle athlete who engages in rigorous sport each day. Family and friends now see Rick as a healthy man who is a community role model of active living; a minor biographical detail in his narrative script is that he also happens to be HIV positive.

Rick's story of HIV and the discovery of sport through recovery links with the theme of a quest narrative (Frank 1995). Rick's journey of self-exploration and expansion through illness is facilitated by his newfound embodiment both as a man with HIV and as a recreational athlete. But at the same time, Rick wilfully uses sport in post-HIV diagnosis life to break free from stereotypes and images of the ill, medicalized, and gay man. According to him,

> The irony of my life now is amazing. At this point in my life, I am healthier in some ways than I ever have been. My heart is more efficient, my muscles are stronger, my skin is cleaner, my endurance is fantastic, and my overall energy is multiplied by a thousand times. . . . Paul started me on this path through basketball, and I'll never be able to thank him enough. I love smashing people's ideas about what a man with HIV should look like and how the doctors told me life with HIV will unfold. In this cosmically bizarre, karmic way, HIV helped me find my body and inner strength. Gay men with HIV are not the people who come to mind when someone says, "virile athlete." But look at me now.

Rick is fully aware that while HIV is controllable through medication and treatment, it is an unpredictable illness. Therefore, while he is still able, he chooses to write his identity through transgressive actions in sport. For him, the ongoing performance of vibrant physicality (Monaghan 2003) is a clear tactic of deviance disavowal. Again, these findings ring with Gillett, Cain, and Pawluch's (2002) conclusion that exercise and sport are socially meaningful for patients with HIV, as embodied vibrancy helps them deal with the debilitating stigmas of illness and docility.

Like Rick and Hugh, Marion, a 23-year-old survivor of breast cancer, describes how her own "will to the body" (Frank 1991) emerged after she was infantilized by doctors and family members through treatment processes. Like so many other cancer survivors, Marion is grateful for the help and support she received before and after her mastectomy, but she was also angered by the degree to which others associated her medically ill body with an incapable self. She described a history of body docility and a complete lack of interest in athletics before her illness. To this end, her involvement in a running club six months after the operation helped her "get away from" her house, her family, the doctors' offices, daily work tasks, and even her own biography. Running with a group of young women for an hour three times a week also provided her with an outlet for releasing her anger by becoming strong. After months of being told about her body's performance (i.e., how it functions, how it looks, how it should feel) by others associated with her cancer, Marion used running to oppose her docile identity. She is now the organizer of a running club for women living with illness.

Common in other transgression narratives are vignettes about how the active body in sport at once destabilizes images of deviant frailty ascribed to patients and claims ownership over illness definition. For Stan, a 51-year-old leukemia survivor, downhill and cross-country skiing are metaphors for the active body. Stan found skiing through the advice of his sister, a long-term athlete who advocates the meditative aspects of physicality. He rejects being physically and socially frail as a potentially lifelong cancer patient, but he does not discount the disease as a significant part of his biological being. Stan does not, in his words, "live around" his cancer; rather, he attempts to "be another kind of cancer patient." He actively uses the interpretive resource (Gubrium and Holstein 1997) provided by his cancer as a means of teaching others not to be ashamed or afraid of bodies invaded by disease. Actively owning the social definition and the use of his ill body is best illustrated, in his case, through skiing:

> Whether I'm hurtling down a hill at top speed or quietly gliding through the backcountry, I am still moving, I still "am." I am a man with cancer. And that cancer is at bay for now, but it's in me. It is me. I am it. There's no quarreling about my body being a host for a disease. This [Stan points to his body] is not my oncologist or my physiotherapist. It is me. I own me until the day I die, and I will move, as a man, as cancer, as dad, and as a skier until I pass on. Skiing teaches me this, to be one, to be whole, to be free through movement. Not to negate what is there and deny your body, but to be present and mindful. I ski with my illness, not in spite or in fear of it. When we are talking about surviving a disease, that's how it's done: by owning every minute with your body. . . . When my body tells me to slow down because I am tired, I do. When I have the energy to ski, I do and enjoy it that much more. The body is truly a blessing.

Stan claims ownership over the body and the self through sport both literally and spiritually. Transgression in this case involves embodying an alternative understanding of biological illness and life with illness and reflecting upon the nature of the diseased body. Embodied sport performances wrestle the ownership of knowing illness away from institutional discourses and allow survivors to construct new codes of body meaning.

Karen, a 45-year-old uterine and breast cancer survivor tells similar stories. For her, sport involvement is about disavowing the docility promoted through medicalization and institutional constructions of diseased bodies. She participates in two masters swimming leagues, and she competes recreationally almost every month. She dabbled with gymnastics for 2 years during her childhood, but she has not participated in the sport since she was 9 years old. Karen started to swim at a local health club several months after her final cancer treatment. One day she felt "pulled" into the gym, located only three blocks from her apartment, and was especially drawn to the pool. "Fate stepped in, I think," she said. "The calming, soothing nature of the water called to me." A year of swimming classes, coaching sessions, and club involvement later, Karen became a specialist in the 100-meter breaststroke and a recreational competitor in a city league for masters swimmers. "C'mon, I had to," she argues. "The irony of the name [of the event] is more than a bit obvious." During our interview with Karen, she acknowledged that swimming is how she conveys her will to live, move, and appreciate life's contingencies: "Sometimes you're up and win, and sometimes you're beaten. The greatest lesson I've learned and now try to teach others is that you are never out until you stop moving."

For other survivors of illness, though, the cultivation of a strong and healthy sports body is a technique of invisibility. Once a person enters into the medical complex for diagnosis and treatment, the body and self are immediately marked as medically and socially different. Christopher, for example, is a 48-year-old who started riding with a cycling group 2 years after doctors removed one of his testicles. He had been diagnosed with testicular cancer only 2 months before the surgery. He felt like a victim, an emasculated man, and a social outsider. Christopher found his inspiration to ride from Lance Armstrong's story, and he joined a local riding club almost a year after his surgery. He explained the experience in the following way:

> I wanted to climb out of my body. Everyone asks you if you're okay, and you spend so much time as the subject of conversation. I've never been the center of attention and I hate it, so you can imagine what that hell was like for me. . . . At first, I didn't tell any of the guys in the [cycling] club about my problem. To them, I'm just Chris, another rider. Doing that saved my sanity, really. . . . Those first rides were nightmares to survive and I was worried about having to sit in the saddle for 3 or 4 hours at a time. But I "found myself" again in the middle of the pack every Sunday with them. I thought about that hour after hour on the bike. God, I'm so grateful just to be one of the pack.

Unlike comeback narratives in sport, Christopher's transgression narrative does not tell a story about a miraculous or heroic recovery for others to emulate. His embodied narrative of health and movement in sport diverts attention away from his previously pathological body. He speaks about simply feeling like a normal man again and being lost in the middle of his weekly riding group, where he is no longer a deviant cancer patient or the center of medical concern.

Keith, a professor of economics, survived a heart attack in 1999 at the age of 52. His bedridden convalescence took nearly 6 months. While reading a local newspaper in bed one day in the spring of 2000, Keith spotted an advertisement for a local tennis club, and he decided to take classes. At the club, he established new friendship networks and cautiously increased his playing volume each month. At present, Keith plays 10 to 12 matches a week. He describes the club as his home away from home, he relishes in the control he now possesses over his body, and he cannot envision a life without the sport.

Keith became so enamored of tennis that he accepted an early retirement offer from his university in the fall of 2007. His desire to break free from the sick role even translated into a desire to be free of the trappings of work-related social identities and task performances. For Keith, tennis is simply a metaphor for actively participating in life while you still can instead of passively lying in bed or sitting at work.

Keith's transgression narrative touches on a common theme. There is a tendency for certain reborn athletes, especially those coming close to death through illness, to adopt the athletic role as a new master status. These athletes swing from one end of the health and activity pendulum to the other. Perhaps as a response to intense body disciplining by medicine and a desire to fully get away from the image of the deviant and sick patient, they overcompensate through extensive sport involvement. Akin to the emaciated triathletes introduced in chapter 5, reborn athletes will change or quit careers, lose touch with past friends, and even alienate family members in the pursuit of physical activity. They develop a sort of physical and social addiction to exercise that is common among those who frame their public identities through embodied sport performances (Atkinson 2007). From a certain perspective, we could argue that they have traded the deviant status of being ill through disease with the deviant status of being obsessed with sport and sports bodies.

Sonya, a 31-year-old cancer survivor also became obsessive about her sport involvement. Formerly overweight in her teenage and young adult years, Sonya found that chemotherapy and cancer treatments produced dramatic weight loss and systematically eroded her appetite. She lost nearly 100 pounds (45 kilograms) through cancer treatment, which she kept off following her recovery. While she at first hated the appearance of her gaunt body, as her recovery progressed and general health improved, she found a new ability to move athletically: "I couldn't believe it . . . out of all of the darkness there was light. When my body balance had been realigned, I could run really well. And eventually I had a thin runner's body." Sonya became so engrossed in being hyperfit and so fearful of losing her thin physique that she ate sparingly while running obsessively. Perhaps not surprisingly, she is now worried about being anorexic and seeks counseling twice a week. Like Stan's tale, Sonya's story illustrates the ways in which some people dealing with social stigmas drift (Matza 1964a) from one deviant identity to another.

In brief, transgression narratives call attention to the body as a site of identity performance through sport. In similar and contrasting ways, transgression narratives detail personal rejections of the docility expected after illness diagnosis. Bodies in motion are presented socially to others as physical evidence, or narrative testimony, of renewed selves, but they are not presented in a comeback or restitution manner. The postdiagnosis body in sport is multiply deviant, as it challenges and subverts traditional medical and sport constructions of ill bodies.

Exit Narratives

Figurationalist Norbert Elias was one of the first sociologists after Durkheim to broach the subject of death and dying. His book, *The Loneliness of Dying* (1986), examines how death and images of death are typically pushed behind the scenes of everyday life and are treated as a form of deviance, as they conjure socially uncomfortable symbols of human frailty. Elias describes modern societies as being particularly emotionally closed off about death and dying, preferring to sideline grieving scenes and emotional releases into private spaces such as a hospitals, funeral homes, or palliative care facilities. His writing is a precursor to Frank's (1995) later analysis of how the medicalization of illness and death isolates people from public view and effectively removes them to hidden places.

The Loneliness of Dying further teaches us about the ways in which the exit of the critically ill patient from the world tends to be scripted by medical experts and not by the patients themselves. In this connection, we draw from Elias' ideas on loneliness to examine how some people, when diagnosed with a terminal illness, choose to construct an emotionally and a socially expressive exit through sport performance. These exit narratives are self-directed and publicly offered stories about how a person's last days may be understood as texts of hope and inspiration.

In general, exit narratives are dialogical with the body's decay or failure in medical scientific terms and are not socially defined by them. We were first inspired to think about the concept of an exit narrative when meeting Mary, an avid ice hockey fan we introduced earlier in this chapter. From Mary, we learned to see an exit process as an opportunity to understand the self in expressive and self-determined ways. Mary taught us that an exit narrative deviates from the traditional mode of telling death through the depressingly clinical perspectives offered by doctors and medical experts or the grieving stories of loved ones. Through exit narratives, sick people claim to tell a different truth about dying. Exit narratives are certainly transgressive as we have shown, but they are also unique, as the following two cases underscore.

Terry Fox was born on the Canadian prairies and raised on Canada's west coast. An active teenager involved in many sports such as rugby, baseball, and basketball, Fox was only 18 years old when diagnosed with osteogenic sarcoma (a form of cancer that makes bones turn soft). As a result, doctors amputated his right leg 6 inches (15 centimeters) above the knee in 1977. Fox was then fitted with an artificial leg. While in the hospital, Fox was so overcome by the experiences of other cancer patients and the inspirational story of Dick Traum—a man who ran the New York City Marathon with a prosthetic leg—that he decided to run across Canada to raise money for cancer research. Fox would eventually call his journey the *Marathon of Hope*. Before undertaking the run, he joined the basketball team of the Canadian Wheelchair Sports Association in British Columbia in 1977, and he played in three national championships with the team. Despite pain produced by a poorly fitted prothesis, Fox completed his first marathon in Prince George, British Columbia, in 1979.

In turning his attention full time to the Marathon of Hope, Fox aimed to raise (CDN) $1 of research money for every member of the Canadian population by running a marathon a day across Canada. At the outset, Fox solicited dozens of public and private companies for funding support, but only a few responded—the Ford Motor Company donated a van, Adidas provided several pairs of shoes, and the Safeway grocery store chain provided food vouchers. After 18 months and more than 3,107 miles (5,000 kilometers) run in preparation, Fox started his marathon in St. John's, Newfoundland, on April 12, 1980, with only a little fanfare and media attention. Public enthusiasm for and awe of Fox's venture grew quickly as he ran through the Atlantic provinces, and the money he collected along his route began to mount. He ran 26 miles (42 kilometers)—and on many occasions more than 30 miles (48 kilometers)—a day through Canada's Atlantic provinces, through Quebec, and into Ontario. By the time Fox reached the Ontario border, the nation had embraced him as a public hero. Canadian dignitaries, charities, and local celebrities donated huge sums of money to Fox's marathon, and the international media picked up his incredible story.

In the early morning of August 31, 1980, Fox woke up just outside of Thunder Bay in Ontario in his Ford marathon van complaining of a cold. Persistent coughing and lung pain during the run that day forced him to consult a doctor, who delivered a chilling diagnosis. On September 1st, after 143 days and 3,339 miles (5,374 kilometers) of running, Fox was forced to stop because cancer had appeared in his lungs. Laying prostrate on a hospital stretcher outside of an ambulance, Fox announced to the nation that after 3,339 miles, his marathon would have to end. During the interview, Fox remarked, "How many people do something they really believe in? I just wish people would realize that anything is possible if you just try. Dreams are made if people try."

A massive outpouring of support followed in Canada, with telethons and other charity events showcasing Fox's situation. Through his stay in the hospital and his treatment for lung cancer, Fox wore his Marathon of Hope T-shirt. The Governor General of Canada, Edward Schreyer, honored Fox as a Companion of the Order of Canada. Even while in the hospital, Fox volunteered to appear in educational films produced by the Canadian Cancer Society.

But 1981 did not usher in better health news for Fox. He received notification in early January that his cancer had spread into his abdomen, but he nevertheless continued to hope. Terry Fox passed away on June 28, 1981, at age 22. He had achieved his dream—he had raised more than (CDN) $24 million for cancer research, precisely matching the number of people living in Canada at that time. Now, 26 years after his death, more than (CDN) $400 million has been raised worldwide for cancer research in Terry's name through the annual Terry Fox Run held across Canada and around the world. In 2005, Fox was named among the CBC Top 10 Greatest Canadians, and he is fondly remembered as one of Canada's greatest heroes.

At the age of 43, Jane Tomlinson of Leeds, England, lost her life to cancer. She was first diagnosed with breast cancer and mastectomized in 1990, at the age of 26. Determined to wage her own war with cancer on her own terms and to help others with similar experiences, she changed career paths and enrolled at Leeds General Infirmary to train as a pediatric radiographer. Doctors discovered lumps in her remaining breast in 1996, and, after rounds of chemotherapy and radiotherapy, they performed a second mastectomy. In 2000, doctors delivered even more bad news—the cancer had metastasized, spreading to her bones and lungs. Jane was told at the time that she had just 12 moths to live.

The *narrative wreckage* that Tomlinson, like so many others, faced through illness could have led her to retreat into herself and die passively. Instead, she decided to author her own exit narrative of hope and inspiration. She embarked on a series

of athletic challenges to raise money for cancer research and for charitable organizations that help the families of people with chronic illness. Tomlinson started
conservatively on her athletic ventures, competing in running events such as the
5K Race for Life and the 5K Leeds Abbey Dash in 2001. But by 2002, Tomlinson's
determination to push her body amplified, and she competed in both the London
Marathon and the New York Marathon. Later that year she presented the Jubilee
Baton, commemorating the Queen of England's 50th anniversary as the monarch,
to the Queen at a festival in Leeds. Later still, she completed the London Triathlon,
the first athlete with an incurable illness to do so.

Undeterred by her failing body, Tomlinson went on to complete a staggering
number of grueling physical challenges that even the most seasoned of athletes
would be proud to list: She finished the Hawaii Ironman (she was the only person
with a terminal illness to do so), cycled 1,060 miles (1,700 kilometers) across
England and 2,000 miles (3,200 kilometers) across Europe (stopping along the
way to climb Mont Ventoux in France), cycled 4,200 miles (6,800 kilometers)
across the United States and 3,100 miles (5,000 kilometers) across Africa, raised
nearly £2 million for charities, ran countless local races of varying lengths in
support of cancer research, wrote two books about her experiences with cancer
and sport, and helped organize a 10K charity run, the Run For All. Along the
way, she periodically received bouts of chemotherapy to treat her cancer and
eventually developed chronic heart disease as a result. For her efforts, Tomlinson received a wide range of accolades, including the BBC Sports Personality
of the Year in 2002, the Helen Rollason Award in 2002, and the Pride of Britain
Award in 2005. She was made a Member of the Order of the British Empire in
2003 and then a Commander of the Order of the British Empire in late 2007
(only 3 weeks before she died).

Tomlinson's heroic and inspirational final years, like those of Terry Fox, certainly defy medical orthodoxy about how an ill body should perform and be
represented. The narrative accounts of Tomlinson and Fox are not a comeback
or restitution brand, however—the certainty of death must have precluded any
such thoughts. While transgressive in many ways—their decisions to engage in
rigorous endurance events as chronically ill young people certainly does not fit
into the standard cultural sick role—the exit narratives that Fox and Tomlinson
publicly told are about becoming and doing in the face of a definitive end to life.
Despite discouragement and sporadic public criticism—for example, incredible
claims were often made in British tabloids about Tomlinson faking her illness,
and she repeatedly faced threatening and accusatory phone calls and e-mails
from enraged sceptics—both athletes chose to face death with a culturally deviant optimism, joy, and concern for the well-being of others. While neither Fox
nor Tomlinson chose to have cancer, they chose to exit life on their own terms as
supporters of the common good. Their exit narratives were other-directed rather
than self-directed, empathic and selfless at time when each had every reason to be
selfish, angry, and closed to the world. To use a classic sport metaphor, Fox and
Tomlinson went down swinging for others facing similar crises in their lives.

THEO~~RETI~~CTIONS
IN~~TER~~SETICAL   # THEORETICAL INTERSECTIONS

Heidegger's (1993) critical examination of technology is substantively unrelated to the subject of deviance or illness in sport. But his idea about the role of technology and our approach to technological innovation (such as the advances achieved through applied medical science) potentially instructs us how to interpret the significance of transgression and exit narratives told through sport as acts of social deviance.

Heidegger describes the Western concept and use of technology as a process of applied discovery. In a traditional scientific sense, it is the process of applying knowledge and technical apparatuses to discover truths about the physical and social worlds. Thus, the scientific application of technology in medicine is literally the bringing forth of a certain kind of understanding of health and illness and of the normative, objective body and the deviant body. However, as Heidegger notes, and Pronger (2002) echoes, nonscientific practices are also technological (in the ancient Greek sense of the word *techne*) modes of revealing truths. Heidegger argues that not everything about the world may be known by measuring or studying it quantitatively through mechanical or scientific means. To this end, he reviews the other side of technology—the revealing of reality through subjective emotional expression and reflection. The ancient Greeks referred to this process as *poiesis.*

Poiesis is the artistic, aesthetic, and emotional technique of revealing social truths—humanistic, moral, ethic, and spiritual social realities. Poiesis is not measurable or accountable as something quantifiable in the world; it reveals, in highly subjective ways, the nonmaterial characteristics of human existence. Poiesis may be an act, a symbol, a thought, or an expression that provides a glimpse of understanding into the human condition that falls outside of conventional scientific and rational ways of knowing life.

Heidegger's (1993) comments are salient to us as sociologists of deviant bodies in sport, as medical and technological ways of knowing the ill body continue to dominate many (sport) cultures. Medical discourses and related technologies for knowing what it means to be an injured or a sick athlete, and they exclude or push to the margins other ways of knowing and experiencing illness through sport. From Heidegger's theoretical point of view, broken athletes are biological resources for testing medicine and applying new medical technologies. Athletes, like others involved in the medical ride, are merely standing reserve armies against which medical knowledge and related technology are tested and improved. Thus medicine and technology, argues Heidegger, *need* to identify, fix, and showcase the correction of deviant bodies. From such a perspective, technology uses ill humans more than ill humans use technology. Lance Armstrong's comeback narrative certainly testifies to the power of technology to define, cure, and mediate illness as a problem in sport. The comeback happens because technology allows it to, and the narrative about survivorship is a medical success story: Armstrong's potential as a normative, a socially contributing, and an inspirational human is revealed or brought forth through the medical salvation of his body.

By contrast, transgression and exit narratives are replete with poiesis. Embodied acts of living through illness, and toward life's physiological end, are not narratives that are framed by medicine and scientific knowledge. They are, in some ways, medically deviant stories that illustrate how humans may explore the experience of illness in unquantifiable ways. Poiesis through sport brings forth truths about human spirit and emotion and the meaning of social life in nonmedical terms. Acts of poiesis, then, defy classification as simply normative or deviant, since these classifications are highly objective and rational ways of knowing the world.

Fox and Tomlinson were individuals who explored the empathic parameters of human existence through athleticism. Their athletic performances are technologies for narrating a lived and felt reality about the human condition that a person may discover as epiphany through illness. To explain poiesis, Heidegger uses the example of a sculptor chipping away at stone to reveal the aesthetic statue inside. The technical act of art, of inspirationally shaping stone, brings forth the essence of the sculpture underneath. The people we interviewed who told us transgression and exit narratives described how technical acts of running, swimming, tackling, and throwing can become forms of poiesis, as they reveal an essence about the human condition that is irreverent to medical classification.

Heidegger also argues that poiesis provides people with moments of catharsis or moments of ecstasis. For example, some people, after being medically colonized and directed as patients, come to sport to seek transcendence from the medically determined self to the emotionally liberated self. We have described these people as *narrators of transgression* in sport. Sport may be cathartic for the individual whose tensions and frustrations about being told how to be "deviantly" ill and how to perform as ill in medically normative ways require ritual and symbolic release. People enter sport to release contained emotions and to experiment with the ecstasy of self-determination that is restricted by the conventional medical ride. In the process, patients deviate from their status as medicalized and self-detached and move toward knowing the self as an openly expressive author of health and illness. In terms of poiesis, transgressing the sick role through sport is a strategy for exploring and redefining what the word *ill* means to people.

In the following discussions, we ask you to consider whether people diagnosed with an illness—and thus medically labeled as *deviant*—have any degree of agency to narrate their own identities through sport as poiesis. Or, are even transgression and exit narratives replete with the stereotypical themes of medical and cultural domination that accompany the standard sick role in Western cultures?

FUNCTIONALISM AND STRAIN THEORY

By building on Merton's (1938) strain theory and Sutherland's (1947, 1973) differential association theory, Cloward and Ohlin (1960) create a version of strain theory about deviant subcultures. They place the emphasis of their theory of differential opportunity systems on how people who feel structural and cultural strain require social contexts for alleviating their strain through deviant adaptation. To pursue dominant status goals through illegitimate means, however, a person must become linked with other deviants. Yet not all who experience strain have access to subcultural communities of deviance through which adaptations can be learned and put in motion. Therefore, while people face blocked access to legitimate means for achieving cultural goals (which produces strain), they may also face blocked access to illegitimate means for achieving goals through deviant behavior. Clearly influenced by Albert Cohen's (1955) construction of subcultural life as a solution to collectively experienced status problems, Cloward and Ohlin's theory underscores how deviant behavior is often a collective group process.

Although fitness facilities and workout spaces abound in North America, people are typically entrenched in workout cultures with a minimal sense of social support and networking. People who are experiencing illness as a status problem and are interested in pursuing athletics as a means of stigma disavowal need to become linked with groups of like-minded actors. In order to be able to utilize sport to transgress the patient role, a person must find the requisite "illegitimate" means to do so. Arguably, the network chains of interdependence created by illness support and fund-raising organizations such as the LAF and the Run for the Cure provide a subcultural solution for such a task. Using Cloward and Ohlin's theory in an innovative way, we might interpret the burgeoning popularity of grassroots organizations like the LAF as a quasi-deviant subcultural model for achieving dominant cultural goals (i.e., health, empowerment, and civic participation) through culturally rule-violating means: that is, by patients and survivors becoming health advocates and lobbyists for change regarding the cultural treatment of anyone diagnosed as ill.

CONFLICT THEORY

In his book *Symbolic Crusades* (1963), Gusfield develops a sociological theory of status politics to understand how social movements form. He contends that in North American society, status interests and conflicts are especially complex because social hierarchies are not entirely based on economics. Similar to Porter (1965) in the Canadian classic *The Vertical Mosaic*, Gusfield argues that the statuses, values, and norms of hegemonic groups have greater cachet than those of others. Members of a lower group, whose statuses, values, and norms are not revered through law or custom, face social discrimination even though they may be in the middle classes economically. Social conflicts are born out of disparities among rank-ordered *cultural* groups. Social movements or symbolic crusades of status frustration are struggles for public recognition and legal endorsement of marginalized cultures.

Gusfield's theory of status order groups may be utilized to study the struggle to obtain social invisibility through sport as a symbolic crusade. Since, from a certain perspective, people diagnosed as ill tend to rank low on the status order, the collective search for normalcy through sport is a quest for status acquisition. Narratives about sport experiences provided by survivors of illness might be examined for content regarding the use of athleticism as a personally symbolic crusade. Similarly, the fight to raise research funding and social awareness for diseases like cancer through sports organizations such as the LAF or races such as the Run for the Cure could be understood as more formalized and public social crusades against the marginalization of survivors of illness.

INTERACTION THEORY

The social psychologist Scheff (1979) offers a theory explaining why emotional narratives of suffering and anxiety contain meaning. For him, such stories have cathartic benefits for audiences. In his book, *Catharsis in Healing, Ritual, and Drama*, Scheff describes personal catharsis as a therapeutic process involving the release of potentially embarrassing or distressing emotions such as grief, fear, and anger. According to Scheff, the performance of catharsis, although often discredited in the sociological literature, is the essential building block of most religious and theatrical performances. Since much of the interaction order (Goffman 1967) is built on the concealment of affect (Elias 1994), people seek social narratives through religion or drama for embodied emotional release like crying or laughter. Catharsis removes embedded anxiety from the psyche and helps produce clear thought. Scheff further contends that in order for catharsis to take place through narrative, a degree of emotional distance from past traumatic events is required.

Future research on post-illness recovery through sport might attend to whether individuals intentionally seek physically grueling activities for catharsis. If we accept Frank's (1991, 1995) description of the disciplining effects of medicalization on patients' ability to express desire, we might expect patients' illness narratives to exude emotional repression. Indeed, medicalization exposes patients to a new interaction order and socializes them into a new set of rules on embodied feeling. By taking direction from Scheff, we might study the experience of intense physicality through sport as an instance of reconnecting mind, body, and feeling through the release of previously contained desires. Individuals do not distance themselves from cathartic interaction, as Scheff might predict, to feel its effects; rather, they place their bodies in the middle of the ritual. Thus we might understand grimacing in pain, breathing heavily, screaming, or crying in athletic competition as catharsis for people who have been coached to keep illness-related emotions in check.

SOCIAL CONTROL THEORY

Matza (1964a) believes that individuals oscillate between conformity and deviance in everyday life. His book *Delinquency and Drift* explains deviance as an ongoing ebb and flow in which people drift in and out normative and counternormative behaviors. He argues that people commit deviant acts (e.g., lying, stealing, interpersonal violence, and so on) because they are motivated and psychologically prepared to do so. After the act is committed and reflected upon as wrong, the person typically feels guilty and assuages the guilt using conforming behavior. People drift into and then out of deviance periodically. Recidivist deviants, however, feel enduring personal desperation. Desperation and associated feelings of fatalism arise when an individual perceives a lack of control over his own life.

A body recovering from stroke and a body able to run more than 42 kilometers are positioned at opposite ends of the health spectrum. They are both somewhat deviant, however, as both deviate from constructions of the normally functioning body. A long-term study of transgression narratives in sport might focus on how the condition of being ill provides the requisite preparation to drift into the role of the reborn athlete. Certainly, as Frank (1995) notes, illness can instill a present-centered fatalism coupled with a perceived lack of personal control. Future research on athletes who explore sport after illness could examine the potential link between the chaos states Frank details and the precursors to drift that Matza identifies. Especially important might be the use of sports competition underpinned by ideologies of meritocracy and hard work in restoring a sense of justice, fairness, and self-determination in life. The drift into a transgressive sporting role might alleviate feelings of desperation and injustice that routinely emerge through illness.

CLASSICAL THEORY

Bentham's (1995) description of the panopticon is a classical assessment of how social order, and consent to order, is manufactured institutionally. Bentham outlines how a prison called the *panopticon* is a metaphor for how discipline and punishment within institutional settings operate via formal and informal techniques. The theoretical panopticon is a two-pronged structure: a tall guard tower encircled by a transparent prisoners' quarters, in which the guards can see in but the prisoners cannot see out. At first, the prisoners comply within the system because they are consciously aware of being monitored by guards. Over time, compliance to prison rules becomes second nature, and conscious thoughts of being monitored turn into habits. Bentham's model offers an explanation for how institutional discipline operates first through external mechanisms and then through inner restraints. Conformity is coercive in the primary stages of socialization and then operates as a socially instilled second nature through instilled restraint mechanisms. We may extrapolate from Bentham's model to view all institutional life as a process of formally learning codes and rules followed by becoming subjects of habituated institutional conformity.

We might argue that medical institutions produce panopticon-like effects through patient diagnosis, treatment, hospitalization, and recovery processes. The athletes interviewed in our research told us stories about how they became subjects of medical discipline, surrendered their bodies to medical experts, and then learned to self-monitor as patients during the recovery process—all while being subject to external public observation and assessment. Recovery processes are examples of learned compulsions to self-treat (i.e., to exercise self-restraint) through medication, self-monitor through prescribed diet and exercise programs, and to engage confessional practices through regular checkups. We might argue that athletes who tell tales of transgression in sport are fully aware of the institutional control game at work via medicalization and are seeking to counteract its hegemonic force through embodied sport. Reborn athletes select alternative ways of experiencing the healing process and immerse themselves in other institutional practices. Sport practices are no less disciplining than medical practices are, but future research in the area could explore if active involvement in sport after illness is a technique designed to combat the institutionally totalizing effects of medicine on the body.

CRITICAL THEORY

Although it is not regularly referenced in the crime and deviance literature, de Certeau's *The Practice of Everyday Life* (1984) is an examination of how people use signs, symbols, texts, or objects in social interaction for their own strategic, and occasionally deviant, purposes. De Certeau's semiotic reading of everyday representation highlights the importance of a sociology of reuse. In the social practice of reuse there is an abundance of opportunities for ordinary people to subvert the rituals and representations that institutions, such as those that make up the medical complex, impose upon them. For de Certeau, the essence of ordinary life is a constant and tactical struggle against the institutions competing to assimilate everyday people into inactive consumers of culture rather than producers of identity. *The Practice of Everyday Life* suggests that the body, for instance, may be reused as a symbol of struggle against institutional homogenization. Individuals actively craft their bodies (de Certeau 1984, 121) to produce individual and cultural interpretations of the world rather than merely receive them. The deviant, then, is the person who actively produces the embodied techniques of her everyday life through socially artistic means.

The future study of transgression narratives told by athletes who were formerly ill could include examinations of how the moving body is an artistic technique of reuse. Hoyle and White's (1999) analysis of how athletes with disability use sport as a technique of empowerment provides insight into how the everyday practice of sport involves people reusing their bodies in socially unexpected ways. Rarely are the people who are diagnosed with chronic illness expected to recover and then perform as athletes. Once assigned the sick role, patients are expected to strive for health and to be conservative in their physical activity (Williams and Bendelow 1998). Athletes who transgress these cultural expectations by immersion in sport actively define post-illness embodiment rather than simply reproduce institutional ways of knowing survivorship.

GENDER AND FEMINIST THEORY

Bordo's (1993) book *Unbearable Weight: Feminism, Western Culture and the Body* is comprised of a cluster of essays on the social construction and expressiveness of the human body. It also borrows from Foucauldian theory and initiates a second-wave feminist understanding of how bodies are sites of oppression and docility for many Western women. For Bordo, even the most extreme forms of body ritual, such as cosmetic surgery, and obsessive forms of physical training are evidence of the desire for women to conform to cultural norms. The practices tend to homogenize women's bodies into ideal feminine forms in which subjectivity, desire, and personal agency through embodiment are traded for cultural acceptance. *Unbearable Weight* maps out how the pathological pursuit of cultural ideals—which Bordo finds understandable, given the kudos received for undertaking conformity-oriented body projects—is the precursor to a full range of female disorders such as anorexia and bulimia. Bordo's interpretation of the cultural foundations of the so-called pathological female body influenced an entire generation of health and illness research and helped establish the field of identity politics research, which has in turn influenced the sociology of deviance.

Bordo's understanding of the body as a site of gender performance could be utilized in a number of ways to examine transgression narratives in sport. For instance, the Run for the Cure could be interpreted as a cultural space for women—who tend to dominate as participants—to pursue sport involvement that does not replicate hegemonic masculine sport ideologies and practices. The Run for the Cure was pioneered by women *for* women and is a setting in which rejections and deconstructions of the ideal, docile feminine body abound. The run and similar athletic events not only transgress docile feminine body practices and images but also challenge institutional discourses about breast cancer (and other diseases) made by experts within the medical industry (Bordo 1993).

INTEGRATED THEORY

While their theoretical contribution might normally be seen as critical criminology, Arrigo and Bernard (1997) draw a postmodern theory of crime and deviance that blends streams of conflict theory, radical criminology, and discourse analysis. Building centrally on the work of Lacan (1977), they emphasize how an integrated postmodern criminology directs attention to how people battle over definitions of social reality—including the realities of crime and deviance—through language. Hegemonic groups, embedded in the economic power bases and supported ideologically through cultural systems of knowing, proffer languages of normalcy and deviancy in everyday life. In the process, they also position people as *normal* or *deviant* through systems of discourse. For example, hegemonic discourses about deviance created by the legal, medical, religious, and academic ways of knowing tend to explain crime by focusing on the essentialized characteristics of the "deviant" offenders themselves. To fully appreciate how deviance is not a state of natural behavior but a construction of discourse, postmodern sociologists of deviance are mindful of how people are positioned as subjects through power networks and are attributed deviant status through "discursive subject positions" (Arrigo and Bernard 1997, 42). An integrated postmodern analysis seeks to decenter subjects (Lacan 1977) in order to understand how discursive structures influence the manners by which they think, feel, and act in the deviance process. Arrigo and Bernard argue that subjects express their own sense of being decentered through deviant behavior by designing and articulating narratives of fear, desire, longing, and passion not normally permitted to them in discourse-proscribed subject positions.

Arrigo and Bernard might understand the transgression narrative in sport as a case study of subject decentering through illness and recovery. The patients with cancer discussed in this chapter were unfulfilled by the narrative scripts they were presented with by doctors and other medical experts. So, they actively decentered their positions as docile patients through embodied sport narratives of transgression. By running a long-distance race or playing a game of rugby, they demonstrated how they perceived the reality of their own body, and thereby they created an alternative discourse to illness. To these individuals, lying in a hospital bed or convalescing through recovery is an unwanted condition, as that embodied narrative does not capture who they really are. Equally, talking about illness from the perspective of a recovering patient serves only to legitimate the authority of medical discourses, as it is a deviant subject position that medical institutions manufacture. For patients the term *recovery* conjures images of a body at loss, and sickness is envisioned as a pathological state requiring remedy. As underlined in Frank's (1995) work, integrated postmodern analyses of illness might seek to unearth heretofore silenced ways of knowing illness through narrative and discourse.

Discussion Questions

1. A central premise in this chapter is that the ill or otherwise broken body is a potential stigma for an athlete. React to and discuss that central idea.
2. Using media sources at your disposal, locate and review a person's illness narrative in sport.
3. Explore the cause-driven athletic events in your community. What are the causes behind the events? Who participates in them, and why?

Recommended Readings

Armstrong, L. 2000. *It's not about the bike: My journey back to life.* New York: Berkley Trade.

> Armstrong's memoir of his public battle with and triumph over cancer is a recognized case of public illness and narrative work. His account is a prime example of how athletes' tales about beating illness and transgressing images of the patient with disability figure prominently in current discourses about the body and its normality.

Collinson, J. 2005. Emotions, interactions and the injured sporting body. *International Review for the Sociology of Sport* 402:221-40.

> Collinson's article on the injury process is an excellent example of how athletes' narrations of the emotional experience of body breakdown teach us to approach injury in nonmedical ways.

Couser, G. 2007. *Recovering bodies: Illness, disability, and life writing.* Madison, WI: University of Wisconsin Press.

> This book showcases people with illness or disability who challenge the stigmas attached to their conditions by telling their lives in their own ways and on their own terms. Discussing memoirs, diaries, collaborative narratives, photo documentaries, essays, and other forms of life writing, Couser shows that these works are not records of medical conditions; rather, they are a means for individuals to recover their bodies (or the bodies of loved ones).

Frank, A. 1995. *The wounded storyteller: Body, illness and ethics*. Chicago: University of Chicago Press.

> Frank's watershed analysis of how illness is constructed and mediated through discourse has influenced theories of the body in several academic fields. Frank questions the neglect of patients' ways of knowing and directing illness knowledge and thereby dislodges taken-for-granted assumptions about medical truths on the meaning of illness and recovery.

Smith, B., and A. Sparkes. 2005. Analyzing talk in qualitative inquiry: Exploring possibilities, problems, and tensions. *Quest* 57:213-42.

> This research article presents five ways in which people's narratives can be analyzed to better understand how life is discursively arranged. These methods include the analysis of conversation, the analysis of discourse, the analysis of the performance of narratives, the analysis of content, and the analysis of structure.

PART

Mediating Sport Deviance

The final set of chapters in this book addresses ways in which deviance within and outside of sport is covered by the media (i.e., mass-mediated) for audiences. Chapter 7 analyzes how, why, and when the criminal justice system has intervened into professional ice hockey over the past decade. The central theme of the chapter pertains to how professional leagues, despite sporadic challenge from the police and the courts, have maintained their overall authority to communicate and thus publicly define what is wanted or unwanted as violence in the sport. The case studies we include illustrate that, at least in ice hockey, there is little to suggest that even the most flamboyant acts of player violence will be viewed by media audiences as serious social problems worthy of criminalization. Chapter 8 presents a case study of how images of terrorism are increasingly infused into mass-mediated global sports events such as the Olympics. Here, we argue that globally popular and mediated sports events have become, in a post–September 11, 2001 world, major sites of hegemonic and counterhegemonic political work. We further contend that it is theoretically naive to assume that sports megaevents are ideologically pure or untouched by political games germinating far away from athletic fields.

Criminal Violence
in Sport

ATHLETES GONE WILD

Consider the following incidents occurring in four different sports in 2006:

- January: In the NCAA Gator Bowl football game between Virginia Tech and the University of Louisville, college junior Marcus Vick of Virginia deliberately cleated and stomped Louisville player Elvis Dumervil. In response, Vick was permanently released from the team. No legal action was taken.

- June: In one of the most tragic cases of on-field violence in recent memory, South African Rugby Union player Riann Loots of the Rawsonville Rugby Club was kicked in the head, while prostrate on the ground, by two members of the opposing Delicious Rugby Club during a league match. Loots died on the field and both of the accused players were immediately suspended from league play. No legal action was taken.

- July: As fans watched the FIFA World Cup final between France and Italy, they saw French superstar Zinedine Zidane maliciously head butt Italian defender Marco Materazzi in the chest, knocking him to the ground. Initial reports of the event alleged that Zidane's attack was a response to taunts from Materazzi regarding the French player's family. Zidane received a red card for the foul and was ejected from the remainder of the World Cup, thus ending an otherwise illustrious career in disgrace. Materazzi received a three-game suspension from FIFA for his on-field comments. No legal action was taken.

- August: Race car driver Paul Tracy of Canada was suspended and fined $25,000 U.S. for deliberately knocking French driver Sébastien Bourdais off course during the Denver Grand Prix. After the race, Tracy confronted Bourdais and challenged him to a fistfight. No legal action was taken.

Although seemingly disparate, these examples of athlete violence illustrate a controversial historical trend. With minor exceptions, sports organizations have successfully maintained their monopoly over dealing with violence occurring within their jurisdictions. They have kept the courts at arm's length, even when their players' conduct violated formal and informal codes of sport or the law of the land. In each of the summarized cases, it may be difficult to comprehend why the offenders were not criminally prosecuted in a court of law. However, as Dunning (1999) points out, even flagrant forms of violence in professional or amateur—and especially contact—sport tend to be controlled by sports organizations and treated as socially special. As sociologists, we find it intriguing to ask why.

These examples also indicate how malicious player–player violence is not restricted to one sport or level of sport but occurs in many sports. In his topographical review of violence in sport, Young (2002a) provides evidence that hyperviolence in sport might be more commonplace than we imagine. Blackshaw and Crabbe (2004) argue that sport violence is so diverse and ingrained across sporting cultures that no single sociological theory of deviance or crime can explain it all.

Yet within the broad area of criminological inquiry, on-field sport violence remains curiously understudied. Few scholars have empirically examined the ways in which criminal violence may be embedded in sport processes (Dunning 1999; Reasons 1992; Young 1993, 2002a, 2004a; Young and Wamsley 1996). While sociologists and criminologists attend to a wide range of rule-breaking behaviors, classifying them into conceptual categories like white-collar crimes, hate crimes, sex crimes, and race crimes, sport crimes and the instituted means of their control have not been taken seriously. Although the criminal activities of athletes away from the playing field, such as sexual assault, gambling, partner abuse, and murder, have received some research attention in recent years, criminologists have been curiously reluctant to interrogate violent behaviors occurring on the sports field as crimes worthy of scholarly attention.

We believe that a socially significant and sociologically fascinating opportunity is being missed here. Specifically, it is unfortunate that sociologists of deviance and crime rarely use sport violence to test their ideas and theories. While sociologists of sport deviance such as Blackshaw and Crabbe (2004) encourage us to venture away from traditional theoretical perspectives on sport deviance and violence, we find merit in exploring both traditional and contemporary theories of crime and deviance in the context of sport research. For instance, read the 10 questions on sport deviance highlighted here, and consider how theories of crime might help answer these questions.

Questions on Sport Deviance

1. Are there common definitions of unwanted violence in sport cultures, and, if so, how are they defined and promoted?

2. What are the institutional mechanisms for controlling violence in sport, and do they create a uniform understanding of acceptable and unacceptable behavior?

3. When, why, and by whom are social control responses in sports organizations initiated?

4. What are the rationales underlying control mechanisms in sports, and how is the effectiveness of the measures evaluated?

5. When is the criminal justice system involved in the regulation of sport violence, and which acts of violence receive criminal prosecution?

6. How have national or local courts responded to violence in sport, and what criminal punishments have been levied against players for on-field acts?

7. What are the social reactions to legal intervention into sport, and what are the outcomes of such reactions within leagues and games?

8. Are multi-institutional programs, including both formal and informal mechanisms for promoting safe play, possible for regulating sport violence?

9. Are there different experiences in the social control of violence between amateur and professional sports?

10. How injurious are particular sports, and to what extent are injury-producing behaviors protected within them?

In this chapter, we explore the prospects of using deviancy theory to explain sport as a social institution with a long-standing authority to define and control aggression and violence. Drawing on an extended case study of ice hockey violence in North America, we explain how sport operates as a total institution (Goffman 1961) that exercises its ability to establish law within games and to police fair play between participants. Examples are provided to question why there seems to be a reluctance to criminally prosecute athletes for on-field violence and why, when athletes are prosecuted, they are punished relatively lightly.

Rink Rage and Criminal Justice

On February 21, 2000, the Boston Bruins visited the Vancouver Canucks in a mid-season NHL contest. With only 2 minutes elapsed in the first period, longtime NHL enforcers—or *policemen* in the accepted vernacular of the sport—Marty McSorley (then age 37) of the Bruins and Donald Brashear (then age 28) of the Canucks clashed horns in a routine display of on-ice pugilism. As described by television broadcasters and affirmed by the Vancouver faithful in attendance, Brashear won the bout handily. Each player received a fighting major penalty of 5 minutes for the incident. On his way to the penalty box, Brashear taunted Bruins players by flexing his biceps. This rather typical ice hockey scenario raised little concern, and there was no indication from anyone involved (players, referees, coaches, or fans) that the fight would be a further source of strain within the game. But with 7 seconds left in an already rough first period, McSorley challenged Brashear to a rematch by cross-checking him. Brashear skated away indifferently and McSorley was sent to the penalty box once again, this time with a double minor penalty for roughing and cross-checking as well as a 10-minute penalty for unsportsmanlike conduct. During the ensuing power play (only 2 seconds later), Brashear crashed awkwardly into Boston goaltender Byron Dafoe during a skirmish in front of the Boston net. Dafoe writhed on the ice, clutching his right knee, and had to be carried from the ice on a stretcher. Referee Brad Watson assessed a 2-minute penalty against Brashear for goaltender interference.

For the rest of the game, McSorley tried to goad Brashear into another fight—partly to seek redemption for his earlier loss and partly to avenge the collision with Dafoe. In the dying seconds of the game, and with the Canucks leading 5 to 2, Brashear and McSorley found themselves on the ice for one last shift. With less than 12 seconds remaining in the final period, McSorley skated out of his team's end of the rink and approached Brashear, who had his back turned. McSorley reached Brashear just inside the Canucks' blue line and clipped him from behind with a two-handed stick slash to the right temple.

Brashear tumbled backward to the ice, unconscious. His head bounced on the ice, and blood poured from his nose. He lay prone and motionless, save for the periodic twitching of his feet and rolling of his eyes. The Canucks' team doctor, Rui Avelar, later testified that Brashear was having a seizure by the time he reached the player. Avelar also confirmed that Brashear had experienced a grade III concussion from the stick's blow. The Canucks' trainers worked on Brashear at midice for more than 10 minutes and eventually removed him from the ice on a stretcher. The hit prompted Vancouver goalkeeper Garth Snow to physically charge McSorley, but referee Brad Watson thwarted the attempt and terminated the game. Fans pelted McSorley with various missiles as the players left the rink and returned to their respective dressing rooms. After the incident, McSorley was assessed a match penalty for attempting to injure and a penalty for game misconduct.

In response to an unprecedented public outcry for stern reprimand by the league, the NHL (led by President Gary Bettman and Executive Vice President Colin Campbell) suspended McSorley indefinitely on March 22, 2000. One day later, the NHL further admonished McSorley by suspending him for the Bruins' remaining 23 games of the 1999-2000 season, costing him more than (CDN) $100,000 in lost wages. As this was the longest suspension for an on-ice incident in league history, the NHL believed the penalty would deter future violence and send out the message that such flagrantly dangerous stickwork was unacceptable. With Brashear returning to the game before the end of the 1999-2000 season, the case appeared to be closed.

However, a Vancouver police sergeant on duty at the February game filed a report about the incident and recommended that the Crown Prosecutors Office in Vancouver charge McSorley with criminal assault. It had been 12 years since the 1988 criminal charge against NHL player Dino Ciccarelli of the Minnesota North Stars for an on-ice stick incident with Luke Richardson of the Toronto Maple Leafs. Ciccarelli was arrested 2 days after the incident and found guilty of assault. At that time, Ontario Provincial Court Justice Sidney Harris cited the need to convey a message to the NHL that "violence in a hockey game or in any other circumstance is not acceptable in our society" (*R v. Ciccarelli* 1988). Harris sentenced Ciccarelli to 1 day in jail and levied a (CDN) $1,000 fine against him. At that point, Ciccarelli became the only NHL player to serve jail time for an on-ice attack. Ironically, however, Toronto police reported that Ciccarelli spent a total of 2 hours in his cell; he was otherwise occupied signing autographs for police officers and hockey fans (Young and Wamsley 1996).

As with all criminal cases that reach the courts, the incident between McSorley and Brashear needs to be seen in context. It occurred only a few years after a widely reported example of player–referee violence in Canadian university ice hockey. On February 24, 1996, at the end of an overtime period in a championship game between the Université de Moncton and the University of Prince Edward Island (UPEI), chief referee Brian Carragher was pinned to the boards and assaulted by eight players from the Université de Moncton. The incident occurred after a controversial goal ended the hockey game in UPEI's favor. Moncton goaltender Pierre Gagnon initiated the assault by grabbing Carragher. Gagnon's assistant coach, Patrick Daviault, and several other players joined in the attack by throwing punches at the referee. Carragher was repeatedly punched in the head and body by the Moncton players and was speared in the groin with a stick. Eventually, Daviault removed a metal mooring from the net and threw it into a pane of glass in front of the goal judge, shattering the glass. Four players from the Moncton team were suspended from intercollegiate competition (their suspensions ranged from 1-5 years), and Daviault received a 1-year suspension. Although police and Crown prosecutors in Charlottetown, Prince Edward Island, initially threatened criminal intervention into the sport in response to the event, none ever materialized.

Two years later, Jesse "The Bull" Boulerice of the Plymouth Whalers in the Ontario Hockey League (OHL) swung his stick at Andrew Long of the Guelph Storm. The blow lacerated Long's face (which required 20 stitches to close), fractured his skull, and produced a blood spot on his brain. Boulerice was suspended for the entire 1998-99 season by the OHL and charged with felony assault by the Detroit police. The charge, which carried a potential 10-year prison sentence, shocked amateur and professional hockey cultures in North America. Boulerice pled no contest to the charge (which is not, in legal terms, an admission of guilt) and received a 9-month suspended sentence from a Detroit county court. The charge is now expunged from his record, and Boulerice has played for a number of other NHL teams. However, as one of the many recidivist offenders in the NHL and a clear example that the league does not have violence under control, Boulerice, now with the Philadelphia Flyers, was suspended for 25 games by the NHL in October 2007 and placed on waivers by his club for yet another vicious incident, this time involving Canucks' player Ryan Kesler.

In the wake of the Université de Moncton and Boulerice incidents, and following considerable resistance from NHL officials, executives, players, and coaches (and indeed many sports fans), Vancouver Crown Prosecutor Michael Hicks filed charges of assault with a weapon against McSorley on March 7, 2000. On September 25, McSorley (represented by legal counsel William Smart) appeared before the Provincial Court of British Columbia to face the charge. In a sport drama that would last 5 days, Marty McSorley, the NHL, and violence in professional ice hockey stood on trial. As a set of court proceedings that attracted an international audience, the trial brought to the fore issues of player violence, player consent to sport violence, and the role of the authorities in governing sport violence. It also led to the asking of questions familiar to professional sport: Do certain acts of player violence constitute criminal behavior, and are there criminal victims in sport?

On October 6th, 2000, McSorley was found guilty of assaulting Brashear with a weapon under section 267(2) of the *Criminal Code of Canada*. Justice William Kitchen sentenced McSorley to an 18-month conditional discharge (essentially probation) and ordered that he not play in any future NHL games involving Brashear. McSorley does not have a criminal record as a result of the decision, and thus he has no difficulty crossing international borders. Prosecuting attorney Michael Hicks later commented that the act was "not a risk the community can accept as within the normal bounds of an NHL game." As the primary defense in the case, Smart argued that NHL players give explicit consent to the risk of such on-ice contact and that McSorley hit Brashear's head as an accident rather than as a premeditated assault. Although Justice Kitchen was not convinced that an accident had occurred, McSorley's 18-month discharge was clearly more lenient than the year-and-a-half imprisonment allowable under Canadian law.

McSorley's slash to Brashear's head was a scene played, and replayed, on international sport television for some time. The incident and its legal outcomes stirred public emotion about the place of ice hockey in North American culture and the social effects of hockey violence. For instance, the March 6, 2000 edition of Canada's *MacLean's Magazine* provocatively referred to ice hockey as a *blood sport*. When examined from every angle, debated by sport pundits, and dissected from a multitude of theoretical points of view, the incident underlined what many hockey fans have known for quite some time: Illegal stickwork and other forms of player violence in the NHL are simply not under control. And equally contested was the wider social utility of the McSorley trial and the issue of whether or not the criminal justice system should have a mandate to control player violence in ice hockey or in sport in general.

Although earlier episodes of NHL violence had also led to criminal charges (Young and Wamsley 1996), the incident between McSorley and Brashear arguably was a turning point in the history of professional ice hockey. A clear and final message had been delivered to the sport to clean up the game or risk further legal intervention. Yet only 4 years later, on March 8, 2004, another flamboyant case of on-ice violence took place during an NHL game in Vancouver. The event would once again illustrate the ability of sport to resist serious criminal intervention.

During a late-season contest, Todd Bertuzzi of the Vancouver Canucks grabbed Steve Moore of the Colorado Avalanche and punched him in the back of the head in the third period of the game. Bertuzzi viciously struck Moore just underneath his helmet and forced him face-first into the ice. Bertuzzi landed on top of Moore and continued to strike punches against his head as he laid semiconscious on the ice. Avalanche teammates piled on top of both players, resulting in an on-ice brawl between the two teams. Moore ended up with two cracked vertebrae, a concussion, and several lacerations as a result of the attack. The NHL immediately suspended Bertuzzi for the 2003-04 season but reinstated him on August 8, 2005. Bertuzzi was charged with common assault by the Provincial Crown in British Columbia, and he pled no contest and eventually received 1 year of probation. Steve Moore has yet to return to professional ice hockey. He filed a civil suit for $20 million U.S. against Bertuzzi and the Vancouver Canucks in the United States, but the case was dismissed by a Colorado court before going to trial. Apparently the parties involved reached a publicly undisclosed settlement outside of court.

Problems clearly arise, as the McSorley and Bertuzzi incidents teach us, when an organization like the NHL is granted carte blanche for determining and policing social policy in a particular sport and the criminal justice system approaches violence in the sport with a laissez-faire mentality. Arguably, objectivity in evaluating the effectiveness of in-house policy for curbing unwanted violence is obfuscated by tradition, rationalized forms of play, and popular sentiments about appropriate player behavior within the game. Despite more than a century of debate concerning violence in ice hockey, relatively little has been done to systematically identify, target, and rectify through multi-institutional means the more serious forms of violence in the game. Despite recent and historical evidence suggesting that even unwanted and serious forms of violence are products of deeply revered socialization processes in the game (Atkinson 2003), insiders and supporters of the standard version of hockey (a tough, hard-checking, fast, and scrappy style of play) have resisted structural changes in the sport. The pervasive mentality in the culture of ice hockey (especially in North America) is to prepare young players for violence in the sport by lowering the age at which they are introduced to rough physical play, such as body-checking.

An important sociological question is how organizations like the NHL achieve hegemony in defining and policing violence. Stated differently, how do ice hockey organizations, despite sporadic cultural critique or challenge by insiders and outsiders, maintain their positions as the public definers of deviance in the game?

Managing Hockey Deviance as a Total Institution

In most societies, there are certain groups that can be categorized as all-encompassing socializing agents. Each group member is bound by a code of behavior, socializes mainly with other members of the group, and is subject to constant monitoring and ideological training by authority figures and group leaders. Groups such as the military branches, religious sects, psychiatric hospitals, and private schools are all examples of social settings in which, upon entry, individuals are resocialized to adopt master statuses of, respectively, solider, convert, patient, or student. In his landmark text, *Asylums,* Goffman (1961, 15) describes such institutions in the following way:

> Every institution captures something of the time and interest of its members and provides something of a world for them; in brief, every institution has encompassing tendencies. When we review the different institutions in our Western society, we find some that are encompassing to a degree discontinuously greater than the ones next in line. Their encompassing or total character is symbolized by the barrier to social intercourse with the outside and to departure that is often built right into the physical plant, such as locked doors, high walls, barbed wire, cliffs, water, forests, or moors. These establishments I am calling *total institutions.*

Goffman (1961, 15-16) identifies five types of total institutions in his classification: (1) those established to care for incapable and harmless persons (e.g., an orphanage), (2) those established to care for incapable and vulnerable persons (e.g., psychiatric institutions), (3) those organized to protect the community against what are felt to be intentional dangers (e.g., prisons), (4) those established to pursue worklike tasks and who justify themselves only on these instrumental grounds (e.g., the military), and (5) those established as retreats from the world (e.g., monasteries).

Goffman's (1961) fourth and fifth types of total institution reflect on life within sports leagues such as the NHL in which microepisodes such as the McSorley and Bertuzzi incidents occur. The application of Goffman's fourth category is easy to see because learning and playing the role of hockey pugilist obviously relates to work, pay, and reputation.

Although Goffman intended his fifth category to represent an ascetically oriented refuge such as a monastery, it might be argued that sports allow for a certain type of retreat from the banality of modern life. As discussed in chapters 1 and 4, figurationalists such as Elias and Dunning (1986) would argue that sport, as a social institution, serves a mimetic function. As such, sports organizations like the NHL possess a taken-for-granted license to create, through the show-casing of violence as part of sport, a retreat from the mundane or predictable world of everyday life, in which acts of physical aggression and the harming of others are normally prohibited.

A close inspection of a sport such as ice hockey reveals the power of sports organizations as total institutions. Thinking sociologically about how definitions of acceptable, wanted, unwanted, and even criminal violence are created in ice hockey, consider the following discussion on how ice hockey (and other) sports organizations manufacture consent to their ideologies and expectations of violence (see figure 7.1). First, as a total institution, ice hockey creates a culture of ideological insularity regarding violence in the sport. This culture is underpinned by a historical ethos of traditional masculinity and aggression. Second, discursive strategies are deployed within the sport in order to publicly frame game violence as noncriminal and socially unthreatening. As such, the violence is tolerable. Third, legal intervention into the sport fails to challenge the hegemony of ice hockey organizations as the definers of deviance and instead reaffirms the authority of the leagues as primary definers. Finally, despite initial public criticism of dangerous and injurious incidents, the mere appearance of responsible stewardship by the leagues and clubs toward offending players serves to dilute public reaction and to galvanize aspects of violence as in some way understandable, or even *wanted*. This in turn further underscores the ability of such bodies to responsibly police themselves.

Gendered Cultures of Insularity in Ice Hockey

For as long as sociologists have inspected the cultural settings that give rise to and provide meaning for sporting practices, gender ideologies, particularly codes of masculinity, have been linked to the performance of athletics. Indeed, there are few other social institutions that have been as extensively probed for their gender trappings (Messner, Hunt, and Dunbar 1999). From the historical analysis of muscular Christianity to the discussion of young men's dominance bonding to the examination of pain and injury processes in competition to the recent contestation of masculine identities through sport, researchers have explained the contextual contingencies underpinning how athletes and sport audiences reproduce gendered codes and values.

Sociologists of sport deviance are rather unique in their empirical investigations of masculinity and its relationship to violence in the spare-time spectrum. Feminist and profeminist research on gender illustrates how interrogations of masculinity begin by acknowledging that hegemonic forms of masculinity characterize most sport institutions (McKay, Messner, and Sabo 2000). Hegemonic masculinity is a conceptually ideal-type gender status in patriarchal cultures. Through complex ideological and discursive frames that produce systems of socialization and institutional support, the hegemonic brand of masculinity establishes, enforces, and legitimates the ascribed authority of a particular kind of male figure. Donaldson (1993, 645-646) describes hegemonic masculinity in the following way:

> It is the common sense about breadwinning and manhood. It is exclusive, anxiety-provoking, internally and hierarchically differentiated, brutal, and violent. It is pseudo-natural, tough, contradictory, crisis-prone, rich, and socially sustained. While centrally connected with the institutions of male dominance, not all men practice it, though most men benefit from it. . . . It is a lived experience, and an economic and cultural force, and dependent on social arrangements. It is constructed through difficult negotiation over a lifetime. Fragile it may be, but it constructs the most dangerous things we live with.

Hegemonic masculinity is a privileging cultural status for many athletic men, as it constructs the normative male identity as one exuding strength, courage, dominance, emotional detachment, and social power and authority. Connell (1995) agrees that most sociological investigations of maleness recognize hegemonic masculinity as the cultural barometer by which all men's gender performances are measured and organized.

Sociological research on men in sport highlights the constitutive social processes involved in intextuating (de Certeau 1984) hegemonic masculinity into cultural practice (see McKay, Messner, and Sabo 2000). As Burstyn (1999) notes, possessing hegemonic masculinity in sport not only is rationalized as integral for winning contests but also is used as a signifier of men's ability to exert social dominance. In plain terms, the stark lesson derived from sport—which is often labeled as *character building* (Miracle and Rees 1994)—is that to be the acceptably masculine man is to be the successful and socially revered man. However, increasing numbers of sociologists of sport such as Burstyn (1999) and Whannel (2002) recognize that not all men can attain or maintain the ideal masculine status within the total institution of sport—that is, most men, including many ice hockey players, are gender deviants when it comes to living up to hegemonic standards. According to writers such as Colburn (1985) and Robidoux (2001), this fact is nowhere more socially obvious than it is in ice hockey cultures, where masculinity in its hegemonic form is both subculturally valued and commercially showcased.

Building on these concerns, White and Young (1997, 1999) describe hegemonic masculinity as a dangerous cultural ideal in sport contexts. They argue that a majority of the player violence and aggression in contact sports is attributable to athletes' overindulgence in hegemonic ideologies of masculinity that are learned as part of the total institution process. Using extended case examples of the physical, emotional, and psychological risks to athletes created by the link between sport and masculinity, White and Young (1999) expose how many male athletes, especially in violent or contact sports, are regularly victimized.

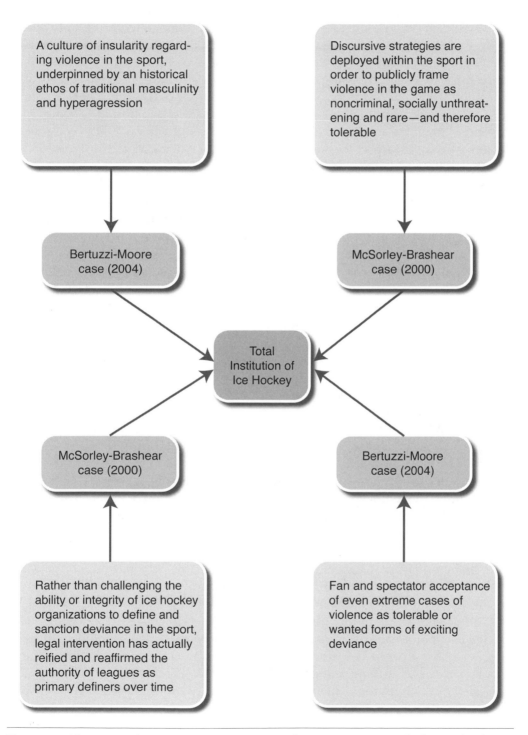

Figure 7.1 The power of a sports organization to manufacture consent to its ideologies of violence.

Rather than privileging male athletes, the acceptance and performance of the hegemonic ideal of masculinity endangers them, as it places men in contexts where physical injury and social marginalization are common.

Ehrenreich (1997) contends that the link between dangerous masculinity and player violence is at its strongest in sport. Although there are clearly other factors pertinent to the emergence of unsanctioned player violence, research on football, soccer, basketball, and boxing demonstrates how subcultural constructions of masculinity are among the major causes of player violence (Dunning 1999; Young 2000). The pursuit of dangerous masculinities leads athletes to treat their bodies as weapons, to utilize aggressive and illegal tactics in competition, and to ostracize others who fail to respect the norms of violence and risk taking tacitly embedded in sport cultures (Messner 1990; Messner and Sabo 1994; Young and White 1997).

Weinstein, Smith, and Weisenthal (1995) argue that a gender code of masculinity teaches young and veteran men in ice hockey a set of normative standards that excuse even the most excessive player behavior. The masculine ethos underpinning the sport is all encompassing, teaching young hockey players to frame most sport experiences along gender lines. Using Goffman's (1961) total institution metaphor, we can start to appreciate how ideologies of masculinity in sports like ice hockey frame violence as an instrumental work task and a gender-appropriate behavior. In this way, violence is also reconcilable in relation to the mythic, hegemonic, and dangerous masculine ideologies underpinning the sport's culture (Gruneau and Whitson 1993).

Victimological perspectives on sport (Faulkner 1973; Young 1991, 1993, 2002a; Young and Reasons 1989) indicate that since most forms of vicious player violence are subculturally accepted by players, tolerated by fans, and commercially lucrative for leagues, little concern has been given to athletes who are emotionally, psychologically, or physically harmed by such behavior. Given Goffman's (1961) description of total institutions, it makes sense that players would not consider violence in the sport as criminal, since they have been deeply socialized to believe precisely the opposite. But, in taking a workers' advocacy perspective, Young (1991, 2002a) builds on Smith's (1983) typology and extends his conceptualization of violence by arguing that athletes do not relinquish their civil rights while on the field, regardless of their acquiescence to dangerous masculine ideologies of hyperviolent play. Young suggests that since athletes are not only asked but also instructionally encouraged, as members of teams, leagues, and workplaces, to participate in contranormative player–player violence, we must be attentive to the ways in which dangerous masculinities become institutionally regulated doctrines (Pascall and White 2000).

To this end, many of the men involved in professional ice hockey disavow *victim* as a potential masculine identity within the game. The professional ice hockey player lives in a context of hypermasculinity, and the very nature of the sport (i.e., that including fistfights, brutal body checks, and other violence) is chiseled out of hyperbolic masculine stereotypes. Among these stereotypes is the notion that a man does not cry, whine, wince, complain, or back down in the face of a physical challenge. As Faulkner (1973), Smith (1983), and Barnes (1988) note, the dangerous masculine culture of professional ice hockey flatly eschews discourses of victimization, preferring to reframe on-ice physicality as character building, toughening, sacrifice, or dedication. Since ice hockey players and their fans often view players as warriors or iron men, the image of the professional ice hockey player as a victim of (criminal) violence is simply incongruent with cultural interpretations of the game (Gruneau and Whitson 1993).

Explanations of player violence offered by coaches, league executives, and broadcasters equally support dangerous masculine practices in ice hockey and restrict the possibility of players being considered as victims of violence (Young 1990). As part of framing ice hockey as an entertainment spectacle worthy of audience consumption, the exaltation of dangerous masculinity establishes a cultural condition in which players are valorized for their consent to physical hurt or victimization. Players are viewed as heroes or weaklings, superstars or wimps, aggressors or losers, and men or sissies, depending on their ability to be a ruggedly masculine player. Conforming to the codes of dangerous masculinity can be informally rewarded within teams through salary and contract incentives, praise, and other forms of preferential treatment (Weinstein, Smith, and Wiesenthal 1995). Similarly, fans and media broadcasters draw attention to the toughness and durability of the masculine or violent player and his ability to withstand ongoing victimization, often mythologizing tough players of the past as masculine legends. Such legends include Gordie Howe, Bobby Orr, Maurice Richard, and Dave "Tiger" Williams (Young 1990). Legal and illegal body checks, fistfights, and injuries are showcased on sport shows—often in segments dedicated to Plays of the Day. At the same time, social reaction to and support for violence in the game creates significant barriers for those athletes holding alternative views on tolerating violence and risk within the game (Young 1993; Young and White 1997).

In brief, a considerable volume of research shows that attitudes and discourses about victimization in professional ice hockey crystallize around a series of interpretive masculine standpoints promoted within a system of totalizing institutional networks. Within such a setting, players, coaches, and league administrators (from team owners to on-ice officials) understand that even excessive violence is part of an acceptable masculine code of toughness within the game.

Neutralizing Ice Hockey Violence

While codes of masculinity learned within ice hockey might serve as an ideological foundation for violence and aggression within the game, critics of hockey and other sports have argued that using a particular brand of masculinity as an excuse for waging violence is not a proverbial *Get Out of Jail Free* card. Nearly a century of research on urban gangs and street crime illustrates that commitment to a subcultural street code of masculine toughness is not a viable excuse for criminal behavior in the eyes of the law (Tanner 2001). How else, then, is violence allowed to endure as a cornerstone of sport?

Likened to the military and other total institutions in which violence is tightly policed in-house, professional ice hockey is based on a system of self-regulation (Horrow 1980). Much of the work involved in keeping the state out of professional hockey relates to a discursive game that NHL insiders play through the media. In postmodern and poststructural analyses of how power works, theorists like Foucault (1977, 1979) call our attention to how the people who are able to control systems of language and representation hold significant power in defining what constitutes right and wrong. In Stebbins' (1996) terms, those 'in control' of leagues provide the language and systems of interpretation for understanding even extreme violence as tolerable difference. The task for the NHL (as well as other ice hockey bodies) as a total institution is to use mass-mediated discourses to convince groups outside of the sport that only its members truly understand how to identify and punish a deviant act of violence in the game.

To this end, insiders strategically reject the viewpoints of others as misinformed. For figurational sociologists, a cultural battle between the NHL *established* and the police and state *outsiders* emerges. Spurred by the arrests of both Marty McSorley and Todd Bertuzzi, rhetoric from NHL players and coaches emphasizes, for example, how outsider interventions by the criminal justice system are unwarranted and unfair. Many NHL players are curious as to why the state deems it necessary to isolate hockey violence and to subvert the institutional control mechanisms in place within the league. Often questioning the *bleeding heart* and liberal mentalities of the criminal justice system, proponents of ice hockey violence reject such interventions. Regarding the case of the Crown prosecution of McSorley, one fan states,

> The law should not be getting involved in sporting events. The leagues should police their own as far as what happens in the context of their sport. In the McSorley case, he did strike another player with a stick. However, this happens many times during the game, just not normally to the head. Will the police prosecute every player when they commit a slash to another player or just slashes to the head? What about one to the arm that breaks a wrist? McSorley was wrong for what he did, but in the real world, after all the judicial posturing and attorneys' fees, he would receive probation. The NHL has already punished him worse, with lost wages while being suspended.
>
> (SI.com 2007)

A media pundit also added,

> NHL officials also decry the state's intervention as illegitimate and myopic, claiming that the courts have no justification to usurp the authority of the league. As Brian Burke, general manager of Brashear's team the Vancouver Canucks (and former NHL executive in charge of league suspensions), noted sarcastically, "Leave this stuff on the ice. Leave it to the NHL. We don't need the Vancouver police department or the RCMP (Royal Canadian Mounted Police) involved in this. . . . If we let them control this, what's next, charging guys for flagrant elbows?"
>
> (Kupelian 2000)

Research in the sociology of deviance leads us to anticipate that the power elite of the NHL draw on techniques of neutralization (Sykes and Matza 1957) to maintain their hegemony to police player–player violence. Challenges from outsiders are deemed alarmist, misdirected, and unfair, and players, officials, and league executives utilize the media to deny serious injury in any on-ice attack, to deny the existence of victims in hockey, to condemn the condemners of violence in ice hockey, and to appeal to higher loyalties regarding the sanctity of the sport. For instance, in a public comment about the 2004 arrest of Hamilton Bulldogs player Alexandre Perezhogin, the president of the American Hockey League (AHL), David Andrews, noted the following:

> Stafford [the victim] was clearly a contributing factor to the incident, but the reaction of Perezhogin was indefensible in terms of both its nature and its real and potential consequences. Mr. Perezhogin has expressed serious remorse over this incident. . . . The severity of the injury to Garrett Stafford, while serious, is not as extensive as previously reported. . . . It's the potential impact of suspensions on professional players of this calibre and at this stage of their careers that must be taken into consideration.
>
> (Canadian Press May 2004)

Notice how Andrews negates the victim and appeals to the higher loyalties of fans to protect Perezhogin's future in the sport. Self-proclaimed ice hockey fan Carl posted the following response to the arrest of Todd Bertuzzi on www.cnnsi.com in June of 2004. Its own techniques of neutralization are not difficult to see:

> This is stupid . . . if Moore would have just taken the beating he was supposed to get then he would not have himself up in the hospital with a broken neck. Bertuzzi was doing something to get back at him for getting his friend and line-mate Naslund. I bet one thing will come of this—Steve Moore will think twice about going after a star player again and maybe if the league had suspended Moore for the hit it wouldn't have come to this and Bertuzzi wouldn't have lost it on the ice. As far as a criminal investigation goes then why don't we investigate every slash, every high-stick that's assault . . . he didn't use a weapon, it was his fist, and the guy didn't die . . . just get over it and let Bertuzzi play.
>
> (SI.com 2004)

Since ice hockey is a culturally revered sport in Canada (in fact, it is the country's national winter sport) and at the same time occupies a precarious position in most American markets, leagues such as the NHL must publicly, in cases where the culture of the sport is questioned, enhance group charisma and deflect group disgrace. With regard to his model of a pronoun-based sociology, Elias (1971) might argue that a positive definition of the *we* (i.e., players, fans, leagues, and officials) institutional identity in ice hockey must be reestablished when players are arrested for on-ice violence; otherwise, the sport may be penetrated by *they* outsiders such as police or courts. In order to accomplish this, *we* insiders in ice hockey seek, in very patterned ways, to deploy insider definitions of violence to maintain a sense of league charisma.

Perhaps the most dominant term used to frame ice hockey violence is *the code* (Robidoux 2001). Conjuring up storybook images of chivalrous knights loyal to cultures of honor and justice, *the code* is used by hockey insiders to frame how violence (even forms violating the official rules of the game) should be respected as an ideology shared among warriors. Adherence to the code sets ice hockey players apart and establishes them as a unique group. As in the military, civilian standards of behavior and the legal systems designed to enforce them are deemed unsuitable in contact sports like ice hockey. In discourses suggesting that Bertuzzi's attack on Moore did not significantly violate the code of accepted violence, NHL players and executives claimed themselves to be the most appropriate judges and juries of violence within the game—not the Crown prosecutors of British Columbia. In the words of Gary Bettman, president of the NHL,

> I think ultimately we'll be judged on our response and the message that it sends. The message that's being sent is this is not a part of our game, it has no place in our game, and it will not be tolerated in our game. From our standpoint, as a sovereign league, we had an appropriate response and we're disappointed the Crown chose to move forward.

> (McElhenny 2000, D3)

Bettman's repeated use of the term *our* is interesting. As a long-standing defense in criminal trials involving on-ice assaults (e.g., *R v. Maki* 1970; *R v. Watson* 1975; *R v. Ciccarelli* 1988; *R v. McSorley* 2000), discourses promoting in-house policing have been successfully utilized by professional sports leagues like the NHL to keep their players out of the criminal justice system. Since outsiders are believed to be uninformed regarding subcultural codes of behavior occurring during a typical game, they are unable to evaluate the intentions underlying acts of violence or the ways in which players experience violence. This is partly achieved by the league using its own terms and categories to frame how we culturally view the problem of violence in the sport.

The hegemony of the NHL is further rationalized on the premise that players will only respect or acknowledge punishment if it is administered by persons familiar with the code. In this discursive strategy, contemporary or legendary hockey icons act as talking heads for the leagues to promote a "We know best" perspective. For example, in an obvious show of support for McSorley, NHL veteran brawler and former player for the Toronto Maple Leafs Tie Domi noted, "I think it's a shame that he [McSorley] was found guilty and I still can't believe he was found guilty. . . . It's absolutely disgusting" (McElhenny 2000, D3).

Clearly, the NHL and other hockey leagues have a strategic goal in claiming ownership over violence problems. Their selective acknowledgment and treatment of violence may be seen as a technique in controlling how to identify and maintain institutional power over player behavior. In the case of the McSorley incident, NHL president Gary Bettman issued statements for both the preliminary assault and the subsequent trial, reinforcing the league's position that certain forms of brutal contact are natural in ice hockey and that the NHL will rigorously police them:

The court today said that its focus was solely on the charge against Mr. McSorley. This was not a trial of the game or the NHL. Clearly, this incident was not representative of NHL hockey or NHL players. While the court's decision today brings closure to this aspect of the incident, it does not alter our position that we will continue to punish severely acts of inappropriate conduct in *our* game.

(Canadian Press 2000b, A4)

McSorley's lawyer, William Smart, added,

If the public doesn't like the slashes, checks and hits common in the league, there are other means to try to change that activity than in a court of law. . . . If that is going to be considered criminal conduct, there aren't enough courtrooms in the country to prosecute all the cases.

(Lewis 2001, E2)

NHL executive and Director of Hockey Operations Colin Campbell offered the following comments on the arrest of Todd Bertuzzi:

It wasn't about whether it should be two games, four games, five games. We felt [Bertuzzi] had given up his right to perform the rest of the season. We had to address the fact should it be the playoffs; shall it be one round, shall it be two rounds? In our opinion, because of the act, because of the injury to the player, because of a number of factors and criteria, we felt that his right to perform the rest of the season, he had to give that up and we have the ultimate right to take that away from him. . . . I don't think [violence] is a problem today in the year 2004, like it might have been in the 1970's and 1980's.

(NHL 2007)

Players and fans alike were clearly willing to fall back on familiar arguments that a core group of NHL policemen could effectively handle on-ice offenders. Using an eye-for-an-eye philosophy, the predominant view was that flagrant violations of the code encourage equally flagrant reactions. Built on perspectives of explicit consent to violence surrounding the game is the understanding that violence begets violence in the total institution. The fact that avid ice hockey fans accept this view illustrates that a total institution is able to extend its ideologies into the public sphere. In response to the arrests of McSorley, Bertuzzi, and Perezhogin, Canadian ice hockey fans frequently indicated such sentiments publicly. Ice hockey fan Matt noted the following about the Perezhogin arrest:

Violence has always been a part of professional hockey and it is not fair to prosecute athletes that may be too violent because the league has the authority to punish these players. Players realize the risks that are in hockey and have such high intensity to compete that there will always be an occasional situation that comes up. However, the fans love violence, players need the freedom to vent frustration, and we don't want laws that will change the face of the game to the point where hockey is no longer hockey. They've (CHA) done a ton to promote safe play in hockey over the last 5 years, so what's the problem? What more can they do? And after all, this is a game for MEN.

(www.fac.cord.edu/pe/)

Through such discourses, the focus in public debates shifted away from the most central figures of the events—Donald Brashear, Steve Moore, and Garret Stafford. Quite tellingly, Brashear's and Moore's initial outcries for harsh punishment quickly gave way to statements of acceptance and avoidance. Justice Kitchen included the following statement as part of the decision in *R v. McSorley* (2000): "My conclusion is that Mr. Brashear simply wants to forget this matter. . . . What this court does seems almost irrelevant to him." With perhaps the exception of the Steve Moore case, the injuries of the players were downplayed in the press, and their experiences with recovery were ignored. As time passed, they were increasingly described as complicit in their own victimization.

The silencing of victims' stories in the press and the lack of attention given to their experiences signifies the power of the total institution to depersonalize and deflect violence. For example, both Brashear and Moore came to be vilified in media accounts. While Sykes and Matza (1957) recognize that victims may be denied in the process of managing deviance, another of their techniques of neutralization—condemning the condemners, or blaming the victims—is also relevant here. In the world of professional ice hockey, blaming the victim is a common technique used by defenders of violence in the game. They use this technique on at least two levels.

First, questions about victims' credibility and innocence are raised. For example, amid the media reports of McSorley's status as the third most penalized player in NHL history arose an emphasis on Brashear's familiarity with dangerously violent play:

> Well, I suppose if this case we're to find McSorley responsible for assault, then the least the Vancouver Police should do is charge Brashear with the same criminal act. If memory serves me right, did he not as well punch McSorley and at least one other player in the same game? If I were to walk down the street and hit an individual, they could have me charged, would they not? So why are there double standards here? This whole case is a disgusting waste of public money, time, and intelligence. I would bet the attending officers at the game would not have laid charges if the tables were turned, McSorley the "goonee" and Brashear the "gooner."
>
> (Robert, hockey fan, CBC.ca 2007)

By assembling an image of Brashear as a thuggish lout well acquainted with injuring others, journalists did little to engender sympathy for the player in ensuing public debates. Further, by discussing the NHL's efforts to correct Brashear's recidivism throughout the years, league officials endeavored to showcase their sensitivity to issues of player violence. In placing Brashear's history with the NHL's legal system in the limelight, league officials strategically identified him (along with McSorley) as a problem offender. Garfinkel (1967) might refer to this strategy as a *degradation ceremony*, a ceremony in which the victim's character is publicly dismantled, leaving him disgraced in front of others. A common technique in most total institutions (Goffman 1961) is to degrade problem inmates and pathologize them as isolated offenders who are atypical of the wider culture of the setting. Compounding Brashear's violent background, many people blamed him for wearing his helmet's chin strap too loosely, thereby preventing his equipment from functioning properly. The suggestion was that his recklessness toward the protection of his own head was a mitigating factor in his injury (i.e., he would not have been injured if he had shown due care toward his own body):

> What Marty did was wrong, no doubt about it. Part of being a professional is keeping your emotions in check at times of extreme stress. Marty was embarrassed due to actions of Brashear after a fight that took place earlier in the game. While I don't believe for a moment that Brashear's actions deserved a vicious blow to the head, he expressed an attitude that is rampant among professional athletes. Lack of respect for "the code" expressed by Brashear played a major role in his getting injured. In addition, had he had his helmet on properly the extent of the injury would have been far less severe.
>
> (Jamie, hockey fan, SI.com 2007)

Moreover, both Brashear's and Moore's characters were scrutinized in public debates. Since Brashear exhibited reluctance to grapple with McSorley for a second time during the February 21 contest and since he had taunted McSorley by dusting off his hands and by taunting the Bruins team following the first fight in the game, his status as an NHL enforcer seemingly conflicted with his actions. Don Cherry, former Boston Bruins coach and host of the immensely popular Canadian Broadcasting Corporation's Hockey Night in Canada intermission segment *Coach's Corner*, reflected on this matter on February 26, 2000: "I'll tell you why it happened . . . he [Brashear] ridiculed an old warrior, an old warrior. . . . You should never ridicule and humiliate a warrior. . . . You play with the bull, and you're gonna get the horns." Essentially, in not permitting his opponent an opportunity for redemption, Brashear violated a fundamental rule within the enforcer code. Brashear's action became described as disrespectful and even cowardly among those in the know about NHL violence. Testimony offered during the McSorley trial by NHL linesman Michael Cvik described Brashear's flouting of violence etiquette and its situational effect on McSorley:

> The two players came together and we go in to try to separate them and as we're trying to separate them, Donald is trying to break away because he doesn't want to become involved [in another fight] at that point. Then we're trying to break them up and we can't because Marty has a hold of Donald's sweater, and Marty says to Donald, "Come on, Don, you have to fight me

again." And Don says, "No Marty, I'm not going to fight you. We're beating you four-nothing. . . ." And at that point, we still can't get them broken apart so I looked at Marty and I said, "Marty, let go of him or I'm going to assess you a misconduct." And at that point, I guess Marty clued in. I was talking to him, he turned to me and he looked at me and he said, "If you're going to give me ten, go ahead, give it to me."

(R v. McSorley 2000)

Along these lines, components of William Smart's defense underlined Brashear's contribution to his own victimization in antagonizing McSorley (*R v. McSorley* 2000). As intended in the tactic of blaming the victim, discourses that disavowed Brashear's status as a good guy deserving of sympathy detracted audiences from the more brutal facts about the violent incident. In a strange way, when Justice Kitchen cited the money lost through suspension, the public humiliation caused by arrest, and the social disgrace imposed by the media, this defined McSorley, the perpetrator, as a victim himself. In engaging in this process, court justices and others obfuscate legal and moral boundaries between offenders and victims. League punishments are thus deemed to be far more severe and socially consequential than court-imposed legal sentences.

Similarly, hockey insiders defended Bertuzzi's attack on Steve Moore as a regrettable but understandable response to Moore's malicious elbow to the head of Vancouver Canucks player (and leading goal scorer in the league) Markus Naslund during a contest two weeks earlier. Moore's elbowing infraction, which received no penalty during the game, sidelined Naslund for nearly one month, and players from the Canucks publicly threatened to *pay back* Moore in a future encounter. Even though few people defined Bertuzzi's hit as unproblematic, many held that Moore had nevertheless set the conditions for his own injury.

Blaming players like Donald Brashear and Steve Moore for their own injuries reinforces a dangerous assumption that there are no victims of sport crimes. If defenders of hockey violence neutralize the stigmatization of the game by scapegoating victims of violence, there are scant grounds for claiming a need for increased criminal prosecution of players committing excessively violent acts. When players are blamed for their injuries—in light of their apparent unwillingness to accept traditional codes of violence in every context—player violence can be reconciled as a problem to be managed within the total institution of hockey.

Ice Hockey and Ironies of Social Control

A review of the existing case law on ice hockey violence reveals a notable trend—players have consistently avoided being defined and punished as bona fide criminals. As both Smith (1983) and Barnes (1988) argued some time ago and Young (1993, 2004a) proposed more recently, legal experts have debated whether violence in the game is best policed from the outside through criminal or civil channels. Criminal law is defined as a nation's recognized body of statute law that establishes what constitutes a legal offence and what precise conditions constitute a crime. These circumstances are generally known as *the elements of the offense.* Unless all the elements are sufficiently established by the prosecuting or Crown authority, the accused is not guilty of the alleged offense. In most Western nations, including Canada and the United States, three elements define an act as criminal: the *actus reus,* or guilty act; the *mens rea,* or guilty mind; and the attendant circumstances.

By contrast, civil law, or *tort law,* is the body of law that provides an injured person with a means to secure financial compensation from the person who caused the injury. Under tort law, when a person is injured either intentionally or through negligence, the offender may be required legally to pay damages. Tort law thus provides a codified system that allows people to receive compensation for the physical, emotional, or psychological injuries they experience at the hands of others. The system of tort law is often viewed to be a deterrent against risky behavior, since it places often heavy financial penalties on socially irresponsible actions. Though tort law and its consequences are an important dimension of sport violence, in this chapter we are less concerned with the use of tort law than with the criminal prosecution of athletes for on-field actions, and specifically violent actions.

History teaches us that while the majority of on-ice violence is not defined as criminal behavior, many violent acts occurring within sports result in charges of criminal assault or assault with a weapon (Young and Wamsley 1996; Young 2004a). In Canada, for example, ice hockey players may be charged with assault under section 265 of the *Criminal Code of Canada,* which states the following (emphasis added):

> A person commits an assault when: (a) without the *consent* of another person, he applies force *intentionally* to that person, directly or indirectly; (b) he attempts or threatens, by an *act or gesture,* to apply force to another person, if he has, or causes that other person to believe upon reasonable grounds that he has, present ability to effect his purpose; (c) while openly wearing or carrying a weapon or an imitation thereof, he accosts or impedes another person or begs.

Section 267 of the *Criminal Code of Canada* defines assault with a weapon (pertinent in the case of ice hockey, as players are often assaulted with sticks) as the following:

> Everyone who, in committing an assault: (a) carries, uses or threatens to use a weapon or an imitation thereof; or, (b) causes bodily harm to the complainant; (c) is guilty of an indictable offence and liable to imprisonment for a term not exceeding ten years.

Canadian ice hockey assault cases such as *Agar v. Canning* (1965), *Martin v. Daigle* (1969), *R v. Maki* (1970), *R v. Green* (1971), *R v. Prénoveau* (1971), *R v. Watson* (1975), *R v. Starrat* (1980), *R v. Ciccarelli* (1988), *R v. Cey* (1989), *R v. Leclerc* (1991), and *R v. Neeld* (2000) represent attempts by the law to curtail criminal violence occurring within the sport at the amateur and professional tiers.

For crime enforcement agents in Canada, the two central and most problematic elements in defining a sport crime are establishing the offender's intent to injure another player and the victim's lack of consent to violent play (parameters required under section 265 of the *Criminal Code of Canada*). Each of these criteria has proven difficult to establish in sport violence cases. A review of the Canadian case law on sport crimes reveals inconsistencies in judicial decisions on what is recognized as criminal behavior. In *R v. Jobidon* (1988), the Supreme Court of Canada ruled that fighting is criminal, despite consent from either of the players. However, Justice Carter said the following in his 1971 decision of *R v. Green:*

> No hockey player enters onto the ice of the NHL without consenting to and without knowledge of the possibility that he is going to be hit in one of many ways when he is on the ice . . . [violence is] an extremely ordinary happening in a hockey game and players really think nothing of it . . . [and it is common when] a man plays boisterously, as he is paid to. I find it difficult to envision a circumstance where an offence of common assault as opposed to assault causing bodily harm could readily stand on facts produced from incidents occurring in the course of a hockey game at that level.

Demonstrating further contradictions, the court ruled in *R v. Leclerc* (1991) that players of contact sport offer "implied consent to those assaults which are inherent and reasonably incidental to the normal playing of the game at this [professional] level." Only two years earlier, in the decision of *R v. Cey* (1989), the court suggested,

> Some actions which can take place in the course of a sporting conflict that are so violent it would be perverse to find that anyone taking part in a sporting activity had impliedly consented to subject himself to them.

In his decision of *R v. McSorley* (2000), Justice William Kitchen (who also served as the presiding court official for the 2004 *R v. Bertuzzi* case) captured the current state of ambiguity regarding how the legal system views criminal behavior in ice hockey:

> The act was unpremeditated. It was impulsive, committed when McSorley was caught in a squeeze—attempting to follow an order to fight with Brashear when there was too little time to do so. The rules by which he was playing I have characterized as indefinite, making compliance by the players more difficult.

Judicial decisions resulting from such cases plainly show that while the violent acts under scrutiny may not be acceptable, toughness and aggression as organizing principles in hockey should not be put on trial. However, these violent acts should not be ignored when interpreting violence in the game as either wanted or unwanted. When Canadian ice hockey players have been brought to criminal courts for excessively violent acts on the ice, court justices have rejected these cases on the grounds that players consent to violent victimization in the game through their acceptance of the codes of aggression structuring athletic competition (Faulkner 1973; Young and Wamsley 1996). Once again, such decisions contribute to the view that player violence in ice hockey is victimless (Bridges

1999; Horrow 1980). It is precisely at this point that the legal notion of *volenti non fit injuria* (or voluntary assumption of risk) becomes implemented to rationalize harmful sport outcomes (Young 1993).

The issue of whether players consent to violence as part of their participation in sport is well debated within the sociology of sport literature (see Barnes 1988; Young 2002a, 2004a). Certainly, players in contact sports such as ice hockey are socialized to accept formal and informal norms condoning personal consent to be hit, checked, slashed, and even punched (sometimes in brutal and injurious ways). Still, in Canadian criminal cases in which excessive ice hockey violence has been deemed unjustifiably assaultive, court justices have pointed out that the principle of *volenti non fit injuria* has its limitations:

> Patently, when one engages in a hockey game, one accepts that some assaults, which would otherwise be criminal, will occur and consents to such assaults. It is equally patent, however, that to engage in a game of hockey is not to enter a forum to which the criminal law does not extend. To hold otherwise would be to create in the hockey arena a sanctuary for unbridled violence to which the law of Parliament and the Queen's justice could not apply.
>
> (R v. Watson 1975)

As established in the 1989 R v. Cey case, and as noted previously:

> Some actions which can take place in the course of a sporting conflict that are so violent it would be perverse to find that anyone taking part in a sporting activity had impliedly consented to subject himself to them.
>
> (R v. Cey 1989)

As witnessed both in lay discussions and in the courts' inability to act consistently on these matters, there is clearly a gray area between the forms of violence an ice hockey player consents to and the forms a player does not consent to. For example, in the incident involving McSorley and Brashear, supporters of McSorley contended that Donald Brashear—a player who had accumulated 1,282 minutes in penalties by this point in his career—should have *expected* to be viciously struck by McSorley given the pattern of violence created during the February 21, 2000, game. Arguing that Brashear should have anticipated an assault given his extensive experience with fighting in hockey, certain groups constructed the incident as brutal but understandable. As Justice Kitchen himself noted in the case,

> The [informal] code of conduct deals mainly with situations where the written rules are breached. . . . For example, the written rules prohibit slashing with the stick, but part of the unwritten code says that slashing is permissible as long as it is during play and not to the head. Of course, when a slash is employed, and is observed by the referee . . . a penalty is normally called.
>
> (R v. McSorley 2000)

A central element in the McSorley defense was the frustration and aggression stirred in him by Brashear's uncharacteristic reluctance to participate in a second fight. In drawing on the commonly adopted theory of hockey rage,

William Smart defended McSorley's actions as merely an extreme expression of a common tactic in hockey—using violence when emotionally aroused or frustrated by physical action in the game. Such justifications gel with Dollard et al.'s (1939) explanation of aggressive acts as a response to situated frustration, Lorenz's (1966) psychoanalytic theory of instinctual aggression as an outcome of close physical combat, and Gurr's (1970) understanding of violence as the outcome of a person's perceived deprivation within an interactive context. These are all views popularized in ordinary hockey discourse, as was evidenced by Detroit Red Wings enforcer Darren McCarty, who suggested, "It's unfortunate. Sometimes the game is really emotional. I know Marty McSorley. I'm sure he didn't mean to do it, but something inside him went off" (Kupelian 2000, D4). Through cleverly orchestrated framing, McSorley became repositioned as the victimized party, whose attempt to regain respect through typically condoned violence was stifled.

Adopting such an argument, players, fans, and legal counsel depicted the incident as an accident, claiming that McSorley did not intend to strike Brashear in the head but across the upper shoulder. In accordance with dangerous masculine codes, the blow should have been perceived by Brashear as a respectable call to fists instead of an intent to *criminally* injure. In coupling the issue of consent with the frustration and accident defense, ice hockey insiders and supporters painted the incident as one undeserving of criminal prosecution. Portraying McSorley as a tough but fair, violent yet honorable, aggressive while proud player, insiders discounted the idea that McSorley had criminally victimized Brashear in a way uncommon or unaccepted in NHL hockey. McSorley's actions were defended as standard practice within the game. Further, since both players involved were well acquainted with the (total institutional) code of violence governing ice hockey, no form of criminal victimization was seen to have occurred.

Testimony offered by Boston Bruins assistant coach Jacques Laperriere suggested that McSorley had been merely following orders in trying to provoke Brashear into another fight so that he could defend the honor of his team (*R v. McSorley* 2000). Indeed, the notion of who is responsible for an on-ice act of aggression has been historically questioned throughout sport case law (Barnes 1988; Young 1993, 2004a). Are coaches, trainers, or team sponsors (all having vested interests in the outcome of a game or the season) complicit in the violent behaviors of athletes they help to socialize? Could not Pat Burns, the coach who sent McSorley onto the ice to fight Brashear in an attempt to recapture team honor (the Bruins were losing to the Canucks late in the third period and had been badly beaten up during the game), foresee a violent outburst between the players? Did Burns not encourage the act? As Young has shown in his discussions of *vicarious liability* and *foreseeability* (1993, 2004a), North American courts have been reluctant to tackle the issue of extended complicity in cases of player violence. If players are in fact socialized to be aggressive in the culture of ice hockey and if agents of socialization are complicit in hyperviolent outbursts, then is not the entire organization of ice hockey criminally responsible? And if it is responsible, how might it be policed?

Legal critics have suggested that meaningful guilty verdicts against ice hockey players are practically impossible. While it might seem easy to establish the first element of a criminal assault in ice hockey (i.e., Bertuzzi smashes Steve Moore in the back of the head and seriously injures him), players have been found innocent of criminal behavior during play on the grounds that, by participating in the contact sport of hockey, players should simply anticipate involvement in dangerous physical exchanges. How, then, can any on-ice act be considered legitimately criminal?

If players consent to the mere possibility of violent victimization, then there can be no requisite guilty mind among offenders. Atkinson's (2006) review of the legal decision in the McSorley case documents how it could not be determined if he in fact intended to injure Brashear. Further, McSorley, like other players in NHL history, claims to have simply *lost it* for a brief time because of situational frustration and aggressive instincts, and so he lost his capacity to act with rational foresight. In this way, players such as Todd Bertuzzi have been excused of criminal misdeeds on the ice on the legal grounds that they could not have foreseen the catastrophic outcomes of their behaviors.

The attendant circumstances of an ice hockey game have been discussed in the process of further justifying the grounds on which unwanted violence in the sport manifests itself. In legal cases dating back to the early 19th century (Young and Wamsley 1996), ice hockey players have been excused of potential crimes since hockey games, by their very nature, are raucous affairs involving brutal body contact. The definitive legal standard for analyzing the circumstances of violence in hockey was set by the decision in *R v. Cey* (1989). The court, in deciding the case and thereby determining what counts as criminally unwanted violence in ice hockey, considered the following factors: the nature of the game (professional, fast, competitive, physically punishing, and thus including expected violence), the presence of regular acts and circumstances of violence in the game (e.g., high-sticking was usual, striking the head was reasonable, blows after the whistle were acceptable), the nature of the violent act under scrutiny and its potential to injure, and the spirit of the violence underpinning the act (whether it was retaliatory or intimidating). Therefore, *R v. Cey* established that when a hyperviolent act occurs in a typically violent sport, there are legal grounds to consider it noncriminal. In working to establish such perceived normativity of violence in hockey, a lack of criminal action in on-ice violence, and the lack of guilty minds among players, practically every defense of players for on-ice actions has established ice hockey as a sport in which even the most dangerous forms of violence are legally defendable as part of the normal circumstances of the game.

In response to years of bad publicity on violence in ice hockey, the Canadian Hockey Association (CHA) and NHL have engaged in extensive public relations campaigns to repolish the sport's tarnished image. The CHA has re-invested and expanded the non-body-contact stream at the amateur level of the sport (traditionally referred to in Canada as *house league)* and has worked with organizations such as General Motors and Tim Hortons to create instructional programs like Safe and Fun Hockey for young players. In Safe and Fun Hockey, there is a zero-tolerance policy against body contact. The program's spokesperson and hockey legend Bobby Orr had a career, as did many other players, that was cut short due to repeated injury from the rigors of the game. Other structural initiatives created by the CHA include Check it Out (designed to educate young players about proper techniques of body contact), Think First, Stop (intended to curb checking from behind), and Relax (encouraging players and parents to simply recognize the fun and play aspects of the sport). Such programs are designed to alter the structure through which violence is introduced at the amateur level as well as influence the wider culture of violence in the sport, especially at the elite and professional levels.

Since 2000 the NHL has done little to de-emphasize overall aggressive play in ice hockey, but it has taken a series of steps to curb high-sticking in the games by beefing up the penalties. Policed by a deterrence model of justice, NHL players are fined and suspended more frequently now than ever before. However, little empirical evidence exists to suggest that the new league rules reduce player injury. NHL statistics indicate that in the 2005-06 regular season, high-sticking infractions and games missed by players due to injuries were both at 7-year highs (National Hockey League 2007). Rules against initiating fights, holding players (or their sticks), and varieties of rough play have, however, curbed some forms of violence in the game, such as fistfights. Such reductions have taken place much to the chagrin of hockey traditionalists, including CBC hockey commentator and Canadian icon Don Cherry. In brief, all of the evidence that we know of strongly suggests that while ice hockey leagues generally respond to excessive violence with an immediate reaction of closer policing, especially during and following legal intervention, the culture of the game, including dangerous notions of hypermasculinity and *the code*, are so entrenched that forms of wanted *and* unwanted violence endure. As the saying goes, "the song remains the same" in the culture of ice hockey in North America.

THEORETICAL INTERSECTIONS

In his influential work on how messages and signs are created and understood, Stuart Hall (1980) outlines how the tasks of media production, transmission, and reception are complex. He illustrates that while the senders of a message encode it with a preferred cultural meaning, audiences do not always use, or decode, the message in the manner intended by the producer. As media researchers, we must pay attention to the potential cracks in the communication process and study how preferred meaning structures embedded in messages are often disrupted by what Hall views as either negotiated or oppositional audience readings. As critical sociologists, we see ourselves as searchers for and readers of oppositional meaning structures contained in mass-mediated constructions of violence in sports like ice hockey.

In the following discussions, we ask you to consider how the respective theoretical positions we outline might encourage researchers to frame violence in sports like ice hockey in ways different from those typically found in dominant media coverage. We encourage you to engage your sociological imagination in order to consider which details about violence in sports like ice hockey are inserted into—or are strategically left out of—encoded mediations of the games.

FUNCTIONALISM AND STRAIN THEORY

Dodge's (1985) theory of positive deviance is a neofunctionalist way of understanding how cases of ice hockey violence play a productive role in justifying the authority of the league as the rule enforcer and emphasizing the limitations of policing the game from the outside. Dodge defines positive deviance as an act of deviation from normality that brings about positive institutional sanctions. Stated another way, the actor's deviation from a commonly accepted group rule allows for a public reaffirmation of the group's normative boundaries. The positive deviant is often an extraordinary figure who actually conforms to group ways of life (i.e., to codes of masculinity, toughness, vengeance, or aggression in ice hockey) to such an exaggerated extent that he far exceeds the usual ways of practicing them. Dodge's call for attention to positive deviance emerges from what he sees as the unduly limited focus on the socially disintegrative aspects of deviance that are "offensive, disgusting, contemptible, annoying or threatening" (Dodge 1985, 17).

There is no doubt that Todd Bertuzzi's attack on Steve Moore stirred immediate public condemnation of Bertuzzi, but public sentiment quickly transformed into an assessment of how the hockey code must be respected by players. From this point of view, Bertuzzi, in a symbolic act of martyrdom, threw his career into harm's way by punishing Steve Moore for his earlier attack on Markus Naslund. Bertuzzi, on-ice defender of the rule of law in the sport and long-term enforcer of the code, graphically illustrated to others the importance of living within a norm-bound system of violence and retribution. Bertuzzi is viewed by NHL insiders and fans as a strong male warrior who takes matters into his own hands during play rather than acquiescing to the officials. He follows both the macho and the team norms of the sport by dramatically avenging Naslund's injury. He later publicly accepts league punishment (even saying it is fair over time), is tried and convicted by the NHL for his transgression, and apologizes to Moore for causing the injury during internationally broadcast press conferences. Bertuzzi's overacceptance of the code and self-enacted enforcer role on the ice reaffirms the exciting nature of brutality in the game, the strength of masculine resolve among players, and the league officials as the ultimate rule enforcers. Acts like Bertuzzi's are also *positive* because they bring players in the league closer together ideologically and insulate the culture of the sport from outside attempts to regulate it.

CONFLICT THEORY

Dahrendorf's conflict theory of authority might paint a completely different portrait of the Bertuzzi affair. In *Class and Class Conflict in Industrial Society,* Dahrendorf (1971) traces the roots of power in social institutions to those who hold authority. Individuals who are able to command others into action possess authority, and their commands are obeyed either by consent or by coercion. In the case of the

NHL, while it might seem that as an enforcer Bertuzzi occupies a position of veteran authority within the league, we might critically ask whose authority he is enforcing. For Dahrendorf, figures like Bertuzzi demonstrate their own subjugation to the dominant culture of masculinity in the sport, to coaches' orders, to teammates' wishes for vengeance, and to the league's power to control players' careers. Bertuzzi acts out violently in order to protect the code of violence in the game and the sovereign authority of the league, but protecting these might not necessarily be in his own best interests as a player.

As a conflict sociologist, Dahrendorf would encourage us to consider what kind of status quo was reinforced by the incident between Bertuzzi and Moore. Players, as a subordinate social class in the league, act in order to maximize team and league profits. Since dramatic cases of on-ice violence bring considerable media attention and sell tickets, dominant league owners profit when violence in the sport is placed under an intense public microscope. In turn, leagues maintain the right to suspend or terminate the contracts of players who violate official league policies on violence. Therefore, league officials in the NHL and other sports organizations derive authority from their control of the culture of violence in the sport and from their ability to resist outside intervention into the sport. Players are merely quasi-groups without the authority to change either policies or accepted customs within the sport. Neither do players individually profit from flamboyant instances of on-ice violence. Spectacular aggression during the games reveals instead the degree of exploitation players experience as members of a power-based ice hockey institution.

INTERACTION THEORY

Kitsuse's (1980) social constructionist stance on tertiary deviance provides a completely different theoretical angle for studying on-ice violence. In his article "Coming Out All Over: Deviance and the Politics of Social Problems," Kitsuse defines tertiary deviance as acts that are redefined by those socially labeled as deviant. When participating in tertiary deviance, people reject the notion that an act or attribute they own discredits them, and they take steps to transform stigmatized identities into valued or useful ones *for them*. Kitsuse extends classic labeling theory by focusing on how acts are interactively defined in social groups, and he emphasizes how systems of discourse emerge in such groups to justify behavior. From Kitsuse's perspective, tertiary deviants are not passive receptors of negative labels; rather, they publicly disavow the stigmatizing label, the persons promoting the label, and the labeling process itself.

Hockey players such as Marty McSorley or Todd Bertuzzi may become tertiary deviants when their on-ice actions of violence are called into question by authority figures outside of the game. Even players not involved in the incidents will *circle the (league) wagons* in such cases and defend rule violators. NHL legend Wayne Gretzky sat behind McSorley during the criminal trial in British Columbia and regularly defended his former teammate in the press. Similarly, hockey *good guys* and fellow Canadian countrymen Joe Sakic, Mario Lemieux, and Trevor Linden rallied behind Bertuzzi during his legal case. Because hockey players are celebrities in countries like Canada, their opinions about standards of violence in the sport (and the most effective means of policing them) are given widespread public credence. When attacked by the criminal justice system, players become tertiary deviants who use their access to public settings and the media to flaunt their ideas and justifications, to a useful as well as an industry-supporting effect.

SOCIAL CONTROL THEORY

Social control theorists Gottfredson and Hirschi (1991) would note that Marty McSorley's assault against Donald Brashear underlines a deeper cultural problem in ice hockey. As outlined in *A General Theory of Crime,* problems of violence manifest themselves when strict codes of discipline and self-control are ambiguous in a social setting. There is a paucity of external control present in the setting, and therefore players will not develop the higher level of self-control that usually manifests itself after people are socialized into a tightly ordered and externally regulated culture. Viewed from a self-control perspective, problems of ice hockey violence reflect failures of institutional control and failures of players to exercise self-restraint. According to Gottfredson and Hirschi's self-control theory, acts of hyperviolence in any context are examples of "acts analogous to crime" (Gottfredson and Hirschi 1991, 72), and they signify that perpetrators cannot curb their basic impulses and desires—such as aggression and risk taking.

Players in sports such as ice hockey will only learn self-controlled behavior if there are rule systems in place that are maintained by authority figures, that operate in predictable ways, and that punish rule violators with rational, reasonable, and consistent sanctions. The violence problem in ice hockey is both a structural condition (i.e., weak authority figures, unpredictable punishment of offenders, missed rule violations by officials and league administrators, unreasonable punishments for some offenders, and irrational targeting of select players) and a cultural condition since the players themselves have a collectively recognized mandate to exert social control using rough play. Players whose work roles define them as enforcers, tough guys, or masculine heroes are not institutionally socialized to develop personality structures characterized by deep self-control, and it is no shock when violent outbursts erupt. Though Wacquant (1995) correctly argues that most athletes are trained to control their violent impulses in sport, ice hockey might be an exceptional case in which particular role players are expected and even encouraged (by coaches, peers, and fans alike) to lose control when prompted.

CLASSICAL THEORY

Deterrence theorists such as Roshier *(Controlling Crime,* 1989) point in yet another direction for making sense of criminal violence in ice hockey. For Roshier, of far greater consequence than the claims-making or self-control conditions precipitating sport violence is the degree to which formal rules in an institution such as the NHL discourage deviance. In a postclassical stream of deterrence theory, Roshier argues that the threat of harsh, quick, and certain punishment must be present in institutional contexts for formal rules to have any credit. Players do not need highly formulated self-control mechanisms—they need only to fear the consequences of rule violations in-house. By clamping down on offenders through serious suspensions and fines, the NHL would send a clearly deterring message to deviants in the sport.

One of the most recurrent criticisms of the NHL's policing of violence has been the league's inconsistent and ineffectual deterrence model of justice. Whereas one player escapes a penalty for an illegal high-sticking incident during a game, another receives a minor penalty. Yet another player receives a penalty and a league suspension of a few games, and another still receives a major suspension. Historical evidence reveals that major suspensions for violent play produce no immediate conformity among NHL players or consistency within the league. For instance, following Marty McSorley's landmark 23-game suspension in 2000, Scott Niedermayer of the New Jersey Devils viciously swung his stick—with a similar style and intent as McSorley's—at Peter Worrell of the Florida Panthers, striking him in the head. Although the NHL had issued a zero-tolerance policy on stick swinging only a week before the March 20 incident, Niedermayer received only 10 games for the act, leaving ice hockey critics and players in Canada perplexed as to what to expect in the future. Such inconsistencies continue.

CRITICAL THEORY

Proponents of the deconstruction theoretical tradition in critical or poststructural sociology, such as Derrida (1978), ask a rather unique set of questions about the mass mediation of events like ice hockey violence. Not yet a dominant theoretical trend in contemporary criminology, Derrida's brand of deconstruction is based on understanding the potential taken-for-granted meanings of social groups and settings. Deconstruction is a practice of social analysis or textual reading that is geared toward exposing how forms of communication are replete with varied messages. Sociologists of crime and deviance might, for example, deconstruct how relations of power and authority between people in work or play settings might affect their understanding of right and wrong.

Derrida's emphasis on deconstruction might encourage a sociologist of deviance to search for how the backgrounds of players involved in on-ice violence subtly frame media reports of sport crimes in hockey and to research whether calls for police intervention against particular players might be based on what Gitlin (1991) calls *inferential racism*. A researcher might have a theoretical hunch that police or public reaction to sport violence is mediated by ethnic ideologies and therefore wish to inspect—line by line and image by image—accounts of player violence in the press through a careful reading of any national or ethnic symbolism. For example, while both Bertuzzi and McSorley were described as good Canadian players in the media coverage of their arrests and trials, the press identified Alexandre Perezhogin as a foreign national or defector and thus more worthy of criminal prosecution (Atkinson 2006). Fan postings on the Internet were generally unsympathetic to the clearly less popular Perezhogin, frequently calling for his permanent expulsion from the North American game and his return to Kazakhstan.

GENDER AND FEMINIST THEORY

Feminist or gender-sensitive theories of crime and deviance, including Hagan's (1989) power control theory, explain the etiology of player violence in a novel way. Hagan's theory explains why men are overrepresented in most crime statistics.

According to him, as children males are socialized to be risk takers and less supervised than their female counterparts. Delinquency is a direct consequence of the socialization patterns young boys are exposed to. Boys in patriarchal institutions such as sport are encouraged toward delinquency since the personality characteristics that will help them succeed as authority figures in athletic contests (i.e., risk taker, aggressive, dominant, physically oriented, self-directed) closely parallel those of the typical deviant. Centrally, then, the men who are freed from constant supervision and control are most likely to become deviants.

Hagan might attribute high rates of recidivism among violent offenders (i.e., as measured by annual penalty minutes, fines, or suspensions) in sports such as ice hockey to how the subcultural code of toughness tacitly undermines official rule structures. The code grants on-ice enforcers latitude in exercising informal control mechanisms in the sport, and thereby entrusts in players an authority to act at will. From a power control perspective, athletes such as ice hockey players develop a heightened level of hubris, or pride-driven arrogance. Players adopting such a hubris consider themselves to be above league control and even above the criminal justice system. In her work on violence and exploitation in junior hockey, Canadian journalist Robinson (1998) argues that hubris is a defining element in the culture of many sports. The hubris produced by an elevated sense of power in the game potentially instructs us as to why NHL insiders respond with shock when athletes are formally charged and prosecuted by the law.

INTEGRATED THEORY

Highlighted in *Crime and Coercion: An Integrated Theory of Chronic Criminality* (2000), Colvin's differential coercion theory is a complex blend of strain and self-control theories. Colvin explains that when people feel extended amounts of social strain, experience low levels of personal efficacy, and perceive self-control to be unbeneficial to their goal attainment or personal satisfaction, they will not abide by norms. He maintains that deviance and crime are caused by exposure to noxious environments and by the formation of maladjusted emotion sets within people. People who are regularly exposed to coercion (which produces strain and low efficacy) develop psychosocial mind-sets marked by acute aggression, fear, and alienation, and these people see little benefit in behaving lawfully. Bonds to others are not maintained, since they are perceived as strain producing and coercive (i.e., an individual is unmotivated to socially attach to the sources of stress). When strain and perceived coercion run high while bonding and self-control run low, deviance results.

Ice hockey analysts have long maintained that cases of on-ice violence are not nearly as stimulus- and response-based (i.e., frustration leads to aggression) as social psychologists suggest (Robidoux 2001). An alternative investigation of ice hockey inspired by coercion theory might focus on whether the culture of the sport is a coercive environment that produces low levels of efficacy among young athletes and whether a coercive pressure is exerted on them to use violence and aggression, in unwanted ways, as part of the institutional ethos of the game. The focus would be in assessing whether coercion and anxiety stimulate low self-control within the group. Pascall and White's (2000) in-depth examination of attrition rates in minor league hockey establishes strong empirical cause to worry about how the culture of violence and aggression in the game is distasteful for many young players or their parents and leads to either violent young offending or player attrition in the sport. Colvin's (2000) theory thus encourages us to research the empirical relationship between coaches and players and the causal role that mentors play in the violence process.

Discussion Questions

1. Is there such a thing, in your opinion, as an on-field sport crime, and should the law intervene in sport violence?

2. Do you think that when players lose control on the field, it has more to do with their individual personalities and characters than it does with the sport cultures in which they are situated?

3. Evidence suggests that while it is not a perfect correlation, men are far more involved in hyperviolent sport acts than women. Is there a theory covered in this chapter that might explain this pattern?

Recommended Readings

Barnes, J.C. 1988. *Sport and the law in Canada*. Toronto, ON: Butterworths.

Barnes' book is a detailed examination of selected Canadian case law related to sport. In it, Barnes provides case analyses of such things as: assumption of risk; liability of participants (player sues player and spectator sues player); liability and negligence of facility operators; liability of schools, coaches, officials, and parents; liability of organizations such as amateur associations and professional teams; and medical negligence.

Goffman, E.1961. *Asylums*. Chicago: Aldine.

Goffman's classic account of life in mental institutions is a pillar in the development of his dramaturgical sociology. In this work, he explores pivotal concepts in research on the processing of selves in total institutions, such as moral careers, the presentation of self, and, of course, dramaturgy.

McKay, J., M. Messner, and D. Sabo. 2000. *Men, masculinities and sport*. Thousand Oaks, CA: Sage.

This edited collection of theoretical and empirical articles on masculinity, power, and sexuality in sport should be primary reading for anyone seriously interested in gender and sport.

Robidoux, M. 2001. *Men at play: A working understanding of professional hockey*. Montreal, PQ: McGill-Queen's University Press.

This book presents an extensive ethnographic account of life on a semiprofessional Canadian ice hockey team. Robidoux adopts a workers' advocacy perspective to illustrate how the business of professional sport is predicated upon the exploitation of young players.

Young, K., and C. Reasons. 1989. Victimology and organizational crime: Workplace violence and the professional athlete. *Sociological Viewpoints* 5:24-34.

> This is one of the first research articles in sociology showcasing a victimological approach to the study of sport violence and injury. Building on a Marxist and cultural studies framework, the authors question what would become of sport if we collectively considered athletes as workers who have the same rights to health and safety that other workers have.

Terror and Security in Sport

© Associated Press

Before the attacks on the United States on September 11, 2001, sociologists of crime, deviance, and social control devoted little attention to acts of terrorism. Certainly in North America, terrorism was perceived as a rare form of deviance and was studied predominantly by political scientists (Turk 2002). Empirically, acts of terrorism have always been difficult to study, with participants often preferring to remain hidden from public view. Likewise, mainstream theoretical perspectives on crime and deviance appear to be inadequate in explaining terrorism, despite the fact that researchers have used central sociological concepts such as conflict, power, and stratification to make sense of the phenomena (Ben-Yehuda 1993).

According to Turk (2002), sociological research on terrorism is largely Marxist or neo-Marxist in approach. Terrorism is typically conceptualized as political deviance waged between warring social, religious, or ethnic groups, one generally invested with an abundance of state-sanctioned power and the other invested with comparatively little. Group struggles are based largely upon the competition for scarce resources such as land or money, or they are the result of ideological differences pertaining to matters of faith, cultural tradition, or identity. Vold (1958) and other conflict theorists offer concepts such as pluralist conflict to predict the rise of terrorism as a response to the perceived ideological oppression of one majority group at the hands of a minority group. Terrorism is enacted as a technique of political posturing against the perceived ruling elite as part of a larger struggle over dominant systems of social organization and control. Similarly, Collins (1975) suggests that terrorism, an obviously ideologically loaded term posing definitional problems for sociologists, is a form of political violence initiated by a group seeking governance over issues, behaviors, or values. His conflict theory of terrorism explains acts of aggression between combating parties as an instrumental part of winning structural and ideological battles.

Another theoretical stream in terrorism research suggests that political acts of violence between groups might be classified as hate crimes. Genocide campaigns, the bombing of civilians, and the execution of targeted political leaders are expressions of group-based intolerance. In a review of the literature on the subject, Krueger and Maleckova (2003) use this approach to argue that terrorism originates not only as a collective response to poverty and political disenfranchisement but also as a response to collective feelings of alienation among the oppressed.

After September 11, scholars, cultural critics, and political pundits scrambled to understand global terror. Writers debate the American-led war on terror in the new millennium (White 2005) or the effects of the September 11 attacks on geopolitical networks and relationships among nations and religions. Others employ the subject of terrorism as a backdrop to explore a cluster of topics, including the politics of surveillance and everyday urban life (Webb and Davis 2006), globalization and the decline of the traditional nation-state (Scheuer 2006), American foreign policy (Pillar 2004), religious fundamentalism (Williams 2005), social risk and human rights decay (Cole and Dempsey 2006), and the representation of outsiders as potential terrorists (Martin and Petro 2006). More than ever, it is clear that terror politics influence modern (and indeed global) governance philosophies and practices.

Generally, sociologists of sport have been slow in turning their attention to terrorism as a form of crime or political deviance in sport settings. However, although sport has not been a primary locus of terrorist activity to date, sports organizers, athletes, political leaders, corporations, and military agents around the globe have been affected by growing concerns about terrorism in sport. Stadia have been reconstructed for security purposes, international events have been canceled or relocated, and miniarmies have been employed to protect participants and spectators at high-profile events such as the FIFA World Cup or the Olympic Games. Given the global popularity of sport and the sheer size of modern sports gatherings, games and events have become high-risk settings for terrorism. A key element in this, of course, is the fact that sport is a central social context for showcasing differences in religions, political systems, traditions, and ideologies among communities of various sizes (e.g., towns, cities, countries, continents, hemispheres) and for the acting out of tension between ethnic groups that positions them on opposite sides (real or imagined) of the global war on terror. For example, on August 7, 2006, former Australian cricketer Dean Jones (then an analyst for South African television's TEN Sports) was fired for referring to a South African player, Hashim Amla, as a terrorist during a live broadcast. On April 23, 2004, former Manchester United F.C. manager Ron Atkinson resigned from his analyst's job with ITV after a racist comment he made about Chelsea's Black French international defender, Marcel Desailly, was inadvertently broadcast.

In this chapter we examine the Olympic Games as a site of political deviance and potential terror in order to further explore the intersections between sport and terrorism. We review the legacy of terrorism at the Games and discuss how terrorism has been woven through global broadcasts as a political maneuver by specific nation-states and their representatives. Since the modern inception of the Games in 1896, each Summer and Winter Games has experienced threats of terrorism. In some cases, the Games have even experienced concrete acts of political violence. While Pierre de Coubertin and others envisioned the modern version of the Games as a global stage for engendering peace among nation-states, others have constructed the event as a site of deviant political and militaristic campaigning. This vignette of the Games helps us track how dominant political tensions among cultural groups weave through sport processes and how the media play an active role in representing the parties involved as either moral or menacing.

Terrorism and the Olympic Games

Whether the association between the Olympic Games and political violence is understood by authorities and international sports organizations as real, imagined, or inevitable, concerns about terrorism and security and the Games now go hand in hand. Although Pierre de Coubertin hoped that international sports events might help pacify conflict between nation-states, modern Olympic competitions undeniably are a platform for staging political struggle, military posturing, and ideological warfare (Young 2000, 2001).

The Olympic Games typically become entangled with political violence and terrorism along one of two axes. In the first instance, the Games may be targeted as a site for overt terrorist action or violence. Politically or religiously motivated individuals or organizations might find suitable targets in athletes participating in the Games, spectators attending the events, or selected corporations sponsoring the contests. Equally, the Olympic Games might become a spillover context for violence in which local military, political, religious, or other conflicts between nations become manifest. Especially as a situation in which athletic contests draw sizeable international audiences into geographical settings already embroiled in strife, the Olympics may be utilized as a vehicle for waging politically charged violence against others or for further engaging conflict between nations (Roche 2002; Atkinson and Young 2003).

In the second instance, the Games may be used by political opportunists as a forum for ideologically underlining the differences between their constituencies and others (see figure 8.1). In this context, and as we outline in the following sections, terrorist activities may be juxtaposed against the explicit and tacit philosophies underpinning sports contests—whether they are "innocent" philosophies such as civil liberties and human freedoms or more contrived goals such as nation building, commercialism, and the hegemonic rule of those with power.

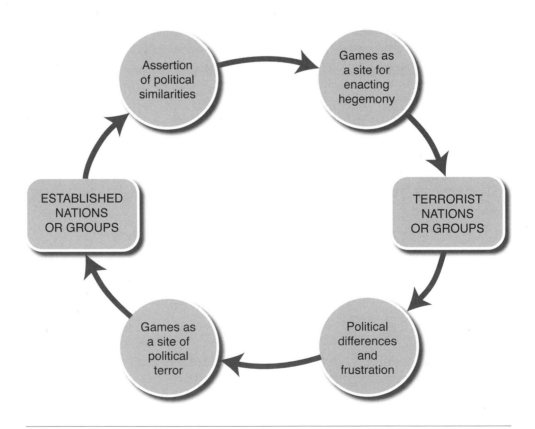

Figure 8.1 Mediating terrorism and political ideology through sport.

Athens, 1896

The political swordplay between established and outsider groups involving political violence or threats of terrorism at the modern Olympics dates back more than a century. The very first Games of the modern Olympic era (Greece 1896) were a stage for military tension between the host nation and Turkey. In 1896, a faction of Greeks traveled to Crete to stage a guerrilla campaign against the Turkish government. At the same time, another Greek army led by the Greek Prince Constantine invaded the Turkish province of Ioannina. A Turkish military force from Monastir eventually pushed the Greek army back to Thessaly, routed a Greek counterattack, and advanced to the Gulf of Volo. The Turks subsequently withdrew in exchange for monetary compensation from Western nations (Senn 1999).

London, 1908

During the 1908 Summer Games in London, tensions between established English Protestants and outsider Irish Catholics again threatened peace. While very few Irish nationalists actually participated in the 1908 Games, worry spread throughout England over an impending Irish terrorist attack in London (Senn 1999). Because of the ardent support for Irish nationalism from the Irish Americans at the Games, members of the British parliament and the British Olympic Organizing Committee feared violence among spectators at Olympic facilities (Roche 2002). The lowering of the American flag to half-mast during the opening ceremonies and recurrent cries of biased British officiating during Olympic events exacerbated the anxieties of local authorities in London (Guttmann 2002). While the events themselves unfolded without disruption, the 1908 Games foreshadowed how the Olympics would become increasingly inserted into the politics of global identity, militarism, and terrorism in the century to come.

Berlin, 1936

The 1936 Berlin Games, often referred to as the *Nazi Games,* heightened international concerns about military conflict in high-profile sport spheres (Mandell 1987). Because the Aryan Nazi philosophy eschewed sentiments of equality and cultural inclusion underpinning the Olympic ethos, the IOC, led by the American Avery Brundage, rallied to secure Germany's peaceful involvement in the Games and its promise that the Games would not be compromised by hostility toward African and Jewish competitors (Bachrach 2000). American politicians and IOC members were concerned with Nazi Germany's ability to host a peaceful and tolerant Games (although only U.S. IOC member Ernst Jahnke suggested boycotting or at least moving the Games, for which he was expelled from the IOC). Against a backdrop of flagrant racism and intolerance and international sentiment that the Nazi Party had utilized the Olympics to promote its economic and philosophical hegemony, the 1936 Berlin Games showcased an emerging nation-state characterized by ethnic prejudice, jingoism, and xenophobia (though it should also be acknowledged that America's athletic heroes were warmly welcomed by many Germans). The dramatic suturing of Nazi politics into the Berlin Games was chillingly brought to life in Leni Riefenstahl's daunting film *Olympia*.

Melbourne, 1956

By the time of the 1956 Games in Melbourne, Avery Brundage and other members of the IOC had pressed for the cessation of all national hostilities during Olympic tournaments (Roche 2002). In the summer of 1956, however, just weeks before the Games were to begin, two military conflicts undermined Brundage's quest for peace in Australia. First, the Egyptian seizure of the Suez Canal and the subsequent military response by the British, French, and Israelis drew a series of established and outsider tensions. The Soviet Union, supported by the United States, demanded an immediate withdrawal of the forces occupying Egypt. The British and French armies eventually vacated Egypt, but five nations still boycotted the Olympic Games in support of the Egyptians (Guttmann 2002). Only a few days later, the Soviet Union mobilized battalions of tanks and other armored vehicles to occupy Budapest. Though Hungary was promised military support from established Western nations, including the United States and England, none arrived, and nearly 200,000 Hungarians were killed or fled to neighboring Austria (Gosper and Korporaal 2000). As a result of global military affairs, the 1956 Games were plagued with intense security concerns, and local organizers in Melbourne spent two weeks worrying if the malice of the battlefields would flow over to the Olympic events (Gosper and Korporaal 2000). They did indeed in an extremely bloody men's semifinal water polo match between Hungary and the Soviet Union, which was eventually suspended.

   Throughout the first half of the 20th century, the Olympic Games were consistently affected by broader matters of national aggression, ideological propaganda, and cultural exclusion. Members of the IOC and national organizing committees developed international programs and security systems to protect the Games from outsider terror and conflict. Boycotts of the Games from both established and outsider nations escalated in number and veracity (Senn 1999). Fears about the Olympics becoming a site for actual aggression against innocent audiences increased, despite the fact that the Olympic events themselves remained free of overt political violence.

Mexico City, 1968

Although the 1968 Summer Games in Mexico have not been closely studied as an instance of political violence, tragic events occurring just three weeks before the Games had clear political trappings. For more than six months before the opening ceremonies, groups of more than 5,000 middle class and pro-Marxist university students (from the Universidad Nacional Autónoma de México and the Instituto Politécnico Nacional) repeatedly gathered near Olympic venues to express dissent against the Mexican government's massive spending on the Games. According to the protesters, the Mexican government, led by President Gustavo Díaz Ordaz, had squandered more than $140 million U.S. on the event—money that could have been utilized to improve pressing social matters such as education, labor opportunities, and health care programs for the large Mexican working class (Mabry 1992). Often perceived as a source of cultural and economic success, the Olympic Games were envisioned by Ordaz's government as a symbolic marker of Mexico's arrival in the sports world, and for this reason, any negative sentiment surrounding the Games was suppressed.

Following a summer of hostilities between protesters and police, Ordaz's government sought to quell the student movement outright. Under government support, the Mexican army cleared out student protesters from the Plaza de Tlatelolco on October 2, 1968, by firing on them with machine guns (Zarkos 2004). The Mexican government officially reported 32 student deaths, though other death counts ran as high as 300. Following the protest, 2,000 students were jailed, and the depleted resistance movement dissipated before the start of the Olympic Games (Mabry 1992).

Munich, 1972

The Munich Games of 1972 arguably involved the most dramatic instance of established–outsider military violence at the Olympics to date. On September 5, 1972, a politically outsider Palestinian group known as *Black September* stormed an Olympic village in Munich, fatally shooting Israeli wrestling coach Moshe Weinberg and weightlifter Yossi Romano and holding others hostage. Black September demanded the release of approximately 200 Palestinian prisoners held in Israel. After a 20-hour standoff at a nearby airfield and a failed rescue attempt by the German authorities, nine more Israeli athletes were killed, along with one German police officer and five of the terrorists. The event, commonly referred to as the *Munich massacre,* led several Arab countries to withdraw from the Games, including Egypt, Kuwait, and Syria, who all feared retaliation (Leonard 1988, 378; Iyer 1996, 19). It also led to the early departure of the Jewish American, seven-time gold medal winner Mark Spitz. The Munich tragedy sent shock waves through established international sport communities and seriously undermined the likelihood of peaceful future Games.

The Cold War and Beyond

The Olympiads of the remainder of the 1970s were relatively calm compared with Munich. Security arrangements in Innsbruck (1976), Montreal (1976), and Lake Placid (1980) were unprecedented in both scope and material resources employed on-site (see Gosper and Korporaal 2000). Perhaps a result of being held on neutral political grounds (Austria and Canada) or heavily militarized grounds (the United States), an air of tight security and political confidence permeated each of these Games. However, the 1980 Summer Games in Moscow and the 1984 Summer Games in Los Angeles further demonstrated the perpetual ebb and flow of established–outsider political tensions that have affected the Olympic Games.

The Moscow Games of 1980 followed the 1979 invasion of Afghanistan by the Soviet Union. Lord Killanin, president of the IOC, repeatedly rebuffed U.S. attempts to have the Games moved out of Moscow. He spent considerable time trying to convince American President Jimmy Carter not to boycott the Games, but Carter launched a global campaign to boycott the Olympics as a gesture of solidarity among established, civilized nations (Senn 1999). American Congressman Walter Mondale underlined the importance of a unified political response to the Soviets by austerely asserting, "What is at stake here is no less than the future security of the civilized world" (Guttmann 2002, 213). The American anti-Moscow lobby drew support from a dozen nations, and a widespread dropout of Olympic participation ensued. Boycotting nations warned others venturing to Moscow that, in the absence of established military superpowers like the United States, hostile attacks against Westerners could occur. Correspondingly, Soviet news broadcasters and politicians warned of the American Central Intelligence Agency's plot to kill Olympic spectators through biological or chemical weapons or via explosives planted at Olympic sites (Guttmann 2002). As a response to the American boycott, the Soviets as well as 13 other nation-states subsequently boycotted the 1984 Games in Los Angeles, claiming that they, too, feared for the safety of their athletes in a reciprocally hostile American setting (Hill 1995).

Throughout the late 1980s and early 1990s, security issues addressed both local protests in host cities and wider global political maneuvering. Established and outsider tensions within cities or host countries were paramount. The Canadian Olympic Association at the Calgary Winter Games of 1988 confronted security issues caused by local protesters concerned with environmental disturbance from the creation of the Olympic event sites (Whitson and Macintosh 1996) as well as by numerous and broadly documented protests related to the aboriginal Lubicon land claim (Wamsley and Heine 1996a, 1996b). Later that year, the Seoul Summer Games unfolded amid fears of military conflict between North and South Korea. Similarly, in 1992, Spanish organizers of the Barcelona Games were besieged with security issues related to local Basque separatist activities (Bernstein 2000).

The 1996 Summer Games in Atlanta highlighted the constantly changing face of violence and terrorism at the Olympics. On July 27, 1996, a pipe bomb exploded near a bandstand in Atlanta's Centennial Olympic Park. Two people were killed and more than 100 others were injured. Atlanta police held 33-year-old security guard Richard Jewell in custody in connection with the bombing, but they subsequently cleared him as a suspect. Unlike coverage of the earlier Munich incident, little information on the Atlanta case has reached the public, and it remains unclear whether the incident may be defined as terrorism at all (Iyer 1996; Price 1996). Following the Atlanta bombing, news stories about thwarted attacks at other Olympic Games surfaced. According to Mizell (2002), unnamed terrorists attempted an attack at the 1998 Olympics in Nagano and at the 1988 Games in Seoul (on at least two occasions). Bill Rathburn, a former police chief and the consultant to the U.S. Department of State during the 1984 Los Angeles Games, suggested that the Weather Underground Organization, a political extremist group based in the United States, had also planned an unsuccessful plastic explosives attack on the Los Angeles Olympics (Mizell 2002).

In light of such real, threatened, and alleged terrorist activities linked to the Olympics, the issue of securing the Games is now paramount to winning the Olympic bid. The mere suggestion that a host city might be politically or militarily vulnerable to a terrorist attack is enough to quash a bid. For example, during the 1997 bid for the 2004 Summer Games, the Swedish Olympic Committee's proposal experienced a fatal blow from a bomb explosion in Stockholm's main Olympic stadium (Reuters 1997). The explosion remains unsolved but is widely thought to be an act of terrorism. In Sweden, the 2004 Games were subsequently referred to as the *Lost Games* (Reuters 1997). By contrast, bids from Sydney (2000), Salt Lake City (2002), and Athens (2004) were all successful partially because of the intensive security programs promised by the respective organizing committees and the degree to which the committees carefully incorporated the need to secure all aspects of the events from terrorist outsiders as an integral component of their Olympic bid (Michaelis 2003).

Given this evidence and the historical trajectory of real or threatened violence at the Games, it seems reasonable to expect that the Olympic Games of the future will continue to face new security obstacles and political challenges. While we do not want to underestimate the effects and importance of other acts of political violence and terrorism around the globe, we believe it fair to say that the events of September 11, 2001, in the United States heavily plotted the course of Olympic security and terrorism issues in the 21st century. New lines of allegiance and tension between established and outsider nations are now contextually drawn and redrawn at post–September 11 Olympic Games.

Today's task of securing the Games interfaces with questions of established and outsider political ideologies, religions, ways of life, and international allegiances. For example, the 2002 Games in Salt Lake City, held less than 5 months after September 11, involved massive security hurdles. The Games spawned an international effort to (re)affirm global allies in a new war on terrorism (Associated Press 2001). In what follows, we unpack security and terrorism discourses related to the Salt Lake City Games as a small case study illustrating how established–outsider political axes may be symbolically crystallized at the Olympics and how terrorist activities may be configured through the mass media. As has been shown elsewhere (Young 2000), while the mass media may not cause sport-related violence such as terrorism, their role in such violence is neither passive nor nonparticipatory.

Terrorism and the 2002 Salt Lake City Games

As the first major international sports event held following September 11, the 2002 Winter Games in Salt Lake City pushed security measures to unprecedented levels. This included spending in excess of $310 million U.S. on securing the event— approximately one-quarter of the overall event budget and the highest amount ever spent for an Olympic Games. The post–September 11 context of the Salt Lake City Games also provided a unique opportunity for the relationship of terror(ism), political ideologies, and sport to be played out in the eyes of the world via the mass media. Segments of the Western media opportunistically framed the 2002 Winter Games as an international summit in which established and outsider relationships in the new war on terrorism became plainly evident. Further, the media deftly constructed the process of securing the Games as a symbolic metaphor for the struggle to secure America and the rest of the "free" world.

Militarism and Defense

In our informal research on the Salt Lake Games, more than 80% of examined global media accounts of security and violence matters characterized Salt Lake City as a *military state* during the Olympic Games. Emphasizing the $310 million U.S. spent on protecting the participants (Benton 2002; Vospeka 2002), the 16,000 security personnel employed, the continuous surveillance by F-16 fighter jets and Black Hawk helicopters, the 45-mile (72-kilometer) no-fly zone encircling the city, the integrated efforts of U.S. military and intelligence ground personnel (including the U.S. Federal Bureau of Investigation [FBI]; Central Intelligence Agency [CIA]; Bureau of Alcohol, Tobacco and Firearms; Marshals; Centers for Disease Control and Prevention; National Guard; Army; and Marines) and their advanced antiterrorism training, and the expansive list of detection technologies utilized to monitor every person's move during the Olympic events (e.g., biometric scanners, portable X-ray equipment, metal detectors, surveillance cameras, computer monitoring systems, and other identification technologies), the public was reassured that "America would be ready" for any terrorist contingency, "ready for anything" (Stearns and Dunn 2002, B3).

When asked about the police and military atmosphere at the Games, American cross-country skier Nina Kemppel noted with confidence, "It's like when I crawl in bed at night and I have my down comforter. It's that kind of comfortable, fuzzy feeling" (Harasta 2002, C2). In what might be seen as an extraordinarily smug boast of readiness, given the events of September 11, 2001, for which the U.S. authorities were clearly unprepared, Federal Aviation Administration spokesperson Mike Fergus commented, "If you violate the restrictions [the no-fly rule around Salt Lake City] you will be able to tell your children and grandchildren you flew formation with the Department of Defense" (Associated Press 2002a, D3). Robert Flowers, head of the Utah Olympic Public Safety Command, underlined the point less ambiguously: "If you fly in our airspace, we're going to shoot you down" (Reaves 2002).

Complementing the pre- and post-Olympic emphasis on the capability of the American protection and intelligence community to secure the event, the media utilized comments by senior American government officials, including President George W. Bush, Homeland Security Director Tom Ridge, Attorney General John Ashcroft, Secretary of Defense Donald Rumsfeld, and Utah Governor Michael Leavitt, to assure global audiences that America would continue to be "the safest place in the world" (Wilson 2001a, E2). The media insisted that people would be so impressed by American security that a case would be made to adopt Salt Lake City as the permanent site for the Winter Olympics

(Canadian Press 2002, A9). Jacques Rogge, president of the IOC, bolstered the international sport community's confidence in American strength, first by refusing to cancel the Games despite pressure and second by publicly commending American security efforts. According to Rogge, "The [Olympic] village is the most secure place in the world. From a security point of view, you could not be better protected" (Wilson 2001a). A common trend across the different media was to punctuate stories with statements made by participating athletes and spectators brimming with confidence and respect for U.S. military resources:

> A lot of people say it will be dangerous, but to me this is going to be the safest place in the world. People who want to scare Americans or the rest of the world are not succeeding. The Olympics are happening and they are going to be a success.
>
> (Catriona Le May Doan, Canadian speed skater, cited in Petrie 2002, D4)

Reports of approximately two dozen planes receiving military escorts away from Salt Lake City before or during the Olympics (CBS Evening News 2002), more than 600 bomb or suspicious package scares in the downtown core (Cantera 2002; Morris News Service 2002), and one anthrax hoax at a local airport (BBC News 2002) served to underscore the perceived efficiency of American defense personnel in dealing with potentially problematic security situations. Not until the final night of the Games did a security problem become widely publicized: a problem involving—rather less threateningly, it must be said—the drunken brawling of more than 20 spectators outside a Budweiser beer tent in the Olympic village (Associated Press 2002b, A7).

Through the recurrent media framing of Olympic policing as a daunting but achievable task in Salt Lake City, preference was given to the degree to which Americans appeared ideologically or practically unfazed by the September 11 attacks. In President George W. Bush's much-quoted words, "We will show the world we can safeguard the Olympics without sacrificing our American ideals—openness, mobility, diversity, and economic opportunity in the process" (Office of the United States and Press Secretary 2002). In the coverage of the massive display of military strength at the Olympics and of America's unwillingness to be frightened away from cultural practices like sport (Associated Press 2002c, A1), the American media emphasized the resiliency of its state. Such was summarized in a September 27, 2001, special edition of the American television program *Extra* titled "America Under Siege," which focused on terrorism at the Games: "Many believe canceling the Games would be giving the terrorists exactly what they wanted. A safe and successful Winter Olympics will prove they can never defeat America."

Thus the media's role in extending established images of America's strength and ability as a global leader was evident in discourses on security and terrorism at the 2002 Olympic Games. As Giroux (2002) and Martin and Petro (2006) observe, media agents are extensions of the international hegemonic power bloc, helping to shape public opinion about security, social efficacy, and cultural stability in the face of political violence. While the ability to protect athletes and spectators attending the Games was the surface issue presented in most media reports, there was also an embedded understanding that the Olympic Games were a test of America's ability to police political violence within its domestic borders. Describing the threat of terrorism at the Olympics as one episode (Iyengar 1996) of national security, the media helped emphasize how the sport process becomes embedded in terrorist and antiterrorist discourses.

Victimization and Recovery

Although media coverage of security at the Salt Lake City Games consistently depicted the United States as a powerful and proud nation, another dominant media frame emphasized America as a recovering—and vulnerable—victim of senseless violence. Tapping into the natural emotional arousal common in sports events like the Olympics, event organizers and media agents deftly linked surging feelings of victimization in the American populace to the feelings regularly stirred by athletic competitions (e.g., excitement, doubt, sorrow, frustration, anger, fear, and so on). In doing so, American athletes and their endeavors became metaphors of the American people's resolve to combat terrorism directly: The athletes were individuals who would compete despite their fear of victimization at the hands of terrorists. Rather than passively accepting the threat to national security posed by international terrorists, the American people showcased their determination to combat victimization through their athletes' commitment to the task at hand. By insinuating that the Olympic Games were an example of the social cohesion and patriotism spawned by the September 11 attacks, the media helped frame the Games as an unyielding response to violent bullying by barbaric outsider states.

News reports of security at the Olympic Games were replete with sentiment about reinvigorated patriotism in America. In the wake of perceived terrorist threats to the Games, the media underscored how Americans were living through times of anxiety, shock, and suspicion. While confident but concerned about security, the Salt Lake Olympic Committee (SLOC) reminded citizens around the world that the United States could be attacked by rogue outsiders at any time (Foy 2001, G3). For this reason, considerable leeway was given to Americans and their displays of patriotism. In an unprecedented exhibition of patriotism by a host nation, Americans were granted special permission by the IOC to present the American flag found in the World Trade Center rubble during the opening ceremonies. Contrasting the tattered (but still intact) symbol of American nationalism with the pageantry and celebration of the Games, comments offered by the media likened the resulting imagery to a universal statement of victims' rights:

> Fireworks ushered in the entrance of [President] Bush and the World Trade Center flag. Organizers hoped to raise the banner during the opening ceremony, but its frail condition made that impossible. A 12-year-old boy, symbolically known as the Child of Light, was then introduced to the world. The child, representing the ability of the human spirit to overcome life's adversities, will remain a theme throughout the Games.

(Associated Press 2002c, A1)

Such displays of patriotism—which, in many ways, violated IOC customs restricting the overt display of nationalism and militarism by a host nation—were rationalized by media agents and excused by sport commentators as natural expressions of defensiveness and fear regarding terrorism in America. The Salt Lake City Games evolved into a context in which acts of American patriotism could be discursively organized as a collective healing opportunity for all victims, or potential victims, of terrorism:

> Olympic organizers, more determined than ever to market the meaning, began talking about the Games as a chance for restoring America's hope. There were recollections of the 1980 U.S. hockey team that won its proxy war against the Soviets, who themselves were then at war in Afghanistan. These Games would transcend even politics and patriotism on their way toward therapy. "This is an important event under any circumstance," Utah Governor Mike Leavitt had said a few weeks after the attacks, "but fate may have fallen upon this state and city to host an event where the world will come together to heal."
>
> (Gibbs 2002, B2)

Equally inspiring in stories about the Games were announcements made by athletes and administrators who were seemingly willing to flout security concerns and threats. Claiming that they simply wanted to be there in a collective show of sympathy and support for Americans, athletes heralded the Games as a universal statement against terrorism:

> It is at this time more important than ever that the Olympic Games in Salt Lake should go ahead. The world needs the message that the Olympics in Salt Lake will send. Athletes want to compete and spectators around the world want to see good triumph over bad.
>
> (Sergei Bubka, Russian pole-vaulter, cited in Wilson 2001b, E10)

In these ways, athletes, as established public spokespersons and international representatives, gave voice to the millions fearful of ongoing security threats. Instead of employing a standard media tactic of sending video postcards back from the battlefield as a means of engendering sympathy for victims of war (Dobkin 1992), the media utilized sound bites from resolute athletes to promulgate ideologies of victimization and courage.

Through the collective sympathy for America and the appreciation offered for the extensive security measures taken to protect those involved, the Olympic Games also evolved into a context for reaffirming political, cultural, and economic loyalties among nations. By thematically emphasizing America's need to protect its friends from similar victimization, the American media helped create new antiterrorist imagined communities (Palmer 2001) built through the Olympic Games. The media emphasized the support of American initiatives and abilities to protect the Games (and prevent further victimization) as confirmatory evidence of international alignment with the American antiterrorist war campaign—tacitly apparent, in and of itself, by the continuance of the Olympics:

> IOC president Jacques Rogge commented, "The Olympic Games are an answer to the present violence and should not be a victim of violence. The Olympic Games in America are the best message of brotherhood, fraternity, and universality. There is no better symbol of the world uniting together around the cause."
>
> (Visser 2001, 53)

Suggesting that the Olympic Games celebrate American ideals, President Bush stated,

> We believe that these ideals—liberty and freedom—make it possible for people to live together in peace, and the Olympics give us a chance in the middle of a difficult struggle to celebrate international peace and cooperation. All people appreciate the discipline that produces excellence and the character that creates champions.
>
> (Fournier 2002, C1).

Implying that everyone participating in the Games, including IOC members, athletes, foreign fans, and corporate sponsors, sympathized with the United States on such controversial matters as terrorism, security, and even definitions of freedom, media accounts and documentaries painted international responses to security and the Games with an extremely homogeneous brush. A master media frame categorizing all participants of the Games as potential victims of violence—and as people who should emulate America's lead as a nation undeterred by, in President Bush's terms, *the evildoers*—emerged. In this process, de Coubertin's ideals underpinning the Olympics were linked with America's resolve to not succumb to the threat of terrorism at the Games or in any other social venue (Vigh 2002, C10). Further, as Scheuer (2004) and other nation-state theorists point out, doing politics at the Olympic Games around the theme of terrorism was as much about illustrating the global hegemony of the United States as it was about securing the Games from terrorism.

Media coverage of security in Salt Lake City consistently pointed out that all members of democratic nation-states should be prepared for victimization by terrorists (Janofsky 2002, A16). Insisting that terrorism was a concern for all nations, and using the recognized ploy of *taking the public voice* (Hall et al. 1978), the media underlined that *we* must exist in a condition of emotional readiness for war. While the Olympic Games were described as a megaevent primed for symbolic terrorist statements, the Games were discursively constructed as a contest in which members of many nations could potentially be targeted for further attacks. As Lloyd Ward, the chief executive officer of the U.S. Olympic Committee, commented, "There's no question that after September 11th, our view of security in the United States, and I would suggest in the world, must be different" (O'Driscoll 2002, C6).

Hence, the support for America offered through the Olympic Games and the concomitant concerns about security managed by the media during the event helped place individuals from ideologically and culturally diverse nations on a similar emotional playing field. Using the international media as the major channel of communication and rallying around the recent terrorism victim, members of the international sport community helped validate Americans' feelings of victimization, reclaimed patriotism, and ideological cohesion.

Our Friends and Enemies

A third frame dominating the media accounts of security at the 2002 Winter Games highlighted preferred Western constructions of the terms *terrorism* and *terrorist* and underlined the distance between nation-state groups in this connection. At the forefront of media coverage of security risks at the Games were concerns about the types of individuals who might exploit the event for the purpose of political terror. Ingrained within such constructions were dominant understandings of the face of terrorism, which at this point in time was al-Qaeda or other fundamentalist Middle Eastern or Asian groups. By attaching the Winter Games (held, ostensibly, in the spirit of peace, harmony, and cultural exchange) to the global struggle against forms of political violence like terrorism, the media coverage of the Games played a key role in drawing international axes and alliances following the tragic events of September 11. Media analyses of security at the Games contained clear understandings of the modern alliances (e.g., the United States and Great Britain) and their rogue enemies (e.g., the Taliban and al-Qaeda) in the new war on terrorism.

For Elias and Scotson (1965), established social groups are deeply embedded in both the base and the superstructural segments of social figurations, and consequently they control many of its ideological state apparatuses such as the media. Established groups have greater access to—though not necessarily outright ownership of—varying institutional opportunities to shape social discourse. In the case of the 2002 Winter Olympics, since the United States hosted the Games, the American voice became established there, not explicitly as the voice of economic or political leadership but as the voice of the host nation. Almost immediately after the declaration that the Games would continue despite mounting security threats following September 11, the American and Canadian media repeatedly offered constructions of the Olympics as *Our Games*, describing them as "A Homeland Winter Olympics: With a Few Guests" (Lopresti 2002, A1). IOC delegates, politicians, and athletes subsequently expressed similar sentiments and consented to the Americanization of the Games in Salt Lake City.

Participation in the Salt Lake City Olympics became interpreted in the media as being accepted into American-led established groups of mutually identified nations united in the fight against terrorism. Outsider groups, in sociological terms, were the more marginal members or the members excluded from the social group of the Olympic figuration of nations. Outsider groups are less embedded in power positions and are dominated on the basis of their limited statuses. They are excluded from participation in socially influential power structures of a figuration, and their voices or ideologies are mainly silenced in the media (Dowling 1986; Elias and Scotson 1965; Hallin 1986). In reports of security at the 2002 Games, few alternative or outsider constructions of terrorism were offered in the Western media. In this case, outsiders to the Olympic figuration were broadly conceived of as renegade political factions like al-Qaeda, military regimes such as the Taliban, or entire nation-states like Iraq or Afghanistan.

One of the few dissenting voices of the Salt Lake City Games came from Gerhard Heiberg, a Norwegian IOC member, who commented that "a country at war cannot organize the Olympic Games" (Wilson 2001b, E10). Heiberg's comment instantly appeared in media around the world, but such was the weight of critical media response that later he felt forced to apologize for his comments and to rescind them. With Afghanistan's exclusion from the Winter Olympic Games—on the basis of the ruling Taliban's prohibition of female participation in sport—there were few opposing viewpoints about terrorism offered by those described as the main enemies of the American state, at least in the Western media. Instead, when such outsider ideologies were reported in the media that we examined, they were strategically described by established agents as socially uncivilized and barbarous. For example, members of the IOC such as Jacques Rogge were outspoken in their condemnation of the Taliban and its Olympic participation policies. In Rogge's words, "[Afghanistan's reinstatement] will only be possible when there is a stable government in place, and when all the conditions that are put by the IOC are fulfilled" (Associated Press 2001, A12).

As Kamalipour (2000) suggests, established representations of terrorism at the Games also drew attention, often with racist stereotypes, to the cunning, surreptitious, and underhanded strategies typically employed by terrorists waging violence. In news reports, audiences were warned about rogue foreign terrorists seeking to sully the message of harmony cultivated by the Games. For example, one particular bomb scare in Salt Lake City became discursively constructed as a sneaky test of American security systems (Cantera 2002, G2). Other accounts, which exploited the newsworthiness of widely documented reports of how persons involved in the terrorist attacks of September 11 had resided in ordinary American neighborhoods, warned citizens that terrorists might be living in isolated areas of their communities, hiding until the Games commenced (CNN News 2002a).

Finally, with the clever intermingling of the Olympic ideals on humanity with American ideals about the appropriate responses to security and violence at the Winter Games, a consistent established message about terrorism was formed. When the popular media substituted the American standpoint on terrorism and defense for the Olympic perspective, dominant American ideologies became translated into international sport discourses. Again, the influential views of IOC members like Jacques Rogge were frequently cited in media accounts as evidence of the ideological partnership between America and the rest of the world: "Your nation is overcoming a tragedy, a tragedy that has affected the whole world. We stand united with you in the promotion of our common ideals, and hope for world peace" (Harasta 2002, C2). Through notions like these, the established American political views on terrorists or enemies of the state became absorbed, regurgitated, and promoted to sport audiences around the world by groups like the IOC.

Fear over terrorist threats and related security issues at the 2002 Winter Olympic Games in Salt Lake City illustrate the relationship between sport, the media, and political violence originating away from the playing field. In the wake of the September 11 attacks on the United States, the 2002 Olympic Games were inserted into a broader context of social, cultural, and ideological struggle, as was also the case with earlier Olympic Games experiencing their own real or threatened political violence (Roche 2002). Concerns about security at the Olympics closely paralleled American fears about terrorism and the degree to which systems of civil protection could be breached by foreign deviants. For these reasons, Olympic security issues, reported and debated widely in the Western media, evolved into a metaphor of Western societies' abilities to defend their social institutions, cultural practices, ideological systems, and, of course, citizens from what President Bush routinely called "the axes of evil."

Security and Future Games

Exactly 100 days before the 2004 Summer Olympics opening ceremonies, three bomb blasts outside a suburban police station threatened civil security in Athens. The event followed a string of terrorist bombings across continental Europe that started in 2001, including a spate of car bombings in Istanbul in 2003, the bombing of four commuter trains that killed more than 100 people in Madrid on March 11, 2004 (Geiger 2004), and the October 12, 2002, nightclub bombing in the town of Kuta on the Indonesian island of Bali, which killed 202 people and injured 209 others. The Athens bombings occurred just 1 week following an announcement that, in an unprecedented demonstration of the economic effects of terrorism, the IOC had purchased a $200 million U.S. insurance policy for the 2004 Summer Games (Wilson 2004).

Security at the 2004 Summer Games (dubbed by some Olympic critics as the *Armed Camp Games;* Spencer 2004) dominated pre-Olympic discourses. The sheer financial and personnel commitment made to the Games was highlighted in news reports which documented the $1.5 billion U.S. devoted to securing the Greek Games and the 70,000 security agents posted at facilities across Greece (Chang 2003; Shipley and Whitlock 2004). News stories consistently emphasized the considerable North Atlantic Treaty Organization (NATO) military involvement, the missile defense systems covering Greek airspace as a part of Operation Active Endeavour (initiated in the Mediterranean following September 11, 2001), and the scores of counterterrorism experts informing city and Olympic officials in Athens (Murphy 2003).

The international mobilization of an Olympic security program for the Athens Games was staggering. Led by American counterterror experts, CIA officials, and the American-based Science Applications International Corporation, the Olympic Advisory Group of political delegates from established allies including Australia, France, Germany, Israel, Spain, Britain, and the United States spent the bulk of 2003 and 2004 allaying anxieties about terrorist problems in Athens (Chang 2003).

One of the group's toughest tasks was to quell threats of a withdrawal from the Games (ironically, by the United States, Australia, and Israel) following widely publicized failures during security tests at Olympic facilities (Spencer 2004; Vistica 2004). Although security threats were mentioned widely in the media, there is little empirical evidence to suggest that they were considered seriously by Olympic sponsors, athletes, or spectators.

Fears regarding security at the Athens Games were a sobering reality for supporters of the Olympics. International sport enthusiasts had to accept that the Olympics Games, as well as other sports megaevents, do not occur within a political vacuum. Ultimately, the 2004 and 2006 Games, like the 1972 Games in Munich, were staged within a global figuration characterized by emerging political tempests and terrorist controversies. Since 2001, ideological and military lines between nations have been redrawn by the global war on terrorism and significantly complicated by events such as the wars in Afghanistan and Iraq, campaigns of genocide in Rwanda, scandals of abuse on prisoners of war perpetrated by American soldiers, and terrorist bombings across Europe and elsewhere. For this reason and others, the Olympic Games are an attractive locus for the expression of political views on wider world events. As the Olympic Games concentrate established allies and outsider populaces into the microcosmic Olympic village, the Games, in Schaffer and Smith's (2000) terminology, are a potential *big killing event*.

In figurational sociological terms, nations may poach the Olympics as a multimediated context for demarcating boundaries between globally identified *established* and globally identified *outsider* nation-states or political groups (Elias and Scotson 1965). Again, since established social groups are deeply entrenched in both the base and the superstructural segments of social figurations, they control many of its ideological apparatuses. Conversely, outsider groups are more marginal members of a social figuration, less embedded in power positions and dominated on the basis of their limited statuses and resources (Dowling 1986; Elias and Scotson 1965).

Historical evidence reveals that certain nations participating in the Olympics are positioned within the IOC as established or outsider parties and that these positions are further crystallized through incidents of (real or threatened) violence at the Games. Such established–outsider positions within the IOC tend to mirror broader ideological and political antagonisms between nation-states that are often played out violently in other spheres of international struggle. While some sociologists of terrorism focus on the individual pathologies of terrorists or their fundamentalist causes, a sociological analysis of terrorism in sport draws equal attention to the social structural and cultural conditions producing terrorist groups. Episodes of real and perceived violence at the Olympic Games illustrate how sport cultures become saturated with the politics of crime, deviance, and social control.

We must consider how the broader figurational politics of militarism and terrorism might be facilitated by the Olympics and how local hostilities between established and outsider groups may be brought to international audiences through the Games. The 2002 Salt Lake City Winter Games may have lulled Olympic officials into a false sense of security, as they were situated in an isolated area within the United States that was relatively free from intense political turmoil and terrorist violence. Securing the Games proved to be achievable in this context. The 2004 Athens Games, by contrast, were positioned within a region beset by political conflict. The budget for securing the 2004 Games was more than three times the size of the Salt Lake City budget—and for good reason. Concerns about the terrorist organization 17 November—alleged to have committed in excess of 23 political assassinations since 1975, including that of U.S. military official Stephen Saunders in 2003—abounded in pre-Olympic discourses (Murphy 2003). 17 November was also blamed for the 2002 and 2003 bombings of Olympic sponsor offices in Greece.

In February 2004, the terrorist group Phevos and Athena (the names of the Olympic mascots for the Athens Games) claimed responsibility for the firebombing of two Greek environment ministry vehicles in Athens (Wilstein 2004). Only one month later, the Athens-based terrorist group Revolutionary Struggle claimed responsibility for a bomb disarmed outside a Citibank outlet situated blocks away from Olympic facilities (TSN 2004). The media circulated reminders of the 1988 Abu Nidal killing and wounding of 108 passengers on a ferry in the Athens port of Piraeus; predictions of the presence of Hamas, Hizbullah, and the Afghan Kurdistan Workers Party (PKK); and stories of rabid anti-American sentiment in Greece since the initiation of Operation Enduring Freedom (Gertz 2003). Equally, they touted warnings about violent anti-World Trade Organization protests in Athens during the Games as yet another security headache (Murphy 2003). Such local concerns about protesters' behaviors were partially fueled by memories of the violent, anti–world trade, anarcho-environmentalist demonstrations in Sydney before the 2000 Summer Games (Lenskyj 2002).

The problem of securing the Games in Athens was complicated by the geographic and physical infrastructure of the city. Critics of the Athens Games pointed to the notoriously poor security of the Athens international airport, the heavy traffic congestion in the city, the floating population of illegal Muslim immigrants in Greece, the relatively porous borders, and the degree to which the country had been an access point for terrorists seeking entry into Europe (Associated Press 2003). Such criticisms were amplified by the tardy construction of the Olympic facilities, the limited and haphazardly successful security tests at the Olympic facilities, and the U.S. Department of State's *Patterns of Global Terrorism Report* of 2002 that pointed to cities like Athens as ripe terrorism targets (Chang 2003). However, despite these problems, the Games were a security success—save for the disruption of a men's platform diving contest in which a Canadian spectator (Ron Bensimhon) wearing a blue tutu jumped into the Olympic Aquatic Centre pool as a publicity stunt for the Golden Palace online casino (www.goldenpalace.com) and for an incident in the men's marathon in which an Irish protestor (Cornelius Horan) calling himself *The Grand Prix Priest* tackled and dragged Brazilian runner Vanderlei de Lima into the crowd during the final stages of the event (Smith 2004). These were hardly significant events in a security sense, though the media predictably cashed in on their newsworthiness, given broader sensitivities to security concerns at the Games.

The spike in concern about security at the Athens Games and at the Olympics in general was counterbalanced by the relatively placid 2006 Games in Torino, Italy. Several events leading up to the 2006 Games, however, reminded organizers not to become complacent with security efforts. Only four weeks before the Games, new threats of terrorism surfaced after Muslim rioting broke out in several European cities. Muslims in cities including London, Paris, Rome, and Istanbul became enraged after several European newspapers published satirical cartoons depicting the prophet Mohammed. The controversial cartoons first appeared in Denmark. In the days leading up to the Olympics, mobs attacked Danish, Norwegian, and Swedish embassies in six European countries. As a result, Danish athletes and five Danish officials in Torino received extra personal security during the Games. The Italian organizing committee had previously spent $170 million U.S. securing the Games and had anticipated civil disturbances by local extremist groups such as the Red Brigades. Italian protestors, disgruntled with everything from the Games' presence in Italy to Coca-Cola's corporate involvement in sport, regularly disrupted pre-Olympic events including the torch relay into Torino.

The actual Torino Games were not without incident, either. In the closing ceremonies, during a final speech by Valentino Castellani, the chairman of the Torino Olympic Organizing Committee, a Spanish man sponsored by www.goldenpalace.com (their logo emblazoned across his T-shirt), invaded the stage. He shouted to the audience, "Passion lives in Torino," which was the slogan of the Torino Olympics, just before security tackled him and dragged him offstage. A 20-year-old Polish adult film actress attempted a similar stage invasion, holding an Italian flag bearing the handwritten inscription *"Mi consenta"* and wearing a drawing by Roman artist Ettore Wallemberg on her skin. Security officials managed to stop her before she reached the stage.

In terms of the role the media played in constructing Athens and Torino as security concerns, the 2004 and 2006 Games clearly were co-opted into the discourses regarding terrorism in sport that were established in Salt Lake City. Much as in the 2002 Games, security at the 2004 Games (and the assessment of its effectiveness) was ideologically framed by established American military experts, NATO members, and other globally recognized politicians. The security effort in Athens was decisively led by American political and military agents, backed by NATO at the request of the United States, and aligned with the framing of the war in Iraq promulgated in Western media.

The problems and discourses of political violence, security, and terrorism we have explored in this chapter are not Athens anomalies but are contemporary global realities that the IOC and other international sports organizations must anticipate and manage. Given the increasing number of nations included in the Olympic Games and the massive international audience the Games procure, established and outsider groups might seek to further exploit the Olympics as a context of military and political struggle. Consequently, staging the Games has become a military exercise, with Olympic sites taking on the appearance of occupied camps policed by highly trained officials from established nations.

THEORETICAL INTERSECTIONS

The Olympic community may be a prototype of what Anderson (1991) calls an *imagined community*. Following Anderson's lead, cultural studies theorists interested in social movements such as the Olympics address how these imagined communities are more fictional representations of cultural affinities between nation-states than they are empirical realities. Anderson's historiography of the emergence of imagined communities succinctly captures the ways in which symbolic representations of spatially and temporally contextualized *we* groups (such as the groups established every two years at an Olympics) are tactically formed by actors to create order and meaning in the world. In the case example discussed in this chapter, the sacrosanct imagined athlete community described as the *Olympic movement* or the *Olympic community* is not an actual conglomerate of ideologically and socially bound actors solely interested in amateur sport; rather, it is a loose organization of diverse peoples who separately and collectively utilize the Games for extending and enforcing their own versions of economic, political, moral, and religious order in the world.

The Games have been, and continue to be, a global stage for friendly nation building, commerce, political campaigning, and ideological dissemination. Standing behind athletes, coaches, and spectators within the imagined Olympic community are government officials, multinational corporate sponsors, and a lengthy list of other interest groups who seek to tacitly link their agendas to mediations of the Olympics. As we have witnessed with increasing regularity throughout the past 40 years, and especially in the very recent past, those who are politically invested within the Games community have used mass mediations to remind audiences of the economic, cultural, and moral superiority of particular nations and the inferiority of others.

In the following sections, we ask you to consider theoretical ways of understanding the political attractiveness of the Games as a site of establishing global or nation-state norms and as a site for demonstrating deviant resistance against members of the perceived global hegemony. Throughout our discussions of the separate theories, we ask you to consider if and how the Games will ever be ideologically unaffected by discourses of terrorism or ever be fully protected from political violence.

FUNCTIONALISM AND STRAIN THEORY

Classic structural-functionalist theories of social integration might view acts of terrorism as ideal examples of social dysfunction. In *The Structure of Social Action* (1951), Talcott Parsons describes a society as a homeostatic system in which social acts and processes either contribute to the overall health of the system or become pathologies that may threaten the system. Deviant behavior within the system results when the system's control mechanisms (i.e., values, norms, shared social codes, and practices) are ineffectual in regulating balanced social behavior. Parsons might suggest the following about the role of terrorism in a social system and the structural pathology it might imply.

Terrorism, as an expression of anger and frustration toward a group that controls the main institutions in a system, highlights a power imbalance among groups within the social structure. Terrorist groups often (but not always) are formed by people without a significant claim to institutional sites of power control like the government, the courts, the police, the economy, or even the media. Research on terrorism tells us that its garden-variety forms involve a culturally or structurally powerless or oppressed group lashing out in anger at the ruling elite. Cases of terrorism in Northern Ireland waged by the Irish Republican Army or in Israel waged by the Palestinian Liberation Army illustrate this point. For Parsons, acts of militantly expressed anger such as terrorism manifest themselves in a system that suppresses healthy forms of anger expression. Thus, terrorism is the product of the relationship between the powerful and the powerless and is not random and meaningless, however catastrophic its outcome. That is to say—and critically—however devastating and reprehensible, terrorism bears meaning to someone. In the case of the Olympic Games, it is the system of national exclusion and inclusion in the IOC or in the Games' membership that may make the event a suitable target of terrorist activity.

CONFLICT THEORY

Conflict theorists such as Quinney (1977) focus on how the state and state-sponsored institutions like sport are ideological instruments of the ruling classes. In *Class, State and Crime,* Quinney suggests that the ruling elite's economic and cultural interests are established and protected through state-run systems of social control, such as the criminal justice system and forms of social welfare. *Deviance* is the institutional label for behaviors that challenge the ruling elite's authority. Acts of terrorism—defined as such by people in positions of power—are deemed as deviant cultural expressions or primitive social behaviors undertaken by those who are culturally maladjusted or unworthy of institutional power.

We take Quinney's instrumental conflict perspective as a theoretical guide to study how terrorism is encoded with cultural meaning through its mass mediation during the Olympic Games. Since the media acts, according to conflict theorists like Quinney, as an ideological state apparatus (Althusser 1977), we can examine if and how preferred (Hall 1980) state definitions of terrorism, violence, and national or ethnic outsiders are promulgated through televised or other textual representations of the Games. As discussed in this chapter, the media may act as a tool of the established power bloc in the process of inserting concerns about terrorism into Olympic discourses, and the media may use Olympic broadcasts to promote political lines of good versus evil among athletes, nations, and cultures.

INTERACTION THEORY

Labeling theorists such as Ben-Yehuda are similarly concerned with how particular acts of violence become identified as terrorism through news channels. In his book, *Assassinations by Jews: A Rhetorical Device for Justice* (1993), Ben-Yehuda focuses on how collectivities such as government agencies selectively target actors as terrorists and stigmatize their political behaviors and expressions as violent, murderous, barbaric, threatening, socially disintegrative, or culturally catastrophic. Labeling not only isolates the offenders culturally but also alienates them from political power networks. Thus, symbolic allegiances among the nonoffending groups are strengthened. Ben-Yehuda suggests that what eventually counts as terrorism is merely a social construction determined by the politics of labeling.

From Ben-Yehuda's theoretical understanding of labeling, the case study of media coverage of terrorism at the Olympic Games suggests that there exists a series of dominant frames about terrorists and terrorism. However, labeling theorists might challenge a critical reader of terrorism texts related to the Olympic Games to examine if there are multiple ideological constructions of terrorism or very few or even only one. The data presented in this chapter on the global coverage of the Olympics illustrate how labeling processes tend to unfold in a unilinear manner, with the targeted group receiving little agency to defend their stigmatization. Dominant nations tend to own or significantly influence media stories related to the Games and to systematically exclude those labeled as threats to the Olympic movement in order to maintain labeling authority over them.

SOCIAL CONTROL THEORY

Social control theorists like Cohen and Felson (1979) explain how deviance is produced when particular social conditions crystallize. The heart of their routine activities theory is that we can explain rates of victimization in a given geographic area by exploring whether three factors are present in that area: motivated offenders, suitable targets, and an absence of guardianship over the targets. The probability of crime is high in an environment where these three factors converge or persist over time. In the language of Cohen and Felson, the *routine activities* of everyday life—such as riding a subway train, using a bank machine, attending a sports event, or leaving the home unattended when going to work—expose individuals to potential offenders. Simply put, the routine activities of social life provide motivated offenders (who are presumed to be everywhere) with opportunities to engage in crime. The theory encourages us to consider how the victims themselves play a role in controlling future deviance by using environmental awareness to protect their personal property and bodies from repeat victimization.

We can easily extract the core principles of the routine activities theory to decipher components of Olympic media coverage of terrorism. Even a cursory review of Olympic media coverage in 2002, 2004, and 2006 uncovers a consistent theme about security and the Games. Across media accounts of the Games as a potential site of terrorism, journalists drew attention to this particular cultural ritual as a logical site of terror work. Due to their sheer size, global scope, and cultural significance, the Olympic Games provide terrorist groups with an ideal opportunity for expressing political statements through violence against attendees. According to the pragmatic rationale of Cohen and Felson, the Games' organizers simply cannot contain offenders' motivation (i.e., to engage in terrorism) or eliminate all potential targets of victimization (i.e., athletes, fans, officials, and so on). So to control terrorist threats at the Games, organizers are publicly charged with the responsibility of eliminating one central element from the triad of crime factors: the absence of guardianship. In the case of the 2004 Games in Athens, the host city was depicted as a setting reputed for safe housing of terrorist groups, and therefore the Games were a setting with an abundance of motivated offenders in the presence of athlete and spectator targets. Media reports of security at the Games, while first suggesting that a series of failures occurred in pre-Olympic tests, ultimately showcased the intensely protectionist (or guardian) air about security in Athens. Stories pointed out that the city, and more specifically all Olympic venues, would be the most heavily policed setting on the planet. In no case would there be an absence of guardianship at the Games, and this factor made the Olympic grounds an unattractive target of politically charged violence. Reports of security measures at the 2004 Games unequivocally proclaimed, much as those pertaining to the 2002 Games did, that the citizens of the world participating in and attending the Olympics would be aggressively protected.

CLASSICAL THEORY

Rational choice theorists such as Cornish and Clarke (1986) would approach the analysis of terrorism at the Olympic Games with a slightly different emphasis than that of social control theorists. In their book *The Reasoning Criminal,* Cornish and Clarke argue that deviance results when an actor views rule violation favorably. In other words, deviance results, regardless of its prohibition, when committing an institutionally defined deviant act will satisfy a social or an emotional need of an actor and when the actor perceives that there is an opportunity for committing the act. The actor will carefully calculate the pros (i.e., personal benefits) versus the cons (i.e., likelihood of apprehension and punishment) of the deviant act and then proceed on the basis of the most attractive outcome. To minimize acts of deviance, control agents should ensure that rule violations are perceived as unpleasing, impossible, or simply too risky. In the language of the classical theorists of deviance, such as Jeremy Bentham and Cesare Beccaria, social control is best achieved when actors are sufficiently deterred from committing deviance by the threat of external and internal punishments.

A rational choice theoretical reading of the media coverage of security at the 2002 and 2004 Olympic Games might expose an attempt by the IOC and nation-states like the United States or Greece to use pre-Olympic narratives for explicitly deterrence purposes. In our review of the selected media coverage contained in this chapter, it is not difficult to decipher a message sent to terrorists of "Do not even bother trying to come here!" weaving through discursive constructions of security and the Olympics. Journalistic emphases on the military presence at the Games, the money spent on high-tech surveillance systems, the multiple nations involved in security, the zero-tolerance policies for suspected persons or troublemakers, and the effectiveness of pre-Olympic security testing were perhaps a carefully scripted message of deterrence to all potential terrorists. By using the global media as a platform for disseminating messages about the strength and resolve of nations participating in the Games, the government, corporate, and Olympic stakeholders who acted as spokespersons of the Games in the media encouraged terrorists to view the host cities and the Games themselves as uninviting sites of violence and dissent.

CRITICAL THEORY

A postmodern reading of terrorism will be far more complex than our previous theoretical dissections of political violence have been. For postmodern criminologists, public surveillance is a mainstay of deviance discovery, regulation, and discipline. In his book *Surveillance After September 11* (2003), Lyon argues that policing and intelligence research to identify potential terror threats has spread to every street corner, office space, home, and public setting in the United States and other countries. The work of Deleuze and Guattari (1987) offers an innovative direction in the study of terrorism and surveillance by focusing on the mushrooming of what they call *rhizomatic systems of surveillance.* In *A Thousand Plateaus,* Deleuze and Guattari (1987) describe surveillance (as a form of social control) as a creeping plant with branches spreading across the landscape. Surveillance operates as a system of information gathering, in which agents of social control may assemble pieces of information about citizens in practically every social setting.

Surveillance is everywhere, but it is often unseen, unspoken, and seemingly innocuous. Following September 11, for example, surveillance data poured in from supermarkets, hotels, restaurants, corner stores, street intersections, and bank card records, and these data were used to trace the activities of the terrorists in the days and hours before the attacks. The use of the electronic images and other forms of information permit intelligence services around the world to monitor people minute by minute and reassemble their behaviors in order to construct an overall chronology of events.

In the case study of the Olympic Games, we can see how state surveillance systems crept into Olympic camps thousands of kilometers away from the proverbial battle fields following September 11. Even the tragic events in Munich in 1972 or in Atlanta in 1996 spiked surveillance procedures at the Olympics. Indeed, there have been few social events as heavily policed as the 2002 Winter Games in Salt Lake City or the 2004 Summer Games in Athens. Such systems of security are designed to be protective toward athletes, officials, and spectators and are political assertions of the right of the United States to monitor all social spaces in the hunt for al-Qaeda or other terrorist cells and networks. As Lyon (2003) illustrates, surveillance was strengthened first at government offices, transnational corporate buildings, airports, and other high-risk places, but eventually it crept into the Olympic villages and facilities.

GENDER AND FEMINIST THEORY

In an overview of how women are subordinated in most social institutions, MacKinnon's *Toward a Feminist Theory of the State* (1989) questions why discourses about acts of political aggression (such as terrorism) typically exclude the subject of women as victims of violence. MacKinnon, a political scientist and pioneer in the sociological analysis of how a state's legal system is underpinned by patriarchy, challenges us to consider how violence and social control become framed by men as a male issue. Throughout the corpus of her work on violence against women such as pornography and rape, MacKinnon's Marxist-Feminist analyses produce a sobering realization that women, as a subordinate social class, have been historically voiceless in public mediations of violence. Since the 1990s, sociologists of deviance and crime have heeded MacKinnon's call to critically inspect this phenomenon.

Analyses of terrorism discourses in and around the Olympic Games might lead us to falsely assume that modern terrorism is a genderless process. Coverage of the 2002 pre-Olympic security efforts and terrorism threats at the Salt Lake City venue scarcely mentioned women, as either perpetrators or victims of violence, in the global war on terrorism. Despite the fact that women have been killed on battlefields as soldiers in the war on terror or deliberately massacred as civilians at the hands of Western-targeted terrorists, terrorism is routinely assembled at the Games as a problem for nations and not for gendered individuals. Few people have analyzed how most historical cases of terrorism played out before or during the Olympics were perpetrated by men or that female athletes at the Games are far more likely to be victimized by males than by other females in acts of terrorism. Cleverly, though, the politically influenced IOC have used media coverage of terrorism at the Games to underscore why countries like Iraq and Afghanistan have been excluded in the recent past: in part, because of state-based policies prohibiting women from participating in Olympic sports. Additionally, and in a patriarchal maneuver that MacKinnon might predict, quotes from Western female athletes were inserted into discourses of security at the Games as public affirmation of the protection they experienced in the hands of the (male) security officers, organizers, and political leaders responsible for securing the event. In a now famous photograph of President Bush standing among American athletes in the Rice-Eccles Olympic Stadium during the opening ceremonies at the 2002 Salt Lake City Games, all of the athletes surrounding him are female.

INTEGRATED THEORY

One of the most widely used and debated integrated approaches to crime, Tittle's (1995) control balance theory focuses on how a person's motivation to commit deviance is determined by the degree of control the person is able to exert over others versus the degree of control the person is subject to in social life. For Tittle, each individual has a control ratio that determines personal action. When a person's state of control is balanced, norm-abiding behavior is expected. When a person experiences an imbalance in the control ratio, through either an excess or a deficit of control, deviance is likely given the situational opportunities to correct the imbalance. Tittle's theoretical assumption largely hinges upon his belief that humans possess an innate desire to be autonomous. As discussed in *Control Balance: Toward a General Theory of Deviance*, deviance exists along a conceptual continuum. Acts of deviance are defined according to the level of excess or deficiency in the perpetrator's control abilities. People with excess control typically engage in deviant acts of exploitation, plunder, or decadence, while people in deficit deviate through predation, defiance, or submissiveness.

Given the core assumptions of Tittle's theory, we could study how acts of terrorism and the mass-mediated threats of terrorism at the Olympic Games are socially categorized by control agents in the West as predatory acts. Data presented in this chapter could be used to illustrate how nameless and faceless potential perpetrators of terrorism are categorized in pre-Olympic discourses as evildoers. Enemies of the "free world" are stereotyped as villains seeking to instill fear in the hearts of democratic peoples by literally hunting them at collective social rituals like the Games. The celebratory, peaceful, globally inclusive, and secular aspects of the Games are described as the actual targets of terrorism in such mediation processes. Terrorists are further described as those preying on innocents in order to correct the control deficit created by their religious, political, economic, and cultural differences.

Discussion Questions

1. Given what we have and might not have discussed in this chapter, think about how sports organizers might define the concept of terrorism.

2. Critically discuss the role of the media in framing the problem of terrorism at the Olympic Games. In particular, ask yourself whether you think the media have overamplified the threat of terrorism at sports events like the Games.

3. Do you think it is right to exclude nations from participating in the Games on the basis of their real or perceived links to terrorist organizations? Why or why not? Can you think of examples of countries that are allowed to participate at the Olympics that are exceptions to this rule?

Recommended Readings

Atkinson, M., and K. Young. 2003. Terror games: Media treatment of security issues at the 2002 Winter Olympic games. *OLYMPIKA* 11:53-78.

> This case study examines how mass mediation of a post–September 11 United States figured prominently in the coverage of the 2002 Winter Olympic Games. The authors adopt a figurational perspective to explore how several emergent ideological frames about the American-led war on terrorism prevailed in television and print coverage of the Games.

Guttmann, A. 2002. *The Olympics: A history of the modern Games*. Chicago: University of Chicago Press.

> Guttmann is widely regarded as a leading sport historian of the Olympics, and this book shows why he has earned such a reputation. Guttmann draws attention to the sociopolitical relevance of the Games as, among other things, a site of cultural tension and struggle between nations.

Senn, A. 1999. *Power, politics and the Olympic Games*. Champaign, IL: Human Kinetics.

> In his overview of the historical emergence of the modern Games, Senn covers some of the most infamous scandals and political controversies of modern Games history. Senn's book is an especially important resource for readers interested in Russian and Eastern European political tensions at the Games.

Walters, G. 2006. *Berlin Games: How the Nazis stole the Olympic dream*. New York: William Morrow.

> Walters' in-depth case study of the 1936 Summer Games is an historical and journalistic account of how the Nazi party seized the Olympics as a propaganda tool and as an ideological state apparatus.

Young, K., and K. Wamsley. 2006. *Global Olympics: Historical and sociological studies of the modern Games*. London: Elsevier.

> This collection of essays on the Olympics traces both the historical emergence of the modern Games and the contemporary scandals underpinning the Games' staging and representation by global media.

CHAPTER 9

Toward a Public Sociology of Sport Deviance

© Associated Press

In this book we have explored a cluster of behaviors related to sport:

- Youth-based resistance movements
- Animal and blood sport violence
- Excessive body behaviors and extreme attitudes toward body weight
- Innovative ways that illness and injury may be reconfigured to reconstruct an athletic self
- Hyperaggression on the field of play and informal and formal responses to such aggression
- The ever-expanding jurisdictions of threat, security, and policing in a changing world of sport and politics

Our contention is that each of these behaviors, in its own way, has been problematized in sport and has resulted in varying amounts of deviance labeling, stigma, disrepute, or punishment. Needless to say, these behaviors do not encompass the full extent of behaviors that have been and continue to be labeled, stigmatized, made disreputable, or sanctioned in sport because, like any other social institution, sport is a world filled with problem behaviors, problem conventions, problem structures, and problem policing. At the time of this writing, sport is confronted with and embarrassed by what seem like ubiquitous problems, which are in fact merely the tip of the sport-deviance iceberg. These include the following:

- Athletes who are out of control both on and off the field and who feel that they have immunity from normal expectations and rules of behavior
- Athletes who are injured, paralyzed, or killed while pursuing riskier and riskier practices in the name of sport and fun
- Problematic fan and crowd behavior that has led to obvious and expensive spikes in stadium security and policing
- An increasingly subterranean world of sport hazing premised on the notion that a sport identity can be achieved only through humiliation, embarrassment, and abuse
- Negative experiences for child athletes, often due to the actions of overbearing and abusive parents and coaches
- Animal use and abuse in sport
- Discrimination of social groups who remain marginalized through sport and the targets of chilly climates
- Practices of educational institutions that overlook rule breaking and deviance in the pursuit of winning, reputation, and ego
- Disadvantaged sweatshop workers producing massively overpriced sport clothing and paraphernalia
- Environments damaged or destroyed in the construction of sport facilities and hosting of sports contests

Focusing on the harsher versions of these practices, Young (2008) conceives of these behaviors as overlapping components in a broader matrix of sport-related violence. This aggregate image is hardly flattering for sport in many contexts, least of all North America.

As a relatively young subdiscipline, the sociology of sport has already produced an impressive body of research to help us understand and react to these—and other—behaviors. But this research cannot operate alone and clearly needs help. To this end, the purpose of this book is to demonstrate that other subdisciplines, especially criminology and deviance, may coalesce with the sociology of sport to better explain and intervene into sport deviance. Showcasing the potential contributions of eight theoretical houses, our Theoretical Intersections segments that conclude each substantive chapter underscore the point that understanding sport deviance and acting responsibly upon it requires a fuller range of sociological tools than may be found in any one subdiscipline.

Together, the substantive case studies and theoretical intersections in this book teach us how we may conceive of deviance in (or out of) sport:

- There are many different approaches to defining deviance. For example, deviance may be viewed as disrespect for one's opponent, as corruption, as scandal, or as behavior that embarrasses or is simply unsophisticated enough to get caught.

- No human behavior may be objectively defined as deviance in all societies. For example, rougher or gentler versions of many sports are prized differentially across cultures, regions, and spaces.

- There is a subjective notion of deviance that emphasizes the relevance of social context and social construction in defining *right* and *wrong*. For example, being a Japanese sumo wrestler or an NFL lineman requires a very different kind of athleticism than an English soccer player or an African long-distance runner requires.

- Deviance works like the beauty axiom—its positive and negative elements exist in the eye of the beholder. For example, during an NHL fistfight, portions of the crowd stand up and cheer, while others want to see this element of the game removed.

- Deviance is historically relative, socially constructed, and culturally varied. For example, certain societies at certain times privilege cooperative and mass participation models of sport, while others at other times prefer elite models, as may be witnessed in the varieties of Olympic Games that have taken place throughout time.

- Deviance cannot be divorced from forms of social ordering and stratification and ideology. For example, soccer hooliganism has been shown to be strongly tied to social class, gender, race, and national identity.

- Deviance may be concealed or flamboyantly displayed. For example, drug cheats are careful who they disclose information to and coaches of violent players disavow their proviolence instructions, while female Olympic sprinters boldly display their sexualized clothing, makeup, or nails and controversial NBA players flaunt their body modifications.

- Unlike criminal behavior, acts of sport deviance may violate laws *or* norms. For example, the use of banned substances in sport may be unfriendly violations of trust *or* violations of the criminal code.

- Any behavior may be considered as deviant and yet be statistically normative. For example, athletes in many sports know which rules may be bent; they become expert recidivist offenders.

- The rewards of deviance may outweigh the costs. For example, varieties of NHL brutality and pugilism are rewarded subculturally, reputationally, and occupationally even, paradoxically, as violent athletes are sanctioned by leagues.

- Finally, as Canadian criminologist John Hagan (1991) reminds us, problem behaviors may be understood on a sliding scale of severity. Behaviors move from conformity (where there is social approval or where the behavior is seen to serve a social function, such as tackling hard on the field of play or training hard to conform to the sport ethic), to social deviation (where people notice that rules are bent but turn a blind eye because such acts are still viewed as relatively harmless, such as when a soccer player steals ground by advancing the ball farther than he should for a free kick or a throw-in or when a fan uses vulgar or threatening language in reaction to a play), to conflict deviance (where there is far more disagreement about the evaluation of social harm and the social norm, such as when a soccer player dives to win a penalty or when a squash player losing a point uses her body cleverly to win a let), to consensus deviance (where there is high agreement about the wrongfulness of the act, which is seen as very harmful, such as when an Olympic sprinter sets world records by using prolonged cycles of banned substances or when an ice hockey player uses his stick to viciously strike an opponent).

The literature on crime, deviance, and social control teaches us that its subject matter is fundamentally social, relative, and situational, as are the resulting public responses. To this end, one of our goals in writing this book is to contribute to public discourses and intervention strategies regarding serious forms of crime and deviance in sport cultures. We present the material in this book not only as sociologists of crime, deviance, and sport but also as academics interested in pursuing a *public sociology*.

In the first volume of the 2007 *Sociology of Sport Journal,* which is perhaps the premier scholarly journal in this subfield, the contributing authors questioned whether the sociology of sport makes a difference in the lives of sports insiders and whether sociologists optimize their research by engaging effectively with their surrounding communities. Carrington (2007) in particular lamented what he perceived to be a degree of academic detachment with which many sociologists of sport approach their research, and he questioned the extent to which their work actually encourages social change. Such a call for a more public sociology of sport in which researchers become advocates of, or catalysts for, political action was not new in 2007, but it did emphasize the point that academic work might have a practical and interventionist purpose beyond the ivory tower.

Throughout this book, we have explored the panorama of sport deviance with due consideration for how Carrington and others, such as Burawoy (2004), understand the mandate of a public sociology. There are certainly areas in the text where we lean toward community involvement with substantial enthusiasm; indeed, what some may refer to as an excess of political or social "involvement" and a lack of academic "detachment" (Elias 1978). Nevertheless, we believe that if the sociology of sport, and sport deviance, is to *matter* publicly, a recalibration of its central themes, purposes, and applications must be undertaken. Stated differently, we see great academic and social merit in becoming "involved" with the people we study in the field of deviancy research in order to better understand their experiences, and advocate for public policy development where desired. Issues that we have examined in this book, such as drug use, the abuse and exploitation of athletes and animals, player violence, resistant and oppositional ways of doing sport, and the entire gamut of wanted and unwanted rule violations, should be considered as interinstitutional policy matters that sociologists, among others, have an ethical and social responsibility to study, understand, and publicly debate.

Almost daily, cases of sport behavior call attention to the importance of re-examining what we mean by *normalcy* and *deviance* and *wanted* and *unwanted* sport behavior. Of course, behaviors considered as such are historically dynamic and culturally specific and come with a full range of social implications. Putting a finger on what Durkheim termed the *normal* and the *pathological* is not easy. Far from requiring an exercise in objectively defining one or the other, it usually means arriving at subjective conclusions about behavior that are based on things like conventions, norms, and mores as well as on the multiple axes along which societies are stratified, such as social class, age, gender, religion, and socioeconomic status. In brief, and as Canadian sociologist of sport Gruneau (1999) argued, sport and sport behavior embodies different meanings for different groups and classes.

As an example, think about the subject of spying on or scouting other players or teams. While in professional sports like ice hockey it is common practice to study video footage of other teams or to send team representatives to watch others practice and to study their secret plays, in other sports such as American football such activities constitute espionage. In 2007, the New England Patriots were caught videotaping the defensive coordinators of rival teams as they sent hand signals to players. The Patriots would study the signals in order to crack the codes and thereby anticipate the plays of the defensive squads. The Patriots were fined $250,000 U.S., head coach Bill Belichick was fined $500,000 U.S., and, perhaps most consequentially, the NFL removed the team's right to participate in the first round of the 2008 draft. Just a few weeks before the Patriots' Spygate scandal, F1 racing team McLaren was assessed a staggering $100 million U.S. fine and stripped of team racing points by the World Motor Sport Council for possession of leaked technical information on rival team Ferrari's car designs. To the best of our knowledge, no sociologist other than John Sugden (2007) has acknowledged and theoretically explored for the politics and processes involved in surveillance and espionage within sport cultures. As sociologists, we are curious as to how spying in one sport culture is relatively tolerable, while in another it garners among the heftiest financial punishment paid in sport history and is enmeshed in scandal.

Existing theory and research on sport deviance does not adequately predict and only partially explains through commonsense approaches why people violate rules within sport. If the sociology of sport deviance is to matter publicly, sociologists of sport need to more adequately explore the way in which we know deviance as an enduring fixture of group life (a task of theory and method) and the practical and active potential of research on sport deviance (a task of praxis). As an embodied, a material, a structured, and a culturally defined process, sport deviance is not only about discourse and the word of the media but also about the way real people act in, shape, and derive meaning from their surrounding communities. As such, sport deviance is socially significant, but more research is needed to demonstrate the extent to which it matters and what can be done about it.

Victimological and Political-Economic Perspectives

A publicly beneficial sociology of sport deviance might commence by exposing the established and outsider logics of power, victimization, and resistance embedded in both wanted and unwanted rule violations. Several decades of research in the sociology of sport produces, as we have endeavored to show in this book, a stockpile of evidence on how deviance or rule violation is a social power play involving some social actors who benefit from sport deviance and crime, some who benefit through victimization, and yet others who resist. However, much more could be said in this regard. Consider the following.

Research on the denial or usurpation of minority rights, identity-based discrimination, physical exploitation and control, and economic misdemeanors needs to be expanded in sport deviance. Heteronormative masculinity, essentialized constructions of femininity, and taken-for-granted associations of biology, ability, and race all need to be interrogated as cultural logics that stratify actors into established and outsider sport groups. Keeping in line with the mandate and philosophy of a responsible and public scholarship, public sociologists of sport deviance might encourage sport consumers to reject cultural norms in sport that marginalize actors either structurally or socially. Through research on normative and deviant sport identities, the global sociology of sport community strives to make sport spaces more inclusive and celebratory of difference. Recent identity rights research in the sociology of sport and current postidentity theorizing (see McDonald 2007) may unfortunately direct attention away from the material, objective, and numeric indicators that highlight the pervasiveness of problems like discrimination, exploitation, and victimization in sport. Discourse-oriented, identity-focused, and media-analytic research, which pervades sociology of sport journals, de-emphasizes the obdurate and structurally patterned bases of social power (Gruneau 1999) and instead focuses on the symbolic representation of power through sport signs and power negotiation through manipulation of group image, counterlabeling, and charisma building.

Bourdieu (1984), Donnelly and Harvey (2007), Bairner (2007), Gruneau (1999), and a host of others question the tendency to downplay the importance of social class as a determinant of sport behavior, and with good reason. Nearly 100 years of research on crime and deviance outside of sport clearly shows that members of socially underprivileged classes are the most likely to commit, and be caught for committing, criminal behaviors. For example, the working classes in North America and the United Kingdom are overrepresented among users of illicit drugs (Liska and Messner 1999). However, studies of the relationship between drug use in sport and social class seem to be waning. Questioning the philosophy of drug use and its representation is important to understanding the role that drugs play in the social world of sport, but an understanding of the precursors, extent, and control of drug use in sport cultures has suffered (Waddington 2000).

From the 1970s onward, subcultural and neotribe research on both sides of the Atlantic highlighted the involvement of the middle class in using the spare-time spectrum for identity-based resistance. Yet there has been a tendency to downplay the importance of middle-class ennui and fragmentation as structural precursors to membership in alternative sport subcultures (see Wheaton 2004). Few critical sociologists of sport link subcultural resistance to sociogenic (that is to say, ongoing structural) and historical change in societies influencing the middle classes. Sociologists of sport have seemingly stripped the *economy* out of *political economy* throughout two decades of research on sport deviance (Bairner 2007). In this respect, a publicly informative sociology of sport deviance would integrate victimological and political-economic perspectives.

A public sociology of sport deviance must also be imbued with several other key features. For instance, it must recognize that existing social problems in sport are materially based and culturally mediated, must produce theoretically informed and empirically verified suggestions for policy change, and must generate models of sport as a site of social integration that celebrates diversity. A public sociology of sport deviance utilizes research on rule violation to assess if and how sport is a site where health promotion is evident and human physical, intellectual, artistic, and moral potentials are explored without fear or prejudice. Critical sociology of sport frequently involves deconstructing identities, practices, institutions, and images of power in sports worlds without suggesting concrete changes to improve sport. A public sociology of sport deviance must venture beyond philosophy and critique; it must, in our view, engage in the process of resolution.

Our dual positions as public sociologists of sport and sociologists of deviance encourage us to employ crime and deviancy theory to explain the antecedents and outcomes of rule violation in sport. Generally speaking, crime and deviancy theories tend to be causal or processually mechanistic (Liska and Messner 1999). Crime and deviancy theories construct general understandings of the human condition, explain pathways into deviance, suggest why rule violators persist in their careers, and suggest interventions (Tittle 1995).

But in a postcausal sociology of sport, where theorizing about the causal determinants of rule-violating behavior seems anathema to the scholarly process, crime and deviancy theories are of little interest. Much of the current crime and deviance research, especially in North America, involves hypothetico-deductive, quantitative approaches geared toward testing the predictive and explanatory power of theory. In contrast, research oriented toward theory and hypothesis testing is infrequently published in the major journals, including the *Sociology of Sport Journal, International Review for the Sociology of Sport*, and *Journal of Sport and Social Issues.* Theories designed to test causes of behavior, describe rule violation, and recommend desistance policies may be unpalatable in a postcausal sociology of sport. Sociologists who study social problems in sport tend to focus on actor constructions and mediations of such problems and rarely, if ever, suggest how certain social structures or cultural practices are causally linked to the problems (and are therefore able to help correct the problems).

Rejecting deviancy and crime research on the grounds of its causal orientation does not reflect what sociologists of sport from nearly every theoretical camp and methodological perspective do in practice. However, criticisms of causal-positivistic research (Pronger 2002) delegitimize alternative ways of knowing sport processes, a curious exercise in theoretical and methodological hegemony. Our work on ticket scalpers, rugby players, drug users, women who relish aggression, animal abusers, urban freeflow runners, and other *sport deviants* strives to understand the process by which social life unfolds, emphasizing how behaviors and their representations structurally and culturally originate, socially unfold, and are interactively received and mediated by audiences. Theory and grounded research on rule violations in sport generate arguments regarding how the sports world is organized and experienced in deeply patterned ways and how the sports world might be experienced if, for example, ticket scalpers did not exploit the homeless in order to secure tickets, dogs were not killed as part of urban gambling cultures, and traceurs were allowed to flow in the city without reprisal from the police.

Social Development Through Youth Sport

From the literature on the sociology of deviance, we find reason to examine sport's potential role as social inoculation against human suffering produced through rule violation. The early Chicago School research on youth delinquency exposed unsupervised leisure time as a context of rule violation for teenagers. Since then, the bulk of crime and deviance theories have either placed the origin of rule violating in adolescence as the definitive life stage for desistance intervention (Sampson and Laub 1993). Wilson, White, and Fisher (2001) study the role of recreational drop-in centers and midnight basketball leagues in Hamilton (Canada) as components of the city's strategy for combating youth drug abuse. Griffin (1998) explores whether adolescent girls' involvement in sport reduces the likelihood of teenage pregnancy. The research of Curtis, McTeer, and White (2003) examines whether young athletes' sport participation is linked with education, employment, and social bonding patterns of success.

If studies of identity rights dominated research on rule violation and resistance in sport throughout the 1990s, studies of youth rights and children's safety in and through sport may be the burgeoning area of the 2000s. From our perspective, the contemporary groundswell of interest in global youth sport cultures fits perfectly with the development of a public sociology of sport deviance.

Sport federations, sports organizations, sports teams, nongovernmental sports offices, and governmental sports agencies as well as international sport advocates have analyzed what best practices may be adopted to protect the rights of children in sport and to ensure that sport is child-centered everywhere it takes place (David 2005). The United Nations' (UN's) 1989 globally ratified document, *The Convention on the Rights of the Child* was a watershed statement on sport as a site of childhood development. It was shortly followed by the 1996 *Panathlon Charter on the Rights of the Child in Sport* (David 2005). Emergent discourses across international organizations and subcommittees like the UN, the United Nations Children's Fund (UNICEF), and the United Nations Educational, Scientific, and Cultural Organization (UNESCO) in the late 1990s described an ideal sport culture as a nondiscriminatory social environment that allows participants to develop as healthy and protected persons (Vanden Auweele 2003). The *Panathlon Charter* in particular stresses social mentorship and bonding through sport and the extensive benefits of providing children with voices to express their own desires for and interests in sport.

By the 2000 UN Millennium Summit and the 2002 UN Special Session on Children, a mantra of social development through youth sport had crystallized. The UN's 2002 document, *A World Fit for Children* and the related Millennium Development Goals (MDGs) were recognized by UNICEF and UNESCO as tools reframing the logic and practice of global sport. In July of 2003, UN Secretary-General Kofi Annan formally addressed members of the international assembly, suggesting how sport may be an ideal vehicle for achieving MDGs. The UN then established the Office of Sport for Development and Peace to broadcast Annan's message. Members of UNICEF agreed with the potential link between MDGs and sport and worked in conjunction with Adolf Ogi, the UN Special Adviser on Sport for Development and Peace, and the UN Inter-Agency Task Force on Sport for Development and Peace to produce *Sport for Development and Peace: Towards Achieving Millennium Development Goals* in 2003. Berna (2007) argues that this document is the first global statement on sport as a basic human right for children and as a cultural site of international peace promotion. The UN continued the campaign by declaring 2005 the International Year of Sport and Physical Education. Politicians, health advocates, national governing bodies, and sports insiders around the globe discussed the effectiveness of youth sport programs in addressing health problems, educational opportunities, economic mobility, environmental protection, crime control, and social fragmentation (Berna 2007).

Seeds of an international youth-sport-as-development social movement had been planted before the UN's half decade of mobilization around the issue. Canada, Norway, and the Netherlands led programs within their countries to examine the promise of sport in fostering social change for youths (DaCosta and Miragaya 2001). The Canadian and Norwegian brainchild, the Right to Play organization (formerly Olympic Aid), had long operated outside of the international policy limelight. International sports organizations like the IOC, the Fédération Internationale de Football Association (FIFA), UK Sport, Sport Without Borders, the Union Européenne de Football Association (UEFA), and the Fédération Internationale de Basketball (FIBA), along with national sport organizing bodies in countries including Canada, Russia, Switzerland, the Netherlands, Egypt, Brazil, the United States, Italy, Hungary, Norway, and more than 70 others, also innovated either one-off sports events or long-term educational and participatory programs to promote sport as a site for achieving social and personal development for young people (Vanden Auweele, Malcolm, and Meulders 2007).

Proponents of a sport-as-safety argument believe that sport programs work as preventive or reactive methods for confronting social problems (David 2005). When sport is structured effectively: it offers education for children who may be alienated from mainstream school opportunities; shelters at-risk children within safely supervised spaces; provides children who have few or no family role models with positive socializing forces; teaches nonviolence, cultural diversity, and interpersonal tolerance; offers a healthy leisure-time option; and reduces child experimentation with drugs and firearms (Phüse and Gerber 2005). Importantly, however, many of these claims are anecdotal, speculative, or simply naive. Inner-city sport programs designed to reduce youth crime in problematic urban areas meet with uncertain results (Murphy 1999). Critics argue that sport may provide temporary relief for at-risk youths but does not alleviate the sociostructural or cultural problems that put them at risk in the first place.

Public sociologists of sport deviance, then, might find productive research in testing whether or not existing theories of crime and deviance explain how sport actually works in youth protection and development. Practically every theory of youth crime and deviance argues that youths require structured and supervised activities and peaceful cultural spaces to counteract biographical experiences such as family violence and fragmentation, peer rule-violating influences, discrimination, economic disparity, exploitation, and abuse that either push or pull children into patterns of unwanted deviance.

Realistically, however, for sport to combat the systematic problems that young people encounter, sport environments should first be cleaned up. Doll-Tepper (2007) calls attention to the following pathological conditions of Western youth sport cultures: the structural problems of access to sport for minority groups and youths with disability, the pervasive gender and sexual discrimination, the adult ideological domination, the high rates of attrition in competitive youth sport due to child anxiety and stress, the instrumentalization of young bodies and minds as part of physical education policies, the sexual and physical abuse of young athletes by coaches, the prevalence of drugs and violence in and around sport venues, and the disappearance of traditional youth games and free play in favor of competitive sport training programs. If sport is to be a safe haven for children, systematic rule violations in sport cultures that produce exploitation must be identified and eliminated. The Panathlon group of the United Kingdom clearly agrees with this statement and has produced six policy documents to be used when assessing problem structures and practices in youth sport: *Equal Opportunities Policy, Child Protection Policy, Mainstream Risk Assessment, Disability Risk Assessment, Fair Play Charter,* and *School, Officials and Organizers Responsibilities Charter* (www.panathlon.co.uk). Nevertheless, theorizing how sport may cure youth problems is partly premature when the sources of inequality, suffering, and exploitation *within* sport are yet to be fully understood.

Promisingly, though, one of the most publicly significant lines of analysis in the youth-sport-protection field is research on sport's possible function in fighting the spread of HIV and AIDS in countries with high rates of infection. Studies of sport in South Africa, Zambia, Kenya, and India (Coalter 2007; Keim 2003) uncover how local and national sports organizations use sport training and competition spaces as sites of education and collective mentoring. The rates of HIV infection are soaring among 15- to 24-year-olds in these countries and cities, and researchers concur that transmission is amplified by youths' lack of knowledge about the disease, by silence about its causes, and by forced sexual activity (especially among young, poor females).

Coalter's (2007) research on multisite case studies of grassroots HIV and AIDS awareness programs in youth football cultures in Africa reveals how sport is used as an effective intervention. Coalter's overview of the Mathare Youth Sports Association, Go Sisters, and Youth Education through Sports programs includes evidence of the effectiveness of peer mentorship about HIV and AIDS through youth football. The respective programs, akin to FIFA's Kicking AIDS Out! campaign, empower young athletes by linking physical, social, and moral development in sport with self-protectionist mentalities of health and safety that are designed to impact youngsters way beyond the playing field. Research from South Africa (Keim 2003) demonstrates how sport involvement delays the onset of risky practices such as early initiation into sex, promiscuity, and unprotected sex. The IOC, the UN, and various other international sports organizations have responded by publishing working documents and policy guides for teaching young athletes about HIV and AIDS and other socially transmitted diseases (Keim 2003). The collective reduction approach champions children's rights to play through opportunity and investment and emphasizes their right to know through education. The majority of educational programs are still in their infancy, however, and their effectiveness will be better assessed over the long term.

Sport for Reducing Social Problems

Numerous authors such as Houlihan and White (2001) claim that sport has untapped potential for social development and international community building among adults. The reduction of social deviance and social problems is surely a part of this potential. May and Phelan (2005) argue that, from a global and economic development perspective, sport encourages social investment in health, education, and physical fitness; local business structures and opportunities; fair competition; bridges across cultural divides built by nonverbal interaction; globally common forms of social bonding and symbol exchange; and a transcendence of traditional social inequalities such as class, race, and gender. Although critics of globalization in sport (such as Maguire 1999) note the extensive imbalances and cultural power plays involved in the present international sports fields and organizations (which are dominated, for the most part, by Western industrial nations), proponents of the sport-as-development model hope that the universal citizenship and interdependence awareness encouraged through sport development projects will highlight human and cultural commonalities rather than deviantize differences.

The present and the future of a public sociology of sport and a public sociology of sport deviance are yet to be written. As we have noted, the discussions of wanted, unwanted, and gray social problems in sport contained in this book are the proverbial tip of the iceberg. Our hope is that others will continue to critique what counts as rule violation and contranormative behavior in sport and contribute to the ongoing formation of a public sociology of sport, using the broadest range of theory and method possible. For us, making use of the literature connected to one of the most mature of all of sociology's subdisciplines—criminology, deviance, and social control—is an obvious place to start. Our task should also begin by acknowledging the existence and the very real implications of social problems, rule violations, and even crime in sport rather than theoretically discounting them as tricks of discourse and mediation.

Discussion Questions

1. Do you see yourself in the role of public sociologist as we have described in this chapter? What are the pluses and minuses of assuming such a stance?
2. Do you think that a community sport program could be developed to combat a social problem in your community? Discuss.
3. Reflect on the theories we have covered in this book. Which one would offer the best basis for a public sociology of sport deviance?

Recommended Readings

David, P. 2005. *Human rights in youth sport.* London: Routledge.

David offers a critical analysis of central problems within youth sport and argues that the future development of sport depends on the creation of a child-centered system. Areas of particular concern in youth sport include overtraining; physical, emotional, and sexual abuse; doping and medical ethics; education; and child labor.

Griffin, R. 1998. *Sports in the lives of children and adolescents.* London: Praeger.

Griffin's book argues that sport is best assessed in relation to how it helps manage the central issues that children and adolescents confront while growing up. His interest in sport for children led him to examine how schools, professional sports, race and class, and popular media affect children's interest and involvement in sports.

Keim, M. 2003. *Nation-building at play: Sport as a tool for re-integration in a post-apartheid South Africa.* Oxford, UK: Meyer and Meyer.

This book showcases Keim's research on schoolchildren's sport, with particular reference to how sport is a solution to social stratification and inequality. The results Keim provide are useful tools for any person involved in school or community sports.

May, G., and J. Phelan. 2005. *Shared goals: Sport and business partnerships for development.* London: IBLF.

May and Phelan demonstrate that sport and physical activity not only improve health but also are a medium for delivering other development objectives such as education, inclusion, and economic situation. They outline the sport development context and make the case for engaging in business partnerships for development around sport.

Vanden Auweele, Y., C. Malcolm, and B. Meulders. 2007. *Sport and development.* Leuven, Belgium: Lannoo Campus.

This edited collection presents important global information on the role of sport in developing impoverished or postdisaster communities. Contributing authors assess how sport may be used to combat the effects of war, famine, disease, poverty, and ethnic prejudice.

References

Adams, C., and J. Donovan. 1995. *Animals and women: Feminist theoretical explorations.* Durham, NC: Duke University Press.

Adler, P., and P. Adler. 2005. Self-injurers as loners: The social organization of solitary deviance. *Deviant Behavior* 26:345-78.

Agar v. Canning. 1965. 54 W.W.R. 302 (M.Q.B); affd. 55 W.W.R. 384 (C.A.).

Agnew, R. 1992. Foundation for a general strain theory of crime and delinquency. *Criminology* 30:47-87.

Alderman, T. 1997. *The scarred soul: Understanding and ending self-inflicted violence.* Oakland: New Harbinger.

Alpert, G., and R. Dunhamn. 1997. *Policing urban America.* Prospect Heights, IL: Waveland.

Althusser, L. 1971. *Lenin and philosophy and other essays.* London: New Left Books.

Althusser, L. 1977. *For Marx.* London: New Left Books.

American Greyhound Council. 2004. Greyhound racing maintains high integrity. Press release. July 14.

Anderson, C., and B. Bushman. 2001. Effects of violent video games on violence behavior, violence cognition, violence affect, physiological arousal, and pro-social behavior: A meta-analytic review of the scientific literature. *Psychological Science* 12:353-9.

Anderson, E. 2000. *Trailblazing: America's first openly gay track coach.* Hollywood, CA: Alyson.

Anderson, E. 2005. *In the game: Gay athletes and the cult of masculinity.* Albany, NY: SUNY Press.

Andrews, D. 1993. Desperately seeking Michel: Foucault's genealogy, the body, and critical sport sociology. *Sociology of Sport Journal* 10:148-67.

Andrews, D. 2006. *Sport-commerce-culture.* New York: Peter Lang.

Armstrong, L. 2000. *It's not about the bike: My journey back to life.* New York: Berkley Trade.

Armstrong, S., and R. Botsler. 2003. *The animal ethics reader.* London: Routledge.

Arrigo, B., and T. Bernard. 1997. Postmodern criminology in relation to radical and conflict criminology. *Critical Criminology* 6:39-60.

Associated Press. 1980. Miss Ruiz loses her title. *New York Times.* April 30: B8.

Associated Press. 2000. Players, NHL: League should handle it. *Calgary Herald.* March 8: E2.

Associated Press. 2001. Bush to bomb through Olympics. *New York Times.* November 17: A12.

Associated Press. 2002a. Olympic security unprecedented in history of sport. *New York Times.* February 8: D2.

Associated Press, 2002b. More than 20 arrested in Salt Lake City. *USA Today.* February 24: A7

Associated Press. 2002c. Winter Olympics open with celebration of U.S. heroes past, present. *Hamilton Spectator.* February 15: A1.

Associated Press. 2003. Istanbul car bomb spark fears over Olympic security. *TaiPei Times.* November 29: 20.

Atkinson, M. 2000. Brother can you spare a seat: Developing recipes of knowledge in the ticket scalping subculture. *Sociology of Sport Journal* 17:151-70.

Atkinson, M. 2002. Fifty million viewers can't be wrong: Professional wresting, sports-entertainment and mimesis. *Sociology of Sport Journal* 19:47-66.

Atkinson, M. 2003. *Tattooed: The sociogenesis of a body art.* Toronto, ON: University of Toronto Press.

Atkinson, M. 2007a. Sport, gender and research method. In *Sport and gender in Canada,* 2nd ed., ed. K. Young and P. White, 29-54. Don Mills, ON: Oxford University Press.

Atkinson, M. 2007b. Punished bodies, enduring selves: Multi-sport as a civilizing process. Paper presented at the annual meetings of the North American Society for the Sociology of Sport, Vancouver, Canada. November 3.

Atkinson, M., and B. Wilson. 2001. Subcultures, bodies, and sport at the millennium. In *Theory, Sport and Society,* ed. J. Maguire and K. Young, 375-395. London: JAI Press.

Atkinson, M., and K. Young. 2001. Flesh journeys: Neo primitives and the rediscovery of radical body modification. *Deviant Behavior* 22:117-46.

Atkinson, M., and K. Young. 2003. Terror games: Media treatment of security issues at the 2002 Winter Olympic Games. *OLYMPIKA* 11:53-78.

Atkinson, M., and K. Young, eds. 2008. *Tribal play: Subcultural journeys through sport.* Bingley, UK: JAI.

Atyeo, D. 1979. *Violence in sports.* New York: Van Nostrand Reinhold.

Bachrach, S. 2000. *The Nazi Olympics: Berlin 1936.* New York: Little, Brown.

Baker, N. 1996. Going to the dogs—Hostility to greyhound racing in Britain: Puritanism, socialism and pragmaticism. *Journal of Sport History* 23:97-119.

Bairner, A. 2007. Back to basics: Class, social theory and sport. *Sociology of Sport Journal* 24:20-36.

Bale, J. 1997. *Keynan Running: Movement, culture, geography and global change.* London: Routledge.

Bale, J. 2004. *Running cultures: Racing in time and space.* London: Routledge.

Balsamo, A. 1996. *Technologies of the gendered body: Reading cyborg women.* Durham, NC: Duke University Press.

Bandura, A. 1973. *Aggression: A social learning analysis.* Englewood Cliffs, NJ: Prentice Hall.

Barnes, J. 1994. *The complete book of greyhounds.* London: Howell.

Barnes, J.C. 1988. *Sport and the law in Canada.* Toronto, ON: Butterworths.

Baudrillard, J. 1983. *Simulations.* New York: Semiotext(e).

BBC. 2003. *Jump London.* Originally aired September 9.

BBC News. 2002. Anthrax scare at Salt Lake city. Originally aired February 13.

Beal, B. 1995. Disqualifying the official: An exploration of social resistance through the subculture of skateboarding. *Sociology of Sport Journal* 12:252-67.

Beal, B., and C. Wilson. 2004. Chicks dig scars: Transformations in the subculture of skateboarding. In *Understanding lifestyle sports: Consumption, identity, and difference,* ed. B. Wheaton, 31-54. London: Routledge.

Beamish, R., and I. Ritchie. 2005. Performance and performance-enhancement in sport: The paradigm shift in the science of "training" and performance-enhancing substances. *Sport in History* 25:434-51.

Beck, U. 1991. *Risk society: Towards a new modernity.* London: Sage.

Becker, H. 1963. *Outsiders: Studies in the sociology of deviance.* New York: Free Press.

Becker, H. 1967. History, culture and subjective experience: An exploration of the social bases of drug-induced experiences. *Journal of Health and Social Behavior* 8:163-76.

Beirne, P. 1999. For a nonspeciesist criminology: Animal abuse as an object of study. *Criminology* 37:117-48.

Benedict, J. 1997. *Athletes and acquaintance rape.* Thousand Oaks, CA: Sage.

Bennett, A. 1999. Subculture or neo-tribes? Rethinking the relationship between youth, style and musical taste. *Sociology* 33:599-617.

Bensley, L., and J. Van Eenwyk. 2001. Video games and real life aggression: Review of the literature. *Journal of Adolescent Health* 29:244-57.

Bentham, J. 1995. *The panopticon writings.* London: Verso.

Benton, J. 2002. A show of force in the name of security. *The Dallas Morning News.* February 9: D2.

Ben-Yehuda, N. 1993. *Assassinations by Jews: A rhetorical device for justice.* Albany, NY: State University of New York Press.

Bermond, B. 1997. The myth of animal suffering. In *Animal consciousness and animal ethics,* ed. M. Dol, 125-36. New York: Van Gorcum.

Berna, A. 2007. Sport as a human right and as a means for development. In *Sport and development,* ed. Y. Vanden Auweele, C. Malcolm, and B. Meulders, 33-41. Leuven, Belgium: Lannoo Campus.

Bernstein, A. 2000. Things you can see from there, you can't see from here. *Journal of Sport and Social Issues* 24:351-69.

Best, J. 2000. *Deviance: Career of a concept.* New York: Wadsworth.

Best, J., and D. Luckenbill. 1982. *Organizing deviance.* Englewood Cliffs, NJ: Prentice Hall.

Bissinger, H. 2000. *Friday night lights.* Dallas: Da Capro Press.

Blackshaw, T., and T. Crabbe. 2004. *New perspectives on sport and deviance.* London: Routledge.

Blumer, H. 1969. *Symbolic interactionism: Perspective and method.* Englewood Cliffs, NJ: Prentice Hall.

Bordo, S. 1993. *Unbearable weight: Feminism, Western culture and the body.* Berkeley, CA: University of California Press.

Bourdieu, P. 1984. *Distinction: A social critique of the judgement of taste.* Cambridge, MA: Harvard University Press.

Brackenridge, C. 1996. *Child protection in sport: Politics, procedures and systems. Report on a Sport Council seminar for national governing bodies.* Cheltenham, UK: C&GCHE.

Brackenridge, C. 2001. *Spoilsports: Understanding and preventing sexual exploitation in sport.* London: Routledge.

Braithwaite, J. 1990. *Crime, shame, and reintegration.* Cambridge, UK: Cambridge University Press.

Branigan, C. 1997. *The reign of the greyhound.* New York: Howell Book House.

Brcic, E. 2006. BALCO: Marion Jones used steroids. *Calgary Herald.* December 3: D3.

Bridges, J. 1999. *Making violence part of the game.* Commack, NY: Kroshka Books.

Brittain, I. 2004. Perceptions of disability and their impact upon involvement in sport for people with disabilities at all levels. *Journal of Sport and Social Issues* 28:429-52.

Brookes, R. 2002. *Representing sport.* London: Arnold.

Burawoy, M. 2004. Manifesto for public sociologies. *Social Problems* 51:124-9.

Burstyn, V. 1999. *The rites of men: Manhood, politics, and the culture of sport.* Toronto, ON: University of Toronto Press.

Butler, J. 1993. *Bodies that matter.* London: Routledge.

Butryn, T. 2003. Posthuman podiums: Cyborg narratives of elite track and field athletes. *Sociology of Sport Journal* 20:17-39.

Butryn, T., and M. Masucci. 2003. It's not about the bike: A cyborg counternarrative of Lance Armstrong. *Journal of Sport and Social Issues* 27:124-44.

Callois, R. 1967. *Les Jeux et le Hommes*. Paris: Gallimard.

Canadian Press. 2000a. McSorley pleads not guilty. *Vancouver Sun*. September 25: D3.

Canadian Press. 2000b. McSorley found guilty of assault with a weapon. *Kitchener-Waterloo Record*. October 6: A4.

Canadian Press. 2002. Ashcroft says security is solid. *Toronto Star*. January 22: A9.

Canadian Press. 2004. Perezhogin out. *Hamilton Spectator*. May 5: D2.

Cantera, K. 2002. Bomb scares could strain Games security. *Salt Lake Tribune*. February 2: A3.

Carrington, B. 2007. Merely identity: Cultural identity and the politics of sport. *Sociology of Sport Journal* 24:49-66.

Cashmore, E. 2002. *Sports culture: An A-S guide*. New York: Routledge.

Castells, M. 1996. *The rise of the network society*. Oxford, UK: Blackwell.

Cauldwell, J. 2006. *Sport, sexualities and queer theory*. London: Routledge.

CBC.ca. 2007. www.cbc.ca.

CBC News. 2001. Norwegian official apologizes. [Online]. www.cbc.ca. November 30.

CBC News. 2003. Alberta hockey coaches suspended for ending violent games. [Online]. www.cbc.ca. January 16.

CBS Evening News. 2002. Sky patrol in Salt Lake. Originally aired February 11.

Chang, A. 2003. Major competition: Athens on high alert as the 2004 Summer Olympics approach. *USA Today*. December 10:D9.

Chase, L. 2006. (Un)disciplined bodies: A Foucauldian analysis of women's bodies. *Sociology of Sport Journal* 23:229-47.

Ciampa, M. 2000. McSorley gives hockey a black eye. *Renaissance Sports* 4:2.

CIBC Run for the Cure. 2007. www.cibcrunforthecure.com.

Clarke, J. 1976. Style. In *Resistance through rituals: Youth subcultures in post-war Britain*, ed. S. Hall and T. Jefferson, 78-95. London: Hutchinson.

Clocksin, B., D. Watson, and L. Ransdell. 2002. Understanding youth obesity and media use: Implications for future intervention programs. *Quest* 54:259-74.

Cloward, R., and L. Ohlin. 1960. *Delinquency and opportunity*. New York: Free Press.

CNN News. 2002a. Ridge praises Olympic security in Salt Lake City. [Online]. www.cnn.com. January 10.

CNN News. 2002b. Ground zero star-spangled banner to wave over Olympics. [Online]. www.cnn.com. February 6.

Coach's Corner. 2000. CBC Hockey Night in Canada. Originally aired February 26.

Coakley, J. 1992. Burnout among adolescent athletes: A personal failure or social problem? *Sociology of Sport Journal* 33:231-47.

Coakley, J., and P. Donnelly. 2005. *Sport in society: Issues and controversies*. Toronto: McGraw-Hill.

Coalter, F. 2007. Sport-in-development: Process evaluation and organizational development. In *Sport and development*, ed. Y. Vanden Auweele, C. Malcolm, and B. Meulders, 13-24. Leuven, Belgium: Lannoo Campus.

Cohen. A. 1955. *Delinquent boys: The culture of the gang*. New York: Free Press.

Cohen, L., and M. Felson. 1979. Social change and crime rate trends: A routine activity approach. *American Sociological Review* 44:588-608.

Cohen, P. 1972. Subcultural conflict and working class communities. In *Working papers in cultural studies 2*. Birmingham, UK: Centre for Contemporary Cultural Studies.

Cohen, S. 1973. *Folk devils and moral panics: The creation of the mods and rockers.* London: MacGibbon and Kee.

Cohen, S. 2003. *States of denial: Knowing about atrocities and suffering.* Cambridge, UK: Polity Press.

Cohen, S., and J. Young. 1973. *The manufacture of news.* Beverly Hills, CA: Sage.

Colburn, K. 1985. Honour, ritual and violence in ice hockey. *Canadian Journal of Sociology* 10:153-70.

Cole, D., and J. Dempsey. 2006. *Terrorism and the Constitution.* New York: New Press.

Collins, D. 1996. Attacks on the body: How can we understand self-harm? *Psychodynamic Counselling* 24:463-75.

Collins, R. 1975. *Conflict sociology.* New York: Academic Press.

Collinson, J. 2005. Emotions, interactions and the injured sporting body. *International Review for the Sociology of Sport* 402:221-40.

Colvin, M. 2000. *Crime and coercion: An integrated theory of chronic criminality.* New York: St. Martin's Press.

Connell, R. 1995. *Masculinities.* Cambridge, UK: Polity Press.

Conrad, P. 2005. *Sociology of health and illness: Critical perspectives.* 7th ed. New York: Worth Publishers.

Cornish, D., and R. Clarke. 1986. *The reasoning criminal.* New York: Springer-Verlag.

Couser, G. 2007. *Recovering bodies: Illness, disability, and life writing.* Madison, WI: University of Wisconsin Press.

Criminal Code of Canada. 2001. Toronto: Edmond Montgomery Publications.

Crosset, T., and B. Beal. 1995. The use of subculture and subworld in ethnographic works on sport: A discussion of definitional distinction. *Sociology of Sport Journal* 14:73-85.

Csikszentmihalyi, M. 1975. *Beyond boredom and anxiety.* San Francisco: Jossey-Bass.

Cunningham, H. 1980. *Leisure in the industrial revolution.* London: Croom Helm.

Curtis, J., W. McTeer, and P. White. 2003. Do high school athletes earn more pay? Youth sport participation and earnings as an adult. *Sociology of Sport Journal* 20:60-76.

DaCosta, L., and A. Miragaya. 2001. *Worldwide experiences and trends in sport for all.* Oxford, UK: Meyer & Meyer.

Dahrendorf, R. 1971. *Class and class conflict in industrial society.* Stanford, CA: Stanford University Press.

Darden, D., and S. Worden. 1996. Marketing of deviance: The selling of gamefowl. *Society and Animals* 4:27-44.

David, P. 2005. *Human rights in youth sport.* London: Routledge.

Davis, C. 2007. Eating disorders, physical activity, and sport: Biological, psychological, and sociological factors. In *Sport and gender in Canada,* 2nd ed., ed. K. Young and P. White, 85-98. Don Mills, ON: Oxford University Press.

Davis, K. 1937. The sociology of prostitution. *American Sociological Review* 2:744-55.

Davis, L. 1997. *The swimsuit issue in sport: Hegemonic masculinity in* Sports Illustrated. Albany, NY: SUNY Press.

de Certeau, M. 1984. *The practice of everyday life.* Berkeley, CA: University of California Press.

DeGrazia, D. 2002. *Animal rights: A very short introduction.* Oxford, UK: Oxford University Press.

Delaplace, J.-M. 2005. *George Hébert: Sculpter du corps.* Paris: Vuibert.

Deleuze, G., and F. Guattari. 1987. *A thousand plateaus.* Minneapolis: University of Minnesota Press.

Denzin, N. 1989. *Interpretive interactionism.* Newbury Park, CA: Sage.

Derrida, J. 1978. *Writing and difference.* London: Routledge.

DeRose, C. 1997. *In your face: From actor to activist.* Los Angeles: Duncan Publishing.

Deutschmann, L. 2007. *Deviance and social control.* 4th ed. Toronto: Nelson.

Diani, M. 2004. Networks and participation. In *The Blackwell Companion to social movements,* ed. D. Snow, S. Soule, and H. Kriesi. 339-59. Oxford, UK: Blackwell.

Dillard, C. 2002. Civil disobedience: A case study in factors of effectiveness. *Society and Animals* 10:47-62.

Dobkin, B. 1992. Paper tigers and video postcards: The rhetorical dimensions of narrative form in ABC news coverage of terrorism. *Western Journal of Communication* 56:143-60.

Dodge, D. 1985. The over-negativized conceptualization of deviance: A programmatic exploration. *Deviant Behavior* 6:17-37.

Doll-Tepper, G. 2007. The potential of sport for wellness in an educational context. In *Sport and development,* ed. Y. Vanden Auweele, C. Malcolm, and B. Meulders, 71-9. Leuven, Belgium: Lannoo Campus.

Dollard, J., L. Doob, N. Miller, O. Mowrer, and R. Sears. 1939. *Frustration and aggression.* New Haven, CT: Yale University Press.

Donaldson, M. 1993. What is hegemonic masculinity? *Theory and Society* 22:643-57.

Donnelly, P., and J. Harvey. 2007. Social class and gender: Intersections of sport and physical activity. In *Sport and Gender in Canada,* 2nd ed., ed. K. Young and P. White (pp. 95-119). Don Mills, ON: Oxford University Press.

Donnelly, P., and K. Young. 1988. The construction and confirmation of identity in sport subcultures. *Sociology of Sport Journal* 5:223-40.

Douglas, M. 1970. *Natural symbols.* New York, NY: Penguin.

Dowling, R. 1986. Terrorism in the media: A rhetorical genre. *Journal of Communication* 36:12-24.

Dunn, R. 1998. *Identity crises: A social critique of postmodernity.* Minneapolis: University of Minnesota Press.

Dunning, E. 1986. Sport as a male preserve: Notes on the social sources of masculine identity and its transformation. *Theory, Culture and Society* 3:79-90.

Dunning, E. 1999. *Sport matters: Sociological studies of sport, violence, and civilization.* London: Routledge.

Dunning, E., P. Murphy, and J. Williams. 1988. *The roots of football hooliganism.* London: Routledge.

Dunning, E., and C. Rojek. 1992. *Sport and leisure in the civilizing process.* London: Macmillan.

Dunning, E., and K. Sheard. 1979. *Barbarians, gentlemen, and players: A sociological study of the development of rugby football.* Oxford, UK: Martin Robertson.

Durkheim, E. 1958. *The rules of sociological method.* Glencoe, NY: Free Press.

Eco, U. 1972. Social life as a sign system. In *Structuralism: The Wolfson College Lectures 1972,* ed. D. Robey, 121-135. London: Cape.

Eichberg, H. 1998. *Body cultures: Essays on sport, space, and identity.* New York: Routledge.

Ehrenreich, B. 1997. *Blood rites: Origins and history of the passions of war.* New York: Henry Holt and Company.

Elias, N. 1978. *What is sociology?* London: Hutchinson.

Elias, N. 1986. *The loneliness of dying.* Oxford: Blackwell.

Elias, N. 1987. *Involvement and detachment.* Oxford, UK: Basil Blackwell.

Elias, N. 1991. *The society of individuals.* Oxford, UK: Basil Blackwell.

Elias, N. 1994. *The civilizing process.* Oxford, UK: Basil Blackwell.

Elias, N. 1996. *The Germans: Studies of power struggles and the development of habitus in the nineteenth and twentieth centuries.* Oxford, UK: Polity Press.

Elias, N., and E. Dunning. 1986. *Quest for excitement: Sport and leisure in the civilizing process.* New York: Basil Blackwell.

Elias, N., and J. Scotson. 1965. *The established and the outsiders.* London: Sage.

Ellis, C. 1998. I hate my voice: Coming to terms with minor body stigma. *Sociological Quarterly* 39:517-43.

Eng, H. 2007. Queer athletes and queering in sport. In *Sport, sexualities and queer theory*, ed. J. Cauldwell, 49-61. London: Routledge.

Engel, M. 2005. The day the sky fell in. *Guardian Magazine.* December 3:12.

Entine, J. 1999. *Taboo: Why Black athletes dominate in sports and why we are afraid to talk about it.* New York: Public Affairs.

Extra (NBC). 2001. "America under siege." Originally aired September 27.

Ezzy, D. 2000. Illness narrative: Time, hope and HIV. *Social Science and Medicine* 50:605-17.

Farr, K. 1988. Dominance bonding through the good old boys sociability group. *Sex Roles* 18:259-77.

Faulkner, R. 1973. On respect and retribution: Toward an ethnography of violence. *Sociological Symposium* 9:17-36.

Favaro, A., and P. Santonastaso. 2000. Self-injurious behavior in anorexia nervosa. *The Journal of Nervous and Mental Disease* 188:537-42.

Favazza, A. 1996. *Bodies under siege: Self-mutilation and body modification in culture and psychiatry.* Baltimore: Johns Hopkins University Press.

Favazza, A. 1998. The coming of age of self-mutilation. *The Journal of Nervous and Mental Diseases* 186:259-68.

Featherstone. M. 2000. *Body modification.* London: Sage.

Finch, A., and S. Nash. 2001. *Greyhound.* London: Trafalgar Square Press.

Fine, G. 1987. *With the boys: Little League baseball and preadolescent culture.* Chicago: University of Chicago Press.

Fishman, M. 1978. Crime waves as ideology. *Social Problems* 25:531-43.

Fiske, J. 1989. *Understanding popular culture.* Boston: Unwin Hyman.

Forsyth, C., and R. Evans. 1998. Dogmen and the rationalization of deviance. *Society and Animals* 6:157-86.

Forsyth, J., and K. Wamsley. 2005. Symbols without substance: Aboriginal peoples and the illusions of Olympic ceremonies. In *Global Olympics: Historical and sociological studies of the modern Games*, ed. K. Young and K. Wamsley, 227-47. Oxford, UK: Elsevier.

Fotheringham, W. 2006. Tour elite thrown out. *Guardian.* July 1:18.

Foucault, M. 1977. *Discipline and punish: The birth of the prison.* London: Penguin Books.

Foucault, M. 1979. *Power/knowledge: Selected interviews and other writings 1972-1977.* Brighton, UK: Harvester Press.

Foucault, M. 1981. *The history of sexuality, volume 1: An introduction.* London: Allen Lane/Penguin Books.

Foucault, M. 1987. *The use of pleasure: The history of sexuality, volume 2.* Harmondsworth, UK: Penguin Books.

Fournier, R. 2002. Bush: Olympics celebrate American ideals. *Detroit News.* February 8:C1.

Foy, P. 2001. Salt Lake chief envisions tighter security. *Detroit News*. October 30:B3.

Frank, A. 1991. *At the will of the body: Reflections on illness.* Boston: Houghton.

Frank, A. 1995. *The wounded storyteller: Body, illness and ethics.* Chicago: University of Chicago Press.

Frank, A. 2004. *The renewal of generosity: Illness, hospitality, and dialogue.* Chicago: University of Chicago Press.

Fromm, E. 1973. *The anatomy of human destructiveness.* New York: Holt, Rinehart & Winston.

Frisch, A. 2004. *The story of Nike.* San Francisco: Smart Apple Media.

Garfinkel, H. 1956. Conditions of successful degradation ceremonies. *American Journal of Sociology* 61:420-4.

Garfinkel, H. 1967. *Studies in ethnomethodology.* Englewood Cliffs, NJ: Prentice Hall.

Geiger, A. 2004. Athens security questioned as Olympics loom. *Los Angeles Times.* April 11:16.

Gertz, B. 2003. Greek spy agency tied to terror group: Athens backed anti-Turkish Kurds. *Washington Times.* September 10:C4.

Gibbs, N. 2002. The Winter Olympics: Hope and glory. [Online]. www.time.com. February 3.

Giddens, A. 1991. *Modernity and self identity.* Cambridge, UK: Polity Press.

Gillespie, G. 2000. Wickets in the West: Cricket, culture and constructed images of 19th century Canada. *Journal of Sport History* 27:51-66.

Gillett, J., R. Cain, and D. Pawluch. 2002. Beyond the biological: Use of physical activity for negotiating illness. *Sociology of Sport Journal* 19:370-84.

Giroux, H. 2002. Terrorism and the fate of democracy after September 11. *Cultural Studies— Critical Methodologies* 2:9-14.

Gitlin, T. 1991. *The sixties: Years of hope, days of rage.* New York: Bantam Books.

Glaser, B., and A. Strauss. 1967. *Discovery of grounded theory. Strategies for qualitative research.* Sociology Press. Chicago: Sociology Press.

Goffman, E. 1959. *The presentation of self in everyday life.* Garden City, NJ: Doubleday-Anchor.

Goffman, E. 1963. *Stigma.* Garden City, NJ: Doubleday-Anchor.

Goffman, E. 1961. *Asylums.* Chicago: Aldine.

Goffman, E. 1967. *Interaction ritual: Essays on face-to-face behavior.* Garden City, NJ: Anchor Books.

Goffman, E. 1974. *Frame analysis.* Cambridge, MA: Harvard University Press.

Gold, M. 1995. *Animal rights: Extending the circle of compassion.* Oxford, UK: Carpenter.

Goodger, J., and B. Goodger. 1989. Excitement and representation: Toward a sociological explanation of the significance of sport in modern society. *Quest* 41:257-72.

Gosper, K., and G. Korporaal. 2000. *An Olympic life: Melbourne 1956 to Sydney 2000.* St. Leonards, Australia: Allen and Unwin.

Gottfredson, M., and T. Hirschi. 1990. *A general theory of crime.* Stanford, CA: Stanford University Press.

Gould, S.J. 1996. *The mismeasure of man.* New York: Norton.

Gramsci, A. 1971. *Selections from prison notebooks.* London: Lawrence & Wishart.

Green, S., and R. Weinberg. 2001. Relationships among athletic identity, coping skills, social support and the psychological impact of injury in recreational participants. *Journal of Applied Sport Psychology* 13:40-59.

GREY2K USA. 2007. www.grey2kusa.org.

GreyhoundracingSUCKS.com. 2007. www.greyhoundracingsucks.com.

Griffin, R. 1998. *Sports in the lives of children and adolescents.* London: Praeger.

Gruneau, R. 1999. *Class, sports and social development.* Champaign, IL: Human Kinetics.

Gruneau, R., and D. Whitson. 1994. *Hockey night in Canada: Sport, identities, and cultural practices.* Toronto: Garamond.

Gubrium, J., and J. Holstein. 1997. *The new language of qualitative method.* New York: Oxford University Press.

Guilbert, S. 2004. Violence in sports and among sportsmen. *Aggressive Behavior* 32:231-40.

Gurr, T. 1970. *Why men rebel.* Princeton, NJ: Princeton University Press.

Gusfield, J. 1963. *Symbolic crusades.* Champaign, IL: University of Illinois Press.

Guttmann, A. 2002. *The Olympics: A history of the modern Games.* Chicago: University of Chicago Press.

Hagan, J. 1989. *Structural criminology.* Piscataway, NJ: Rutgers University Press.

Hagan, J. 1991. *The disreputable pleasures: Crime and deviance in Canada.* Toronto: McGraw-Hill Ryerson.

Hall, A. 1996. *Feminism and sporting bodies: Essays on theory and practice.* Champaign, IL: Human Kinetics.

Hall, S. 1980. Encoding/decoding. In *Culture, media, and language,* ed. S. Hall, 128-38. London: Hutchinson.

Hall S., C. Crichter, T. Jefferson, J. Clarke, and B. Roberts. 1978. *Policing the crisis: Mugging, the state and law and order.* London: MacMillan.

Hall, S., and T. Jefferson. 1976. *Resistance through rituals: Youth subcultures in post-war Britain.* London: Hutchinson.

Hallin, D. 1986. *The uncensored war: The media and Vietnam.* New York: Oxford University Press.

Harasta, C. 2002. Olympic miracle: Everyone was safe. *Dallas Morning News.* February 25:C2.

Haraway, D. 1991. *Simians, cyborgs, and women: The reinvention of nature.* London: Free Association Books.

Hardy, L. 1992. Psychological stress, performance and injury in sport. *British Medical Bulletin* 48:615-29.

Hargreaves, J., and P. Vertinsky. 2006. *Physical culture, power and the body.* London: Routledge.

Hathaway, A., and M. Atkinson. 2001. Tolerable differences revisited: Crossroads in theory on the social construction of deviance. *Deviant Behavior* 23:119-42.

Hawley, F. 1993. The moral and conceptual universe of cockfighters: Symbolism and rationalization. *Society and Animals* 1:159-68.

Haug, F. 1987. *Critique of commodity aesthetics: Appearance, sexuality, and advertising in capitalist society.* Minneapolis: University of Minnesota Press.

Hausenblas, H., and A. Carron. 1999. Eating disorder indices and athletes: An integration. *Journal of Sport and Exercise Psychology* 21:230-58.

Hebdige, D. 1979. *Subculture: The meaning of style.* New York: Methuen and Company.

Hebert, S. 2001. Policing the contemporary city: Fixing broken windows or shoring up neo-liberalism? *Theoretical Criminology* 5:445-66.

Heidegger, M. 1993. The *question concerning technology and other essays.* New York: Harper & Row.

Heino, R. 2000. What is so punk about snowboarding? *Journal of Sport and Social Issues* 24:176-91.

Hemingway, E. 1932. *Death in the afternoon.* New York: Scribner.

Herman, J. 1994. *Trauma and recovery: The aftermath of violence: From domestic abuse to political terror.* New York: Basic Books.

Hill, C. 1995. *Olympic politics.* Manchester, UK: Manchester University Press.

Hirschi, T. 1969. *Causes of Delinquency.* Berkeley, CA: University of California Press.

Hoberman, J. 1992. *Mortal engines: The science of performance and the dehumanisation of sport.* New York: Free Press.

Hoberman, J. 1997. *Darwin's athletes: How sport has damaged Black America and preserved the myth of race.* Wilmington, MA: Houghton Mifflin.

Hoberman, J. 2005. *Testosterone dreams.* Los Angeles: University of California Press.

Hockey, J. 2005. Injured distance runners: A case of identity work as self-help. *Sociology of Sport Journal* 21:38-58.

Hodgson, S. 2004. Cutting through the silence: A sociological construction of self-injury. *Sociological Inquiry* 74:162-79.

Holt, R. 1990. *Sport and the British: A modern history.* New York: Oxford University Press.

Hood, A. 2006. Drug scandals change the face of the Tour. *Velo News.* June 30:2.

Hoop Dreams. 2004. Directed by Steve James. Distributed by Fine Line Features.

Horrow, R. 1980. *Sports violence: The interaction between private law making and the criminal law.* Arlington, VA: Carrollton Press.

Houlihan, B. 1999. *Dying to win: Doping in sport and the development of anti-doping policy.* Strasbourg, Austria: Council of Europe.

Houlihan, B., and A. White. 2001. *The politics of sport development.* London: Routledge.

Howe, D. 2004. *Sport, professionalism and pain: Ethnographies of injury and risk.* London: Routledge.

Howell, C. 2001. *Blood, sweat and cheers: Sport and the making of modern Canada.* Toronto: University of Toronto Press.

Hoyle, J., and P. White. 1999. Sport, women and disability: Some exploratory notes. In *Sport and gender in Canada,* ed. P. White and K. Young, 254-267. Don Mills, ON: Oxford University Press.

Hughes, R., and J. Coakley. 1991. Positive deviance among athletes: The implications of overconformity to the sport ethic. *Sociology of Sport Journal* 8:307-25.

Humane Society of North America. 2002. More arrests made in the case of thousands of slain greyhounds. Press release. November 8.

Humane Society of the United States. 2007. www.hsus.org.

Humphreys, D. 1997. Shredheads go mainstream? Snowboarding and alternative youth. *International Review for the Sociology of Sport* 32:147-60.

Hyun, H. 1995. Environmental movements against golf course development in Korea since the late 1980s. *Korea Journal of Population and Development* 24:57-70.

Iyengar, S. 1996. Framing responsibility for political issues. *The Annals of the American Academy of Political and Social Science* 546:59-70.

Iyer, P. 1996. Lost magic: Terror at the Games. *Time* August 5:14-21.

Janofsky, M. 2002. Security kicks in before the Winter Games. *New York Times.* February 5:A16.

Jarvis, N. 2007. Ten men out: Gay sporting masculinities in softball. In *Sport, sexualities and queer theory,* ed. J. Cauldwell, 62-75. London: Routledge.

Jennison, G. 2004. *Animals for show and pleasure in ancient Greece.* Philadelphia: University of Pennsylvania Press.

Johnston, L., and D. Carroll. 2000. The psychological impact of injury: Effects of prior sport and exercise involvement. *British Journal of Sport Medicine* 34:436-9.

Jones, P. 1997. *Winner's guide to greyhound racing.* New York: Cardoza.

Joukowsky, A., and L. Rothstein. 2002. *Raising the bar: New horizons in disability sports.* New York: Umbrage.

Joyner, M. 2003. VO₂MAX, blood doping, and erythropoietin. *British Journal of Sports Medicine* 37:190-3.

Kamalipour, Y. 2000. The TV terrorist: Media images of Middle Easterners. *Global Dialogue* 2:89-96.

Katz, J. 1988. *Seductions of crime.* New York: Basic Books.

Keim, M. 2003. *Nation-building at play: Sport as a tool for re-integration in a post-apartheid South Africa.* Oxford, UK: Meyer and Meyer.

Kelling, G., and J. Wilson. 1982. Broken windows. *Atlantic Monthly* 249:29-38.

Kenney, D., and R. McNamara. 1999. *Police and policing.* Westport, CT: Praeger.

Kerr, J. 2004. *Rethinking violence and aggression in sport.* London: Routledge.

Kestenbaum, E. 2003. *Culture on ice: Figure skating and cultural meaning.* Middletown, CT: Wesleyan University Press.

Kew, F. 1997. *Sport, social problems and issues.* Oxford, UK: Butterworth Heinneman.

Kheel, M. 1999. An eco-feminist critique of hunting. *Journal of the Philosophy of Sport* 23:30-44.

Kimbrell, A. 1995. *The masculine mystique: The politics of masculinity.* New York: Ballantine.

Kimmel, M., and M. Messner. 1992. *Men's lives.* New York: Macmillan.

King, R. 2004. This is not an Indian: Situating claims about Indianness in sporting worlds. *Journal of Sport and Social Issues* 28:3-10.

King, S. 2001. An all-consuming cause: Breast cancer, corporate philanthropy, and the market for generosity. *Social Text* 19:115-43.

Kitsuse, J. 1980. Coming out all over: Deviants and the politics of social problems. *Social Problems* 28:1-13.

Klausner, S. 1968. *Why men take chances: Studies in stress-seeking.* New York: Anchor Books.

Klein, A. 1993. *Little big men: Bodybuilding subculture and gender construction.* Albany, NY: State University of New York Press.

Knapp Commission. 1972. *Knapp Commission Report on Police Corruption.* New York: George Braziller.

Knapp, G. 2003. USA covered up positive tests. *San Francisco Chronicle.* April 18:C1.

Krueger, A., and J. Maleckova. 2003. Education, poverty and terrorism: Is there a causal connection? *Journal of Economic Perspectives* 17:119-44.

Kupelian, V. 2000. Players outraged by slash. *Detroit News.* February 23.

Kyte, J. 2000. Too bad for Marty McSorley. *Ottawa Citizen.* October 7.

Lacan, J. 1977. *Écrits: A selection.* New York: Sheridan.

Lance Armstrong Foundation. 2007. www.laf.org.

Landers, D. 1976. *Social problems in athletics: Essays in the sociology of sport.* Champaign, IL: University of Illinois Press.

Lapchick, R. 2002. *Smashing barriers: Race and sport in the new millennium.* New York: Madison.

Law, J. 2004. It's a jungle gym out there. *Globe and Mail.* May 13:D9.

Le Breton, D. 2000. Playing symbolically with death in extreme sports. *Body and Society* 6:1-11.

Lemert, E. 1967. *Human deviance, social problems, and social control.* Englewood Cliffs, NJ: Prentice Hall.

Lenart, S., and H. Targ. 1995. The media war against Nicaragua. *Peace Review* 7:347-53.

Lenskyj, H. 2002. *Best Games ever? The social impacts of Sydney 2000.* New York: SUNY Press.

Lenskyj, H. 2003. *Out on the field: Gender, sport and sexualities.* Toronto: Women's Press of Canada.

Leonard, W. 1988. *A sociological perspective of sport.* New York: MacMillan.

Levine, E. 2005. *Death and the sun.* Boston: Houghton Mifflin.

Lewis, M. 2001. Getting Marty off. *The Canadian Lawyer* 24:63-5.

Liao, H. 2006. A brief review of Olympic urbanization. *International Journal of the History of Sport* 23:1232-52.

Liberman, N. 2003. Sports video games still scoring big. *Street and Smith's Sports Business Journal* 6:7-13.

Lindburg, D. 1999. Zoos and the rights of animals. *Zoo Biology* 1:18-9.

Liska, A., and S. Messner. 1999. *Perspectives on deviance.* Englewood Cliffs, NJ: Prentice Hall.

Little, M., and E. Sayers. 2004. Where there's life . . . hope and the experience of cancer. *Social Science and Medicine* 59:1329-37.

Livestrong. 2007. www.livestrong.org.

Lo, L. 1994. Exploring teenage shoplifting behavior: A choice and constraint approach. *Environment and Behavior* 26:628.

Lofland, J., and L. Lofland. 1995. *Analysing social settings.* Belmont, CA: Wadsworth.

Loland, N. 2000. The art of concealment in a culture of display: Aerobicizing women's and men's experiences and use of their own bodies. *Sociology of Sport Journal* 17:111-29.

Lopresti, M. 2002. A homeland Winter Olympics: With a few guests. *USA Today.* February 9:A1.

Lorenz, K. 1963. *On aggression.* San Diego: Harcourt Brace.

Lupton, D. 1996. *Food, the body, and the self.* London: Sage.

Lupton, D. 2003. *Medicine as culture: Illness, disease and the body in Western societies.* London: Sage.

Lyng, S. 1990. Edgework: A social psychological analysis of voluntary risk taking. *American Journal of Sociology* 95:851-86.

Lyon, D. 2003. *Surveillance society: Monitoring everyday life.* London: Open University Press.

Mabry, D. 1992. *The Mexican University and the state: Student conflicts, 1910–1971.* College Station, TX: Texas A & M University Press.

MacKinnon, C. 1989. *Toward a feminist theory of the state.* Cambridge, MA: Harvard University Press.

MacLean's Magazine. 2000. Blood sport. March 6.

Maffesoli, M. 1996. *The contemplation of the world: Figures of community style.* Minneapolis: University of Minnesota Press.

Maguire, J. 1992. Towards a sociological theory of sport and the emotions: A process-sociological perspective. In *Sport and leisure in the civilising process: Critique and counter-critique,* ed. E. Dunning and C. Rojek, 96-120. London: Macmillan.

Maguire, J. 1993. Bodies, sport cultures and societies: A critical review of some theories in the sociology of the body. *International Review for the Sociology of Sport* 28:33-50.

Maguire, J. 1999. *Global sport: Identities, societies, civilization.* Cambridge, UK: Polity Press.

Maguire, J., and L. Mansfield. 1998. No-body's perfect: Women, aerobics, and the body beautiful. *Sociology of Sport Journal* 15:109-37.

Malcolmson, R. 1973. *Popular recreations in English society, 1700-1850.* Cambridge, UK: Cambridge University Press.

Mandell, R. 1987. *The Nazi Olympics.* Champaign, IL: University of Illinois Press.

Mangan, J., and L. DaCosta. 2001. *Sport in Latin American society.* London: Frank Cass.

Markula, P. 2003. The technologies of the self: Feminism, Foucault and sport. *Sociology of Sport Journal* 20:87-107.

Markula, P. 2006. The dancing body without organs: Deleuze, femininity and performing research. *Qualitative Inquiry* 12:3-27.

Marshall, J. 1991. Justin Fashanu: Soccer's enigmatic gay star. *Gay Times* 9:154.

Martin v. Daigle. 1969. 1 N.B.R. (2d) 755, 6 D.L.R. (3d) 634 (N.B.C.A).

Martin, A., and P. Petro. 2006. *Rethinking global security.* Newark, NJ: Rutgers University Press.

Maslow, A. 1970. *Religion, values and peak experiences.* New York: Viking.

Matheson, J. 2005. *The greyhound: Breeding, coursing and racing.* Chicago: Vintage Dog Books.

Matza, D. 1964a. *Delinquency and drift.* New York: Wiley.

Matza, D. 1964b. Juvenile delinquency and subterranean values. *American Sociological Review* 26:712-9.

Maughan, R., L. Burke, and E. Coyle. 2004. *Food, nutrition and sports performance.* London: Routledge.

May, G., and J. Phelan. 2005. *Shared goals: Sport and business partnerships for development.* London: IBLF.

McClelland, L., and A. Crisp. 2001. Anorexia nervosa and social class. *International Journal of Eating Disorders* 29:150-6.

McCormick, J. 1999. *Bullfighting: Art and technique and Spanish society.* New York: Transaction.

McDonald, M. 2007. Beyond the pale: The Whiteness of sports studies and queer scholarship. In *Sport, sexualities and queer theory,* ed. J. Cauldwell, 33-44. London: Routledge.

McElhenny, J. 2000. Players say McSorley verdict opens can of worms. *Vancouver Sun.* October 7.

McKay, J., M. Messner, and D. Sabo. 2000. *Men, masculinities, and sport.* Thousand Oaks, CA: Sage.

McMurtry, W. 1974. *Investigation and inquiry into violence in amateur hockey.* Report to the Honourable Rene Brunelle, Ontario, Minister of Community and Social Services. Toronto, ON: Ontario Government Bookstore.

Melucci, A. 1996. *Challenging codes: Collective action in the information age.* Cambridge, UK: Cambridge University Press.

Merton, R. 1938. Social structure and anomie. *American Sociological Review* 3:672-82.

Messner, M. 1990. When bodies are weapons: Masculinity and violence in sport. *International Review for the Sociology of Sport* 25:203-21.

Messner, M. 1992. *Power play: Sport and the problem of masculinity.* Boston: Beacon Press.

Messner, M. 2002. *Taking the field: Women, men and sports.* Minneapolis: University of Minnesota Press.

Messner, M., D. Hunt, and M. Dunbar. 1999. *Boys to men: Sports media messages about masculinity.* Oakland: Children Now.

Messner, M., and D. Sabo. 1994. *Sex, violence, and power in sports: Rethinking masculinity.* Champaign, IL: Human Kinetics.

Miah, A. 2004. *Genetically modified athletes: Biomedical ethics, gene doping and sport.* London: Routledge.

Michaelis, V. 2003. Security in Athens: $1 billion. *USA Today.* September 27:D2.

Milovanovic, D. 1997. *Chaos, criminology and social justice.* Westport, CT: Greenwood.

Miller, P. 2003. *Race and the sport color line.* London: Routledge.

Miracle, A., and R. Rees. 1994. *Lessons of the locker room: The myth of school sports.* Amherst, NJ: Prometheus Books.

Mitchell, T. 1991. *Blood sport: A social history of Spanish bullfighting.* Philadelphia: University of Pennsylvania Press.

Mizell, L. 2000. Bigger crime needed to put sports in courts. *St. Petersburg Times.* October 12.

Mizell, L.D. 2002. *Target USA: The inside story of the new terrorist war.* New York: Wiley.

Monaghan, L. 2002. Vocabularies of motive for illicit steroid use among bodybuilders. *Social Science & Medicine* 55:695-708.

Monaghan, L. 2003. Danger on the doors: Bodily risk in a demonised occupation. *Health, Risk & Society* 5:11-31.

Morris News Service. 2002. Stink bomb scare hits Olympics. *Savannah Morning News.* February 21:14.

Mottram, D. 2005. *Drugs in sport.* London: Routledge.

Muggleton, D. 2000. *Inside subculture: The postmodern meaning of style.* Oxford, UK: Berg.

Muggleton, D., and R. Weinzierl. 2004. *The post-subcultures reader.* New York: Berg.

Munro, L. 2001. *Compassionate beasts: The quest for animal rights.* Westport, CT: Praeger.

Murphy, B. 2003. Greek Olympics terror threat concerns FBI. *Hamilton Spectator.* September 7:E2.

Murphy, P., J. Williams, and E. Dunning. 1990. *Football on trial: Spectator violence and development in the football world.* London: Routledge.

Murphy, S. 1999. *The cheers and the tears: A healthy alternative to the dark side of youth sports today.* San Francisco: Jossey-Bass.

Nelson, H. 2001. *Damaged identities, narrative repair.* Ithaca, NY: Cornell University Press.

Nettleton, S., and M. Hardley. 2006. Running away with health: The urban marathon and the construction of charitable bodies. *Health* 10:441-60.

Niedzviecki, H. 2004. *Hello, I'm special.* New York: Penguin Books.

Nixon, H. 1996. Explaining pain and injury attitudes and experiences in sport in terms of gender, race, and sports status factors. *Journal of Sport and Social Issues* 20:33-44.

Northfield, D., and T. Bell. 2001. Is Salt Lake prepared to protect the masses? *NGW Online News.* November 19.

Noyes, D. 2006. *One kingdom: Our lives with animals.* Boston: Houghton Mifflin.

Oakley, R. 2003. Huge security for Athens Olympics. [Online]. www.cnn.com. September 13.

O'Driscoll, P. 2002. No major security plans expected. *USA Today.* January 29:C6.

Office of the United States Press Secretary. 2002. *Preparing for the world: Homeland security and Winter Olympics.* Statement released January 10.

Olweus, D. 1993. *Bullying at school: What we know and what we can do.* Cambridge, UK: Blackwell.

Olympia. 1938. Directed by Leni Riefenstahl. Distributed by Olympia-film Berlin Productions.

Overman, S. 1997. *The influence of the Protestant ethic on sport and recreation.* Brookfield, VT: Ashgate.

Palmer, C. 2001. Outside the imagined community: Basque terrorism, political activism, and the Tour de France. *Sociology of Sport Journal* 18:143-61.

Panathon International. 1996. *Panathlon Charter on the Rights of the Child in Sport.* London, UK.

Paraschak, V. 2007. Doing race, doing gender: First Nations, sport, and gender relations. In *Sport and gender in Canada,* 2nd ed., ed. K. Young and P. White, 137-54. Don Mills, ON: Oxford University Press.

Park, R., and E. Burgess. 1924. *The city.* Chicago: University of Chicago Press.

Park, R., E. Burgess, and D. McKenzie. 1925. *The city.* Chicago: University of Chicago Press.

Parsons, T. 1951. *The structure of social action.* New York: McGraw-Hill.

Pascall, B., and S. White. 2000. *Violence in hockey.* Commissioned by the Honourable Ian Waddell, Minister Responsible for Sport, British Columbia, Canada.

People for the Ethical Treatment of Animals. 2007. www.peta.org.

Petrie, M. 2002. Security tight, spirits high. *Calgary Herald.* February 5:D4.

Petrovic, A. 2004. Managing sports fields to reduce environmental impacts. *Acta Horticulturae* 661:405-12.

Phüse, U., and M. Gerber. 2005. *International comparison of physical education: Concepts—Problems—Prospects.* Berlin: Aachen.

Pike, L. 2005. Doctors say "just rest and take Ibuprofen." *International Review for the Sociology of Sport* 40:201-19.

Pillar, P. 2004. *Terrorism and US foreign policy.* Washington, DC: Brookings Institution.

Pluss, C. 2005. Constructing globalized ethnicity: Migrants from India and Hong Kong. *International Sociology* 20:201-5.

Polhemus, T. 1994. *Street style: From sidewalk to catwalk.* London: Thames and Hudson.

Popovic, M. 2006. Heroes of consumer society: Snowboarding and the counterculture myth. Paper presented at the annual meeting of the North American Society for the Sociology of Sport, Vancouver, Canada. November 3.

Porter, J. 1965. *The vertical mosaic.* Toronto: University of Toronto Press.

Postigo, H. 2003. From Pong to Planet Quake: Post industrial transitions from leisure to work. *Information, Communication, and Society* 6:593-607.

Preece, R., and L. Chamberlain. 1993. *Animal welfare and human values.* Waterloo, ON: Wilfred Laurier University Press.

Price, S. 1996. Stained games. *Sports Illustrated.* August 5:22-31.

Pronger, B. 1990. *The arena of masculinity: Sports, homosexuality, and the meaning of sex.* New York: St. Martin's Press.

Pronger, B. 1999. Fear and trembling: Homophobia in men's sport. In *Sport and gender in Canada,* ed. P. White and K. Young, 182-95. Don Mills, ON: Oxford University Press.

Pronger, B. 2002. *Body fascism: Salvation in the technology of physical fitness.* Toronto: University of Toronto Press.

Prus, R. 1987. Generic social processes: Maximizing conceptual development in ethnographic research. *Journal of Contemporary Ethnography* 16:251-91.

Putnam, R. 1995. *Bowling alone: America's declining social capital.* New York: Simon & Schuster.

Quinney, R. 1977. *Class, state and crime.* New York: David McKay.

R. v. Bertuzzi. 2004. B.C.J. No. 2692, 2004 BCPC 472.

R v. Cey. 1989. 48 C.C.C. (3d) 480 (Sask C.A.).

*R v. Ciccarelli.*1988. O.J. No. 2388 (O.P.C).

R v. Green. 1971. O.R. 591, 2 C.C.C. (2d) 442, 16 D.L.R. (3d) 137 (Prov. Ct.).

R. v. Jobidon. 1988. 2 S.C.R. 714.

R. v. Leclerc. 1991. 7 C.R. (4th) 282, 4 O.R. (3d) 788, 67 C.C.C. (3d) 563, 50 O.A.C. 232 (C.A.).

R v. Maki. 1970. 3 O.R. 780, 1 C.C.C. (2d) 333, 14 D.L.R. (3d) 164 (Prov. Ct.).

R v. McSorley. 2000. B.C.J. No. 0116 (B.C.P.C).

R v. Neeld. 2000. B.C.J. No. 57676-01 (B.C.P.C).

R v. Prénoveau. 1971. R.L 21 (C.s.p).

R v. Starrat. 1980. 1 O.R. 227, 5 C.C.C. (2d) 32 (C.A).

R v. Watson. 1975. 26 C.C.C. (2d) 150 (O.P.C).

Rail, G. 1990. Physical contact in women's basketball: A first interpretation. *International Review for the Sociology of Sport* 25:269-85.

Rail, G. 1998. *Sport and postmodern times.* New York: SUNY Press.

Reasons, C. 1992. The criminal law and sports violence: Hockey crimes. Unpublished paper. University of British Columbia.

Reaves, J. 2002. Olympic security: How far should it go? [Online]. www.time.com. January 30.

Regan, T. 2000. *The case for animal rights.* Berkeley, CA: University of California Press.

Reid, T. 2004. Rape case against Bryant dropped. *Washington Post.* September 2:A1.

Reinharz, S. 1992. *Feminist methods in social research.* New York: Oxford University Press.

Reinking, M., and L. Alexander. 2005. Prevalence of disordered eating behaviors in undergraduate female collegiate athletes and nonathletes. *Journal of Athletic Training* 40:47-51.

Reuters. 1997. Explosion at Swedish stadium blunts Olympic hopes. *Globe and Mail.* August 25:A12.

Rhoden, T. 2006. *Forty million dollar slaves.* New York: Crown.

Richardson, L. 2003. Looking Jewish. *Qualitative Inquiry* 9:815-21.

Rinehart, R., and S. Sydnor. 2003. *To the extreme: Alternative sports, inside and out.* Albany, NY: SUNY Press.

Ritchie, I. 2007. Drugs/substance use in sports. In *The Blackwell encyclopedia of sociology*, ed. G. Ritzer, 1239-42. Oxford: Blackwell Publishing.

Robidoux, M. 2001. *Men at play: A working understanding of professional hockey.* Montreal, PQ: McGill-Queen's University Press.

Robinson, L. 1998. *Crossing the line: Violence and sexual assault in Canada's national sport.* Toronto: McClelland & Stewart.

Roche, M. 2002. The Olympics and global citizenship. *Citizenship Studies* 6:165-81.

Roshier, R. 1989. *Controlling crime.* Chicago: Lyceum Books.

Rollin, B. 2001. Rodeo and recollection: Applied ethics and Western philosophy. *Journal of the Philosophy of Sport* 23:1-9.

Rushton, J.-P. 2000. *Race, evolution and behavior.* New Brunswick, NJ: Transaction.

Ruud, J. 1996. *Nutrition and the female athlete.* Boca Raton, FL: CRC Press.

Sabo, D. 1986. Pigskin, patriarchy and pain. *Changing Men: Issues in Gender Politics* 2:24-5.

Sacco, V. 2005. *When crime waves.* Thousand Oaks, CA: Sage.

Sage, G. 1999. Justice do it! The Nike transnational advocacy network. *Sociology of Sport Journal* 16:206-35.

Sampson, R., and J. Laub. 1993. *Crime in the making: Pathways and turning points through life.* Cambridge, MA: Harvard University Press.

Samuels, D. 1999. Going to the dogs: Greyhound racing. *Harper's Magazine.* November 1, 50-9.

Sardiello, R. 1998. Identity and status stratification in the deadhead subculture. In *Youth culture: Identity in a postmodern world*, ed. J. Epstein, 118-47. Oxford, UK: Blackwell.

Savulescu, J., and M. Clayton. 2004. Ergogenic aids: A review of basic science, performance, side effects, and status in sports. *British Journal of Sports Medicine* 38:666-70.

Schaffer, K., and S. Smith. 2000. *The Olympics at the millennium: Power, politics and the Games.* New Brunswick, NJ: Rutgers University Press.

Scheff, T. 1979. *Catharsis in healing, ritual, and drama.* Berkeley, CA: University of California.

Scheuer, J. 2006. *Through our enemies' eyes.* Baltimore: Potomac Books.

Scully, M. 2004. *Dominion: The power of man, the suffering of animals and the call to mercy.* New York: St. Martin's Press.

Seale, C. 1998. *Constructing death: The sociology of dying and bereavement.* Cambridge, UK: Cambridge University Press.

Seale, C. 2001. Sporting cancer: Struggle language in news reports of people with cancer. *Sociology of Health and Illness* 23:308-29.

Seitlin, J. 2004. State records show 21 cases of positive cocaine tests at dog track. *Bonita News.* June 12:D2.

Senn, A. 1999. *Power, politics and the Olympic Games.* Champaign, IL: Human Kinetics.

Shaffir, W., and S. Kleinkneckt. 2002. The trauma of political defeat. *The Canadian Parliamentary Review* 25:149-61.

Shaw, C. 1930. *The jack roller.* Chicago: University of Chicago Press.

Shaw, C., and H. McKay. 1942. *Juvenile delinquency and urban areas.* Chicago: University of Chicago Press.

Sheard, K. 1999. A stitch in time saves nine: Birdwatching, sport, and civilizing processes. *Sociology of Sport Journal* 16:181-205.

Shepard, P. 1996. *The other: How animals made us human.* Washington, DC: Island Books.

Shepherd, N. 2002. Anarcho-environmentalists: Ascetics of late modernity. *Journal of Contemporary Ethnography* 31:135-57.

Sheppard, R. 2002. Skating with the mob. *Maclean's.* August 12:56.

Shields, R. 1992. *Places on the margin. Alternative geographies of modernity.* London: Routledge.

Shilling, C. 1993. *The body and social theory.* London: Sage.

Shipley, A., and C. Whitlock. 2004. In Athens it's safety at all costs. *Washington Post.* August 12:A01.

Shogan, D. 1999. *The making of high performance athletes: Discipline, diversity, and ethics.* Toronto: University of Toronto Press.

SI.com. 2004. www.cnnsi.com.

Silk, M., and D. Andrews. 2006. The fittest city in America. *Journal of Sport and Social Issues* 30:315-27.

Simon, R. 2004. *Fair play: The ethics of sport.* Oxford, UK: Westview Press.

Smith, B., and A. Sparkes. 2005. Analyzing talk in qualitative inquiry: Exploring possibilities, problems, and tensions. *Quest* 57:213-42.

Smith, M. 1975. The legitimation of violence: Hockey players' perceptions of their reference groups' sanctions for assault. *Canadian Review of Sociology and Anthropology* 12:72-80.

Smith, M. 1983. *Violence and sport.* Toronto: Butterworths.

Smith, R. 2004. 1.5 billion for this? *Sports Fan Magazine.* August 27:1.

Smith-Maguire, J. 2007. *Fit for consumption.* London: Routledge.

Snow, R. 2004. *The history and sport of cockfighting.* London: Twiddling Pencil Publishers.

Sontag, S. 1991. *Illness as metaphor/AIDS and its metaphors.* Harmondsworth, UK: Penguin Books.

Sparkes, A. 2004. Bodies, narratives, selves and autobiography: The example of Lance Armstrong. *Journal of Sport and Social Issues* 28:397-428.

Sparkes, A., and B. Smith. 2003. Men, sport, spinal cord injury and narrative time. *Qualitative Research* 3:295-320.

Spector, M., and J. Kitsuse. 1977. *Constructing social problems.* Menlo Park, CA: Cummings.

Spencer, S. 2004. Armed to the rings: Soldiers outnumber athletes at Athens. *The Toronto Sun.* May 8:60.

Spitzer, S. 1975. Toward a Marxian theory of crime. *Social Problems* 22:638-51.

Stearns, J., and T. Dunn. 2002. Salt Lake city ready for anything. *Reno Gazette.* February 7:B3.

Stebbins, R. 1996. *Tolerable differences: Living with deviance.* Whitby, ON: McGraw-Hill.

Stebbins, R. 1997. Lifestyle as a generic concept in ethnographic research. *Quality and Quantity* 31:347-60.

Stebbins, R. 2006. *Serious leisure: A perspective for our time.* New Brunswick, NJ: Aldine.

Sternheimer, K. 2003. *It's not the media: The truth about popular culture's influence on children.* New York: Westview.

Sugden, J. 2007. Sport and spies. Paper presented at the Annual Meetings of the North American Society for the Sociology of Sport, Pittsburgh. October 31-November 3.

Sullivan, M. 2000. *The ultimate greyhound.* London: Howell.

Sutherland, E. 1947. *The professional thief.* Chicago: University of Chicago Press.

Sutherland, E. 1973. *Principles of criminology.* Chicago: University of Chicago Press.

Swain, J., and S. French. 2000. Towards an affirmative model of disability. *Disability and Society* 15:569-82.

Sykes, G., and D. Matza. 1957. Techniques of neutralization: A theory of delinquency. *American Sociological Review* 22:664-70.

Tanner, J. 2001. *Teenage troubles: Youth and deviance in Canada.* Toronto: Nelson.

Taylor, I. 1971. Soccer consciousness and soccer hooliganism. In *Images of deviance,* ed. S. Cohen, 134-65. New York: Penguin Books.

Taylor, I., Walton, P. and J. Young. 1973. *The new criminology: For a social theory of deviance.* London: Routledge and Kegan Paul.

Theberge, N. 2002. *Higher goals: Women's ice hockey and the politics of gender.* Albany, NY: SUNY Press.

Thornton, A. 2004. Anyone can play this game: Ultimate Frisbee, identity and difference. In *Understanding lifestyle sports: Consumption, identity and difference,* ed. B. Wheaton 175-96. London: Routledge.

Thornton, S. 1995. *Club cultures: Music, media, and subcultural capital.* Cambridge, UK: Polity Press.

Tittle, C. 1995. *Control balance: Toward a general theory of deviance.* Boulder, CO: Westview Press.

Tokish, J., M. Kocher, and R. Hawkins. 2004. Ergogenic aids: A review of basic science, performance, side effects, and status in sports. *American Journal of Sports Medicine* 32:1543-53.

Toorock, M. 2005. Parkour philosophy. [Online]. www.americanparkour.com. June 9.

Trujillo, N. 1990. Hegemonic masculinity on the mound: Media representations of Nolan Ryan and American sports culture. *Critical Studies in Mass Communication* 8:280-308.

Turk, A. 1969. *Criminality and legal order.* Chicago: Rand McNally.

Turk, A. 2002. Sociology of terrorism. *Annual Review of Sociology* 30:271-86.

Turner, V. 1969. *The ritual process: Structure and anti-structure.* New York: Aldine Publishers.

TSN. 2004. www.tsn.ca. March 15.

United Nations. 1989. *Convention on the rights of the child.* Geneva, Swizterland.

United Nations. 2002. *A world fit for children.* Geneva, Swizterland.

United Nations. 2003. *Sport for development and peace: Towards achieving millennium development goals.* Geneva, Switzerland.

U.S. Department of State. 2002. *Patterns of terrorism report.* Secretary of State and the Coordinator for Counterterrorism.

Vanden Auweele, Y. 2003. *Ethics in youth sport.* Leuven, Belgium: Lannoo Campus.

Vanden Auweele, Y., C. Malcolm, and B. Meulders. 2007. *Sport and development.* Leuven, Belgium: Lannoo Campus.

Vaz, E. 1982. *The professionalization of young hockey players.* Lincoln, NE: University of Nebraska Press.

Vigh, M. 2002. Feds promise SLC heads up. *Salt Lake Tribune.* January 19:C10.

Visser, D. 2001. IOC chief satisfied with Salt Lake security. *Globe and Mail.* October 28:53.

Vistica, G. 2004. Tests find porous security for Athens Olympics. *Washington Post.* October 11:A11.

Vold, G. 1958. *Theoretical criminology.* Newark, NJ: University of Delaware Press.

Vospeka, R. 2002. Olympic security planners finally relax. *Vancouver Sun.* February 25:H7.

Wacquant, L. 1995. Pugs at work: Bodily capital and bodily labor among professional boxers. *Body and Society* 1:65-94.

Waddington, I. 2000. *Sport, health and drugs: A critical sociological perspective.* London: Taylor and Francis.

Waddington, I., and E. Dunning. 2003. Sport as a drug and drugs in sport: Some exploratory comments. *International Review for the Sociology of Sport* 38:351-68.

Walter, T. 1999. *On bereavement: The culture of grief.* Buckingham, UK: Open University Press.

Walters, G. 2006. *Berlin Games: How the Nazis stole the Olympic dream.* New York: William Morrow.

Wamsley, K., and M. Heine. 1996a. Tradition, modernity, and the construction of civic identity: The Calgary Olympics. *OLYMPIKA* 5:81-90.

Wamsley, K., and M. Heine. 1996b. Don't mess with the relay, it's bad medicine: Aboriginal culture and the 1988 Winter Olympic Games. In *Olympic perspectives,* ed. R. Barney, S. Martyn, D. Brown, and G. MacDonald. London, ON: International Centre for Olympic Studies.

Watson, R., and J. McLellan. 1986. Smitting to spitting: 80 years of ice hockey in Canadian courts. *Canadian Journal of History of Sport* 17:10-27.

Webb, M., and B. Davis. 2006. *Illusions of security. Global surveillance and democracy in the post 9/11 world.* New York: City Lights Books.

Weber, M. 1930. *The Protestant ethic and the spirit of capitalism.* London: Allen and Unwin.

Weinstein, M., M. Smith, and D. Wiesenthal. 1995. Masculinity and hockey violence. *Sex Roles* 33:831-47.

Whannel, G. 2002. *Media sport stars: Masculinities and moralities.* London: Routledge.

Wheaton, B. 2004. *Understanding lifestyle sport: Consumption, identity and difference.* London: Routledge.

White, D. 1986. Sports violence as criminal assault: Development of the doctrine by Canadian criminal courts. *Duke Law Journal* 47:1030-4.

White, J. 2005. *Terrorism and homeland security.* New York: Wadsworth.

White, P., and K. Young. 1997. Health and the new age ascetic. In *Taking sport seriously: Social issues in Canadian sport,* ed. P. Donnelly, 74-95. Toronto: Thompson.

White, P., and K. Young. 1997. Masculinity, sport and the injury process: A review of Canadian and international evidence. *Avante* 3:1-30.

White, P., and K. Young. 1999. Is sport injury gendered? In *Sport and gender in Canada.* Don Mills, ON: Oxford University Press.

White, P., K. Young, and J. Gillett. 1995. Body work as a moral imperative: Some critical notes on health and fitness. *Loisir and Société* 18:159-83.

Whitson, D., and D. Macintosh. 1996. The global circus: International sport, tourism and the marketing of cities. *Journal of Sport and Social Issues* 20:278-95.

Whyte, W. 1943. *Street corner society.* Chicago: University of Chicago Press.

Wiggans, P., and D. Miller. 2005. *Sport and the color line.* London: Routledge.

Wigge, L. 2000. Stick it to the players who swing their sticks. *Sporting News.* March 6:3.

Williams, J. 2003. *A game for rough girls.* London: Taylor and Francis.

Williams, J., E. Dunning, and P. Murphy. 1984. *Hooligans abroad: The behaviour and control of English fans in continental Europe.* London: Routledge and Kegan Paul.

Williams, P. 2005. *The Al Qaeda connection.* New York: Prometheus Books.

Williams, R. 1977. *Marxism and literature.* Oxford, UK: University of Oxford Press.

Williams, S., and G. Bendelow. 1998. *The lived body: Sociological themes, embodied issues.* London: Routledge.

Willis, P. 1978. *Profane culture.* London: Routledge and Kegan Paul.

Willis, P. 1980. Notes on method. In *Culture, media, language,* ed. S. Hall, 88-95. London: Hutchinson.

Willis, P. 1997. Theoretical confessions and reflexive method. In *The subcultures reader,* ed. K. Gelder and S. Thornton, 246-251. New York: Routledge.

Wilson, B. 1997. Good Blacks and bad Blacks: Media constructions of African American athletes in Canadian basketball. *International Review for the Sociology of Sport* 32:177-89.

Wilson, B. 2002. The anti-jock movement: Reconsidering youth resistance, masculinity and sport culture in the age of the Internet. *Sociology of Sport Journal* 19:207-34.

Wilson, B. 2006. *Fight, flight, or chill: Subcultures, youth, and rave into the 21st century.* Montreal, PQ: McGill-Queen's University Press.

Wilson, B. 2007. Oppression is the message: Media, sport, spectacle and gender. In *Sport and gender in Canada,* ed. P. White and K. Young 212-33 Toronto: Oxford University Press.

Wilson, B., and R. Sparks. 1996. It's gotta be the shoes: Youth, race and sneaker commercials. *Sociology of Sport Journal* 13:398-427.

Wilson, B., P. White, and K. Fisher. 2001. Multiple identities in a marginalized culture: Female youth in an "inner city" recreation/drop-in centre. *Journal of Sport and Social Issues* 25:301-23.

Wilson, J., and R. Herrnstein. 1985. *Crime and human nature.* New York: Simon & Schuster.

Wilson, S. 2001a. Olympics chief: Games will go on in Salt Lake. *Los Angeles Times.* September 21:E2.

Wilson, S. 2001b. Norwegian official apologizes for Salt Lake stir. *Los Angeles Times.* October 24:E10.

Wilson, S. 2004. IOC deal for cancellation insurance. *USA Today.* April 19:D3.

Wilstein, S. 2004. Olympics looking like a big fat Greek mess: Athens appears to be way behind in preparations. *Toronto Star.* March 2:E1.

Wise, S. 2000. *Rattling the cage: Toward legal rights for animals.* Cambridge, UK: Perseus Books.

Woodward, J. 2004. Professional football scouts: An investigation of racial stacking. *Sociology of Sport Journal* 21:356-75.

Wortz, L. 2006. What's up with Parkour? *Toronto Star.* May 16:C1.

Young, K. 1983. The subculture of rugby players: A form of resistance and incorporation. Master's thesis, McMaster University, Hamilton, ON.

Young, K. 1990. *Treatment of sports violence by the Canadian mass media.* Report to Sport Canada's Applied Sport Research Program. Ottawa: Government of Canada.

Young, K. 1991. Violence in the workplace of professional sport from victimological and cultural studies perspectives. *International Review for the Sociology of Sport* 26:3-14.

Young, K. 1993. Violence, risk, and liability in male sports culture. *Sociology of Sport Journal* 10:373-96.

Young, K. 1997. Women, sport, and physicality: Preliminary findings from a Canadian study. *International Review for the Sociology of Sport* 32:297-305.

Young, K. 2000. Sport and violence. In *Handbook of sports studies,* ed. J. Coakley and P. Donnelly, 382-407. London: Sage.

Young, K. 2001. Toward a more inclusive sociology of sports-related violence. Paper presented at the annual meeting of the North American Society for the Sociology of Sport, San Antonio. October 31.

Young, K. 2002a. From sports violence to sports crime: Aspects of violence, law, and gender in the sports process. In *Paradoxes of youth and sport,* ed. M. Gatz, M. Messner, and S. Ball-Rokeach, 207-24. New York: SUNY Press.

Young, K. 2002b. Standard deviations: An update on North American sports crowd disorder. *Sociology of Sport Journal* 19:237-75.

Young, K. 2004a. The role of the courts in sport injury. In *Sporting bodies, damaged selves: Sociological studies of sports-related injury,* ed. K.Young, 333-53. Oxford, UK: Elsevier.

Young, K. 2004b. *Sporting bodies, damaged selves: Sociological studies of sports-related injury.* Oxford, UK: Elsevier.

Young, K. 2008. From violence in sport to sport-related violence. In *Sport and society: A student introduction,* ed. B. Houlihan, 174-204. London: Sage.

Young, K., and C. Reasons. 1989. Victimology and organizational crime: Workplace violence and the professional athlete. *Sociological Viewpoints* 5:24-34.

Young, K., and K. Wamsley. 1996. State complicity in sports assault and the gender order in 20th century Canada: Preliminary observations. *Avante* 2:51-69.

Young, K., and K. Wamsley. 2006. *Global Olympics: Historical and sociological studies of the modern Games.* Oxford, UK: Elsevier.

Young, K., and P. White. 1995. Sport, physical danger, and injury: The experiences of elite women athletes. *Journal of Sport and Social Issues* 19:45-61.

Young, K., and P. White. 2007. *Sport and gender in Canada,* 2nd ed. Don Mills, ON: Oxford University Press.

Young, K., P. White, and W. McTeer. 1994. Body talk: Male athletes reflect on sport, injury and pain. *Sociology of Sport Journal* 11:175-94.

Zarkos, J. 2004. Raising the bar: A man, the flop and the Olympic gold medal. *Sun Valley Guide.* May 17:28.

Index

Note: The italicized *f* and *t* following page numbers refer to figures and tables, respectively.

About the Authors

Michael Atkinson, PhD, is a senior lecturer in the School of Sport and Exercise Sciences at Loughborough University in Leicestershire, UK. He has served on the editorial boards of *Sociology of Sport Journal* and *Deviant Behavior*. Atkinson is a member of the North American Society for the Sociology of Sport and the International Society for the Sociology of Sport.

In 2004, Atkinson was awarded the Social Sciences and Humanities Research Council of Canada's Aurora Award. He resides in Quorn.

Kevin Young, PhD, is a professor in the department of sociology at the University of Calgary in Alberta, Canada. He has served on the editorial boards of several journals, including *International Review for the Sociology of Sport*, *Sociology of Sport Journal*, *Soccer and Society*, and *Avante*. Young has also served on the executive board of the North American Society for the Sociology of Sport and as vice president of the International Sociology of Sport Association. Young is editor of the book series *Research in the Sociology of Sport*.

Young enjoys all sports, loves the outdoors, and is a passionate supporter of Liverpool Football Club. He resides in Calgary.